FRENCH CRUISERS
1922–1956

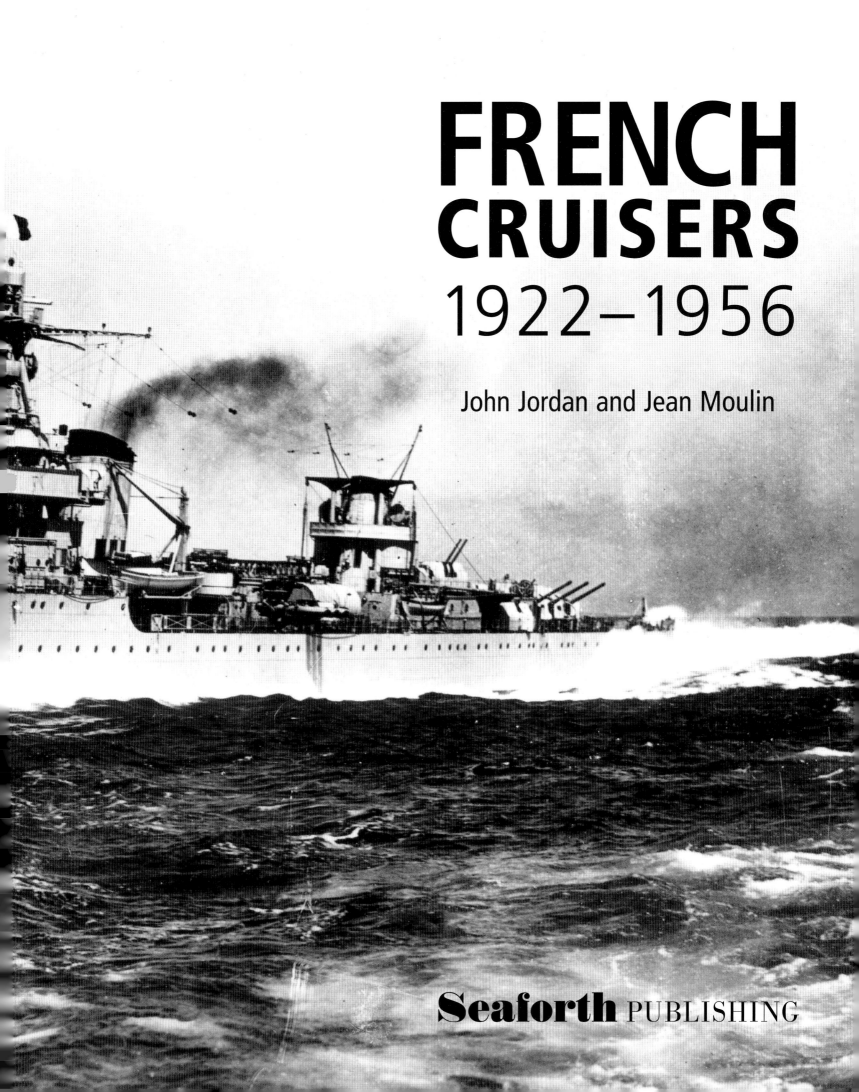

FRENCH CRUISERS
1922–1956

John Jordan and Jean Moulin

Seaforth PUBLISHING

Copyright © John Jordan & Jean Moulin 2013
Watercolour paintings © Jean Bladé 2013

First published in Great Britain in 2013 by
Seaforth Publishing
An imprint of Pen & Sword Books Ltd
47 Church Street, Barnsley
S Yorkshire S70 2AS

www.seaforthpublishing.com
Email info@seaforthpublishing.com

British Library Cataloguing in Publication Data
A CIP data record for this book is available from the British Library

ISBN 978-1-84832-133-5

Typeset and designed by Stephen Dent
Printed in Singapore by Imago

Frontispiece:
Emile Bertin on 9 August 1939, making 35 knots.

CONTENTS

Preface 6

Acronyms and Abbreviations 7

PART I: TECHNICAL SECTION

Introduction 8

Chapter 1   The *Duguay-Trouin* Class 24

Chapter 2   *Duquesne* and *Tourville* 41

Chapter 3   The *Suffren* Class 54

Chapter 4   *Pluton*, *Jeanne d'Arc* and *Emile Bertin* 83

Chapter 5   *Algérie* 107

Chapter 6   The *La Galissonnière* Class 121

Colour plates 129

Chapter 7   The *De Grasse* Class 143

Chapter 8   The C5 and *Saint Louis* Designs 159

PART II: HISTORICAL SECTION

Chapter 9   The Period 1926–1939 164

Chapter 10   The Period 1939–1943 176

Chapter 11   The Period 1943–1945 196

Chapter 12   The Period 1945–1956 212

Sources 228

Index 229

PREFACE

T HIS BOOK IS IN MANY RESPECTS A NATURAL sequel to *French Battleships 1922–1956*, written with Robert Dumas and published by Seaforth Publishing in September 2009. However, it required a very different approach. Only four French battleships were designed and completed during the period in question, whereas the same period saw the construction of no fewer than twenty cruisers for the Marine Nationale belonging to nine different classes. Whereas the battleships all sailed for North Africa in June 1940, and subsequently became the focus of substantial efforts by the Allies to eliminate or at least neutralise them, the cruisers found themselves distributed between Allied and French metropolitan and colonial ports from Saigon to the West Indies at the time the Armistice took effect, and this had a major impact both on their subsequent careers and on their very survival. Seven of the most modern and most powerful French cruisers would be scuttled at Toulon in November 1942, others would be impounded for almost three years in the British fleet base of Alexandria; three would be despatched from Toulon to defend the ports of West Africa, while three would find themselves out on a limb in the far reaches of the French empire. Following the liberation of North Africa in 1942–3, the four surviving modern light cruisers would be extensively modernised in the United States. The older units, which had dated anti-aircraft batteries and had seen little proper maintenance since June 1940, rejoined the Allied cause in a trickle, to be employed within the limits of their capabilities on patrol missions.

The complexity of the history of these ships, particularly during the wartime and post-war periods, precluded the organisation adopted for *French Battleships*, in which each of the 'technical' chapters was followed by a historical chapter recounting the peacetime and wartime careers of the individual ships. Instead the eight chapters outlining the design philosophy and the technical characteristics of each of the classes/ships in question are followed by a historical section which covers, in broadly chronological sequence, the often eventful careers of all of the cruisers laid down during the inter-war period. The 'technical' section of the book (Part I) is largely the work of John Jordan with the support and advice of Jean Moulin, himself an established author of numerous French-language monographs on the cruisers and the *contre-torpilleurs*. Jean Moulin has also provided the 'historical' section (Part II), which has been translated from the French by John Jordan.

The present book aims to summarise for English-speaking readers the considerable quantity of information, backed up by recently-released official documentation, made available in a series of monographs on the cruisers published in France since the mid-1990s. Coverage includes the three ships of the *De Grasse* class, the first of which was laid down in August 1939, and which have been the subject of detailed studies by John Jordan and Bruno Gire, and the *Saint Louis* class heavy cruiser design of 1939–40, which was extensively researched by Jean Moulin.

In addition to telling the story of the French cruisers, Jean Moulin's historical section focuses closely on issues of infrastructure, tactical organisation and even national culture which are not always well understood on this side of the Channel. There is also a strong insight into the complexities of the political situation and its impact on the Marine Nationale both during and after the Second World War. It is hoped that this book will give the reader a better understanding not only of the design philosophy and technical characteristics of these ships, but also of the history and traditions of the Marine Nationale during the twentieth century.

THE DRAWINGS

The line drawings and labelled schematics by John Jordan, most of which have been specially prepared for this book, are based on official plans and other documentation currently held by the Centre d'Archives de l'Armement (CAA) at Châtellerault; many of the plans have been openly published on the website of the Service Historique de la Défense. Some of these plans and documents have only recently been made available as part of the *Fonds Potsdam*, an archive of material assembled by the German *Kriegsmarine* during the Occupation and transferred to Berlin, where it was seized by the Russians; the materials were returned to France after the fall of the Berlin Wall and have now been reclassified and distributed among the various French national archives.

The colour section showcases the work of marine artist Jean Bladé, formerly the Surgeon General for the French armed forces. These beautiful watercolours, some of which were painted during Jean's time in the Navy (1922–65), not only constitute a valuable record of the cruisers and their activities, but give a distinctive feel for what service in these ships was like during the inter-war and wartime period.

ACKNOWLEDGEMENTS

The authors would like to express their thanks to the following organisations which have assisted them with their research:

The Service Historique de la Défense:
  Centre d'Archives de l'Armement et du Personnel Civil (CAA) at Châtellerault
  Département Marine at Vincennes, Paris
The Association pour la Recherche de Documentation sur l'Histoire de l'Aéronautique Navale (ARDHAN).

Sincere thanks are also due: to Dr Jean Bladé, who provided the painting of *Emile Bertin* which illustrates the jacket as well as the colour artwork in the centre section of the book; to Marc Saibène, Robert Dumas, Philippe Caresse, Gérard Garier and Peter Cannon for their assistance with photographic illustration. All uncredited photographs are from the private collections of the authors, for which all rights are reserved. Bruno Gire kindly permitted us to use his plan and profile drawings of the *De Grasse*, and also provided documentation and other unpublished plans of the ship. The authors also wish to extend their thanks to Rob Gardiner (Seaforth Publishing), who has offered support and advice throughout the project, and to Steve Dent, both for the intelligence and creativity he has displayed in designing the layouts and for the infinite patience with which he has accommodated the inevitable last-minute amendments. Without the collaboration of these people this book would not have been possible.

John Jordan & Jean Moulin
October 2012

ACRONYMS AND ABBREVIATIONS

ORGANISATIONS ETC

AOF	=	*Afrique Occidentale Française* (French West Africa)
CAA	=	*Centre d'Archives de l'Armement*
CEP	=	*Centre d'expérimentation du Pacifique* (Pacific Experimental Centre)
CFLN	=	*Comité français de libération nationale* (French Committee of National Liberation)
CIN	=	*Centre d'instruction naval* (Naval Instruction Centre)
CIOA	=	*Centre d'instruction des opérations amphibies* (Amphibious Operations Training Centre)
CPE	=	*Commission Permanente des Essais* (Trials Commission)
CSM	=	*Conseil supérieur de la marine* (Navy Board [advisory])
DNEO	=	*Division navale d'Extrême-Orient* (Far Eastern Naval Division)
EATM	=	*Ecole d'application du tir à la mer* (gunnery school ship)
EMG	=	*Etat-major general de la marine* (Naval General Staff)
EOR	=	*Ecole des officiers de reserve* (School of Officers of the Reserve)
GPRF	=	*Gouvernement provisoire de la République Française* (Provisional Government of the French Republic)
MDAP	=	Mutual Defense Assistance Program
STCN	=	*Service technique des constructions navales* (Constructors' Department)

TECHNICAL

ACAD	=	*automatique contre-avions double* (automatic twin AA mounting)
AMC	=	armed merchant cruiser
AP	=	armour-piercing
CAD	=	*contre-avions double* (AA twin mounting)
CAQ	=	*contre-avions quadruple* (AA quad mounting)
CAS	=	*contre-avions simple* (AA single mounting)
CV	=	*chevaux*, 1CV = 0.98632shp
DA	=	*disponibilité armée* (care and maintenance)
DCT	=	director control tower
DP	=	dual-purpose
FTP	=	follow the pointer
HA	=	high-angle (guns)
HE	=	high explosive
HP	=	high pressure

LP	=	low pressure
Mle	=	*Modèle* (model)
MP	=	medium pressure
OEA	=	*Obus Explosif en Acier* (HE shell)
OEcl	=	*Obus Eclairant* (starshell)
OI	=	*Obus Incendiaire* (incendiary shell)
OPf	=	*Obus de Perforation* (armour-piercing shell)
psi	=	pounds per square inch
RPC	=	remote power control
rpg	=	rounds per gun
rpm	=	rounds per minute
SAP		semi armour-piercing (shell)
shp	=	shaft horsepower
UTS	=	Ultimate Tensile Strength

RANKS

CA	=	*Contre amiral* (Rear-Admiral)
CO	=	commanding officer
CPO	=	Chief Petty Officer
VA	=	*Vice amiral* (Vice-Admiral)
VAE	=	*Vice amiral d'escadre* (Squadron Vice-Admiral)

NAVAL FORMATIONS

DC	=	*division de croiseurs* (cruiser division)
DCL	=	*division de croiseurs légers* (light cruiser division)
DCT	=	*division de contre-torpilleurs* (destroyer division)
DCX	=	*division de croiseurs auxiliaires* (armed merchant cruiser division)
DL	=	*division légère* (light division)
DSM	=	*division de sous-marins* (submarine division)
EL	=	*escadre légère* (light squadron)
FHM	=	*Forces de haute mer* (high seas forces)
FI	=	*Force d'intervention* (intervention force)
FMA	=	*Forces maritimes d'Afrique* (African maritime forces)
FMEO	=	*Forces maritimes d'Extrême-Orient* (Far Eastern Maritime Forces)
FNFL	=	*Forces navales françaises libres* (Free French Naval Forces)
FNGB	=	*Forces navales en Grande Bretagne* (Naval Forces in Great Britain)
FNI	=	*Force navale d'intervention* (Naval Intervention Force)
FNTF	=	French Naval Task Force
GASM	=	*Groupe d'action anti-sous-marine* (Anti-Submarine Group)

INTRODUCTION

Above: The launch of the 10,000-ton cruiser *Foch* from the *Point du Jour* covered slipway at Brest on 24 April 1929. The slipway had been built in the early 1900s ready for the laying down of the pre-dreadnought battleship *Danton*. Note the plaques above the entrance recording the hulls built there. From top to bottom: the battleships *Danton*, *Jean Bart*, *Bretagne*, *Flandre* (*Normandie* class – launched but not completed); the cruisers *Duquesne*, *Suffren*, *Colbert* and *Foch*.

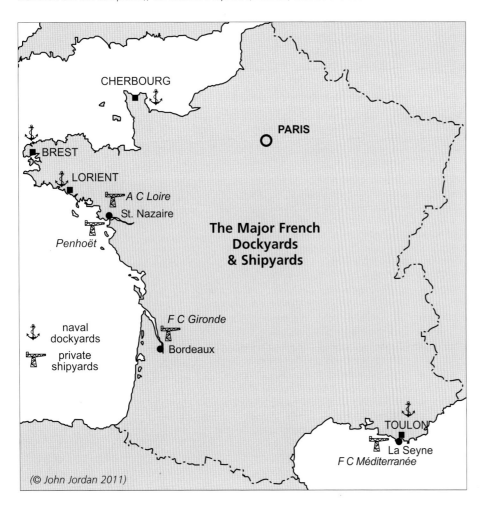

CHERBOURG

PARIS

BREST

LORIENT

A C Loire

St. Nazaire

Penhoët

The Major French Dockyards & Shipyards

F C Gironde

Bordeaux

⚓ naval dockyards

🏗 private shipyards

TOULON

La Seyne
F C Méditerranée

(© John Jordan 2011)

CONSTRUCTION

Brest Naval Dockyard was the lead yard for all classes of cruiser built for the Marine Nationale during the inter-war period. Individual ships of the various classes might be ordered from other yards, including private shipyards, but Brest would always lay down the first ship and would be responsible for providing detailed plans to other shipyards to ensure commonality of fittings and equipment and 'quality control'. The hulls of cruisers built at Brest were all laid down on the *Cale du Point du Jour*, a covered slipway located on the River Penfeld in the upper reaches of the dockyard, just beyond the famous Transporter Bridge (demolished in 1947 following bomb damage). Once launched, the hulls were towed downriver to the fitting-out quay, the *Quai d'armement*, which was surmounted by a large hammerhead crane referred to as the *Grande grue* (see map). Once the ship was complete she was moved to the *Rade-Abri*, the sheltered anchorage close to the dockyard, ready for sea trials. Brest built two of the three ships of the *Duguay-Trouin* class, the first Treaty cruiser *Duquesne*, all four ships of the *Suffren* class, the one-off *Algérie*, and the first of the six-ship 7600-ton class, *La Galissonnière*.

The second in rank of the French naval dockyards for surface ship construction was Lorient, also in Brittany, which became the lead yard for the *contre-torpilleurs* built during the inter-war period. Its major facility was a large, modern covered building dock, the *Forme de Lanester*, which could accommodate the hull of a single large ship or two smaller hulls side by side. Ships were floated out into the River Scorff, then towed downriver to the fitting-out quay, equipped with a hammerhead crane similar to the one at Brest (see map). Ships completed at Lorient generally ran their machinery trials from that port before being transferred to Brest for the final fitting of equipment such as fire control installations. Lorient built the second ship of the *Duguay-Trouin* class, *Lamotte-Piquet*, the second of the Treaty cruisers, *Tourville*, the minelayer *Pluton*, and the second of the 7600-ton cruisers, *Jean de Vienne*. The dockyard also laid down the first of the cruisers of the *De Grasse* class, the remaining two being ordered from private shipyards.

The only private shipyard to receive an order for a cruiser during the 1920s was the Ateliers et Chantiers de St. Nazaire-Penhoët, which built the training cruiser *Jeanne d'Arc* (authorised under the 1926 Estimates). Perhaps as a result of this shipyard's experience in building *contre-torpilleurs*, St. Nazaire-Penhoët also received the order for the prototype fast light minelaying cruiser armed with 152mm guns, *Emile Bertin* (authorised in 1930), and subsequently built the 7600-ton cruiser *Georges Leygues*.

Congestion in the naval dockyards during the late 1920s and early 1930s led the Navy to cast its net wider when, following the London Treaty of 1930, it decided to order a series of six 7600-ton cruisers, which were authorised under the 1931 and 1932

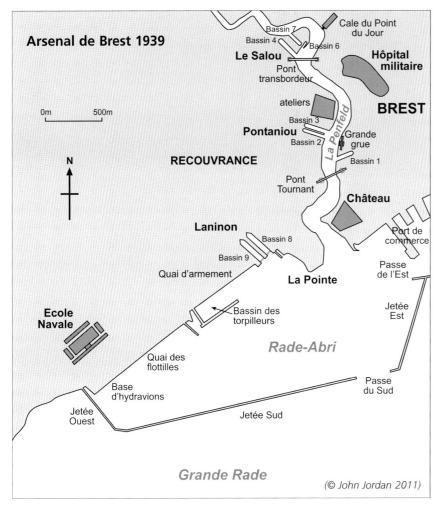

Arsenal de Brest 1939

(© John Jordan 2011)

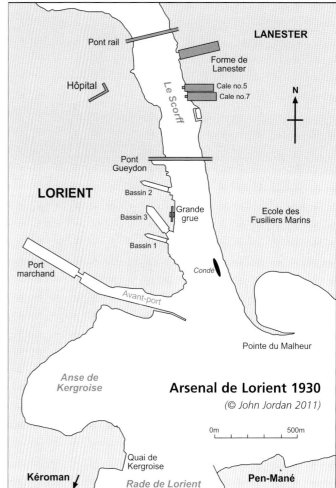

Arsenal de Lorient 1930

(© John Jordan 2011)

Estimates. Three of the ships are accounted for above; orders for the remaining three were placed with: Ateliers et Chantiers de la Loire (St. Nazaire), Forges et Chantiers de la Gironde (Bordeaux), and Forges et Chantiers de la Méditerranée (La Seyne – opposite the naval dockyard at Toulon).

AC Loire had built some of the earlier *contre-torpilleurs*; in terms of its geographical location it was adjacent to the Penhoët shipyard, and during the 1930s the two yards would increasingly collaborate on shipbuilding projects, including the construction of the battleship *Jean Bart*. FC Gironde had built four modern fleet torpedo boats and had recently completed the seaplane carrier *Commandant Teste*, which had a number of 'cruiser' features. FC Méditerranée had built battleships in the past, and was currently building four modern *contre-torpilleurs*. The latter two yards would subsequently receive orders for the second and third cruisers of the *De Grasse* class, *Châteaurenault* and *Guichen*.

Longitudinal framing was employed throughout in the construction of cruisers during the inter-war period. Transverse frames normally had a spacing of 2m, and were numbered in metres from the aft to the forward perpendicular (thus Frame 50 was 50m from the aft perpendicular). There were generally sixteen main transverse bulkheads (*cloisons principales*) which extended from the ship's bottom to the upper deck. Beneath the Main Deck these were penetrated only by cables and pipework to create seventeen watertight compartments, and key bulkheads – such

as those at the forward and after ends of the machinery spaces and those between the propulsion 'units' – were generally reinforced. The double bottom extended for most of the ship's length and was used to stow liquids such as oil fuel and reserve feed water for the boilers.

The steels used for construction and protection were classified according to their Ultimate Tensile Strength (UTS) – the maximum stress a material can withstand while being stretched or pulled before 'necking' (when the cross-section begins to contract significantly). The unit of measurement used by the French was kilogrammes per millimetre squared (kg/mm², often shortened to 'kg').

During the early 1920s French metallurgy lagged some way behind that of Britain and the United States.[1] Mild steel with a rating of 50kg (= 32 tons/in²) was used for ship construction. This compared with a corresponding figure of 37–44 tons/in² for the new 'D' steel used in the first British Treaty cruisers,[2] for which the plates could be rolled thinner for the same tensile strength. Had a steel with similar properties been adopted for the French ships there would have been significant weight savings on the hull, which for a Treaty cruiser

---

[1] Further evidence can be found in the construction of French guns, which had to be built up from far more components than their British and American counterparts.

[2] It was also used extensively in Japanese and Italian ships built during the 1920s.

Right: *Colbert* fitting out
under the *Grande grue* at
Brest in June 1929. In the
background, on the opposite
bank of the Penfeld, are the
boiler, machinery and plate
shops which served the
dockyard.

Right: *Colbert* fitting out under the *Grande grue* at Brest in June 1929. In the background, on the opposite bank of the Penfeld, are the boiler, machinery and plate shops which served the dockyard.

accounted for some 50 per cent of standard (Washington) displacement. This could then have been invested in protection; in the event the weight of protection accorded to the early *Duquesne* and *Tourville* was less than in any other contemporary foreign cruiser. The light (20–60mm) protective plating provided in these and later cruisers was of 60kg steel (38 tons/in²), comparable in tensile strength to the British 'D' steel. It was not used for construction until the *De Grasse* class of the late 1930s. Armour quality steel rated at 80kg (51 tons/in²) was first employed in the last of the Treaty cruisers, *Algérie*, and subsequently in the light cruisers of the *La Galissonnière* class. In *Algérie* it was employed not only for the thick belt and armoured deck (110mm and 80mm respectively), but for the turrets, ring bulkheads, ammunition trunks, conning tower and the key transverse bulkheads. Some prototype plates of cemented armour were ordered for use in the later *De Grasse*, but there is no evidence that they were fitted.

During the 1920s the French naval dockyards and shipyards still employed riveting throughout, but electric welding was successfully introduced for the non-strength elements of the hull of *Algérie*. In the same ship there was widespread use of the light alloy duralumin for internal partitions and fittings, a practice which had begun with the later ships of the *Suffren* class. These measures brought spectacular reductions in hull weight compared to the earlier ships[3] which could then be invested in additional protection.

INTERNAL LAYOUT

Decks within the hull (*ponts*) were distinguished from decks within the bridge structure (*passerelles*). For all French cruisers of the period the Main Deck (*Pont principal*) was the main internal deck, running the full length of the ship, and the deck above it, which was

---

[3] The weight of *Algérie*'s hull was 3800 tonnes as
compared with 4800 tonnes for *Duquesne* and *Tourville*.

the weather deck, was termed the First Deck (*Premier pont*). All the major classes of inter-war cruiser except *Algérie* had a raised forecastle (*Teugue*), which in the area of the forward superstructure was often referred to on official plans as the *Pont passerelle*.

Below the Main Deck were one or two Platform Decks (*Faux-ponts*), depending on the size of the ship, and the Hold (*Cale*) where the magazines and shell rooms were located. Above the Forecastle – First Deck in *Algérie* – were the bridge decks (*passerelle inférieure, intermédiaire, de navigation*), the upper one fronted by an enclosed compass platform (see drawing).

French Treaty cruisers were designed for an average complement of 650, of whom 30 might be officers (35 for a flagship), 15 Chief Petty Officers (CPOs – *premiers maîtres*), 100 Petty Officers (*maîtres* and *seconds maîtres*), and 500 quartermasters and seamen. Accommodation was arranged on the traditional pattern, and in many respects mirrored British practice. The admiral's quarters (and in some cases the CO's) were generally on the First Deck within the after superstructure. The officers' accommodation was aft on the Main Deck. The cabins were to the sides; 'services' – offices, washplaces and bathrooms – were on the centre-line, flanked by two broad passageways (*coursives*). There were separate wardrooms for junior and for senior officers; the former was generally above the stern, the latter close to the senior officers' accommodation, which was beneath the admiral's quarters.

Accommodation for the crew was divided between the forecastle (First Deck) and the Main Deck, with some variation in layout between the different classes of ship which reflected the space available. The after end of the forecastle was generally the location for an extensive medical complex, which included a consulting room, an operating theatre, a sick bay (*infirmerie* – normally eight beds), and an adjacent mess for those temporarily excused duty (*exempts de service*). The cabins for the CPOs were often on this level, with the larger messes for the petty officers closer to the bow. The CPOs had their own dining room. The remainder of the crew's accommodation was on the main deck, from forward of the officers' quarters to the bow. Seamen's messes were for up to ninety men, although forty to fifty was a more common figure. The messes for petty officers were smaller, accommodating perhaps twenty-four men; those for the *Maîtres* generally had superimposed bunks, whereas the *seconds maîtres* slung hammocks, like the seamen. There were generally two to four double cabins for *agents civils*, who might be members of the government or fleet chaplains, but might equally be civilians who worked on board in some capacity.

Washplaces, bathrooms, showers and heads were generally located close to the accommodation for the appropriate rank. The galleys (*cuisines*) and the bakery (*boulangerie*) were generally grouped around the fore-funnel on the First Deck, their distinctive chimneys being led up at the 'corners' of the funnel. There was a laundry (*buanderie*), a barber's (*coiffeur*) and a shop (*coopérative*), generally located at the foot of the bridge structure.

In some ships modifications to established practice were necessary because of the unusual configuration of their hull or superstructures. In *Algérie*, which had no forecastle, the CPOs' cabins and dining room had to be relocated to the Platform Deck aft, beneath the officers' accommodation. And in the 7600-ton cruisers, which had an aircraft hangar in place of the after deckhouse, the admiral's and CO's quarters had to be moved down to the Main Deck below.

Below the Main Deck the layout was entirely conventional, with the machinery spaces occupying

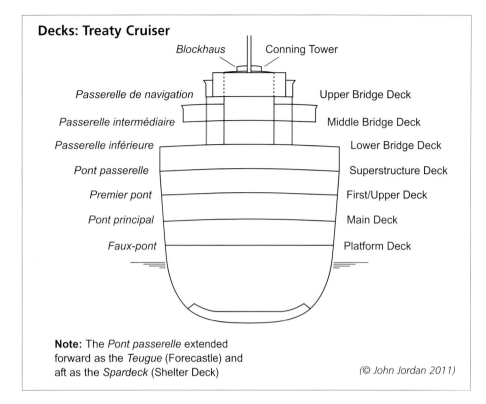

Decks: Treaty Cruiser

Blockhaus	Conning Tower
Passerelle de navigation	Upper Bridge Deck
Passerelle intermédiaire	Middle Bridge Deck
Passerelle inférieure	Lower Bridge Deck
Pont passerelle	Superstructure Deck
Premier pont	First/Upper Deck
Pont principal	Main Deck
Faux-pont	Platform Deck

Note: The *Pont passerelle* extended forward as the *Teugue* (Forecastle) and aft as the *Spardeck* (Shelter Deck)

(© *John Jordan 2011*)

the midships section and the magazines fore and aft. In most ships the machinery spaces were divided into two independent 'units', each with its own boilers, turbines, pumps and condensers. However, the French never interrupted the run of machinery spaces by

Internal Layout

Suffren

La Galissonnière

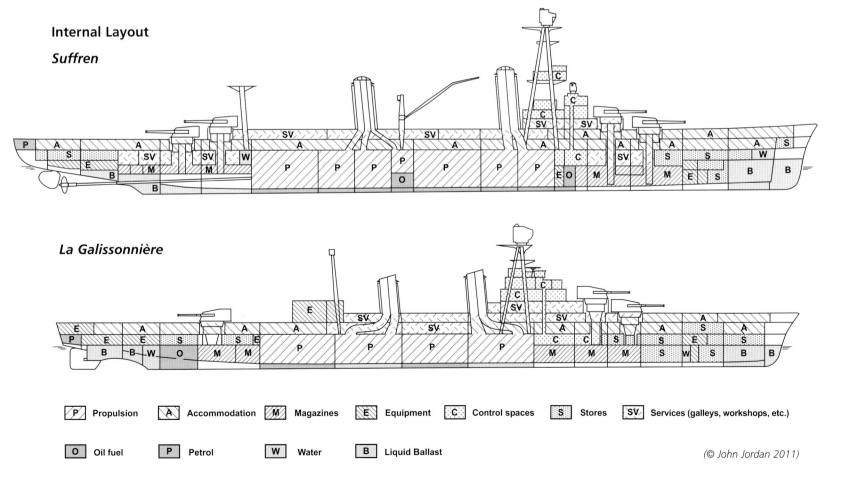

P	Propulsion	A	Accommodation	M	Magazines	E	Equipment	C	Control spaces	S	Stores	SV	Services (galleys, workshops, etc.)

O	Oil fuel	P	Petrol	W	Water	B	Liquid Ballast

(© *John Jordan 2011*)

Above: Painting duty on the hull of the cruiser *Foch* some time between 1933 and 1935. In peacetime each of the 10,000-ton cruisers was home to 650 officers and men. *(Henri Landais collection)*

Above: An officer's cabin aboard *Algérie*. *(Alain Marchand)*

inserting a midship magazine for the high-angle (HA) guns, as did the British with the 'Counties'. This had implications for the locations of the guns themselves, which in the French Treaty cruisers were mounted fore and aft to reduce to a minimum the horizontal movement of ammunition from the hoists. The lower decks in the bow were used for stores and provisions, those in the stern for additional stores and the steering compartment

Fuel oil was stowed in tanks in the double bottom and broader bunkers at the sides of the ship. Because

of fears of combustion fuel oil was not stowed abeam or beneath the magazines. In addition to the side and bottom tanks, there were generally large athwartship fuel tanks forward and/or aft, separated from the magazines by a double bulkhead with a void space between. Reserve feed water was stowed in the bottom or side tanks adjacent to the machinery spaces. There were large tanks for water for general use by the crew fore and aft, but drinking water was stowed fore and aft in separate containers. There were also separate containers for lubrication oils, generally abaft the after engine room. Besides the coal used for boiler firing and protection in the *Suffren* class (see Chapter 3), ships generally carried a small quantity of coal in a side bunker forward or amidships for use in the foundry and – in the ships laid down prior to 1930 – the steam pinnaces.

The bottom tanks in the bow and stern were generally left empty, but could be quickly filled with seawater ballast to correct trim following a torpedo hit. The later French cruisers also had an elaborate list compensation system amidships.

MACHINERY
Propulsion
French cruiser propulsion machinery during the interwar period was subject to technological developments and damage control considerations similar to those evident in the other major navies. Of these the most important were the trend towards high-pressure, high-temperature steam conditions, and the subdivision and layout of the machinery spaces.

All French boilers of the period were small-tube types designed by Indret, the Navy's propulsion establishment on the Loire (near Nantes). The boilers adopted for the early *Duguay-Trouin* class were of the Guyot-du Temple type and were rated at a conservative 18.5kg/cm² (265psi). The boiler fitted in the two *Duquesne*s and the four *Suffren*s was similar in design, but operated at the slightly higher pressure of 20kg/cm² (285psi). Each pair of boilers was located within its own containment box so that the *rue de chauffe* (the working path which ran across the boiler faces) remained at atmospheric pressure.

For the *Algérie*, *Emile Bertin*, and the six light cruisers of the *La Galissonnière* class, which were laid down from early 1931, there was a major leap in technology with the adoption of superheating. These boilers were all rated at 27kg/cm² (385psi) and 325° Celsius. They were smaller and lighter than the earlier boilers for a given power output; this reduced machinery weight, and also resulted in greater flexibility in the layout of the machinery spaces. Finally, for the *De Grasse* class, the Marine Nationale went to 35kg/cm² (500psi); the boilers in these ships were similar in size to those of the *La Galissonnière* class, but could produce sufficient steam for an additional 26,000CV as designed.

Steam turbines were almost evenly divided (even within otherwise homogeneous classes) between the Rateau-Bretagne impulse and the Parsons reaction types. All had single reduction gearing to ensure a respectable endurance. The standard turbine set had high-pressure (HP) and low-pressure (LP) turbines in series, with the reverse turbine in the LP housing and a separate cruise turbine for long-range fuel economy. French turbines were generally well-designed, but both

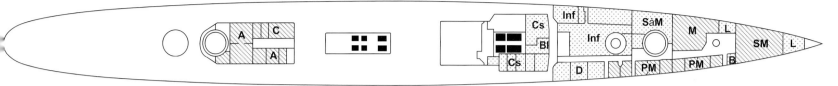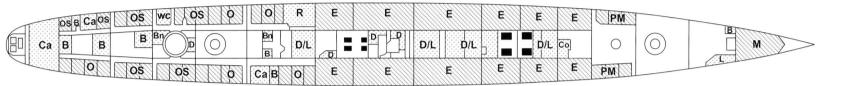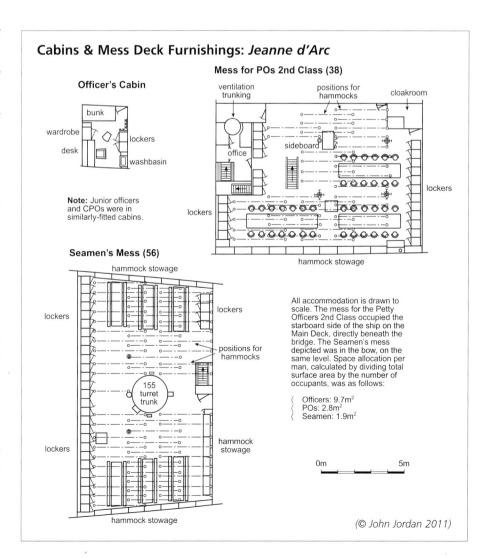

Accommodation: *Colbert*

First Deck

Main Deck

SERVICES

Inf	*Infirmerie* (sick bay)
Ca	*carré* (wardroom)
SàM	*salle à manger* (dining room)
L	*lavabos* (washplace)
D	*douches* (showers)
Bn	*bains* (bathrooms)
Bl	*boulangerie* (bakery)
Cs	*cuisine* (galley)
R	*salle de récréation* (recreation room)
B	*bureau/office* (office)
Co	*coopérative* (shop)

ACCOMMODATION

A	*amiral* (Admiral)
C	*commandant* (CO)
O	*officiers* (officers)
OS	*officiers subalternes* (junior officers)
PM	*premiers maîtres* (CPOs)
M	*maîtres* (POs 1st class)
SM	*seconds maîtres* (POs 2nd class)
E	*équipage* (q/m + seamen)

(© John Jordan 2011)

boilers and turbines were often built by a variety of private contractors and shipbuilders. This policy had its intended effect of distributing the workload across an ever-widening naval industrial base, but the lack of standardisation was often costly in terms of reliability and ease of maintenance.

The early French cruisers relied on a high degree of subdivision rather than protection for their survival. The *Duguay-Trouin*s and the *Duquesne*s had 20–30mm plating on turrets, magazines and conning towers but the machinery spaces were completely unprotected. The four boiler rooms in these ships, each housing two boilers side by side, were only 8–9m long, while the earlier ships also had their four turbine sets accommodated in three engine rooms of 10–11m. To secure improved survivability in the *Duquesne*s the French adopted the 'unit' arrangement of propulsion machinery, with each pair of boiler rooms followed by a 15-metre engine room housing two sets of turbines, the forward set powering the wing shafts. This arrangement was continued in the four *Suffren*s, despite the introduction of light protection for the machinery spaces and the move to three shafts, the centre shaft being powered by two boilers in separate boiler rooms providing steam for one set of turbines.

In the *Algérie*, for the first time, an armoured 'citadel' was adopted which covered not only the magazines but the machinery spaces. There was also a fully-fledged underwater protection system throughout. With horsepower further reduced from 90,000CV to 84,000CV, the unit layout was abandoned in favour of the traditional in-line arrangement, the three boiler rooms being grouped together beneath a single funnel with the two engine rooms abaft them.

The contemporary minelaying cruiser *Emile Bertin*, on the other hand, was designed for high speed, and like the earlier French cruisers was virtually unpro-

Cabins & Mess Deck Furnishings: *Jeanne d'Arc*

Officer's Cabin

Mess for POs 2nd Class (38)

Seamen's Mess (56)

Note: Junior officers and CPOs were in similarly-fitted cabins.

All accommodation is drawn to scale. The mess for the Petty Officers 2nd Class occupied the starboard side of the ship on the Main Deck, directly beneath the bridge. The Seamen's mess depicted was in the bow, on the same level. Space allocation per man, calculated by dividing total surface area by the number of occupants, was as follows:

Officers: 9.7m^2
POs: 2.8m^2
Seamen: 1.9m^2

(© John Jordan 2011)

tected. The three boiler rooms for her six paired boilers were 50 per cent longer than in the early ships (15m), but were again in a unit arrangement with the turbines for the wing shafts forward of the after boiler room.

The post-London Treaty light cruisers of the *La Galissonnière* class, and their linear successors of the *De Grasse* class, had armour protection almost on the level of the *Algérie*, but had insufficient breadth of hull for a full anti-torpedo system. Their propulsion machinery was derived from the *Emile Bertin*, but was less powerful and more compact, with only two shafts (versus four) and two fewer boilers. The result was a unit propulsion layout with a single 16m boiler room followed by a single engine room (the turbines being offset to port or to starboard) making up each of the two units.

The French did not make the mistake of attempting longitudinal division of the machinery spaces, as in the Imperial Japanese Navy, neither did they adopt the wing compartments which were a feature of Royal Navy cruisers with the unit machinery layout. All their designs except the *Duguay-Trouins*, however, featured protective longitudinal bulkheads either just inboard or just outboard of the torpedo bulkhead abeam the boiler rooms in order to limit the flooding of these spaces.

Onboard services

Steam for onboard services was provided by a single auxiliary boiler, which could be lit independently when the ship was alongside; it was used to fire the main propulsion boilers, to provide steam for auxiliary machinery such as the windlass and the after capstan, for services for the crew, and for heating of the living spaces. It was generally smaller than the units which provided steam for the turbines, and was fitted in wherever there was a suitable space; it was located in one or other of the engine rooms in the early ships, which had relatively small and cramped boiler rooms, but in the later light cruisers was accommodated in one of the main boiler rooms, to port or to starboard of the main boilers, which were offset accordingly. The auxiliary boiler fitted in the *Algérie* was a more substantial model, and was installed alongside the single larger-capacity (propulsion) boiler in the third boiler room.

The foundry and the galleys were fuelled by coal, for which separate bunkers were provided forward (see *Duquesne*) or amidships (see *La Galissonnière*). The galleys of the later cruisers were normally fuelled by oil, although the fuel shortages of 1941 saw the conversion of the galleys of some ships, notably the Toulon-based *Marseillaise* and *Jean de Vienne*, to burn coal.

Electrical supply

Power for the guns, fire control systems, propulsion machinery, rudders, and for other onboard services including lighting, was provided from a 230–235V electrical circuit. At sea the supply was generated by four turbo-dynamos powered by steam from the turbines. When the ship was alongside power was provided from one or both of two diesel generators.

Distribution of the turbo-dynamos and diesels was determined by two factors: damage control, for which separation and emergency back-up systems were required; and the need to divide the main generators between the forward and after parts of the ship, where the main consumers of electrical power (turrets, fire control directors and rudder servo-motors) were located, in order to minimise cable runs. The early cruisers of the inter-war period had two turbo-generators in the after engine room, while the forward pair was located in a separate dynamo room forward, around (or just abaft) the ammunition trunk for turret II.[4] The *Duquesne*s and the four *Suffren*s had the forward turbo-dynamos co-located for the first time with the diesel generators in a large, aerated dynamo room which also housed the main switchboard. Cabling and the steam lines for the turbo-generators were run along the inboard sides of the main longitudinal bulkheads in separate tunnels. The turbo-dynamos and diesel generators could be linked together in pairs, and generally shared a common switchboard.

In the cruiser *Algérie*, damage control arrangements were improved by separating the two diesel generators from the forward turbo-generators and locating them at a higher level, on the First (Upper) Deck just forward of the torpedo tubes, to port. This arrangement was taken a stage further in the *La Galissonnière* class. In these ships the turbo-dynamos were distributed between the two large engine rooms, to port and to starboard of the main turbines, which were offset due to the adoption of a two-shaft unit propulsion layout. This freed up space forward on the Platform Deck for a more extensive suite of control spaces, which now included spaces for the remote power control servo-motors and converters. The two main diesel-generators were located on the Main Deck amidships, to port, and there was a third diesel on the First (Upper) Deck, in a deckhouse to starboard of the fore-funnel. This unit was intended to provide emergency power in the event of extensive damage and flooding below. This arrangement was to have been repeated in the *De Grasse* class.

In common with the experience of other major navies, electrical power requirements increased over the period. The turbo-dynamos of the early ships were rated at 200kW per unit, whereas in the later *Algérie* and *De Grasse* this figure was increased to 300kW. The standard diesel-generator was rated at 100kW (120kW overload for a one hour), but whereas the early ships had only two units, later ships had three.

PROTECTION

Early French cruisers of the inter-war period relied on subdivision rather than armour for protection. High speed and armament were prioritised, which left little weight available for protection given the 10,000-ton displacement limit imposed by the Washington Treaty. In these early ships strenuous efforts were made by the designers to reduce the length of the individual machinery spaces, particularly boiler rooms, to enable the ships to resist flooding from a single torpedo hit amidships. The only protection comprised layered 30mm plating on the turrets and conning towers, and 20–30mm boxes around the magazines. Despite rela-

---

4 The main gun turrets aboard French major warships were designated as follows from fore to aft: *Extrême avant* (Ext. AV), *Avant* (AV), *Arrière* (AR), *Extrême arrière* (Ext. AR). Alternatively, they were given the roman numerals I, II, III and IV respectively. The latter system is the one used in this book.

tively thick scantlings, even small-calibre shell could easily penetrate the hull close to the waterline, making the ships vulnerable not only to the fire of other cruisers but also of flotilla craft.

This was quickly recognised as unsatisfactory, and for the *Suffren* class which followed the *Duquesne*s it was decided to sacrifice high speed for protection. Ship horsepower was reduced by 25 per cent, and the weight saved was used to provide a narrow 50mm waterline belt 2.6m high over the machinery spaces. The boxes around the magazines had protection of the same thickness. The total weight of protection in this 'second generation' of Treaty cruisers (554 tonnes in *Suffren*, 671 tonnes for *Colbert*, plus 91 tonnes for the main turrets) was a significant increase on the corresponding figure for the *Duquesne*s (368 + 91 tonnes), but did not yet approach the figures for contemporary foreign cruisers.[5]

More weight was found in the next two ships by reviewing the quantities of consumables declared under standard displacement – a practice which paralleled that in other navies. The weight of the hull and its fittings was also reduced by extensive use of duralumin alloy for internal partitions and fittings, as in the *contre-torpilleurs* of the period. However, rather than go down the conventional path of an external belt, the French opted for an internal armoured 'caisson' which enclosed all the machinery spaces to the height of the Main Deck.

Foch had vertical plating 54mm thick, and in *Dupleix* this figure was increased to 60mm. The total weight of hull protection virtually doubled, to 1283 tonnes in *Foch* and 1462 tonnes in *Dupleix*. In contrast hull weight declined from 4967 tonnes in *Colbert* to 4000 tonnes in *Dupleix*, a reduction of 20 per cent. In the proposed C4 design based on the *Dupleix*, the weight of protection would have been 1820 tonnes, while the weight of the hull declined still further, to 3784 tonnes.

In the event the Marine Nationale opted for a complete and radical redesign for the final Treaty cruiser, the *Algérie*. By adopting a flush deck and a modern in-line propulsion plant employing superheating, sufficient weight was saved for a conventional modern protection system, with an armoured 'citadel' which formed a carapace over the machinery spaces and the magazines and an anti-torpedo system which featured liquid loading. A 110mm NC armour belt 3.7m high was complemented by an 80mm armoured deck, while the conning tower and the turret faces were protected by plates 100mm thick. Behind the armour belt and beneath the waterline there was a layered anti-torpedo protection system comprising the now-customary 'sandwich' with void compartments either side of the oil fuel bunkers, backed up by a 40mm torpedo bulkhead with a 'holding' bulkhead inboard of it to prevent water invading the machinery spaces. The total weight of protection rose to 2035 tonnes – 20 per cent of standard displacement.

Following the London Treaty of 1930 the French followed developments in the British Royal Navy in opting for cruisers of more modest size (less than 8000 tons) armed with 152mm (6in) guns. However, despite the reversion to a raised forecastle, the six

ships of the *La Galissonnière* class were similarly protected to the *Algérie*, with an armoured citadel covering the machinery spaces and magazines. The boiler rooms and engine rooms for their two-shaft propulsion plant were longer than in earlier French cruisers, but now that the machinery spaces were within an armoured citadel, length and subdivision were less important considerations. However, the reduction in beam precluded an effective underwater protection system. The total weight of protection as designed (figures from 15 April 1936) was 1660 tonnes, 21.5 per cent of standard displacement (7720 tonnes). The later *De Grasse* class would have had a similar level of protection.

COMMAND SPACES

All French cruisers of the inter-war period had conning towers, from which the ship could be operated during an engagement. The conning tower was a relatively compact space, with curved walls to provide maximum strength, so it could accommodate only a handful of picked staff to support the Captain and, if flag staff were embarked, the Admiral.

The conning towers on the cruisers differed from those on the modern battleships in a number of important respects. Both types were on two levels, but on the cruisers the 'fighting' and 'tactical' functions were kept separate.[6] The upper level housed the *Poste de manoeuvre*, from which the ship was conned, and the *Poste de tir* (fire control station). The instruments for the latter were on a raised platform towards the rear of the conning tower; directly above it was a cupola, armoured on the same scale as the upper level of the conning tower, which was provided with observation slits. The captain's station was at the centre of this raised platform, from which he could oversee all the key operations. There was access via heavy armoured doors to the compass platform at the forward end, and to the captain's sea cabin and charthouse at the after end. Access to the lower level of the conning tower was via an internal ladder.

The lower level was the domain of an embarked flag officer. It housed the *Central opérations*, with the flag plot, and the *Central transmissions*, which handled reception and transmission of all messages to and from other ships and shore stations. The *Central transmissions* incorporated an encryption/decryption station (*Chiffre*) equipped with the necessary codebooks and transmitting equipment. In many ships there was access forward to an enclosed admiral's bridge (directly beneath the compass platform) and aft to the admiral's sea cabin and charthouse. If the ship concerned was not a flagship these facilities were normally under the command of the Executive or First Officer, the *Officier en second*, whose primary task in combat was to ensure close co-operation with the other ships in the division and other friendly units in the area.

Only the upper level of the conning tower, which

---

[5] Protection for the British *Kent*s weighed 1025 tons.

[6] In the battleships the ship was conned from the lower level, and the Operations Centre (the province of the admiral) was on the upper level directly abaft the stations of the CO and the Gunnery Control Officer. For the layout of a battleship conning tower see John Jordan & Robert Dumas, *French Battleships 1922-1956*, p.45 and p.114.

Conning Tower: 7600-ton Cruiser

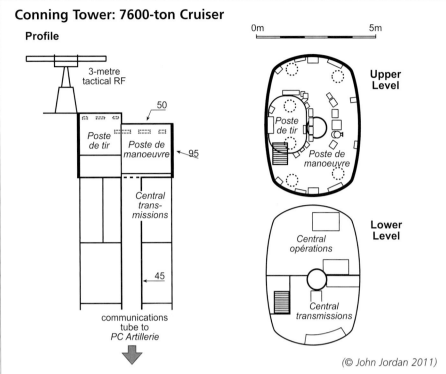

(© John Jordan 2011)

In combat the ship was fought from the conning tower, which was normally under armour. The upper level housed the *Poste de manoeuvre*, from which the ship was conned, and the *Poste de tir* (fire control station), which was normally on a raised platform. The *Poste de manoeuvre* was generally equipped with a steering bar and repeater, two gyrocompass repeaters, a transmitter of helm orders, engine order transmitters for each group of turbines with repeaters, speed and ahead/astern indicators, a board for reading signals and a blackboard to write orders. The *Poste de tir* was normally on a raised platform towards the rear of the conning tower. Directly above it was a cupola, armoured on the same scale as the upper level of the conning tower, which was provided with observation slits. The captain's station was at the centre of this raised platform, from which he could oversee all the key operations; his position was equipped with two periscopic glasses and a collapsible chart table. To either side of him there were the port and starboard fire control stations, each of which was equipped with a periscopic glass, telephones, loudspeakers, push-buttons for communication, and a fire control console.

The lower level housed the Operations and Transmissions Centres, the latter including a Decryption/Encryption Centre. The Operations Centre was equipped with a plotting table, a repeater showing engine rpm, and fire control consoles. The main W/T reception office was normally located directly abaft the conning tower on the lower level.

Foch: Command Decks

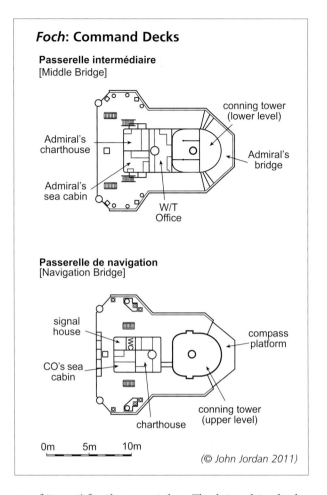

(© John Jordan 2011)

housed the most important 'battle' functions, the manoeuvring of the ship and fire control, was under armour. In the early ships only light splinter protection was provided in the form of 30mm (15mm + 15mm) steel plating. However, the later *Algérie* and the six light cruisers of the *La Galissonnière* class had the upper level of the conning tower protected by heavy NC plating: 100mm walls and a 70mm roof in the *Algérie*, reduced only slightly to 95mm walls with a 50mm roof in the light cruisers. The communications tube, linking the upper level of the conning tower with the transmitting station, which in the later ships was under armour beneath the main deck, had only light 20mm protection in the early ships but more heavily armoured in the later ships: 50mm in the *Algérie* and 45mm in the light cruisers.

Atop the conning tower, and generally mounted on the cupola itself, was a rangefinder. The rangefinders on the early cruisers were 4-metre coincidence models. They were superseded on the four *Suffren*s by a similar model with a 5-metre base. Both models were trainable through 360 degrees and had an enclosed, weather-

proof 'turret' for the rangetaker. The later ships had a lightweight 3-metre 'open' rangefinder which was trialled on the *Foch*. The primary purpose of the rangefinder was observation of the target – hence its location directly above the *Poste de tir* – and torpedo fire control, but it could also be used for 'tactical' purposes to inform the captain of the ship or an embarked admiral.

The conning tower provided in the *Duguay-Trouin* class established the pattern for the cruisers laid down during the 1920s. However, it was relatively cramped, and the conning towers installed in the *Duquesne*s and the early *Suffren*s were significantly larger. The first major change in design came with the *Dupleix*, in which the conning tower was shorter but significantly broader. This seems to have facilitated a much-improved internal layout, with better views forward and to the sides. It was adopted for the later *Algérie* and the *La Galissonnière* class.

The final change came with the *De Grasse* design, in which the conning tower was integrated more closely with the forward tower. It was both broader and narrower, with the *Poste de manoeuvre* on a raised platform occupying the central section and overlooking the compass platform, and *Postes de tir* to port and to starboard at the outer (curved) extremities.

ARMAMENT
Main battery
The *Duguay-Trouin*s were among the first cruisers in the world to have their main armament exclusively in power-operated twin turrets fore and aft. They set the pattern for French cruiser construction during the

1920s, the Treaty cruisers of the *Duquesne* class being essentially enlarged and upgunned versions of the earlier ships.

The 155mm (6.1in) gun adopted for the *Duguay-Trouins* was not previously a naval calibre, earlier cruisers having been armed with the 164.7mm gun (6.5in – in both turrets and casemates), while the abortive scout cruisers of the *Lamotte-Piquet* class projected as part of the 1912 Naval Programme would have been armed with the same 138.6mm (5.5in) gun employed as the secondary armament of the French dreadnoughts. The 155mm was the standard Army medium/heavy calibre, and the gun on the *Duguay-Trouins* was derived from land-based models. The turret itself was a scaled-down battleship model, using a standard two-stage replenishment hoist system in a trunk which rotated with the turret. The projectiles and bagged propellant charges, stowed in shell rooms and magazines in the bowels of the ship, were raised to the working chamber (the lowest platform of the turret structure) via twin dredger-type cage hoists housed within a cylindrical ammunition trunk. They were then transferred to the upper cage hoists, which emerged outside the breeches of the guns. The shell and the two half-charges were then transferred to loading trays and rammed into the breech, ready for firing.

The French had used twin and single powered turrets extensively for their earlier armoured cruisers, and had acquired considerable experience in their design and operation. Turrets – particularly if armoured – had the advantage of providing complete protection for the gun crew, and the electrically-powered replenishment and loading machinery reduced their workload, so that a steady rate of fire could be sustained for longer periods. However, despite the reduction from four quarter-charges to two half-charges and the slightly reduced height of the ammunition hoists, the firing cycle of the cruiser turrets was little better than that of contemporary battleships. The 155mm turrets in the *Duguay-Trouins* had a firing cycle of only three to four rounds per gun per minute, and the 203mm (8in) turret of the Treaty cruisers was similar in this respect.

The 152mm (6in) gun adopted following the London Treaty of 1930 was also a non-traditional French naval calibre, and appears to have been adopted simply for commonality with the other major navies – of the treaty powers only the Japanese opted for the maximum 155mm calibre permitted by the London 1930 treaty. Both the gun and turret were of completely new design and broke with previous practice. The 152mm was the first French medium-calibre gun to have the semi-automatic sliding breech patented by the Imperial German Navy and which had so impressed the Marine Nationale when it inherited the large destroyer *S 113* – she became the *Amiral Sénès*. The sliding breech was much quicker in operation than the traditional Welin interrupted-screw model retained in the 155mm and 203mm guns, and therefore had the potential to increase the rate of fire provided the replenishment cycle could also be speeded up. For the new triple turret – another first in the Marine Nationale – two-stage cage-type hoists were abandoned in favour of continuous 'pusher' hoists, which could be angled to come up beside the gun. The hoist for the 152mm shell emerged on the left and the hoist for the propellant – now in a single aluminium

bronze case rather than separate bagged half-charges – on the right. Projectile and cartridge were then tipped by hand onto a slide which ran alongside the gun to the power-operated loading gear. The much-increased rate of fire possible with the new arrangements – a theoretical eight rounds per minute for the low-angle turrets installed in the *Emile Bertin* and the *La Galissonnière* class – led to proposals for a dual-purpose turret, which was subsequently adopted for the battleships of the *Richelieu* class. However, the dual-purpose (DP) turret Mle 1936 was more complex, significantly heavier, and required a barbette of increased diameter. It was considered for the *De Grasse* class but rejected for the above reasons, and the turret adopted for the latter would have been restricted to 70 degrees elevation.

Fire control

Director fire control, although well-established in the British Royal Navy for both main and secondary batteries, was not adopted by the Marine Nationale until after the First World War. Following trials with Vickers directors and locally-developed models in the surviving French dreadnoughts during the early 1920s, a new director control tower similar in conception to that developed for the Royal Navy entered service with the *Duguay-Trouins* from 1929. The French directors were unusual in being fitted with both a 5-metre coincidence rangefinder (for target

Below: The *Duguay-Trouins* were among the first cruisers in the world to have their main armament exclusively in power-operated twin turrets fore and aft. *Duguay-Trouin* is seen here in August 1945. The director is unmodified, but there is now an American SF-1 surface surveillance radar on the topmast; the latter was fitted in February 1944. *(ECPAD)*

range) and a 3-metre stereoscopic model for scartometry (the measurement of the distance between shell splashes and the target). The directors supplied range and bearing data, together with gun angle (*hausse*) to a transmitting station (*Poste central artillerie*) below decks, which in the later cruisers was under armour. The mechanical computer in the transmitting station (Mle 1923 in the *Duguay-Trouin*s, Mle 1924 for the Treaty cruisers) established a training angle for the turrets and elevation for the guns, taking into account deflection and parallax, and transmitted these to the turrets via a follow-the-pointer (FTP) system or, in the event of systems failure, a special telephone network designated '*téléphone* 17'. During the late 1930s remote power control (RPC), which enabled turrets to be trained and guns to be kept on the target irrespective of platform movement, was introduced, but it was often difficult to find the necessary space for servomotors in the older cruisers and the systems installed in the newer ships were generally not liked. Even where fitted RPC was regarded as unreliable; it was often disabled during combat and, in many cases, subsequently removed.

Once director control was adopted for the main guns, the post of the Gunnery Control Officer was transferred from the conning tower to the director control tower (DCT) itself. Despite this, the armoured conning tower (see Command Spaces above) continued to be the main centre from which the ship was fought when in combat. Each of the two firing positions (*Postes de tir*) in the conning tower was equipped with periscopic glasses. These enabled the *Poste de tir* to generate an angle of train which was then transmitted to the *PC artillerie*. Both the director control tower and the conning tower were equipped for remote firing of the guns (taking into account movement of the platform).

The emergency fire control position was at the rear end of turret III, which in the Treaty cruisers was equipped for the purpose with a second 5-metre SOM coincidence rangefinder – in later ships it would be superseded by a stereoscopic model with an 8-metre base, as would the 5-metre C model in the director control tower. There was a third 5-metre C (later 8-

metre S) rangefinder atop turret II. Both turrets could send range and bearing data to the transmitting station, but only turret III had a control position which enabled it to coordinate the firing of all four turrets. The turret rangefinders permitted independent training up to 15 degrees on either side of the turret axis. This allowed the rangefinder to remain on the target when the turret was trained to take into account deflection.

High-angle guns

The early French inter-war cruisers (up to and including *Suffren*) were equipped with the single 75mm/50 gun Mle 1922/24, which also equipped the *contre-torpilleurs* and *torpilleurs* of the period. The *Duguay-Trouin*s had four, disposed amidships abeam the funnels, with 3-metre coincidence rangefinders to provide range for surface engagement. The larger Treaty cruisers had eight, disposed in four groups of two fore and aft, on the forecastle deck at the base of the bridge and at the after end of the boat deck respectively. Three-metre rangefinders for high-angle (HA) control were fitted in the bridge wings as a temporary measure, but it was always envisaged that these would be replaced by directors specially designed for HA fire using newly-developed 3-metre stereoscopic rangefinders. Delays in the development and production of the director meant that it was available only from 1933, and all the early 10,000-ton cruisers plus the *Colbert* had to be retro-fitted with the equipment following completion.

From the *Colbert* onwards the standard HA weapon was the 90mm/50 Mle 1926, first in a single then in a twin mounting. The *Algérie* had the 100mm/45 Mle 1930 in an open twin mounting similar to that of the 90mm twin, while the cruisers of the *De Grasse* class would have had a more advanced 100mm model in a fully-enclosed, high-performance twin mounting.

All of these HA guns proved to be reliable and reasonably effective weapons, but the constant quest for incremental improvements brought with it a lack of standardisation which was costly in terms of development, procurement, logistics and maintenance. The Royal Navy of the inter-war period adopted the 4in calibre from the outset for its cruisers, progressing from single to twin mountings; the US Navy opted initially for a 5in/25 single mounting, moving to the 5in/38 for the cruisers built in the 1930s; and the Italians stuck with their 100mm/47 (3.9in) twin mounting for all their inter-war cruisers. By contrast the Marine Nationale, with far fewer cruisers than the USA or Britain, had in service or under development three different gun calibres in no fewer than five different mountings by 1939.

High-angle fire control

The standard HA director was long in development and had to be retro-fitted in most of the ships designed to receive it. It was initially fitted with a 3-metre OPL stereo rangefinder (see drawing and caption in Chapter 1) and installed either in the upper bridge wings (most ships), abeam the fore-funnel (*Suffren* and *Dupleix*) or atop the tripod foremast or tower (*Foch* and *Algérie*). The associated fire control table, Mle 1930, was not ready for installation until 1934. Ships with only four HA guns (the *Duguay-Trouin*s and *Emile Bertin*) had only one fire control table, which meant that only a single target to port or to starboard could be engaged at any one time. As first delivered the upper part of the director

Below: *Marseillaise* with the later-pattern director control tower, equipped with an 8-metre stereoscopic rangefinder, atop the tripod foremast. The port-side HA director can be seen to the left of the crane, at the after end of the bridge wings. (*ECPAD*)

was open to the weather. However, in the late 1930s most directors were roofed over with steel and glass.

Light anti-aircraft guns

Beginning with the Treaty cruisers, the Marine Nationale complemented its HA guns with light anti-aircraft (AA) weapons comparable to those entering service with the other major navies. Initially the standard gun was the 37mm/50 Mle 1925 in a single mounting (*contre-avions simple* – CAS), a reliable weapon with a modest rate of fire of around 20rpm. With the midship section of the inter-war cruisers cluttered by boats, catapults and bulky reconnaissance aircraft it was often difficult to find a suitable location for these guns. In consequence they were generally mounted on the forecastle and quarterdeck, where they enjoyed good all-round firing arcs but were exposed to the elements. Small 1-metre rangefinders with headphone links were generally provided for each pair of guns. These proved unsatisfactory during combat due to noise levels.

From the early 1930s a new machine gun, the 13.2mm/76 Hotchkiss, became available in twin (*contre-avions double* – CAD) and quad (*contre-avions quadruple* – CAQ) mountings. Its light weight meant that it could be fitted higher in the ship, and twin mountings were often fitted atop the conning tower or in the bridge wings. Essentially a 'last-ditch' weapon, firing through open sights, it had a high rate of fire but lacked the necessary punch and range against modern high-performance metal-skinned aircraft. The mountings were retro-fitted in existing cruisers from around 1933, and the later Treaty cruisers, starting with *Colbert*, were intended to complete with two or four quad mountings, although due to production difficulties these were not generally available until 1941.

By the early 1930s it was becoming apparent that anticipated improvements in aircraft performance meant that the rate of fire of the 37mm CAS would be inadequate. As a temporary measure it was decided to develop a 37mm CAD which essentially comprised two 37mm CAS on a common mounting, pending the investigation of other more advanced solutions. However, production delays meant that the twin mounting was only available in numbers from the late 1930s, and some ships did not receive their planned outfits until after the Armistice of 1940.

From 1941 a new light MG, the Browning 13.2mm – a development of the US 0.5in model – began to be produced in numbers, and single mountings (CAS) were used to supplement existing AA weapons and bolted on wherever space could be found, often on the initiative of the on-board personnel.

The necessary improvements in the close-range AA capabilities of French cruisers were late in arriving and piecemeal in their implementation. Only the *Algérie* and the *Colbert* received a major, planned revision of their light AA arrangements prior to the scuttling at Toulon in November 1942, and even this refit was modest in its scope and ambition. Since the terms of the Armistice prohibited any increase in military capabilities, the only measure possible was a redistribution of the existing AA weaponry to provide superior arcs. Both ships had their mainmast suppressed, and in its place a tiered deckhouse (referred to as a 'pergola') was constructed to house the after light AA. This was complemented by a plat-form above the bridge for the forward gun mountings.

Only the modern light cruisers which survived the scuttling at Toulon and were refitted in US naval dockyards received a radical and comprehensive modernisation. Aircraft hangars, catapults and cranes were stripped out and the deck-space gained utilised to fit four/six large quad 40mm Bofors mountings in tubs, each with its own Mk 51 tachymetric director; these were complemented by multiple stand-alone 20mm Oerlikon guns for close-in defence. The French were so impressed with the capabilities of the 40mm quads they attempted to acquire further mountings for the older surviving heavy cruisers, going so far as to construct the necessary tubs aboard these ships in readiness for their projected delivery during 1944–5. In the event, however, the USA refused to supply the mountings, and British/Canadian single Bofors Mk III guns were fitted in their place.

Torpedoes

From the outset torpedoes were considered by the French to be an important part of the cruiser's armoury. They were to have been fired at relatively long range as 'browning shots' against enemy line formations. The new torpedoes developed after the First World War were notable for their 550mm (21.65in) bodies, which constituted a major advance on the 450mm (17.7in) diameter of earlier French torpedoes in terms of range and size of warhead, but also meant that they needed a bigger ship to carry them in the required numbers. The first post-war model, the Mle 1919D, carried a 238kg warhead of picric acid, and had two speed settings: 6000m at 35kts, and 14,000m at 25kts. It was superseded by the much-improved Mle1923D, which had a more powerful warhead of 415kg of TNT, and range settings of 9000m at 39kts and 13,000m at 35kts.

The cruisers of the *Duguay-Trouin* class set the pattern with four triple torpedo tube mountings amidships, served by a large torpedo workshop on the centre-line with four reload lockers each holding three spare torpedoes inboard of the tubes. There were concerns regarding the vulnerability of the ship to the explosion of her own torpedoes in the event of action damage, so individual steel lockers were provided on the deck edge amidships for the torpedo warheads. These were hinged on the outboard side so that in the event of fire the warheads could be tipped into the sea.

Size and weight constraints prevented the Treaty cruisers of the *Duquesne* and *Suffren* classes from embarking such a substantial torpedo payload, but arrangements were otherwise similar. In the *Duquesne*s there were triple torpedo tube mountings to port and starboard with a capacious torpedo workshop on the centre line between them. A single athwartships locker containing three reloads was placed centrally in the workshop, with torpedo maintenance and reloading stations on either side aligned with each mounting, the tubes being offset *en echelon*. This arrangement was repeated in *Suffren*, but in the later three ships of the class it was simplified, the two torpedo tube mountings being mounted opposite one another with only a single maintenance/reloading station between. *Algérie* was similar, except that the torpedo workshop was forward of the tubes, at the after end of the bridge structure, and the reloading station was on the open upper deck between the tubes.

In the light cruisers built during the 1930s deck space considerations related to the need to accommodate and operate large, capable reconnaissance aircraft precluded the large torpedo loadouts and elaborate torpedo maintenance and reloading facilities of the earlier ships. The only torpedoes embarked on these ships were carried in their tubes, and in the *La Galissonnière* class these were in twin rather than triple mountings.

UNDERWATER SENSORS

The French were very conscious of the submarine threat following their experience in the First World War, when no fewer than three battleships (*Gaulois*, *Suffren* and *Danton*) were sunk by German U-Boats and others seriously damaged. It was initially envisaged that all of the new cruisers would have both active and passive underwater detection systems to minimise the threat of torpedo damage from unseen opponents. There was space provision for a retractable tube for an ultrasound 'pinger' with its associated sonar room (*cabine d'écoute*), generally just forward of the foremost boiler room, and for Walser passive hydrophones (a development of a system developed during the Great War) beneath the hull at the mid-point between the bridge structure and the bow. It was envisaged that the primary purpose of these systems was to provide early warning of the presence of a submarine; the cruiser would then undertake evasive measures rather than attempt to prosecute the contact, leaving the latter mission to any flotilla craft in company.

However, French ambitions were not matched by results. The installation of ultrasound 'pingers' was begun in 1929 aboard the new destroyers of the *Bourrasque* class, but was quickly abandoned due to technical difficulties. At the same time Walser-type passive hydrophones were trialled aboard the *contre-torpilleur Panthère* and the destroyer *Siroco*, but proved to be virtually useless when the ship was underway, any signal being completely masked by the self-noise generated by the ship's machinery and the movement of the hull through the water. The spaces built into the ships were retained to await future developments, but when an effective detection apparatus finally became available in late 1939 – the British ASDIC 128, renamed 'Alpha' in French service – priority for fitting was naturally accorded to the older French *contre-torpilleurs* of the *Jaguar* class and the destroyers.

The other underwater systems to be fitted as standard in French cruisers were the Fessenden apparatus, developed during the Great War to communicate with friendly submarines, and the Warluzel depth-sounder developed during the 1920s, for which booms and winches were fitted on either side of the bridge. As the space for the retractable ultrasound tube was generally located to starboard, the Fessenden apparatus was often located in the port-side compartment directly opposite.

AIRCRAFT

The Marine Nationale of the inter-war period was fully committed to naval aviation, and envisaged that all future ships of cruiser size and above would carry and operate aircraft for reconnaissance and spotting duties. The first reconnaissance seaplane to be developed for deployment aboard cruisers, the Schreck FBA 17, a wood-and-canvas single-engine biplane, under-

went its first catapult launch on 22 October 1926. The FBA 17 subsequently conducted trials aboard the cruiser *Primauguet* using a prototype 20-metre catapult powered by compressed air, which was installed on the quarterdeck. Similar catapults were installed on her two sisters in the Spring of 1929, but although the boat crane was lengthened to handle the aircraft it could not place the aircraft atop the catapult, so a collapsible crane was subsequently installed on the port side of the quarterdeck. The 1600kg capacity of the catapult and cranes, together with the less-than-satisfactory handling arrangements, were an undoubted constraint, and these three ships always carried fewer, smaller aircraft than the later cruisers.

In contrast, aviation facilities were incorporated into the design of the Treaty cruisers of the *Duquesne* class from the outset, effectively replacing the two after torpedo tube mountings and their reloads. A 22-metre catapult of a new type powered by gunpowder was located at the after end of the shelter deck, between the second funnel and the mainmast. Two reconnaissance seaplanes could be operated, one of which was stowed on the centre-line between the funnels and the other on the catapult itself. The boat crane was extended to enable it to lift aircraft manoeuvring alongside into the rest position; there was a separate derrick on the mainmast to lift aircraft directly onto the catapult. Although by no means ideal due to the interposition of the second funnel between the stowage position and the catapult, this arrangement was a big improvement on the *Duguay-Trouin*s. The dangerously volatile aviation fuel was stowed, as in the *Duguay-Trouin*s, in separate tanks high in the stern.

Although *Tourville* embarked an FBA 17 for a short period during 1929, the *Duquesne*s were designed to operate the larger CAMS 37A flying boat, which had folding wings, bomb racks and a crew of three: an observer/bomb-aimer, a pilot and a rear machine-gunner. With a maximum take-off weight in excess of 3000kg, the CAMS 37A was too large and too heavy to be accommodated aboard the earlier ships. It did not like being catapulted, and by the early 1930s was being relegated to shore duties, being replaced in the shipborne reconnaissance role by the purpose-designed Gourdou Leseurre GL 810/811/812 series of three-seat float monoplanes.

The next Treaty cruiser, *Suffren*, was generally similar in her topsides layout to *Duquesne* and *Tourville*, but in place of the single centre-line catapult of the latter there were twin catapults to port and to starboard, the number of aircraft being correspondingly increased from two to three. The 'rest' position for the third aircraft was still between the funnels, and because the catapults had been moved forward and to the sides they could now be served by the single extended boat crane.

In *Colbert*, the fourth of the French Treaty cruisers, the position of the boats and the catapults was reversed, with the latter located between the funnels and the 'rest' position between the after funnel and the mainmast. This enabled both catapults and boats to be served by twin 'goose-neck' cranes located outboard of the second funnel. This arrangement proved particularly successful and was adopted for the fifth and sixth ships, *Foch* and *Dupleix*. The construction of these three ships spanned the changeover from the CAMS 37A to the GL 810 float monoplane, and although the official profile and plan views of *Suffren*, *Colbert* and *Foch* show the CAMS 37A on their catapults, all three ships would operate the GL 810 from the outset, the first production aircraft being embarked on *Colbert* for trials in April 1930.

The early variant of the Gourdou-Leseurre monoplane had fixed wings, and the aircraft therefore had to be stowed *en echelon* atop the catapults to prevent the wings from overlapping. The later GL 811 and GL 812 variants had folding wings. A smaller variant, the GL 832, with an all-up weight of just under 1700kg, was specially developed for the older light cruisers, the first operational aircraft being embarked in the *Lamotte-Piquet* prior to her deployment to the Far East in 1936. The GL 810/811/812, a comparatively robust aircraft with a metallic fuselage, proved particularly successful in service, and would be the primary French shipborne reconnaissance aircraft from 1931 until 1939, when it was replaced by the high-wing Loire 130 seaplane. The latter was a heavier aircraft, with a maximum take-off weight of 3500kg (vs 2460kg for the GL series), and could be launched only following catapult upgrades which took place from 1937 onwards.

The last of the Treaty cruisers, *Algérie*, had a radically different topside layout to the earlier ships, and the need to save weight for protection and an enhanced AA armament meant that she was reduced to a single catapult to port, just abaft the single funnel. The catapult was a new model using compressed air, and was served by the larger of the two cranes supported from the searchlight platform amidships. Only two aircraft (GL 811/812 types) were normally embarked, the second aircraft being stowed on the shelter deck abaft the funnel.

Despite the reduction in displacement of the cruisers built after 1930, the six ships of the *La Galissonnière* class, which were intended to scout for the fleet, had the most comprehensive aviation arrangements yet. Designed to operate the new Loire 130 reconnaissance seaplane, they were also to carry two float fighters capable of shooting down enemy long-range bombers and reconnaissance aircraft. The aircraft eventually selected for this role was the Loire 210, a single-seat monoplane of modern construction with a maximum take-off weight of 2180kg. Two Loire 130 aircraft could be accommodated, wings folded, in a capacious double hangar aft; one of the Loire 210 float fighters would be carried on rails atop the hangar, and the fourth atop the single catapult. Originally this was to have been mounted between the hangar and the after turret, but a lack of centre-line space meant that it was relocated atop the turret itself. The catapult was a new telescopic model, with a folded length of 14.6m, and was powered by compressed air. In the event the Loire 210 experienced serious structural problems during its development and was abandoned, so that in service the ships generally operated only two Loire 130 seaplanes.

Concerns regarding the vulnerability of the cruisers while they were stopped recovering their aircraft led to the adoption of 'landing mats' of German design which were deployed from the stern. The aircraft taxied onto the mat on landing and was recovered over the stern by crane with the ship making between 10 and 15 knots. The mats, which were manufactured in France under licence, were of ribbed canvas and measured 12m by 8m. The recovery system had a considerable

impact on the design of the after part of the ships, which had a transom stern to accommodate and stream the mat, a supplementary folding crane at the stern to hoist the aircraft on board, and rails set in the quarterdeck which ran from the stern to the hangar.

Despite the effort and expense invested in these facilities – there were no fewer than five cranes on these ships! – they did not prove a success. The catapult and the aircraft atop it were subject to severe vibration, and the heavy folding catapult placed an unwelcome load on the training motors of the turret itself. The mats proved difficult to deploy and recover, and because they had to be stowed wet on the stern drum they rotted away over time; all had been removed by February 1942, and the three ships which survived the scuttling at Toulon had their hangars, catapults and cranes removed during their modernisation in the United States in 1943, in order to make room for powerful new batteries of AA guns.

The final class of ships ordered, the three cruisers of the *De Grasse* class, would have had twin hangars amidships, on either side of the single funnel, and twin catapults at the after end of the boat deck. Recovery arrangements would have been as in the *La Galissonnière* class. The midships arrangements were extremely cramped – a single fixed athwartships catapult on the British pattern would arguably have been far better – and the hangars were suppressed to save weight. With the failure of the mat recovery system the nameship *De Grasse*, the only ship of the class to be launched, had her stern modified, receiving a traditional 'cruiser' stern in place of the designed transom.

BOATS

It was common for French cruisers, like their British counterparts, to moor at a buoy in an anchorage rather than come alongside when in port. Toulon had a set of finger piers, known as the *Appontements Milhaud*, which could accommodate a cruiser or a

Above: Pierre Cot, the French Air Minister, embarks on one of *Suffren*'s GL 810 floatplanes ready for a catapult launch in late July 1933. *(New York Times)*

Colbert: Boat Deck

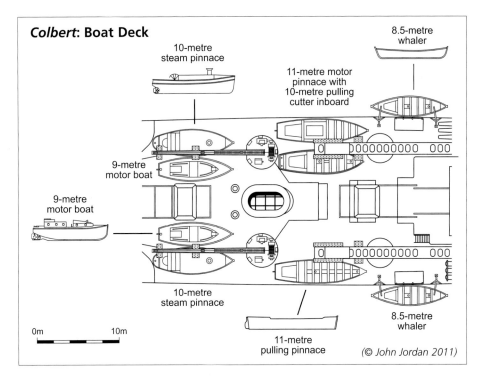

10-metre
steam pinnace

8.5-metre
whaler

11-metre motor
pinnace with
10-metre pulling
cutter inboard

9-metre
motor boat

9-metre
motor boat

10-metre
steam pinnace

8.5-metre
whaler

11-metre
pulling pinnace

0m   10m

(© John Jordan 2011)

battleship on either side. However, even in France's premier Mediterranean base, it was normal for cruisers to moor in the *Grande Rade*, the large enclosed anchorage on the seaward side of the dockyard. This was even more true for Brest, whose historical dockyard was on both sides of a narrow river, the Penfeld, and when performing their regular imperial policing duties, the cruisers would often be expected to anchor in bays where portside facilities were minimal, and crews had to be taken ashore for leave and recreation by boat. Boats were therefore an important part of a ship's equipment, and careful consideration was always given by the designers to the *Drome d'embarcations* and its handling arrangements.

In the cruisers designed from the 1922 *Statut Naval* to the end of the decade, the boats were of four main types. To ferry the crew ashore there were large open boats called *chaloupes* (pinnaces) or *canots* (cutters) with lengths varying between 9m and 11m (the *chaloupes* were longer). In the early days they were generally powered by oars, but some had petrol motors, and during the 1930s they were increasingly powered by diesels.

The second standard type of boat was the *canot à vapeur* (steam pinnace), driven by a reciprocating engine. These fast 10-metre boats were often used for inshore policing duties, for which purpose they could be armed with a 47mm gun at the bow.

The CO, admiral (if embarked) and officers were generally allocated fast motor boats with petrol engines (*vedettes à essence*). Initially these were generally of a standard 9-metre type, but subsequently a smaller 7-metre model became common, and cruisers completed during the 1930s often carried 5-metre motor boats. The 9-metre and 10.8-metre motor boats eventually supplanted the steam pinnace, and were often used to tow the embarked aircraft when operated from the surface in an anchorage. Petrol for the motor boats and motor launches was stowed in separate tanks high in the stern, as was the aviation fuel.

All the above boats were generally stowed on

crutches and handled by boat cranes. Where it was difficult to fit all boats within reach of the crane, some boats were stowed on trolleys which ran on rails. In early cruisers the boat cranes had extensions which enabled them to handle the ship's aircraft, but in later ships the functions were usually kept separate.

The two 8.5-metre (later 8-metre) whalers (*baleinières*) were primarily for rescue purposes. Unlike the other boats they were stowed on davits, usually at weather-deck level, so that they could be launched quickly regardless of sea conditions.

The hulls of the ship's boats were generally painted in the same colour as the hull and superstructures of the mother ship (i.e. *gris clair no.1* for most of their service), with plain wood or white interiors. The cabins of the motor boats were mahogany. The 'Captain's gig' and 'Admiral's barge' were often painted a distinctive colour; blue (sometimes black) hulls were common, as was a white roof.

PAINT SCHEMES

Ships completed before 1930 had their hull and upperworks painted blue-grey (*gris bleuté*). The underside of the ships was red-brown, with a black band at the waterline. From 1930 blue-grey was replaced by a standard light grey designated *gris clair no.1*. Funnel caps and anchors were painted black. Concentration dials initially had black faces and white numbers/hands, although Mediterranean-based ships later had white faces with black numbers/hands. Rangefinder arms were generally painted white to reflect the heat and thereby prevent distortion in the optics.

Decks were generally of bare steel on the forecastle forward of the breakwater, with wood planking from the breakwater to the stern. The first two 7600-ton cruisers had Bordeaux red linoleum on the quarterdeck in place of the wooden planking, but this was not liked and the remaining four ships reverted to wood planking from just forward of the hangar to the stern.

From 1938–42 the anchors on Mediterranean ships were painted light grey to match the hull. From early 1940 ships based in the Atlantic (primarily the *Force de Raid*) were painted in a darker grey. When they returned to Toulon following the Armistice of June 1940 they reverted to their original light grey livery. The only ship to receive a camouflage scheme during the early war period was *Montcalm*, which was given a disruptive scheme of dark grey and light grey for the Norwegian Campaign of April/May 1940.

The cruisers modernised in the United States during 1943 received the US Navy's standard Measure 22, with a Navy Blue hull and upperworks of Haze Gray. Bare steel decks were painted Deck Blue. *Gloire* received an experimental disruptive 'dazzle' scheme of Black, Ocean Gray and Haze Gray, which she carried until June 1944. Measure 22 was retained in the immediate post-war period, but from 1950 the surviving cruisers were repainted in a standard light grey with black funnel caps and anchors.

RECOGNITION MARKINGS[7]

White funnel bands were already in use by the late 1920s, when the first of the *Duguay-Trouin*s entered

---

[7] This section is based on Jean Guiglini, *Les Marques Particulières des Navires de Guerre Français*, Service Historique de la Marine 2002.

Flagships

Vice Amiral d'Escadre **Contre Amiral**

 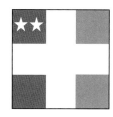

A three-ship division of cruisers was commanded by a Rear-Admiral (*Contre Amiral*). The admiral commanding a Squadron generally held the rank of 'Squadron Vice-Admiral' (*Vice Amiral d'Escadre*). This was the flag flown by the cruiser *Algérie* in her role of flagship of the 1st Cruiser Squadron (VAE Lacroix) in 1942.

(© John Jordan 2011)

Funnel Bands

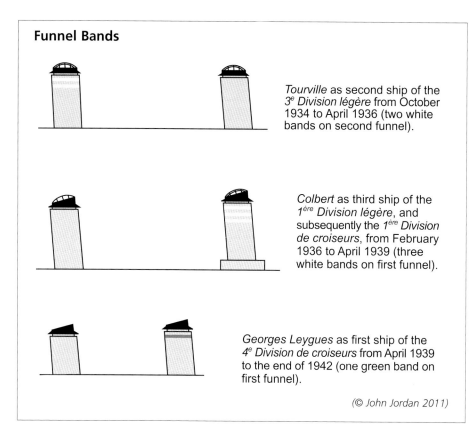

Tourville as second ship of the *3ᵉ Division légère* from October 1934 to April 1936 (two white bands on second funnel).

Colbert as third ship of the *1ᵉʳᵉ Division légère*, and subsequently the *1ᵉʳᵉ Division de croiseurs*, from February 1936 to April 1939 (three white bands on first funnel).

Georges Leygues as first ship of the *4ᵉ Division de croiseurs* from April 1939 to the end of 1942 (one green band on first funnel).

(© John Jordan 2011)

service, to distinguish each ship from the others within a division, but until 1939 the system of markings was determined by the admiral commanding the squadron. The *Duguay-Trouin*s rarely operated as a division except in the early stage of their careers. From 1928–31 the flagship of the division had no funnel bands, the second ship a single funnel band and the third ship two bands, all using the first funnel. From 1931–2 one ship of the class had a single band on the first funnel, the other on the second.

With the entry into service of the 10,000-ton cruisers, markings became more standardised. From 1930 the three ships of the 1st Light Division (*Suffren*, *Duquesne*, *Tourville*) had one, two or three white bands on the first funnel to indicate their position in the division. The bands were 52cm wide, and the first was 45cm from the top of the funnel casing, with 54cm between bands. When the next three ships (*Colbert*, *Foch* and *Dupleix*) entered service they made up a new 1st Light Division, and the three older ships became the 3rd Light Division (see Chapter 9). The same system was retained, but the ships of the 3rd Light Division now had their bands moved to the second funnel. If a fourth ship was temporarily attached to a division (e.g. *Colbert* when she first entered service and again in early 1939) she carried four bands on her funnel.

This system survived the change from Light Divisions to Cruiser Divisions in 1937 (the 3rd Light Division became the 2nd Cruiser Division). However, it was practical only while there were two divisions of cruisers in the Mediterranean Squadron, and with the entry into service of the six cruisers of the 7600-ton type in 1937–8 it was clear that a new system would have to be devised. From February 1939 it was decreed that the allocation of recognition markings would be determined by the Navy Ministry, not by the individual fleet commander, and Admiral Darlan produced a revised scheme which was to be applied from April 1939. In the new scheme all ships would have their bands on the fore-funnel, but these would be coloured as follows:

1st DC (10,000t): white
2nd DC (10,000t): black
3rd DC (7600t): yellow
4th DC (7600t): green
5th DC (8000t): red

This scheme was retained until the end of 1942.

Tricolour recognition bands (blue/white/red from fore to aft) were painted on turrets II and III during the Spanish Civil War 1937–8, and again from 10 July 1940 following the Armistice. These were retained until the end of 1942. The ships serving in the Far East during the Sino-Japanese War (*Lamotte-Piquet* 1937–8, and *Primauguet* 1938–9) had large tricolour bands painted on the roofs of all four turrets.

Below: The tripod foremast and funnel cap of *Gloire* at Dakar during 1942 with the battleship *Richelieu* in the background. The three green funnel bands mark her out as the third ship of the 4th Cruiser Division. *(ECPAD)*

CHAPTER 1

THE *DUGUAY-TROUIN* CLASS

INTRODUCTION

The three 8000-tonne light cruisers of the *Duguay-Trouin* class were the first cruisers laid down in France since 1906, and were radically different from their predecessors. They were also of advanced design when set against their foreign contemporaries. The British 'E' class, laid down in 1918, were more heavily protected, but their build was traditional and their seven 6in guns were in single open-backed mountings. The US Navy's Scout Cruisers of the *Omaha* class, laid down 1918–20, were similar in size and speed and had an impressive armament, but eight of their twelve 6in guns were in double-storey casemates, a dated feature which reduced the number of guns which could fire on the broadside.

The design of the *Duguay-Trouin* class was the culmination of a lengthy development process. During the early 1900s the Marine Nationale had persisted with the construction of large, powerful armoured cruisers, the latest of which had been completed well after the early British and German battlecruisers entered service. The construction of these ships was still occupying the naval dockyards and absorbing a large part of the naval budget at a time when the British and German navies were building light cruisers armed with 4in/10.5cm and 6in/15cm guns and powered by turbines to scout for their respective battle fleets and to lead the destroyer flotillas. This imbalance

became an issue for the Marine Nationale by 1912, and the ambitious *Statut Naval* of the same year proposed the construction of ten fast *éclaireurs d'escadre* ('fleet scouts') to be in service by 1920. After considering a 6000-tonne scout cruiser, the French finally opted for a smaller ship intermediate in size and capabilities between the British *Arethusa* and the German *Magdeburg* and *Karlsruhe* classes. The first of three cruisers of the *Lamotte-Piquet* class, designated *convoyeurs d'escadrilles* ('flotilla leaders'), was due to have been laid down at Toulon Naval Dockyard in November 1914; the other two ships were to be allocated to private shipyards. In the event these ships became early victims of the suspension in construction imposed shortly after the outbreak of war in August 1914, and the Marine Nationale was to end the Great War without a single modern light cruiser in service.

The *Lamotte-Piquet* design was entirely conventional (see drawing). The main armament of eight 138.6mm (5.5in) guns was disposed in single shielded mountings superimposed fore and aft, with four mountings in the waist amidships.[1] The 138.6/55 Mle 1910 was intermediate in calibre between the British 4in and 6in and

1 Some French sources have stated that these guns were in casemates, but this is by no means clear from the plans of the ship; the mountings had full shields and there was no protective plating outboard of them.

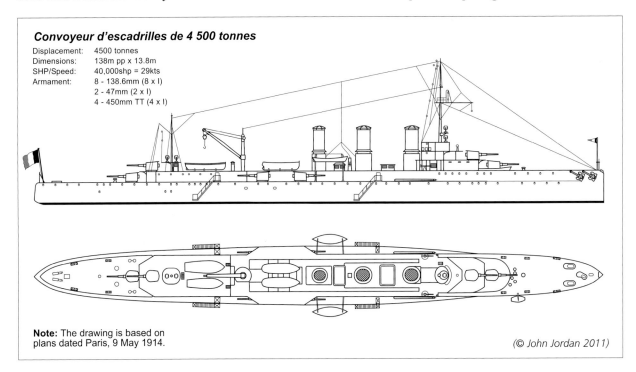

Convoyeur d'escadrilles de 4 500 tonnes

Displacement: 4500 tonnes
Dimensions: 138m pp x 13.8m
SHP/Speed: 40,000shp = 29kts
Armament: 8 - 138.6mm (8 x I)
2 - 47mm (2 x I)
4 - 450mm TT (4 x I)

Note: The drawing is based on plans dated Paris, 9 May 1914.

(© John Jordan 2011)

the German 10.5cm and 15cm guns, and was the same model mounted as secondary armament in the French dreadnoughts of the *Courbet* and *Bretagne* classes. Besides two 47mm guns for saluting, there were four above-water tubes for 450mm torpedoes,[2] located on the Main Deck directly above the engine rooms. Like their German counterparts – but in contrast to the British fleet cruisers, which were powered by fast-running destroyer turbines – they would have been only partially oil-fired, with four boilers with mixed firing complemented by eight coal-fired boilers. Maximum speed as designed was an impressive 29 knots, but protection was minimal, comprising a 28mm side belt over the machinery with end bulk-heads of 14/16mm. Surprisingly, given their relatively high designed speed, the French ships had a tradi-tional hull form with a straight stem, whereas both the British and the Germans adopted a raked bow with substantial sheer and flare for their own light cruisers.

The *Service technique des constructions navales* (STCN – Constructors' Department) met again in July 1915 to review the *Lamotte-Piquet* design, and proposals were made for a slightly larger ship, the major changes in the design being a reduction from four to two shafts and the provision of four 65mm HA guns, the mainmast being suppressed to clear arcs for the latter. The proposals were not adopted, and the light cruiser project lay in abeyance until September 1919, when a sketch design for a new light cruiser was drawn up in connection with the first post-war naval construction programme. The programme, presented on 13 January 1920 by the new Navy Minister Georges Leygues under the title *Projet 171*, proposed the aban-donment of the construction of the incomplete battle-ships of the *Normandie* class, the conversion of the fifth of the class (*Béarn*) to an aircraft carrier, and the construction of a new generation of light craft, to include six cruisers and twelve *torpilleurs-éclaireurs* ('scout torpedo boats').[3]

DESIGN AND CONSTRUCTION

The new cruiser design was derived from the 1915 proposal, but with a number of important changes: the eight 138.6mm main guns were to be in twin power-operated turrets superimposed fore and aft; the 65mm HA were to be replaced by a new 75mm model; and there were to be no fewer than twelve torpedo tubes capable of launching the powerful new 550mm Mle 1919 torpedo, in four triple trainable upper-deck mountings, thereby matching the latest British cruisers of the 'D' class. However, when in 1920 the characteristics of the British 'E' class and the US Navy's *Omaha* class became known, it quickly became apparent that any new French cruiser would need both a major increase in gunpower and much higher speed than had been envisaged in the original proposal.[4] This implied a larger – and more expensive – ship.

---

[2] The British cruisers had 21in (533mm) tubes in trainable upper deck mountings, the Germans fixed submerged 50cm tubes.

[3] The *torpilleurs-éclaireurs* would subsequently be reclassified as *contre-torpilleurs*.

[4] The 'E' class was armed with seven 6in guns and had twelve 533mm torpedo tubes; maximum speed was 33 knots. For the *Omaha*s the corresponding figures were: ten 6in guns, ten 533mm TT and 34 knots.

THE POST-WAR CRUISER DESIGNS

	Projet 171 (1919)	2nd Project (1920)	Final Project (1921)
Displacement:	5270t	7980t	8000t
Length pp:	145m	175m	175m
Beam:	14.5m	17.4m	17.2m
Draught:	5.2m	–	5.6m
Speed:	30kts	33kts	34kts
Horsepower:	54,000CV	85,000CV	102,000CV
Armament:	Eight 138.6mm (4 x II)	Eight 155mm (4 x II)	Eight 155mm (4 x II)
	Four 75mm HA (4 x I)	Four 75mm HA (4 x I)	Four 75mm HA (4 x I)
	Twelve 550mm TT (4 x III)	Twelve 550mm TT (4 x III)	Twelve 550mm TT (4 x III)

Source: Guiglini & Moreau, *op. cit.*

It was now proposed to replace the eight 138.6mm guns by 155mm guns, more than doubling the weight of the main armament at a stroke.[5] The HA and torpedo armaments remained the same, but an increase of four knots in speed meant almost doubling the output of the machinery, with four shafts instead of two. Displacement grew from 5270 tonnes to 8000 tonnes, length from 145m to 175m, horsepower from 54,000CV to 102,000CV (see table), and cost from 40 million French francs to 70 million francs. There remained a requirement for six ships, but cost and infrastructure constraints became important issues. Finally a first *tranche* was agreed, comprising only three cruisers (*vice* six), six *contre-torpilleurs* (*vice* twelve), twelve *torpilleurs d'escadre* ('fleet torpedo boats') and twelve submarines (*vice* thirty-six), together with the reconstruction of *Béarn*. This programme was approved in March/April 1922, shortly after the conclusion of the Washington Conference, and the construction of a further nine submarines was authorised the following year. However, subsequent French plans were recast in the light of the Washington Treaty provisions, and the *Duguay-Trouin* design was superseded by a larger, more heavily-armed type which would become the *Duquesne* class (see Chapter 2).

The first hull, that of *Duguay-Trouin*, was laid down in August 1922 at the Arsenal de Brest. *Primauguet* followed her on the slipway one year later, while the

Above: *Duguay-Trouin* (left) and her sister *Primauguet* fitting out under the big hammerhead crane, the *Grande grue*, at Brest in 1926. *Duguay-Trouin* already has her 155mm guns in place in the turrets.

---

[5] The weight of a twin 138.6mm mounting would have been in the region of 35 tonnes; a twin 155mm turret weighed approximately 80 tonnes.

***Primauguet*:**
Profile & Plan views

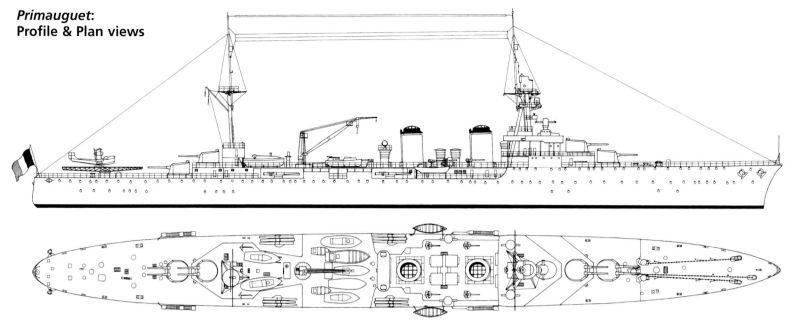

The plan view of *Primauguet* is based on the official deck plans produced by Brest Naval Dockyard and dated 26 July 1926. It shows 'notional' HA directors in the bridge wings (see also drawing of bridge decks). The profile view, which in the absence of the original was compiled from a variety of sources, shows *Primauguet* following the experimental installation of an aircraft catapult on the quarterdeck, 1 April 1927.

(© John Jordan 2010)

***Duguay–Trouin*:**
Inboard Profile

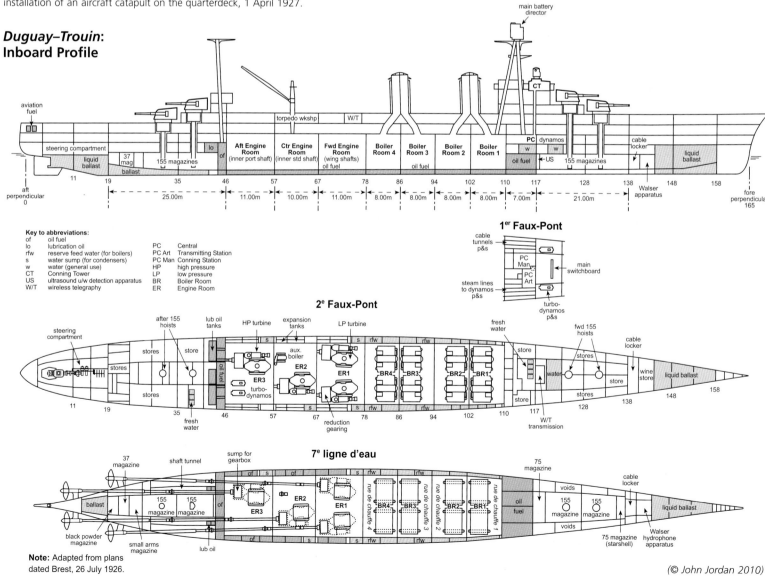

Key to abbreviations:

of	oil fuel	PC	Central
lo	lubrication oil	PC Art	Transmitting Station
rfw	reserve feed water (for boilers)	PC Man	Conning Station
s	water sump (for condensers)	HP	high pressure
w	water (general use)	LP	low pressure
CT	Conning Tower	BR	Boiler Room
US	ultrasound u/w detection apparatus	ER	Engine Room
W/T	wireless telegraphy		

Note: Adapted from plans dated Brest, 26 July 1926.

(© John Jordan 2010)

Duguay–Trouin: Hull Sections

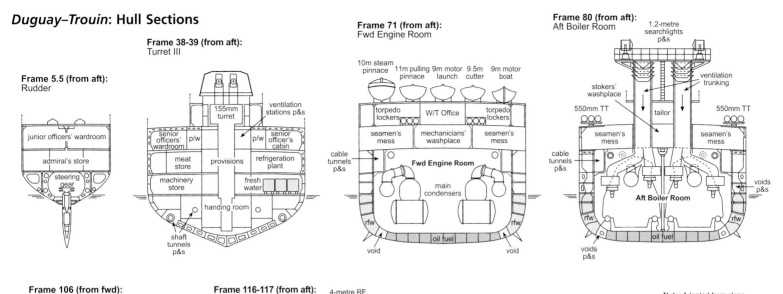

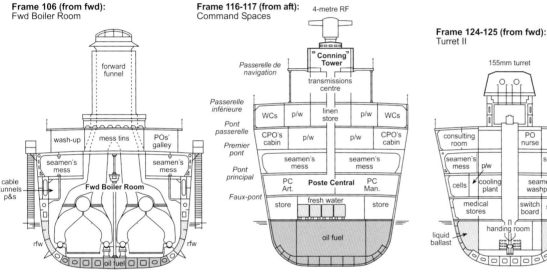

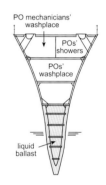

(© John Jordan 2010)

second ship, *Lamotte-Piquet*, was laid down in January 1923 at the Arsenal de Lorient. Each of the hulls took approximately three years to complete, but the development of some key items of their equipment proved more problematic, and although the ships were officially accepted into the fleet in 1926–7, they were not fully ready for service until late 1929. In particular there were delays in the delivery of the fire control system for the main guns; the main fire control director was installed only in 1928–9, and the late decision to incorporate aviation facilities was responsible for a number of unforeseen modifications.

NAMES

The three ships of the class were named after three famous Breton seamen who served with the French Navy. René **Duguay-Trouin**, (1673–1736) was a famous French corsair from Saint Malo. He had a brilliant career first as a privateer and then in the King's navy, being appointed *Lieutenant-général des armées navales du roi* (Lt-General of the King's Fleets), and a Commander in the Order of St Louis.

Count Toussaint-Guillaume **Picquet** de **la Motte** (1720–91) was born in Rennes. During the American Revolutionary Wars, he distinguished himself as a member of Admiral d'Estaing's squadron in Martinique and played an important role in the battle of Grenada

and the siege of Savannah. He too subsequently rose to be *Lieutenant-général des armées navales*.

The third ship of the class, **Primauguet**, bore the nickname of Hervé de Portzmoguer (c1470–1512), a Breton naval commander renowned for his raids on the English and for his death in the battle of St Mathieu.

HULL AND GENERAL CONFIGURATION

In contrast to the conservative design of the proposed pre-war scouts, the hull form of the new ships was in advance of any cruiser type under construction abroad. High freeboard allied to a raised forecastle made for a ship with excellent sea-keeping qualities. The fine lines of the forward part of the ship, adopted to secure the desired high speed, were complemented by a clipper bow with gentle sheer and marked flare which kept the forecastle dry even in heavy weather. The turning circle, much-criticised in the contemporary *contre-torpilleurs*, was deemed exceptional, averaging 750m with 25 degrees of helm on a length of 175m pp at a speed of 28 knots. The only criticism noted by successive commanding officers was the high centre of gravity, which on a reduced fuel load often resulted in a roll of 14–18 degrees and made the ships less-than-steady gunnery platforms.

The main guns were in twin turrets superimposed

Above: *Lamotte-Piquet* making 32.5 knots on her power trials. Unlike her two sisters, she was built at Lorient Naval Dockyard. *(CN, courtesy of Marc Saibène)*

Opposite: An early view of *Lamotte-Piquet* shortly after her arrival at Toulon; the photo was taken in early 1929. The main battery director is in place, and there is an FBA 17 reconnaissance seaplane between the boat crane and the mainmast, but the catapult has yet to be fitted on the stern. *(Marius Bar)*

fore and aft, with the triple torpedo tubes at upper deck level, in the waist of the ship. The silhouette was kept deliberately low, thereby enhancing the image of a fast ship. A capacious bridge structure was built around the widely-spaced feet of a heavy tripod mast designed to secure a firm foundation for the main fire control director. This was complemented by a pole mainmast aft. An armoured conning tower was incorporated into the bridge structure, topped by a 4-metre 'tactical' rangefinder.

The boiler rooms were grouped together forward. Despite the doubling of horsepower, a reduction from twelve boilers in the 1914 design to eight in the *Duguay-Trouins* made possible a reduction to two broad funnels, each incorporating the uptakes for four boilers. The funnels were little higher than the bridge structure in an effort to keep the funnel gases well clear of the director atop the tripod foremast. There was prominent ventilation trunking forward and abaft both funnels, the after air intake doubling as the platform for the after 1.2-metre searchlight projectors. The four single 75mm HA guns were located on the shelter deck abeam the funnels. Abaft the twin funnels, directly above the engine rooms, was a spacious boat deck served by a single long-arm crane.

MACHINERY

The propulsion plant of the new ships comprised eight Indret small-tube boilers of the Guyot-du Temple type and four sets of Parsons single-reduction turbines, powering four shafts. Total machinery weight was 2497 tonnes, accounting for 28.5 per cent of displacement. The boilers were disposed in pairs in four adjacent boiler rooms amidships. Each set of four was arranged back to back, with the uptakes grouped together and led up into one of the two broad funnels. The boilers were exclusively oil-fired and had an operating pressure of 18.5kg/cm^2.

The three engine rooms were in line directly abaft the boiler rooms. The forward engine room housed the two sets of turbines powering the wing shafts. The centre engine room housed the turbines powering the starboard inner shaft, and the after engine room the turbines for the port inner shaft. Each set of turbines comprised an HP and an LP turbine operating in series and driving one of the four shafts via single-reduction gearing. The reversing turbine was located in the exhaust housing of the LP turbine, and there was a separate cruise turbine for economic operation at low speeds. The original propellers were of a three-bladed type with a diameter of 3.70m; however, following her

---

Duguay–Trouin: Master Frame

Premier Pont

air intakes

20

22

20

Pont Principal

12

14

16

cable tunnel

14

Boiler Room 4

7

10

rfw

16

oil fuel

bilge keel

18

Note: Adapted from plans dated Brest, 30 July 1924.

(© John Jordan 2010)

sea trials *Duguay-Trouin* was fitted with four-bladed propellers of 3.9m diameter.

The length of the machinery spaces – 39 per cent of the ship's length (pp) – was dictated by the narrow hull adopted in order to secure high speed. In the later French cruisers with four shafts the turbines for the inboard shafts would be located side by side in the same engine room; however, there was insufficient beam for this in the *Duguay-Trouins*. On the other hand, the length of each of the seven main machinery compartments was kept to a minimum to give tight compartmentation. Each of the four boiler rooms was 8m long, while the engine rooms were kept to 10–11m.[6] Each set of turbines had its own lube oil pumps and condensers, and could be operated independently of the others. In theory these 'passive' damage control provisions improved survivability in a ship which was otherwise virtually unprotected.

Locating a single set of turbines in each of the after engine rooms also created sufficient space to accommodate the auxiliary machinery necessary to provide heating for the crew spaces and electrical power for lighting, training of the guns and torpedo mountings, and fire control. There was an Indret auxiliary boiler with two steam collectors in the centre engine room, and two 265kW turbo-generators in the after engine room, close to the after turrets. The other two turbo-generators were beneath the forward end of the bridge, and therefore adjacent to the forward turrets and the main fire control systems. This arrangement kept electrical cabling to a minimum and provided 'distributed' generating power with independent switchboards in the event of action damage. The generators could be run individually or coupled together. This arrangement would be repeated in later ships but with the addition of diesel generators.

Maximum fuel capacity was 1400 tonnes, of which 1200 tonnes was usable. Petrol for the motor boats and for the aircraft was stowed in special tanks located high in the stern; there were two tanks each with a

---

[6] In the *Duquesne* and *Suffren* classes they were 50 per cent longer.

MACHINERY TRIALS

Full Power Trial (6 hours)

	Primauguet 24 Jun 1926	Lamotte-Piquet 16 Jul 1926	Duguay-Trouin 23 Jul 1926
Displacement:	8378t	8286t	8362t
Draught:	4.85m	4.86m	4.88m
Maximum speed:	33.07kts	33.??kts	33.60kts
Maximum power:	116,849CV	115,209CV	117,821CV
Average speed:	33.04kts	33.??kts	33.44kts
Average power:	116,305CV	115,100CV	116,235CV
Endurance (500t oil fuel):	361nm	n/a	327nm
Endurance (1200t oil fuel):	785nm	n/a	866nm

Fuel Consumption Trial at Cruising Speed (8 hours at 15 knots)

	Primauguet 30 Jun 1926	Lamotte-Piquet 20 Jul 1926	Duguay-Trouin 20 Jul 1926
Displacement:	7889t	8062t	8036t
Draught:	4.63m	4.78m	4.71m
Average speed:	15.08kts	15.19kts	15.11kts
Average power (2 boilers):	5212CV	5433CV	4378CV
Consumption/nm:	284.04kg	264.58kg	219.28kg
Endurance (500t oil fuel):	2280nm	1890nm	1760nm
Endurance (1200t oil fuel):	4224nm	4536nm	5472nm

Endurance & Consumption Trial (24 hours at 30 knots)

	Primauguet 3–4 Jul 1926	Lamotte-Piquet 24–5 Jul 1926	Duguay-Trouin 26 & 29 Jul 1926
Displacement:	9158t	8867t	9003t
Draught:	5.24m	5.13m	5.11m
Average speed:	30.12kts	30.12kts	30.??kts
Average power (8 boilers):	65,810CV	63,680CV	63,535CV
Endurance (500t oil fuel):	622nm	658nm	606nm
Endurance (1200t oil fuel):	1454nm	1580nm	1492nm

Source: Guiglini & Moreau, *op. cit.*

Note: Although 'shaft horsepower' (shp) is generally used in English-language reference sources, all figures in this book are given in the French *chevaux* (CV). The conversion formula is:
1CV = 0.98632shp (thus 116,849CV above = 115,250shp).

TURNING TRIALS

Date	Speed	Angle of rudder	Turning circle	Angle of heel	Time to turn 360°
11 Feb 1927	28 knots	25° port	650–800m	7–10°	9 mins
11 Feb 1927	22 knots	25° stb	700–950m	1–3°	11 mins

Source: Guiglini & Moreau, *op. cit.*

BUILDING DATA AND GENERAL CHARACTERISTICS

Name	Builder	Laid down	Launched	In service
1922 Programme				
Duguay-Trouin	Arsenal de Brest	4 Aug 1922	14 Aug 1923	2 Nov 1926
Lamotte-Piquet	Arsenal de Lorient	17 Jan 1923	21 Mar 1924	5 Mar 1927
Primauguet	Arsenal de Brest	10 Aug 1923	21 May 1924	1 Oct 1926

Displacement:	8000t standard
	8760t normal
	9655t full load
Length:	175.3m pp, 181.0m oa
Beam:	17.2m
Draught:	5.3m max. (normal)
Machinery:	Eight Guyot-du Temple small-tube boilers, 18.5kg/cm^2; four-shaft Parsons geared steam turbines for 102,000CV; speed 34kts (designed)
Oil fuel:	1400 tonnes; radius 3600nm at 15kts, 800nm at 33kts
Armament:	Eight 155mm/50 Mle 1920 in twin mountings Mle 1921 (1000 rounds + 30 starshell); four 75mm/50 Mle 1922 HA in single mountings Mle 1922 (540 rounds + 120 starshell); twelve tubes for 550mm torpedoes Mle 1923D in four triple mountings Mle 1922T (+12 reloads)
Protection:	*Magazines*: 20mm
	Deck: 10mm/20mm
	CT: 30mm
	Turrets: 30mm
Complement:	591 as flagship

Weights

Hull:	3170t
Protection (hull):	105t
Protection (armament):	61t
Armament (incl. torpedoes):	867t
Propulsion:	2497t
Fittings/Provisions:	1560t
OF:	500t
Normal Displ.	8760t

Note: Characteristics are generally Legend; the armament is that fitted on (or shortly after) completion. Adjustments to the complement were sometimes made at the request of the CO before the ship entered service; the complement often fluctuated during service.

Below: *Primauguet* on 16 October 1929, following her return to Toulon in the autumn of 1929. Unusually, the main battery director and topmasts are painted white. Note the FBA 17 aircraft atop the stern catapult. (*Marius Bar*)

capacity of 1770 litres for the boats, and a single tank with 2930 litres for the aircraft. A small quantity of coal – 22.4 tonnes – was also provided to fire the foundry, the galleys and the steam pinnaces.

Results on trials proved slightly disappointing. The designed figure of 102,000CV was comfortably exceeded, with *Duguay-Trouin* attaining 117,821CV on the six-hour full power trial conducted on 23 July 1926 (see table). However, the maximum speed attained was 33.4 knots, while her two sisters made just over 33 knots. Nevertheless, the cruisers could comfortably maintain speeds in excess of 30 knots in service with only half power. Successive commanding officers praised the flexibility and reliability of the machinery (qualities not always attributable to French marine engineering of the inter-war period). The *Duguay-Trouin* class also proved to be economical steamers, projections from trials suggesting an endurance of between 4224nm (*Primauguet*) and 5472nm (*Duguay-Trouin*) at 15 knots. At 30 knots just under 1500nm was projected. Trials data for the *Duguay-Trouin* are in the accompanying table.

GROUND TACKLE AND NAVIGATION
The three main anchors (two bower, one sheet) were in hawsepipes forward: two to starboard and the third to port. They were of the Byers type and each weighed 5780kg. The single stern anchor weighed 1900kg. Two kedge anchors, of 1200kg and 890kg respectively, were carried atop the shelter deck aft.

There were four magnetic compasses: one on the bridge, one in the conning tower, one on the after superstructure, and one close to the servo-motors for the rudder. The Anschütz gyroscopic compass was in the *PC Manoeuvre*.

The single counter-balanced rudder had a surface area of 20.75m^3. It was electrically powered with manual backup. There were two independent 220V electric motors linked by differential gearing in the steering compartment; they could be operated from the *PC Manoeuvre*, the conning tower, or the steering compartment itself.

PROTECTION
Protection was minimal, accounting for less than 2 per cent of displacement (166 tonnes). The side plating was 20mm thick at its upper edge, declining to 14mm at the waterline. The upper deck (First Deck) above the machinery spaces and the magazines was of 20mm steel with the outboard edges reinforced to 22mm, and the main deck was 12–14mm (see Master Frame half-section drawing). The side walls of the magazines were of 20mm plating, and there was plating of a similar thickness on the Second Platform Deck above the magazines. There was 14mm plating above the steering gear aft.

The 155mm gun turrets had 30mm armour (15mm + 15mm), and the barbettes (20mm + 10mm) and the conning tower (30mm walls and roof) had protection of similar thickness. This was adequate against the lighter 4in and 8.8cm/10.5cm guns of the standard British and German war-built destroyers, but the latest British ships of the 'Modified W' class were armed with the much heavier 4.7in (120mm) gun, and this would become the norm in post-war destroyer construction.

Against the latest cruisers, armed with 6in guns and larger, the light plating of the *Duguay-Trouin* class could provide only splinter protection. However, since none of the early post-war cruisers, including the 10,000-ton Treaty cruisers, was given armour sufficient to protect them against their own kind ('eggshells armed with hammers' was one popular contemporary description), it would be unfair to make this a specific criticism of the French ships. Like other cruisers of their generation they were designed to outrun ships they could not out-fight. In compensation they were well sub-divided, with no fewer than 17 transverse watertight bulkheads and a double shell worked in abreast the boiler and engine rooms, and the 'stiffening' provided by their light 20/30mm plating at least made for a sturdy, robust hull which was appreciated by successive commanding officers.

ARMAMENT
Main battery
The 155mm calibre adopted for the main armament of the new cruisers was the standard calibre in use with the French Army for its field guns; it was also the closest existing calibre to the British/American 6in (152mm) and German 15cm guns. The 155/50 Mle 1920 gun, which was mounted in twin turrets in the *Duguay-Trouin* class and in single casemate mountings in the converted aircraft carrier *Béarn*, was constructed with a liner, an autofretted A tube, a jacket in two lengths and a breech ring. The traditional Welin interrupted screw breech block opened upwards, being balanced about its horizontal axis of rotation. There was an automatic hydropneumatic breech flushing system.

The eight guns were mounted in pairs in a twin turret Mle 1921 which weighed around 80 tonnes complete. The enclosed gunhouses were gas tight with forced ventilation. The guns were in separate cradles each with a toothed elevating arc. Training and elevation were electrically powered with hydraulic drive, and maximum elevation was 40 degrees. Remote power control would later to be fitted for training only.

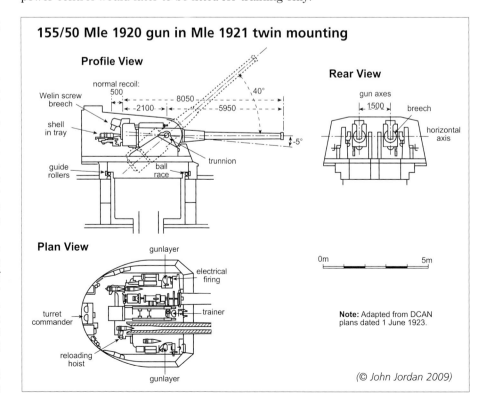

155/50 Mle 1920 gun in Mle 1921 twin mounting

Profile View

Rear View

Plan View

Note: Adapted from DCAN plans dated 1 June 1923.

(© John Jordan 2009)

The standard OPf shell – the authors have been unable to locate the year number – was a semi-armour-piercing (SAP) model, with a 3.34kg bursting charge of picric acid (*Mélinite*); the BM11 propellant charge was in halves. High explosive (HE) shell were also provided; the latter had a nose fuse and weighed 59kg (130lb). Shells and charges were hoisted together in cages, with the shell in the upper of the three compartments. The lower hoists were of the dredger type; on arrival at the working chamber the shells and charges were transferred to waiting posi-

tions, and from these to the upper cage hoists. When the latter emerged on either side of the guns, the shells were moved by tongs into loading trays which traversed into position for loading by spring rammers; the charges were rammed by hand. Each gun was provided with 125 combat rounds. In addition fifteen starshell and twenty practice rounds were provided for each of the upper turrets (II and III), and sixty

155/50 MLE 1920

Gun Data

Construction:	Autofretted 'A' tube with jacket and liner
Breech mechanism:	Upward-opening Welin screw
Weight of gun:	8.87t
Ammunition type:	Separate
Projectiles:	OPf Mle 192? (56.5kg)
	OEA Mle 19?? (59.0kg)
	OEcl Mle 192?
Propellant:	BM11 in two half-charges (19.81kg)
Muzzle velocity:	850m/s
Max. range:	26,100m (40°)

Mounting Data

Designation:	Twin Mle 1921
Weight of turret:	80t
Distance apart gun axes:	1.50m
Protection:	30mm (15mm + 15mm)
Loading angle:	??
Elevation of guns:	−5° / +40°
Max. training speed:	6.4°/sec
Max. elevating speed:	6°/sec
Firing cycle (per gun):	3–4rpm

Notes:
OPf	*Obus de Perforation*	Armour Piercing
OEA	*Obus Explosif en Acier*	High Explosive (HE)
OEcl	*Obus Eclairant*	Starshell

All weights in metric tons (tonnes).
Speeds in metres/degrees per second.

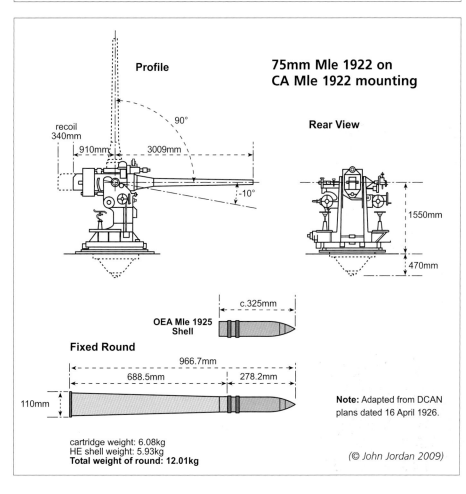

155mm SAP shell OPf Mle 1924?

Note: Adapted from DCAN plans dated 1 June 1923.

Half Charge

-----585mm-----
170mm
charge weight: 11kg

Case for Six Half Charges

345mm   530mm   632mm
weight empty: 19kg
weight full: 85kg

ballistic cap (windshield)
hardened shell cap
bourrelet
shell body
driving bands
base plug

800mm

shell weight: 56.5kg
burster: 3.34kg Mélinite

(© John Jordan 2009)

Profile

75mm Mle 1922 on CA Mle 1922 mounting

recoil 340mm
90°
910mm   3009mm
-10°

Rear View

1550mm
470mm

c.325mm
OEA Mle 1925 Shell

Fixed Round

966.7mm
688.5mm   278.2mm
110mm

Note: Adapted from DCAN plans dated 16 April 1926.

cartridge weight: 6.08kg
HE shell weight: 5.93kg
Total weight of round: 12.01kg

(© John Jordan 2009)

75/50 MLE 1922/1924

Gun Data

Construction:	Autofretted barrel
Breech mechanism:	Schneider concentric ring
Weight of gun:	1.07t
Ammunition type:	Fixed
Projectiles:	OEA Mle 1925 (5.93kg)
	OEcl Mle 1923
Propellant:	BM5 (2.18kg)
Complete round:	
Weight:	12.01kg
Dimensions:	967mm x 110mm
Muzzle velocity:	850m/s
Max. range:	15,000m (45°)
Ceiling:	7500m (90°)

Mounting Data

Designation:	CA Mle 1922
Weight of mounting:	n/a
Loading angle:	-10° / +75°
Elevation of guns:	-10° / +90°
Firing cycle (per gun):	15rpm theoretical
	8rpm practical

Notes:
OEA	*Obus Explosif en Acier*	High Explosive (HE)
OEcl	*Obus Eclairant*	Starshell

practice rounds for each of the lower turrets (I and IV).

The complexity of the reloading mechanism reduced the firing cycle to three rounds per minute; this was a disappointment, as the initial contracts stipulated 5–6rpm. Regular breakdowns were also experienced throughout the ships' service lives, a problem never satisfactorily resolved.

Anti-aircraft weapons

The four single 75mm/50 guns were of the new Mle 1922 specially developed following the First World War to provide surface ships with an anti-aircraft capability (they were also installed in the *torpilleurs* and *contre-torpilleurs* of the 1922 Programme). The gun was essentially a modification of the 75mm Mle 1902 Schneider reduced to a length of 50 calibres; only the mounting was different. It was intended to engage hostile aircraft with time-fused HE shells at extended ranges, and had a firing cycle of 8–12rpm. The gun could be elevated to 90 degrees and could be loaded at angles up to 75 degrees. Against surface targets it had a theoretical maximum range of 14,900m; maximum effective range against aircraft was 7500m. It could also fire starshell for night-time target designation. A total of 540 contact- or time-fused HE rounds was provided for the four guns, together with 120 starshell and 96 exercise rounds. The guns were disposed on either side of the funnels, and the 75mm magazines were located immediately forward of the boiler rooms.

Provision was also made for six Hotchkiss twin 8mm machine guns, although the mountings were not fitted until 1928–9. These proved virtually ineffectual against even the aircraft of the day, and were replaced by the twin Hotchkiss 13.2mm weapon during the 1930s.

Fire control

Fire control for the main armament was exercised from the main DCT, which was located atop the tripod fore-

mast some 26m above the waterline. It was fitted initially with a 4-metre coincidence rangefinder of French design and manufacture[7] for target ranging and a Zeiss 3-metre stereo model for target observation; the primary purpose of the latter was to measure the distance between shell splashes falling short and the target (scartometry). Delays in the delivery of the equipment meant that all three ships ran trials without their main directors, which were installed only in 1928–9. A severe fire aboard *Duguay-Trouin* during a refit at Toulon in 1929–30 resulted in damage to the

Above: *Duguay-Trouin* moored at the Quai des Quinconces during a visit to Bordeaux, 6–9 July 1934.

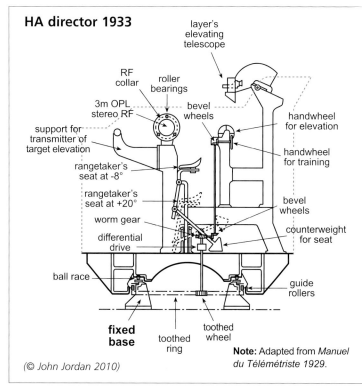

HA director 1933

layer's elevating telescope

RF collar — roller bearings

3m OPL stereo RF — bevel wheels

handwheel for elevation

support for transmitter of target elevation

handwheel for training

rangetaker's seat at -8°

rangetaker's seat at +20°

bevel wheels

worm gear

differential drive

counterweight for seat

ball race

guide rollers

fixed base

toothed ring

toothed wheel

Note: Adapted from *Manuel du Télémétriste 1929*.

(© John Jordan 2010)

The standard French HA director was developed during the mid/late 1920s, but delays in production meant that it was not ready for installation until about 1933. The director was fitted with an OPL (Optique de Précision Levallois-Perret) 3-metre stereo rangefinder Mle 1926, which could elevate from −10° to +90°. The support was fixed to the rotating floor of the director, and the rangefinder was held in place by two collars with guide rollers. The rangetaker's seat could be raised or lowered to enable him to follow the movement of the target aircraft in comfort, his weight being balanced by a counterweight. The role of the rangetaker was simply the measurement of range.

The trainer used a handwheel to train the director in bearing via a bevel and worm gear linkage, a toothed side wheel engaging with a toothed ring fixed to the base seating. The director was mounted on a fixed seating with a ball race; there was a single set of (vertical) guide rollers. The rangefinder was linked by a rigid transmission to the elevation transmission of the director (not shown in drawing); it was trained in azimuth and elevated at the same time as the director.

[7] The rangefinders installed in French battleships of First World War vintage had been purchased directly from the British company of Barr & Stroud. These included 6ft (2m) and 15ft (4.57m) coincidence models. The new French models were developed by the Société d'Optique et de Méchanique de Haute Précision (SOM).

Above: Two views of *Primauguet* during a visit to Shanghai in June 1935. She has had her foretopmast suppressed but is otherwise largely unmodified. Note the early type of concentration dial on the forward side of the foremast, with numbers 0–9. The bow view illustrates the flare and sheer which, together with the raised forecastle, made these ships such good sea-boats, able to sustain high speed even in heavy seas. In this photo the minesweeping paravanes are deployed. *(Marc Saibène collection)*

director, which had to be disembarked for repair; it was replaced only in 1933 during a major refit at Brest.

The DCT provided range and bearing data for a Mle 1923 fire-control computer located below decks. A second 4-metre coincidence rangefinder was installed in a trainable housing atop the conning tower, and a further pair were located on the outer edge of the shelter deck between the 75mm guns; these proved to be unusable when the 75mm guns were fired, and were removed during the Second World War.

Concentration dials for formation firing were installed fore and aft at the base of the foremast and mainmast respectively. Three 1.2-metre searchlight projectors were provided for target illumination at night; the forward projector was installed atop a platform directly beneath the foretop, while the after projectors were located side by side atop the after boiler room ventilation housing immediately abaft the second funnel. Remote power control for training was provided during the mid-1930s.

The *Duguay-Trouin*s were to have been fitted from the outset with HA directors of a new design with integral 4-metre rangefinders. The original plans show

these directors, designated *tourelles de télépointage C.A.*, in the upper bridge wings (the similar rangefinder housings on the shelter deck described above are designated *tourelles de télémétrie*). Development was protracted; HA directors were not fitted until 1933–4, and these were bulkier and of completely different design to the ones shown in the original plans (see Modifications).

Torpedoes
The heavy torpedo armament of the 8000-tonne cruisers was influenced by the latest British and American cruisers. Four triple tubes Mle 1922T of the type installed in the contemporary *torpilleurs* and *contre-torpilleurs* were fitted at upper deck level in the waist of the ship, each with a training arc of 40–140 degrees. No fewer than twenty-four torpedoes were carried, twelve of which were housed in the tubes with a further twelve reloads stowed in lockers on the upper deck, each of which held three torpedoes (see drawing). The warheads were normally stowed in separate steel lockers on the deck edge between the tubes. The 550mm torpedo Mle 1923D, a development of the postwar Mle 1919, was heavier than most of its foreign contemporaries[8] and had an impressive performance. It was fitted with a 308kg TNT warhead and had two speed settings: 39 knots for 9000m range, and 35 knots for 13,000m

The location of so many torpedoes and their warheads above the weather deck amidships presented a major fire hazard, especially in combat, although the ships' designers took care to place the warhead lockers on the deck edge so that any explosion would be vented upwards and outwards, thereby minimising damage to the ship's vitals; the lockers were hinged to enable the warheads to be quickly jettisoned over the side in the event of fire. The arrange-

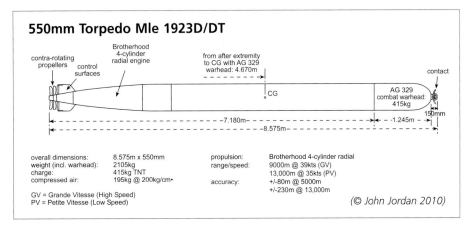

550mm Torpedo Mle 1923D/DT

overall dimensions:	8.575m x 550mm	propulsion:	Brotherhood 4-cylinder radial
weight (incl. warhead):	2105kg	range/speed:	9000m @ 39kts (GV)
charge:	415kg TNT		13,000m @ 35kts (PV)
compressed air:	195kg @ 200kg/cm•	accuracy:	+/-80m @ 5000m
			+/-230m @ 13,000m

GV = Grande Vitesse (High Speed)
PV = Petite Vitesse (Low Speed)

(© John Jordan 2010)

[8] Only the IJN's 61cm Type 8 torpedo was larger.

ment was nevertheless much criticised by the trials commission (*Commission permanente d'essais*), and was not repeated on any of the subsequent French cruiser classes, which had a much-reduced complement of torpedoes.

The torpedo fire control position was located in the armoured conning tower, and firing data was provided

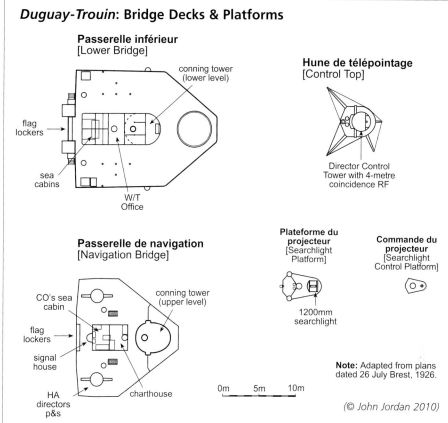

Duguay-Trouin: Bridge Decks & Platforms

Passerelle inférieur
[Lower Bridge]

conning tower (lower level)

flag lockers

sea cabins

W/T Office

Hune de télépointage
[Control Top]

Director Control Tower with 4-metre coincidence RF

Passerelle de navigation
[Navigation Bridge]

CO's sea cabin

flag lockers

signal house

HA directors p&s

conning tower (upper level)

charthouse

Plateforme du projecteur
[Searchlight Platform]

1200mm searchlight

Commande du projecteur
[Searchlight Control Platform]

Note: Adapted from plans dated 26 July Brest, 1926.

0m   5m   10m

(© John Jordan 2010)

The HA directors shown on these original plans are purely 'notional'. The directors eventually fitted had a completely different configuration; they were also far bulkier and heavier. The after ends of the bridge wings had to be extended and the weight of the new directors borne by broad cylindrical supports which rested on the upper deck.

Above, left: Close-up of the HA director seen from above aboard *Lamotte-Piquet* in 1939. The integral rangefinder is a 3-metre stereo model manufactured by the French company Optique de Précision Levallois-Perret (OPL); the controls and mechanisms for the director layer (see drawing) are under canvas.

Left: The main gunnery director of *Lamotte-Piquet*, photographed from an American aircraft at Shanghai on 27 February 1937. The principal rangefinder (lower rear compartment) is a 4-metre coincidence model, as is that in the rangefinder turret atop the conning tower. The smaller rangefinder (lower forward compartment) is a Zeiss 3-metre stereo model used for scartometry (see text). *Lamotte-Piquet* had recently been fitted with two HA directors, of which the starboard-side director is clearly visible at the after end of the bridge. *(US Navy)*

Right: *Duguay-Trouin* at Le Havre on 23 July 1934, following the major refit which saw the installation of two HA directors at the after end of the bridge wings. Note the massive pillar needed to support the weight of the new director. Note also the shielded 75mm single mounting and the 4-metre rangefinder associated with the 75mm mountings in anti-surface fire. *(Moreau, courtesy of Marc Saibène)*

by the 4-metre rangefinder located above it. Secondary 'rapid-fire' torpedo fire control positions similar to those installed in the *contre-torpilleurs* were later fitted in the bridge wings.

UNDERWATER DETECTION APPARATUS

The official plans of *Duguay-Trouin* show a space reserved for installation of a tube for an ultrasound 'pinger' to starboard, just forward of the athwartships

fuel bunkers directly beneath the bridge. They also show a larger compartment farther forward for the Walser passive hydrophone system (see inboard profile and hold deck plans); the drawings suggest there would have been four of the 1.3-metre circular arrays, two to port and two to starboard. There is no indication that either of these systems was ever installed, as trials during 1929–31 aboard destroyers and other small craft were unsuccessful.

AVIATION INSTALLATIONS

During construction it was decided to fit a catapult for a reconnaissance seaplane experimentally on *Primauguet*. The catapult, a Penhoët compressed-air model with an overall length of 20.27m (catapult beam: 19.17m), was installed on 1 April 1927, and could launch aircraft with a maximum weight of 1600kg at 93km/h. It was installed on the ship's axis on the quarterdeck 16.4m from the stern.

Trials were conducted with first a Bresson 35, then an FBA 17, which was to become the standard aircraft embarked in these ships until the mid-1930s. The trials were regarded as generally successful, and the catapult was installed on the *Primauguet*'s two sisters in March–April 1929 following their completion. The only significant modification to the catapult was a reduction in the height of its cylindrical base from 2.5m to 1.23m in an effort to minimise vibration.

Aircraft stowage and handling arrangements proved more problematic and were subject to a number of improvements. The absence of a hangar meant that the aircraft was exposed to the elements on the open quarterdeck. In 1927 it was decided to fit a 4.3-metre extension to the boat crane to enable it to lift the seaplane from the water and place it on a pivoting pedestal to be installed atop the shelter deck between the crane and the mainmast; lift capacity was 1500kg. However, the crane still had insufficient reach to place a seaplane on the catapult, and during 1932–4 a collapsible crane 11.5m long was installed on the port

FINAL FITTING OUT: KEY ITEMS OF EQUIPMENT

	Duguay-Trouin	Lamotte-Piquet	Primauguet
Crane lengthened (4.5m):	1927	Early 1927	1927
DCT fitted:	12 Apr 1928	8 Jun 1928	1 Jul 29
Catapult fitted:	15 May 1929	Apr 1929	Early 1929
DF antenna/cabin installed:	[postponed]	[postponed]	Mid-1929

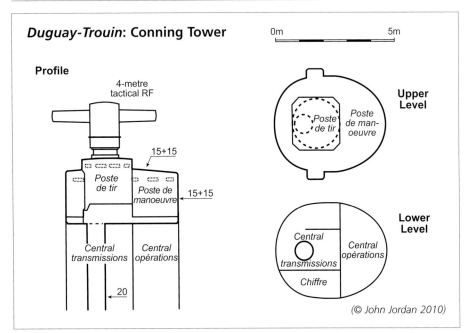

Duguay-Trouin: **Conning Tower**

(© John Jordan 2010)

Duguay-Trouin: Torpedo Maintenance & Reloading

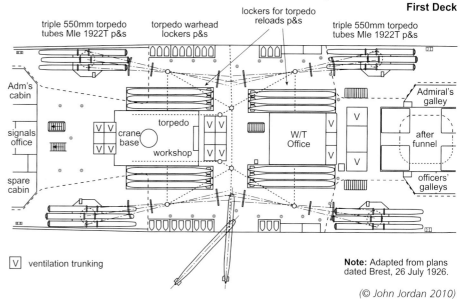

First Deck

triple 550mm torpedo tubes Mle 1922T p&s

torpedo warhead lockers p&s

lockers for torpedo reloads p&s

triple 550mm torpedo tubes Mle 1922T p&s

Adm's cabin

signals office

spare cabin

torpedo crane base workshop

W/T Office

Admiral's galley

after funnel

officers' galleys

[V] ventilation trunking

Note: Adapted from plans dated Brest, 26 July 1926.

(© John Jordan 2010)

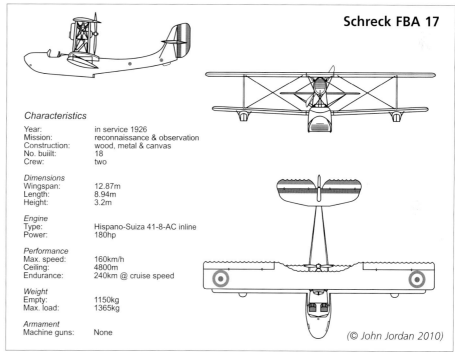

Schreck FBA 17

Characteristics

Year: in service 1926
Mission: reconnaissance & observation
Construction: wood, metal & canvas
No. buiilt: 18
Crew: two

Dimensions
Wingspan: 12.87m
Length: 8.94m
Height: 3.2m

Engine
Type: Hispano-Suiza 41-8-AC inline
Power: 180hp

Performance
Max. speed: 160km/h
Ceiling: 4800m
Endurance: 240km @ cruise speed

Weight
Empty: 1150kg
Max. load: 1365kg

Armament
Machine guns: None

(© John Jordan 2010)

side of the quarterdeck specifically to handle the aircraft. From this time the ships generally deployed with two FBA 17 seaplanes, one of which was carried atop the catapult and the second stowed on the shelter deck. From 1935 these were progressively replaced by the Potez 452 seaplane[9] or the Gourdou-Leseurre GL 832 float monoplane, a smaller, two-seat version of the GL 810 already in service aboard the 10,000-ton cruisers.

The aviation fuel tank, which had a capacity of 2700 litres, was located directly beneath the stern to starboard of two 1770-litre petrol tanks to fuel the ship's motor boats. The three tanks were surrounded by fireproof insulating material. Fire prevention measures included the replacement of used fuel by inert gas, and the ability to pump the contents of the tank rapidly into the sea.

The decision to fit the catapult on the quarterdeck effectively displaced the direction-finding equipment it was initially planned to install. It was temporarily relocated atop the aircraft pedestal in *Primauguet*, but this was clearly unsatisfactory and installation was postponed indefinitely for the two remaining two ships. It was finally decided to install the antenna and its asso-

ciated cabin in the centre of the ventilation trunking between the funnels.

The aircraft arrangements were to be considerably modified in France's first Treaty cruisers, *Duquesne* and *Tourville*, which were otherwise similar to the cruisers of the 1922 Programme in their topsides layout. The catapult was installed atop the shelter deck between the after funnel and the mainmast, the boats and their associated crane being relocated to positions between the funnels (which were more widely spaced). This arrangement provided the seaplanes with more protection from the elements.

BOATS
The close spacing of the funnels enabled all the ship's boats to be located atop the central part of the shelter deck. The outfit when the ships were first completed was as follows:

---

[9] The Potez 452 was a single-motor, two-seat high-wing seaplane with a maximum weight of 1750kg (1130kg empty); wingspan was 13m. A total of sixteen were built for the Navy. One was embarked on *Duguay-Trouin* for catapult trials in 1936, another embarked on *Primauguet* for her deployment to Indochina in 1938, and two aircraft (nos.11 and 15) operated from *Lamotte-Piquet* in Indochina in 1938-9.

Above, left: A stern view of *Lamotte-Piquet* with a GL 832 monoplane embarked. The photo was taken during March 1940, when *Lamotte-Piquet* was docked for maintenance at Hong Kong. Note the white-painted concentration dial on the after side of the mainmast.
(D Brennan, courtesy of Pete Cannon)

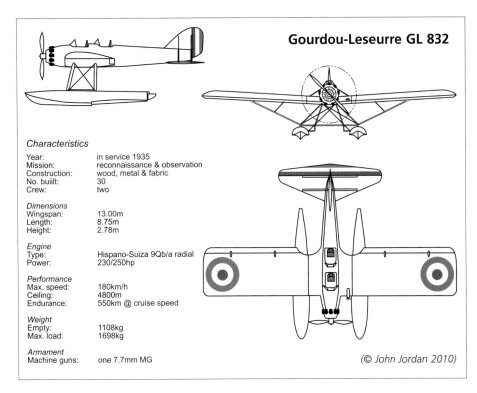

Gourdou-Leseurre GL 832

Characteristics

Year:	in service 1935
Mission:	reconnaissance & observation
Construction:	wood, metal & fabric
No. buiilt:	30
Crew:	two

Dimensions

Wingspan:	13.00m
Length:	8.75m
Height:	2.78m

Engine

Type:	Hispano-Suiza 9Qb/a radial
Power:	230/250hp

Performance

Max. speed:	180km/h
Ceiling:	4800m
Endurance:	550km @ cruise speed

Weight

Empty:	1108kg
Max. load:	1698kg

Armament

Machine guns:	one 7.7mm MG

(© John Jordan 2010)

– One 11-metre pulling pinnace
– Two 10-metre steam pinnaces
– One 9.5-metre cutter
– One 9-metre motor launch
– Two 9-metre motor boats
– Two 8.5-metre whalers
– Two 5-metre dinghies

With the exception of the two whalers, which were on davits outboard of the funnels, the boats were handled by the single crane with a reach of 11.7m located on the centre-line; lift capacity was 12 tonnes. The same crane would later be extended to enable it to handle aircraft (see above). The boat outfit would prove inadequate when the ships were subsequently employed as flagships (see Modifications).

MODIFICATIONS 1930 TO 1942

Significant modifications were made to all three ships during the 1930s as a result of experience with the ships in service. At the same time newly developed equipment was incorporated where possible to bring them up to date. *Duguay-Trouin*, which was deployed exclusively in home waters and underwent a major refit at Brest in 1932–3, served as the prototype for these modifications, which were subsequently extended to her two sisters.

The command spaces were found to be inadequate, particularly as the new cruisers were frequently employed as flagships.[10] The navigation bridge was therefore enlarged to provide an operations/signal distribution centre, and an admiral's bridge was fitted around the vertical leg of the tripod foremast. In order to accommodate the additional boats required by the admiral and his staff (one 9-metre and two 7-metre motor boats) the shelter deck was extended to the ship's sides above the after torpedo tubes to port and to starboard. These sections were removable to facilitate reloading of the tubes when alongside.

The ship's anti-aircraft provision was already deemed inadequate by the early 1930s, and a number of measures were taken to improve her capabilities. The new HA fire control director with integral 3-metre OPL Mle 1926 stereo rangefinder (see drawing) was now ready. It was significantly larger and heavier than envisaged in the original design, and required substantial changes in order to accommodate it. The after ends of the bridge wings were enlarged and the weight of the new directors was borne by broad cylindrical supports which rested on the upper deck. There was only a single associated HA fire control computer, so only a single target could be engaged to port or to starboard.

The 75mm guns were fitted with light duralumin shields for splinter and spray protection, and the relatively ineffectual 8mm machine guns were replaced by

---

[10] A typical flag staff comprised a senior officer (normally a rear-admiral), a *Capitaine de frégate* as Chief of Staff, four other officers, and 17/18 other rates, a total of 23–24.

Right: *Primauguet* was selected for the trials of the first catapult, which was installed on the quarterdeck and had a cylindrical pedestal 2.5m high; the height was later reduced to 1.23m to eliminate vibration. The aircraft atop the catapult is an FBA 17. *(Albert Moreau/Jean Guiglini collection)*

four of a projected six Hotchkiss twin 13.2mm MG Mle 1929: one atop the bridge, one atop the after deckhouse abeam the mainmast, two at the outer edges of the boat deck, and two abeam the bridge structure at the level of turret II (these would be the last to be installed, due to a shortage of mountings).

During the same refit a new main DCT was installed to replace the one damaged by fire in 1930. The MF/LF direction-finding antenna and its associated cabin were finally installed between the funnels, and the new collapsible aircraft crane was fitted on the port side of the quarterdeck. The topmasts were lowered, and a steel bulwark was constructed at the after end of the forecastle to port and to starboard.

In 1935 the second phase of the anti-aircraft improvements was undertaken, also at Brest. Remote power control for training was fitted to both the 75mm HA guns and to the after searchlight projectors. At the same time the foretopmast, which had been found to obstruct the main DCT on after bearings, was completely removed, and the mainmast top lowered. The catapult was modified to launch the GL 832 and Potez 452 monoplanes, and secondary torpedo fire-control positions were installed in the bridge wings.

Lamotte-Piquet was taken in hand by Lorient Naval Dockyard in 1933–5, with a view to bringing her up to the same standard as her sister-ship. She received all the modifications extended to *Duguay-Trouin* during her 1932–3 and 1935 refits. In addition she was fitted with a new DCT of the type fitted in the 10,000-tonne cruisers. *Primauguet*, however, received only the 75mm gun shields (steel not duralumin) and the collapsible aircraft crane before she deployed to the Far East in 1932 (the navigation bridge was also enlarged), and remained virtually unmodified until 1936 when she returned to metropolitan France. She was subse-

quently refitted at Lorient in 1936–7, and was brought up to the standard of her two sisters. She received the new HA fire control arrangements, although the RPC installation was not completed until 1940, and 3-metre rangefinders were fitted provisionally in the bridge wings pending the development of a new enclosed HA director. At the same time the Hotchkiss 13.2mm twin MG were installed. Like *Lamotte-Piquet*, *Primauguet* also received a main DCT *type croiseurs de 10,000t*, but with an 8-metre OPL stereo RF for ranging, the 3-metre stereo RF being retained for scartometry. The original 4-metre coincidence rangefinders on the shelter deck were replaced by stereo models at the same time. The new rangefinders proved to be much more effective, and similar modifications were

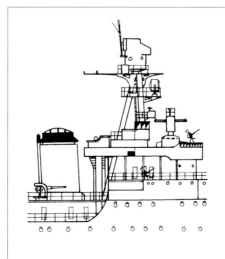

Duguay-Trouin: Bridge 1935

Part-view of *Duguay-Trouin* during the mid-1930s following her major refit. The compass platform has been extended and enclosed, and an admiral's bridge constructed around the forward leg of the tripod foremast. The after ends of the bridge wings have been extended in order to accommodate the newly-fitted HA directors, supported from below by heavy cylindrical pillars. The 75mm HA mountings have been fitted with shields, and 13.2mm Hotchkiss MG have been installed atop the bridge and abeam the bridge structure.

(© John Jordan 2010)

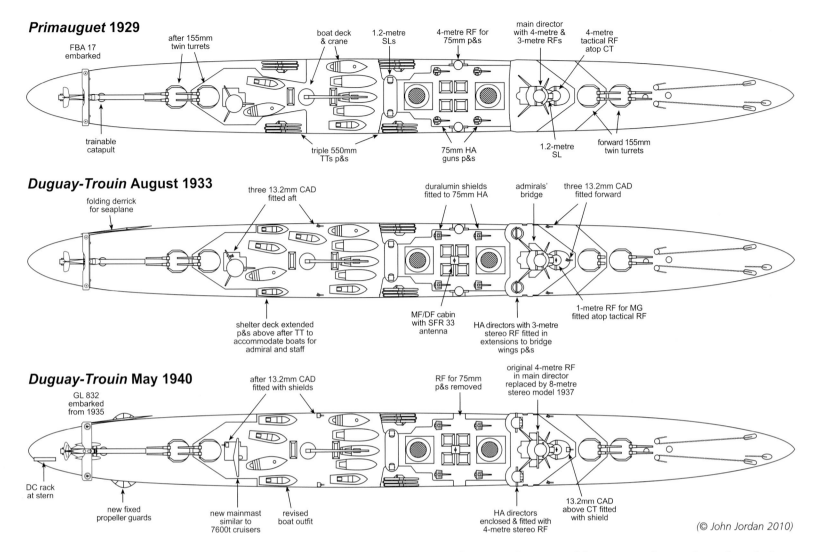

Primauguet 1929

FBA 17
embarked

after 155mm
twin turrets

boat deck
& crane

1.2-metre
SLs

4-metre RF for
75mm p&s

main director
with 4-metre &
3-metre RFs

4-metre
tactical RF
atop CT

trainable
catapult

triple 550mm
TTs p&s

75mm HA
guns p&s

1.2-metre
SL

forward 155mm
twin turrets

Duguay-Trouin August 1933

folding derrick
for seaplane

three 13.2mm CAD
fitted aft

duralumin shields
fitted to 75mm HA

admirals'
bridge

three 13.2mm CAD
fitted forward

shelter deck extended
p&s above after TT to
accommodate boats for
admiral and staff

MF/DF cabin
with SFR 33
antenna

HA directors with 3-metre
stereo RF fitted in
extensions to bridge
wings p&s

1-metre RF for MG
fitted atop tactical RF

Duguay-Trouin May 1940

GL 832
embarked
from 1935

after 13.2mm CAD
fitted with shields

RF for 75mm
p&s removed

original 4-metre RF
in main director
replaced by 8-metre
stereo model 1937

DC rack
at stern

new fixed
propeller guards

new mainmast
similar to
7600t cruisers

revised
boat outfit

HA directors
enclosed & fitted with
4-metre stereo RF

13.2mm CAD
above CT fitted
with shield

(© John Jordan 2010)

extended to *Duguay-Trouin* at Toulon in 1937–8 and to *Lamotte-Piquet* at Saigon in 1939–40.

The new enclosed HA directors, which had a metal roof and glass to the rear, were installed in *Duguay-Trouin* and *Primauguet* only in early 1940, but were not fitted in *Lamotte-Piquet*, which was in the Far East and destined never to return to France. At the same time the 4-metre base stereo rangefinders originally located on the shelter deck were removed, and installed in place of the 3-metre RF in the new HA directors. Other

early war modifications to the two home-based ships included the installation of fixed propeller guards above the outer shafts similar to those of the 10,000-tonne cruisers, and the replacement of the original mainmast in *Duguay-Trouin* by a new lightweight model similar to that of the cruisers of the *La Galisson-nière* class (see Chapter 6), which had been trialled in *Primauguet* since her refit in 1936–7. *Duguay-Trouin* also carried fifteen 35kg depth charges for protection against submarines.

Right: *Duguay-Trouin* in the *Rade-Abri* at Brest during the winter of 1935/36. She has been extensively modified since her completion: the foretopmast has been suppressed, HA directors have been fitted at the after end of the bridge wings, and there are extensions to the bridge structure and to the after end of the shelter deck to improve flag facilities. Note the single broad white band on the second funnel. *(Marc Saibène collection)*

CHAPTER 2

DUQUESNE AND *TOURVILLE*

INTRODUCTION

In agreeing qualitative limits for ships beneath the capital ship category which stipulated a maximum displacement of 10,000 tons and a maximum gun calibre of 8in (203mm), the Washington Conference effectively created a new category which became known as the 'Treaty cruiser'. From this point onwards all five of the major navies would consider any cruiser with lesser qualities to be an acknowledgement of material inferiority.

To a certain extent design of the new ships was a step in the dark. Only the British, with the *Hawkins* class, the French (*Duguay-Trouin* class), and the Japanese (*Furutaka* class) had suitable designs on the drawing board which, if scaled up, would provide a suitable template for the Treaty cruiser; the Americans, although supportive of – and partly responsible for – the new qualitative limits had only paper sketches, and the latest Italian cruisers were small, fast scouts.

In the Spring of 1922, following the conclusion of the Washington Conference, the French Naval General Staff[1] met to consider the outcomes of the conference and to draw up a new naval programme. The cornerstone of the latter was to be the construction of no fewer than twenty-one cruisers designed to the qualitative limits permitted by the Treaty. The future of the capital ship in the face of the increasing capabilities of aircraft was deemed to be uncertain. The submarine, on the other hand, was considered by many of those present to be the ideal weapon for a power of the second rank, and had the added advantage of being relatively affordable. The traditional role of the cruiser, that of protecting trade and sea lines of communication while threatening those of a potential enemy, continued to be vital for a maritime power like France with an extensive world empire to police. High speed, which made possible both rapid intervention and escape from contact with superior units (including enemy battlecruisers), was to be prioritised in the design of the new ships, as was defence against submarines, which was essential for their survival in narrow waters.

In its report the General Staff stated that the maximum displacement of 10,000 tons imposed itself, and that the difference between the 8000 tons of the *Duguay-Trouin* and the higher displacement was simply what one would expect if gun calibre were increased from 155mm to 203mm. It considered therefore that when considering the balance between speed and protection, speed would have to be prioritised to the virtual exclusion of protection as in the current ships.

The *Duguay-Trouin* was particularly well-suited to the scaling-up process. It was the only design with eight guns in twin turrets fore and aft – a choice which proved popular among other navies for their Treaty cruisers.[2] And it was undoubtedly fast – all five of the major navies initially viewed 33 knots as being the minimum desirable maximum speed.[3]

In July 1924, when all three hulls of the *Duguay-Trouin* class had been launched, and *Duquesne* and *Tourville* were not yet on the slipways, the French magazine *L'Illustration*, following an interview with a Marine Nationale source,[4] defined the missions of the new ships as follows:

– strategic scouting *at a large radius from the battle fleet* (author's italics);
– seeking out and maintaining contact with the enemy;
– the support of light surface forces and submarines, patrol ships and convoy escorts;
– the destruction of enemy ships threatening French sea lines of communication;
– the fast transport of troops between North Africa and France;

Above: *Duquesne* moored in the *Rade-Abri* at Brest in 1930, shortly after her entry into service. The single white band on her fore-funnel marks her out as the flagship of the 1st Light Division. *(Philippe Caresse collection)*

---

[1] *Etat-major général de la marine* or EMG.

[2] Both the British and the Italians adopted this arrangement; the Japanese, pushing at the margins as ever, opted for a third turret forward to complement the two aft.

[3] The three latest British battlecruisers of the *Renown* and *Hood* classes, which it was important to be able to outrun, had a maximum speed of 30–31 knots.

[4] Article by Raymond Lestonnat, 5 July 1924; the bullet points are a précis of the key missions.

Duquesne: Profile & Plan views

Profile and plan views of *Duquesne* as first completed, based on the official plans produced by Brest Naval Dockyard and dated 20 August 1930. The aircraft atop the single catapult is the CAMS 37A reconnaissance seaplane; it would shortly be superseded by the GL 810 float monoplane.

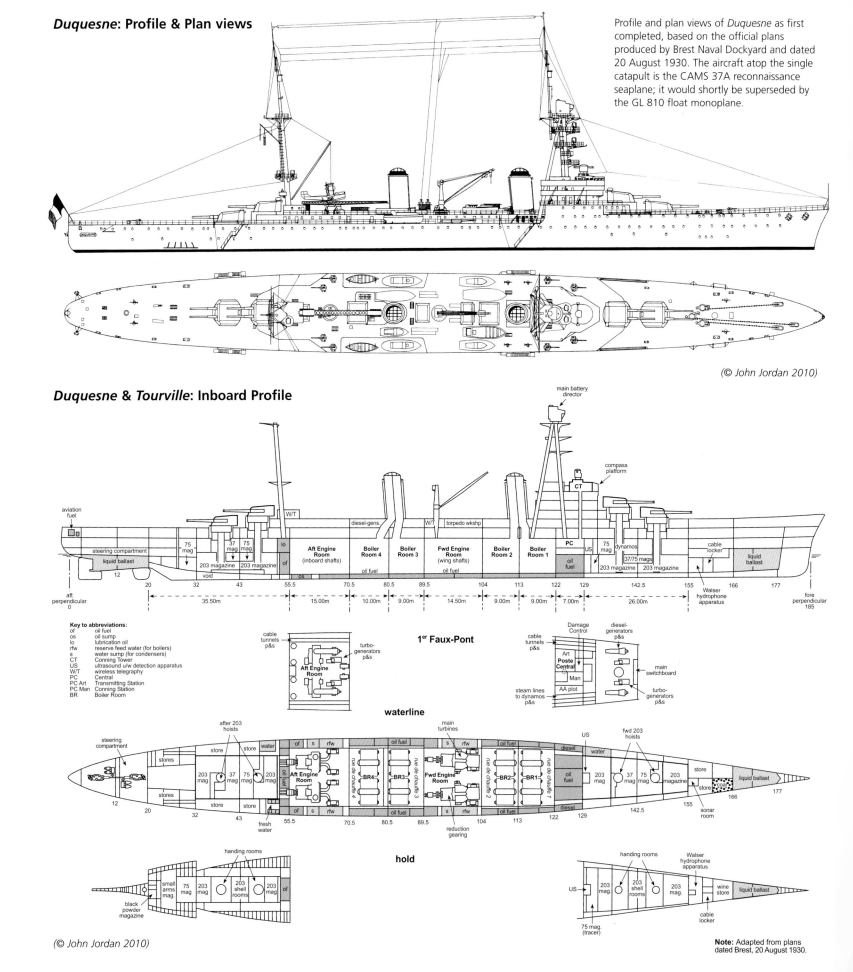

(© John Jordan 2010)

Duquesne & *Tourville*: Inboard Profile

Key to abbreviations:

of	oil fuel
os	oil sump
lo	lubrication oil
rfw	reserve feed water (for boilers)
s	water sump (for condensers)
CT	Conning Tower
US	ultrasound u/w detection apparatus
W/T	wireless telegraphy
PC	Central
PC Art	Transmitting Station
PC Man	Conning Station
BR	Boiler Room

1er Faux-Pont

waterline

hold

(© John Jordan 2010)

Note: Adapted from plans dated Brest, 20 August 1930.

Duquesne: Hull Sections

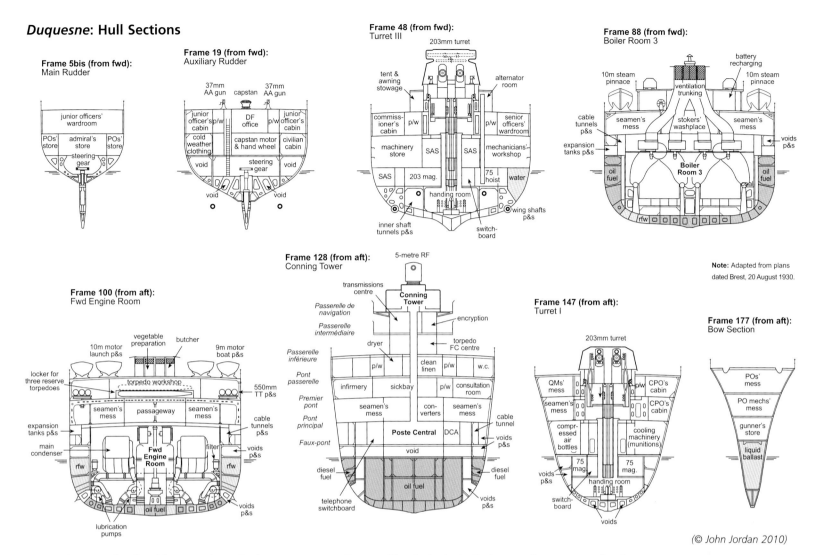

Frame 5bis (from fwd):
Main Rudder

Frame 19 (from fwd):
Auxiliary Rudder

Frame 48 (from fwd):
Turret III

Frame 88 (from fwd):
Boiler Room 3

Frame 100 (from aft):
Fwd Engine Room

Frame 128 (from aft):
Conning Tower

Frame 147 (from aft):
Turret I

Frame 177 (from aft):
Bow Section

Note: Adapted from plans dated Brest, 20 August 1930.

(© John Jordan 2010)

– and showing the flag (the French wished to impress friendly nations and the colonies with modern vessels).

Duquesne and *Tourville* would be classified, like their immediate predecessors, as *croiseurs légers* ('light cruisers', as opposed to *croiseurs cuirassés*, 'armoured cruisers'), and this classification would remain with them until the London Treaty of 1930 divided cruisers into the (a) and (b) categories according to their main guns, when *Duquesne* and *Tourville* were reclassified *croiseurs de 1ère classe*, and the three *Duguay-Trouin*s became *croiseurs de 2e classe*.

DESIGN AND CONSTRUCTION
The Staff Requirement drawn up on 6 July 1922 was as follows:

– eight 203mm (8in) guns, each with 150 rounds, in three or four lightly armoured turrets;
– four 100mm HA guns, each with 500 rounds;
– two quadruple 550mm torpedo tubes, with four reserve torpedoes;
– four Thornycroft 24cm anti-submarine mortars;
– a range of 5000nm at 15 knots.

It was envisaged that for the early ships of the type protection would be limited to tight underwater compartments against torpedoes (as in the

*Duguay-Trouin*s), but that consideration might be given to increasing protection at a cost of 2 knots speed. The STCN was therefore asked to draw up two preliminary designs: the first was to have the maximum speed compatible with the stated armament and no protection; the second was to have the speed of the first design reduced by 2 knots, the weight saved being put into protection.[5]

With hindsight it would appear that the weight penalties involved in increasing the calibre of the main guns from 155mm to 203mm were probably underestimated by the General Staff. Even if the requirement for a larger hull strengthened to withstand the much greater stresses when firing the bigger gun is put to one side, the weights involved were totally disproportionate. Each twin 203mm turret weighed 180 tonnes, whereas the much smaller 155mm turret fitted in the *Duguay-Trouin* weighed only 80 tonnes. Each 203mm round comprised a shell weighing 123kg with a 53kg charge, whereas the 155mm shell weighed only 57kg and was propelled by a 20kg charge. The General Staff also wanted 150 rounds per gun, whereas in the *Duguay-Trouin*s that figure was 125. Overall weights for the main artillery

---

[5] Contemporary studies for the early British Treaty cruisers embodied similar requirements; however, in contrast to the Marine Nationale the Royal Navy opted for more protection and reduced speed.

of these respective ships (including ammunition) were therefore approximately 930 tonnes versus 400 tonnes – an increase of 135 per cent!

Moreover, in November 1922 the General Staff modified some of their initial requirements. The ships were now to have a much-enhanced anti-aircraft armament comprising eight single 100mm dual-purpose guns, each with 500 rounds, plus eight single 40mm AA each with 1000 rounds and twelve single 8mm MG. There was also to be a seaplane for recon-naissance (a trainable catapult using compressed air was trialled aboard the cruiser *Primauguet* from April 1927). In compensation, the quadruple torpedo tubes would become triples.

The additional four 100mm mountings requested, together with their ammunition, would cost around 20 tonnes each, the eight 40mm around 16 tonnes, and the seaplane and catapult perhaps 60–70 tonnes, for a total of 155–165 tonnes. The weight saving from reducing the torpedo tubes from quadruple to triple mountings was minimal, particularly as there would now be six reloads, hence no reduction in the number of torpedoes carried (each torpedo weighed approxi-mately 2 tonnes). In a displacement-limited design such as a Treaty cruiser, these could be the straws that broke the camel's back, and so it proved.

Because the Washington Treaty definition of 'stan-dard displacement' was purely artificial, as it excluded such essential items as fuel and reserve feed water, the STCN constructors worked to a maximum 'normal' displacement figure of 11,000 tonnes, which was to include 500 tonnes of fuel oil and 240 tonnes of reserve feed water plus 100 tonnes for 'miscellaneous' items (if these are subtracted from the total, we arrive

at a figure of 10,160 tonnes, equivalent to 10,000 'long' tons). Once all the new demands were accommodated it was found that only 1740 tonnes remained available for machinery. Using Washington Treaty criteria the machinery installation of the *Duguay-Trouin*s was calculated at 2085 tonnes for an output of 102,000CV, and it was estimated that 120,000CV would be required if the new, larger ships were to make 34 knots. The STCN estimated that if the weight/power ratio remained constant, 1740 tonnes would provide only 85,000CV for a maximum speed of 31.5 knots.[6] It began to look as if 34 knots would be unattainable even without protection. It was further calculated that the minimum machinery weight to produce the required power output, even using the latest propul-sion technology, was 1946 tonnes, which would bring the ships 200 tonnes over the Washington limit.

Superheating was considered but was rejected, as the technology was not yet mature and there were concerns regarding its reliability. In the event a more compact machinery solution was made possible by instituting an open competition among potential contractors. AC Bretagne came up with a four-shaft solution producing 115,000CV for 34 knots at normal displacement (33.1 knots at full load) based on eight small-tube boilers rated at 20kg/cm^2 (those in the *Duguay-Trouin* class were rated at a more conservative 18.5kg/cm^2) and four identical sets of turbines, with cruise turbines only on the inner shafts to achieve the stipulated 5000nm at 15 knots.

---

[6] The machinery of the British *Kents*, which had similar performance figures (80,000shp for 31.5 knots), weighed 1850 tons (= 1880 tonnes).

BUILDING DATA AND GENERAL CHARACTERISTICS

Name	Builder	Laid down	Launched	In service
1924 Programme				
Duquesne	Arsenal de Brest	30 Oct 1924	17 Dec 1925	25 Jan 1929
Tourville	Arsenal de Lorient	4 Apr 1925	24 Aug 1926	12 Mar 1929

Displacement:	10,000 tons standard 11,404 tonnes normal 12,435 tonnes full load
Length:	185m pp, 191m oa
Beam:	19.00m
Draught:	6.45m max. (normal)
Machinery:	Eight Guyot du Temple boilers, 20kg/cm^2 (215°); four-shaft Rateau-Bretagne geared steam turbines for 120,000CV; speed 34kts (designed)
Oil fuel:	1842t oil; radius 5000nm at 15kts, 1800nm at 29kts, 700nm at 33kts
Armament:	Eight 203mm/50 Mle 1924 in twin mountings Mle 1924 (150rpg); eight 75mm/50 Mle 1924 HA in single mountings Mle 1922 (500rpg); eight 37mm/50 Mle 1925 AA in single mountings (1000rpg); six tubes for 550mm torpedoes Mle 1923D in triple mountings Mle 1925T (3 reloads)
Aircraft:	Two GL 810 HY seaplanes
Protection:	*Magazines*: 20–30mm *CT*: 30mm *Turrets*: 30mm
Complement:	605 (637 as flagship)

Weights (*Duquesne*)

Hull:	4783t		Oil Fuel:	900t
Protection (hull):	368t		Reserve Feed Water:	240t
Protection (armament):	91t		Miscellaneous:	104t
Armament:	1224t		**Normal Displ.**	**11,404t**
Propulsion:	2271t			
Torpedoes/Aircraft:	111t		Oil Fuel:	941t
Fittings/Provisions:	1242t		Ammunition:	78t
Miscellaneous:	70t		Miscellaneous:	12t
Washington Displ.	**10,160t**		**Full Load Displ.**	**12,435t**

Source: Official *devis d'armement* (via Robert Dumas).

Some further (minor) weight savings were made when it was decided to replace the proposed 100mm gun with the 75mm/50 Mle 1922 on a Mle 1924 single mounting, and the 40mm AA gun by the new 37mm/50 Mle 1925. The four Thornycroft A/S mortars were also suppressed, though a later installation was not precluded as the ships were designed with provision for an ultrasound underwater detection system forward.

Protection in the first draft design was on a par with that of the *Duguay-Trouin* class, with tight compartmentation and reinforced longitudinal bulkheads 2–3m inboard of the outer hull to protect the magazines and machinery. The STCN had wanted to provide 30mm splinter protection over the machinery spaces, but this had to be abandoned when the *Conseil Supérieur*[7] demanded a general 'beefing up' of the protection over the after magazines and steering gear, and requested that the thickness of certain key transverse bulkheads be increased from 8mm to 20mm in order to restrict flooding.

The STCN responded by recommending a reduction of 2 knots in speed to secure adequate protection for the ship's magazines and some protection for the machinery spaces, which were vulnerable even to destroyer shell. However, the General Staff, which had received reports that the new Italian cruisers would be capable of 34 knots, vetoed the request.

The total weight accorded to protection in *Duquesne* and *Tourville* was 460 tonnes – a mere 4.5 per cent of

displacement. Although this constituted an improvement on the *Duguay-Trouin* class it was a significantly lower figure than France's competitors managed.[8] It was decided to order the first two units immediately as a counterweight to the Italian ships, but to keep protection under review for later units.

The order for *Duquesne* was placed with Brest Naval Dockyard; *Tourville* was ordered from Lorient. *Duquesne* was laid down in late 1924, *Tourville* in 1925, and both ships entered service in early 1929 (see table).

NAMES

Abraham **Duquesne**, marquis du Bouchet (c.1610–88) was the son of a naval officer and became a sailor himself, spending his early years in merchant service. He fought against the Spanish, then served for a time in the Swedish Navy. On his return, he distinguished himself in the Third Dutch War, fighting as second in command of the French squadron against the Dutch Admiral de Ruyter, who had the united fleets of Spain and the United Provinces under his command. A Protestant, he refused to renounce his faith, which deprived him of the rank of vice-admiral and a marshal's bâton.

Anne-Hilarion de Costentin, comte de **Tourville** (1642–1701) was a naval commander who also served

---

[7] The *Conseil supérieur de la marine* (CSM) was an advisory body composed of senior admirals which provided advice to the Navy Minister, and direction to the French corps of constructors, the STCN.

[8] The Royal Navy, which like the Marine Nationale played by the rules, managed to incorporate 1025 tons of protection (10.3 per cent of displacement) into the *Kents*; however, this was at the cost of a significant reduction in power and speed. The Italian *Trentos* had 890 tonnes of protection, but were probably over the Treaty limits by a similar margin on completion.

with distinction under King Louis XIV. He fought against the British and the Dutch at the Battles of Beachy Head (French: Bévéziers) and Barfleur, and on 27 June 1693 he defeated a convoy of fifty-nine English ships commanded by George Rooke at Cape St Vincent. He was made a Marshal of France in 1693.

HULL AND GENERAL CONFIGURATION

Duquesne and *Tourville* had essentially the same hull configuration as the *Duguay-Trouin*s, which combined high freeboard forward with marked sheer and flare. The French were the only nation to pursue the raised forecastle option in their first generation of Treaty cruisers; the British, the Americans and the Italians all opted for a flush deck, while the Japanese persisted with their distinctive 'wavy line' upper deck which, theoretically, combined the longitudinal strength of the flush deck with the high freeboard forward of the 'forecastle' type, while at the same time economising on hull weight.

Duquesne and *Tourville* were good seaboats; they could sustain 30 knots even in adverse weather, and prominent bilge keels reduced their roll to an acceptable level. However, accommodation was relatively cramped because of the loss of a deck amidships and aft, and this combined with inadequate ventilation of the living spaces to make the ships less than comfortable when they served on foreign stations. Moreover, the break in the forecastle resulted in a structural weakness amidships which may have been aggravated by the flare of the bow section. Working of the hull in heavy seas following *Tourville*'s world cruise in 1929 required some subsequent strengthening.

As in the *Duguay-Trouin*s there was a heavy tripod foremast to support the DCT for the main guns, and a heavy pole mainmast. The masts and funnels were raked at an angle of 5 degrees. The bridge structure was built around the legs of the tripod, and there was no after structure equipped with a secondary fire control position as was common in other navies.

The adoption of a 'unit' layout for the machinery had a major impact on the general arrangement of the midship section, both below and above decks. The widely spaced funnels effectively divided the shelter deck into two. The section between the second funnel and the mainmast was used for the aviation installations, which in the *Duguay-Trouin*s had been divided between the shelter deck and the stern; a single catapult was mounted, served by a lifting derrick fixed to the base of the mainmast. The ship's boats were carried on the shelter deck between and abreast the funnels and in two cutaways in the sides of the shelter deck abeam the second funnel. These were served by a single centre-line crane similar in configuration to that of the *Duguay-Trouin*s.

Whereas in the earlier ships the four HA guns had been located close together outboard of the funnels, the double complement of 75mm guns mounted in *Duquesne* and *Tourville* was divided into two groups of four, the forward group being located on the Lower Bridge Deck with the after group at the after end of the shelter deck, abeam the catapult. This resulted in a significant improvement in firing arcs, enabling targets close to the ship's axis fore and aft to be engaged. Surprisingly, HA directors do not feature on the original plans, although they would be fitted in due course (see below).

MACHINERY

The eight Guyot-du Temple small-tube boilers, built by Indret, were divided equally between four boiler rooms, of which the first two served the forward engine room and the midships pair the after engine room. In each of the boiler rooms the two boilers were disposed side by side with a common *rue de chauffe* which ran across both boiler faces. The *rue de chauffe* was served by turbo-ventilators, and the boilers were within gas-tight boxes which served to create tolerable working conditions for the crew, who were also thereby protected from boiler flashbacks. The boilers in boiler room 1 were arranged so that they backed on to the boilers in boiler room 2; this enabled the uptakes to be grouped together and led up into the fore-funnel. The same arrangement was duplicated aft, resulting in two broad, widely-spaced funnels. There were four Rateau turbine groups, each of which was capable of independent operation with its own turbopumps and condenser. Each grouping comprised a pair of main impulse turbines with reverse turbines incorporated into the main casing. The single reduction gearing reduced the 2800rpm rotation of the turbines to an acceptable 280rpm for the shafts, which were fitted with three-bladed propellers 4.2m in diameter. The two forward turbine groups, which drove the wing shafts, were located abaft the forward boiler rooms. The two after turbine groups incorporated the cruise turbines, and drove the inner shafts. Each of the main turbine groups was rated at 30,000CV for a total designed power output of 120,000CV; each of the cruise turbines was rated at 2,900CV. Propeller guards were fitted to both ships in 1930.

Despite the claims of 36+ knots made following speed trials, the performance of these ships proved to be slightly disappointing. The Marine Nationale was really hoping for 34 knots at normal displacement over the full eight-hour period, but *Duquesne* managed 34.12 knots with 131,770CV for only four hours, and *Tourville* achieved only 33.22 knots with 126,919CV

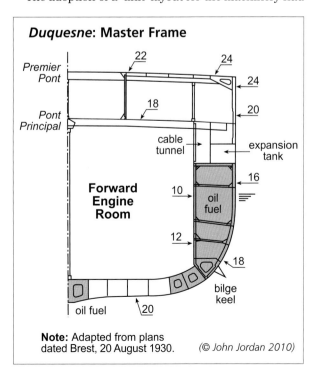

Duquesne: Master Frame

Premier Pont

22   24

24

Pont Principal

18   20

cable tunnel

expansion tank

16

Forward Engine Room

10

oil fuel

12

18

bilge keel

oil fuel   20

Note: Adapted from plans dated Brest, 20 August 1930.

(© John Jordan 2010)

over six hours.[9] Nevertheless, 31 knots was comfortably sustained at full load, and both ships steamed for 24 hours at an average of 30 knots with only half the nominal horsepower available (see table).

Electrical power was provided while underway by two pairs of turbo-dynamos, and while alongside by two diesel generator groups. The latter, together with the forward pair of turbo-generators, were located in a special compartment forward of the main machinery spaces which had natural ventilation when alongside; the other pair of turbo-generators was located in the after engine room on a platform above the turbines at First Platform Deck level (see drawings).

GROUND TACKLE AND NAVIGATION

The arrangement of the anchors, capstan and cables duplicated that of the *Duguay-Trouin*s, The bower and sheet anchors (in hawsepipes; two to starboard, one to port) were of a modified Byers type; each weighed 5970kg. The single Hall stern anchor weighed 1900kg, and a single 1600kg kedge anchor was stowed amidships to port. There was a 34-tonne steam windlass on the forecastle and a small capstan aft.

Unusually there were two centre-line rudders, one with a surface area of 11m², the other of 22m². They were powered by four Thomson servo-motors which could be controlled from the bridge, from the conning tower or locally. The ships, according to one Commanding Officer,[10] manoeuvred 'like torpedo boats', even in harbour, although their fine lines resulted in a comparatively large turning circle, a common feature of French warships of the period.

PROTECTION

Construction was on the longitudinal principle, and, as with the *Duguay-Trouin* class, the hull was tightly sub-divided. The sixteen main transverse bulkheads

---

[9] In a later trial on 31 March *Tourville* attained 34.45 knots with 136,742CV for one hour with forcing.

[10] *Capitaine de vaisseau* Quedec, 12 June 1946, Saigon.

MACHINERY TRIALS: *TOURVILLE*

	Full Power (6 hours) 17 Mar 1928	Forcing (1 hour) 31 Mar 1928
Displacement:	11,395t	9646t
Draught:	6.10m	5.37m
Average speed:	33.23kts	34.49kts
Average power:	126,918CV	136,742CV
Fuel consumption/hour:	–	–
Endurance (500t oil fuel):	700nm	–

	Endurance (24 hours at 30knts) 27–28 Mar 1928	Fuel Consumption (5 hours at 15kts) 9 Mar 1928
Displacement:	11,401t	11,383t
Draught:	6.07m	6.06m
Average speed:	30.04kts	14.86kts
Average power:	67,405CV	7104CV
Fuel consumption/hour:	1013kg	247.98kg
Endurance (500t oil fuel):	1800nm	5000nm

Source: Garier & Cheyron, *op. cit.*

were continuous from the keel to the upper deck, and were watertight up to the main deck. Each of the seventeen compartments thus created had its own pumps and ventilation. The transverse bulkheads fore and aft of the engine rooms were reinforced to 20mm by sheets of 60kg steel in an effort to restrict flooding to three adjacent compartments in the event of torpedo or mine damage. The unit machinery arrangement, with alternating boiler rooms and engine rooms, was adopted to further enhance the survivability of the ship; even after a torpedo hit this ensured that at least two boilers and one set of turbines would be available to get the ship home.

Below: A splendid view of *Duquesne* on 24 June 1932. There is a GL 810 floatplane on the catapult, and a second in the 'rest' position abaft the fore-funnel. The foretopmast has already been shortened. Note the single 37mm AA mountings on the forecastle. (*Marius Bar*)

In the absence of armour that could resist the shells of opposing cruisers, these ships relied like their immediate predecessors on their high speed to keep them out of harm's way, and their tight underwater subdivision to contain any damage sustained and to ensure survivability. Nevertheless, there was some light splinter protection over their most vulnerable spaces to enable them to engage light flotilla craft with a degree of confidence. The magazines, which accounted for some 25 per cent of the ships' length, had 30mm bulkheads of 60kg steel on either side with 20mm crowns and end bulkheads. Given that these protective 'boxes' were well inboard and separated from the hull sides by a combination of voids and spaces filled with equipment, this protection should have been adequate to keep out splinters from destroyer shell bursting on the outer hull plating (generally 16–20mm thick) or the upper deck (22–24mm). The steering gear was covered by 17mm plates, and the gunhouses and the conning tower had layered 30mm protection comprising two 15mm plates of HT steel riveted together.

ARMAMENT

Main battery

The 203mm Mle 1924 gun was a new model specially developed for this class. It was of simple construction with a thick autofretted A tube, shrunk jacket and breech ring; the Welin-type interrupted screw breech block opened upwards. Initially an AP shell of 123.1kg and an HE shell of 123.8kg were provided. The next series of shells, developed during the late 1920s, was lighter, but the OPf Mle 1936 AP shell developed prior to the Second World War was significantly heavier (see table). The propellant, as for the 155mm Mle 1920 of the *Duguay-Trouins*, was in two half-charges. There was a spring rammer for the shells, the charges being loaded manually. Range at the maximum elevation of 45 degrees was 31,400m for the early AP shell, and 30,000m for the HE shell, with a muzzle velocity of 850m/s. Both muzzle velocity and the weight of charge were reduced (to 820m/s and 47kg respectively) for the heavier Mle 1936 shell, which had a colorant added in March 1939 so that the cruisers could more easily iden-

203/50 MLE 1924

Gun Data

Construction:	Autofretted 'A' tube with shrunk jacket and liner
Breech mechanism:	Upward-opening Welin screw
Weight of gun:	20.72t (incl. breech)
Ammunition type:	Separate
Projectiles:	OPf Mle 1927 (123.1kg)
	OEA Mle 1927 (123.82kg)
	OPf Mle 19?? (119.07kg)
	OEA Mle 19?? (119.72kg)
	OPf Mle 1936 (134kg)
Propellant:	BM13 in two half-charges (53kg for OPf Mle24, 47kg for OPf Mle36)
Muzzle velocity:	850m/s for OPf Mle 1927
	820m/s for OPf Mle 1936
Max. range	31,400m (45°)

Mounting Data

Designation:	Twin Mle 1924
Weight of turret:	180t
Distance apart gun axes:	1.88m
Protection:	30mm
Loading angle:	-5° / +10°
Elevation of guns:	-5° / +45°
Max. training speed:	6°/sec
Max. elevating speed:	10°/sec
Firing cycle (per gun):	3–4rpm

Notes:

OPf	*Obus de Perforation*	Armour Piercing
OEA	*Obus Explosif en Acier*	High Explosive (HE)

tify their respective shell splashes when firing in formation. *Duquesne* was red, *Tourville* yellow and the third ship in the division, *Suffren*, presumably fired green.

The twin turret Mle 1924 was likewise specially developed for these ships, and seems to have been successful, as it was retained for all French Treaty cruisers up to *Algérie*. The guns were in separate cradles with individual toothed elevating arcs, although they could be coupled together for salvo fire; during the mid-1930s remote power control (RPC) was fitted for training. The guns could be elevated to +45

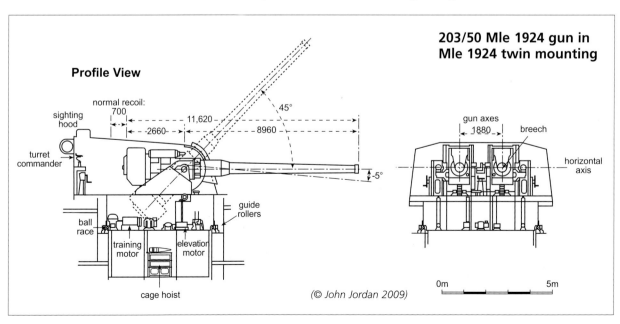

Profile View

203/50 Mle 1924 gun in Mle 1924 twin mounting

(© John Jordan 2009)

degrees and depressed to -5 degrees, with loading carried out between +10 degrees and -5 degrees employing catapult rammers. The shell rooms were below the magazines, except that some of the forward magazine stowage was on the same deck-level as the shells. Dredger hoists from the magazine handing room ran up to the working chamber, where ammunition was transferred to the upper cage hoists. These emerged outside the guns; shells were then transferred to swinging arms which locked to the guns for loading. The firing cycle as designed was 5–6 rounds per minute; in practice it was less.

Anti-aircraft weapons

The 75mm/50 Mle 1924 was a slightly modified version of the Mle 1922 fitted in the *Duguay-Trouin*s. The eight single mountings on *Duquesne* and *Tourville* were grouped in pairs abeam the bridge structure and at the after end of the shelter deck. The fixed rounds were raised by hoists in cases from the magazines fore and aft, and were fused on deck. Protective shields were fitted to the guns in late 1933.

Eight single 37mm/50 Mle 1925 light AA mountings were fitted from completion: two on the forecastle, two on the quarterdeck, and the other four on the shelter deck abeam the first funnel. In 1933–4 the forecastle and quarterdeck mountings were relocated to the shelter deck, abeam the boat crane. At the same time four of the new 13.2mm/76 Hotchkiss Mle 1929 twin mountings were installed on the quarterdeck. These replaced the original 8mm Mle 1914 MG, which were acknowledged to be ineffectual against contemporary aircraft. Two further twin 13.2mm mountings were fitted in the lower bridge wings to cover forward arcs in 1937, and these were fitted with shields the following year. In 1940 *Tourville* also received shields for her quarterdeck mountings.

Fire control

As with the *Duguay-Trouin* class there were delays in the development and the delivery of fire control systems, and both ships ran sea trials without them. The director control tower for the main guns was

37/50 MLE 1925

Gun Data

Weight of gun:	158kg
Ammunition type:	Fixed
Projectiles:	OEA Mle 1925 (0.73kg)
	OI Mle 1924 (0.73kg)
Propellant:	BM2 in cartridge (0.2kg)
Complete round:	
Weight:	2.8kg
Dimensions:	408mm x 61mm
Muzzle velocity:	810m/s
Max. range:	8000m theoretical
	5000m effective

Mounting Data

Mounting designation:	CAS Mle 1925
Weight of mounting:	470kg
Elevation of guns:	-15° / +80°
Firing cycle:	20rpm

Notes:

CAS	*Contre-Avions Simple*	AA single mounting
OEA	*Obus Explosif en Acier*	High Explosive (HE)
OI	*Obus Incendiaire*	Incendiary shell

203mm shell: OPf Mle 1927

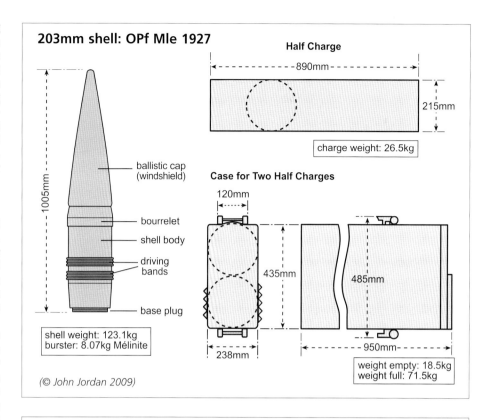

shell weight: 123.1kg
burster: 8.07kg Mélinite

charge weight: 26.5kg

weight empty: 18.5kg
weight full: 71.5kg

(© John Jordan 2009)

Duquesne: Director Control Tower

The director control tower *type croiseur de 10 000 tonnes* was divided into two compartments (upper/lower): the upper for the fire control team, the lower for the rangefinding team and the director layer and trainer. The main rangefinder was a SOM coincidence model with a 5-metre base, which was located in the after part of the lower compartment. It was held in place by two collars fixed to the director housing, each collar comprising a bronze frame with the rangefinder supported on three roller bearings. In the forward part of the lower compartment there was a Zeiss 3-metre stereo rangefinder for scartometry, secured in place as for the 5-metre rangefinder.

The upper compartment probably had positions for the (Assistant) Gunnery Control Officer, the Rate Officer and the Spotting Officer. There were three windows in the upper part of the compartment for the key personnel, and optical equipment included spotting glasses, and periscopes for the Control Officer and the Cross-Leveller.

The entire structure rotated around an extension to the mast on a ball race, with two sets of guide rollers top and bottom. The trainer used a handwheel to train the director in bearing via a worm screw and bevel gear linkage, a toothed side wheel engaging with a toothed ring fixed to the mast. The rangefinders were trained in azimuth with the director, and in elevation by the rangetakers using a standard lever mechanism.

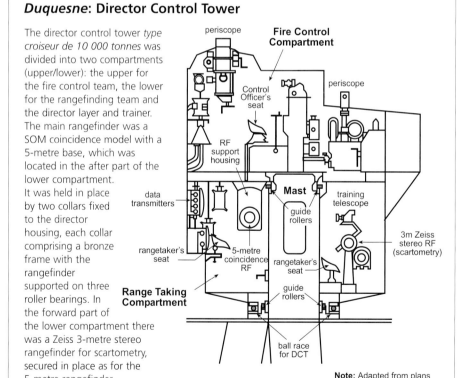

(© John Jordan 2011) **Note:** Adapted from plans dated Brest, 20 August 1930.

similar to that of the earlier ships but incorporated a longer-base 5-metre SOM coincidence rangefinder. It was not fitted atop the heavy tripod foremast until 1929–30. Delivery of the 5-metre tactical rangefinder in its weatherproof trainable housing atop the conning tower was likewise delayed. In the interim *Duquesne* was fitted with an older-model Triplex rangefinder, and her sister with an SOM 3-metre coincidence model. When the fire control installation was complete, data from these sensors was handled by a fire control computer Mle 1924, with two smaller and less-capable 'aviso'-type calculators as emergency back-up. The 5-metre rangefinders atop turrets II and III and the rangefinder atop the conning tower could also feed range and bearing data into the fire control computer. Those atop the turrets were initially in a fixed housing but were replaced in 1933–4 by a newer model which could be trained independently through 15 degrees.

Concentration dials were fitted fore and aft to facilitate formation firing, and there were four 1.2-metre Sautter-Harlé searchlight projectors for night firing on platforms angled port and starboard on the forward side of the tripod mast and around the pole mainmast.

The projectors were remotely controlled from platforms directly beneath them to prevent the operators from being blinded.

Duquesne and *Tourville* were completed without specialised fire control facilities for their 75mm HA guns. However, at their first major refits in 1932–4 they were fitted with two HA directors with integral 3-metre base rangefinders port and starboard; each had its own associated fire control position equipped with an 'aviso'-type plotting table. The directors were fitted at the after end of the bridge and were supported, as in the *Duguay-Trouins*, by pillars which rested on the upper deck, at the base of the tripod foremast. In *Tourville* the directors were at the intermediate bridge deck level, whereas in *Duquesne* they were one deck higher; this would be a key distinguishing feature from the mid-1930s until the ships' demise. At the same time the 75mm mountings were fitted with RPC for training.

Torpedoes

The heavy torpedo armament of the *Duguay-Trouins* had been much criticised (see Chapter 1), and the outfit in *Duquesne* and *Tourville* was altogether more

Below: Left: An excellent view of *Duquesne* dating from her deployment as part of the French force monitoring maritime traffic during the Spanish Civil War; note the tricolore recognition markings on turrets II and III. The foretopmast has been shortened, and the after 37mm single mountings Mle 1925 moved from the quarterdeck to the boat deck. The photo was taken on 11 May 1937. The single white band on the second funnel marks her out as the flagship of the 3rd Light Division, subsequently the 2nd Cruiser Division. *(Marius Bar)*

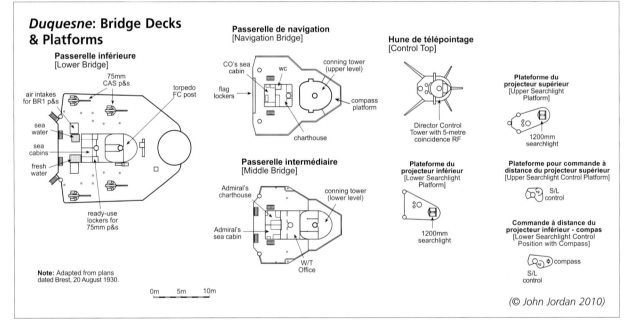

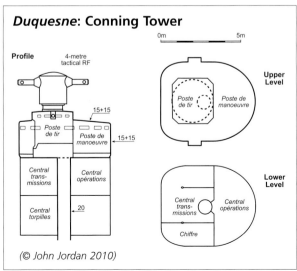

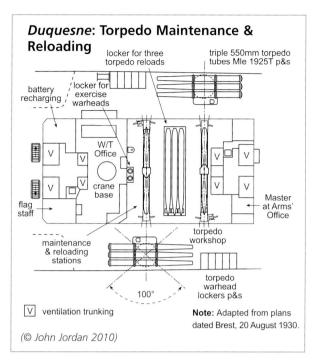

Duquesne: Torpedo Maintenance & Reloading

- locker for three torpedo reloads
- triple 550mm torpedo tubes Mle 1925T p&s
- battery recharging
- locker for exercise warheads
- W/T Office
- crane base
- flag staff
- Master at Arms' Office
- maintenance & reloading stations
- torpedo workshop
- 100°
- torpedo warhead lockers p&s

V ventilation trunking

Note: Adapted from plans dated Brest, 20 August 1930.

(© John Jordan 2010)

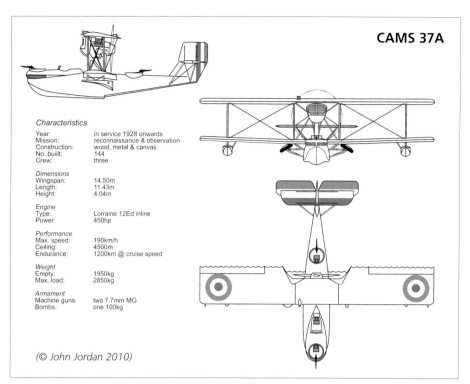

CAMS 37A

Characteristics

Year:	in service 1928 onwards
Mission:	reconnaissance & observation
Construction:	wood, metal & canvas
No. buiilt:	144
Crew:	three

Dimensions

Wingspan:	14.50m
Length:	11.43m
Height:	4.04m

Engine

Type:	Lorraine 12Ed inline
Power:	450hp

Performance

Max. speed:	190km/h
Ceiling:	4500m
Endurance:	1200km @ cruise speed

Weight

Empty:	1950kg
Max. load:	2850kg

Armament

Machine guns:	two 7.7mm MG
Bombs:	one 100kg

(© John Jordan 2010)

modest. There were two triple torpedo tube mountings of a new model, Mle 1925T, for 550mm torpedoes; these were located port and starboard on the upper deck between the funnels. In the 'locked' position the starboard-side tubes were trained forward, and the port-side tubes aft, with armoured deck-edge lockers adjacent for safe stowage of the 308kg explosive warheads in peacetime. The tubes could be trained and fired from the armoured conning tower or locally, range and bearing data being provided by the 5-metre base rangefinder atop the conning tower.

Three reserve torpedoes were carried; these were located in the torpedo maintenance shop between the tubes. In the *Duguay-Trouin*s the torpedoes were reloaded by a system of overhead pulleys and cables, which was difficult to do in a seaway. However, in the *Duquesne*s the spare torpedoes were stowed athwartships in the maintenance shop, and could be loaded directly into the tubes via the maintenance beds; the latter had limited traverse which enabled them to be aligned with any of the three tubes (see drawing).

The torpedo was again the Mle 1923D, which had a Schneider 4-cylinder engine fuelled by alcohol, and two speed settings: 9000m at 39 knots or 13,000m at 35 knots.

AVIATION INSTALLATIONS

There had been no provision for aircraft in the original *Duguay-Trouin* design. When the first trainable catapult, using compressed air, was trialled aboard *Primauguet* in 1927 the only possible location was the quarterdeck. Although the performance of the catapult itself was promising, the quarterdeck location was criticised because the comparatively low freeboard aft meant that the aircraft was unduly exposed to the elements. An aircraft stowed atop the catapult was also exposed to blast from the after guns. Collapsible cranes had to be specially developed and installed for handling; even so, the transfer of the spare aircraft from its resting position at the after end of the shelter deck was a complex procedure.

For the *Duquesne* class it was decided to locate the catapult atop the shelter deck itself, between the second funnel and the pole mainmast. The aircraft were normally handled by a hinged derrick with a reach of 14m and a lift capacity of 5 tonnes, which was hinged at the base of the mainmast. The catapult, a new model powered by gunpowder capable of launching aircraft up to 2500kg, was not ready for installation until 1929–30, so in the interim the FBA 17 and Cams 37A reconnaissance seaplanes were launched from the water. Once the catapult had been installed these obsolescent models were replaced by the purpose-built Gordou-Leseurre 810 float mono-plane. The GL 810–811 series[11] equipped both ships until 1937, when the catapults were temporarily removed. They were replaced the following year, having been modified to handle the heavier Loire 130.

Two aircraft were normally embarked: one was stowed with wings fully deployed atop the catapult; the other on the boat deck just abaft the fore-funnel. The boat crane would subsequently be lengthened to enable it to lift the ship's aircraft aboard or set it down on the surface. The aviation fuel, together with petrol for the motor boats, was again stowed in separate isolating tanks high in the stern with full fire precautions.

BOATS

The outfit when the ships were first completed was as follows:

- one 11-metre pulling pinnace
- one 11-metre motor launch
- two 10-metre steam pinnaces
- one 10-metre cutter
- two 9-metre motor boats
- one 7-metre motor boat
- two 8.5-metre whalers
- two 5-metre dinghies

---

[11] The GL 811 had folding wings.

The boats were stowed on the shelter deck between the two funnels, and abeam and abaft the second funnel, the steam pinnaces and whalers being located in cutaways on the upper deck so as not to obstruct the training arcs of the catapult. With the exception of the two whalers, which were on davits, the boats were handled by a single crane located on the centre-line just forward of the second funnel. The latter was a slightly larger 'Applevage'[12] model than the one fitted in the *Duguay-Trouins* to give the necessary hull clearance; it had a reach of 12.3m and a lift capacity of 12 tonnes.

---

[12] It was manufactured by the *Société de construction et de location d'appareils de levage et de matériel de travaux publics.*

MODIFICATIONS 1930 TO 1942

It was found that the outer propellers extended beyond the hull to such a degree that it was necessary to fit propeller guards to the after part of the hull; this was done at Brest in late 1930. At the same time the boat crane was extended to enable it to handle aircraft.

A major refit to both ships was carried out in 1932–4, during which the anti-aircraft capabilities were considerably modified and upgraded. Spray/splinter shield were fitted to the eight 75mm HA guns, and the projected HA directors were finally fitted at the after end of the bridge. The after four single 37mm Mle 1925 were relocated to the edges of the boat deck abeam the centre-line crane, and in their place on the quarterdeck four twin 13.2mm Hotchkiss Mle 1929 MG were fitted. At the same time the foretopmast was suppressed to clear arcs for the main gunnery director, and new 5-

Below: Onboard photo of *Tourville* in the Toulon Roads dating from 13 February 1933, taken from the mainmast. Note the newly-fitted HA directors in their distinctive tubs seated around the legs of the foremast and the massive pillars supporting them. Abaft the HA director tubs, on the upper deck, are four of the eight 37mm Mle 1925 AA guns. *(Marius Bar)*

Below: The after part of *Duquesne* taken from the tripod foremast in early 1939, showing the boat/aircraft crane and the second funnel, the single white band marking her out as the flagship of the 2nd Cruiser Division; the single centre-line catapult is masked by the funnel. Note the shielded 75mm HA mountings aft. The photo gives an excellent view of the outfit of boats: outboard, abeam the funnel at First Deck level, are the two 10-metre steam pinnaces with the 8.5-metre whalers on davits abaft them. Inboard, abeam the funnel are a 10-metre pulling cutter (to port) and a 7-metre motor boat (to starboard). Forward of the latter two boats is the upper-deck stowage for hammocks. *(Gérard Garier collection)*

Duquesne September 1939

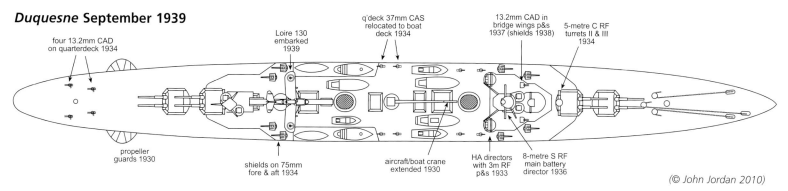

four 13.2mm CAD
on quarterdeck 1934

Loire 130
embarked
1939

q'deck 37mm CAS
relocated to boat
deck 1934

13.2mm CAD in
bridge wings p&s
1937 (shields 1938)

5-metre C RF
turrets II & III
1934

propeller
guards 1930

shields on 75mm
fore & aft 1934

aircraft/boat crane
extended 1930

HA directors
with 3m RF
p&s 1933

8-metre S RF
main battery
director 1936

(© John Jordan 2010)

metre rangefinders with 15-degree traverse were fitted in place of the original fixed housings on turrets II & III.

Around 1936 a new long-base stereoscopic rangefinder, the OPL PC2 Mle 1935, became available. This 8-metre model began to replace the original 5-metre models in the main DCT in the *Duguay-Trouins* and in all the 10,000-ton cruisers, beginning with *Duquesne* and *Tourville*.

The catapults were temporarily disembarked in 1937 and were modified to enable them to handle the larger Loire 130 reconnaissance seaplane. At around the same time there were modifications to the bridge structure which included the installation of two twin 13.2mm Hotchkiss MG in the lower bridge wings; these were fitted with shields the following year.

PROPOSAL FOR CONVERSION TO AIRCRAFT CARRIERS

When *Duquesne* and *Tourville* were completed in 1928 they were only marginally less well-protected than their foreign contemporaries. However, by the mid-1930s the Italian Navy had completed the four ships of the *Zara* class, which had an armour belt 150–100mm thick and 70–65mm armoured decks. These were cruisers designed to fight, not run. *Duquesne* and *Tourville* would be at a clear tactical disadvantage in such a contest, and their speed advantage, eroded by age, was barely sufficient to outrun the Italian ships in a tail chase.

In 1935 there was a proposal to convert them into aircraft carriers, France's single fleet carrier *Béarn* having proved too slow to operate tactically with the Marine Nationale's latest ships, and studies were duly commissioned. All except one of the four preliminary designs were for a carrier/cruiser hybrid, with either turret I or turret IV being retained. The flight deck

CARRIER CONVERSION PROPOSALS

Variant	Main Guns	AA	Flight Deck	Hangar
1	2 x 203mm (turret I)	12 x 100mm (6 x II)	139m x 22m	98m x 14.2m
		4 x 37mm (4 x I)		
2	2 x 203mm (turret IV)	(as 1)	139m x 22m	102m x 14.2m
3	None	(as 1)	176m x 22m	116.5m x 14.2m
4	2 x 203mm (turret I)	(as 1)	139m x 22m	102m x 14.2m

Source: Garier & Cheyron, *op. cit.*

would have been 139m long and 22m wide, with a hangar 98–102m long but only 14.2m wide. In the fourth sketch design all four turrets were removed, giving a 176m flight deck and a 116.5m hangar. Exhaust gases were to have been discharged through horizontal funnels on the starboard quarter. There were to be six twin 100mm/45 Mle 1930 HA mountings (the same model as that installed in the cruiser *Algérie*), with four single 37mm Mle 1925. Displacement would have increased to 12,000 tonnes, but the fine hull-form adopted for *Duquesne* and *Tourville* to secure high speed meant that the ships would have had a hangar capacity of only 12–14 aircraft.

Eventually this project was abandoned, and it was decided instead to build two purpose-built carriers of 18,000 tonnes, with double hangars to accommodate a more satisfactory total of forty aircraft. *Joffre* and *Pain-levé* (as they were subsequently named) were duly approved as part of the 1938 *tranche* and the former laid down in late 1938, but construction of *Joffre* was abandoned in June 1940 and her sister-ship was cancelled. The proposal to convert *Duquesne* and *Tourville* to aircraft carriers was to resurface in 1945, but was not pursued. By this time the ships were of limited military value, and their machinery was in serious need of refurbishment.

Left: *Tourville* in the Spring of 1939. Modifications since completion include shortened topmasts, the installation of HA directors (at the middle bridge level in line with the fore-funnel), and a revised layout of the light AA guns. She has trainable 5-metre rangefinders atop turrets II and III, and a new stereo rangefinder with an 8-metre base has replaced the original 5-metre coincidence model in the director control tower. Note the two black bands on the first funnel which mark her out as the second ship of the 2nd Cruiser Division. *(Marc Saibène collection)*

CHAPTER 3

THE *SUFFREN* CLASS

INTRODUCTION

Once the design for France's first pair of Treaty cruisers had been finalised the Naval General Staff immediately began to consider how the programme would proceed, and it was decided that a single ship of a modified design would figure in the 1925 *tranche*. On the one hand there were concerns regarding the low level of protection it had been possible to provide for *Duquesne* and *Tourville*, particularly once it became known that the Italians had managed to incorporate a 70mm belt with a 50mm armoured deck in their own first Treaty cruisers, the *Trento* and *Trieste*;[1] on the other the General Staff was anxious that the high speed of the *Duquesne*s should not be seriously compromised in the new design. The first note to the STCN addressing the proposed characteristics of the new cruiser was dated 11 February 1924, some three months before the order for the first two ships was placed. Like their counterparts in the Royal Navy and US Navy, the French designers were condemned to an endless game of 'catch-up', the latest thinking having to be embodied in new designs long before their predecessors could be completed, and often before they had even been laid down.

The characteristics requested by the Naval General Staff for the new cruiser were as follows:

– a standard (Washington) displacement of 10,160 tonnes (= 10,000 long tons);
– a main armament of eight 203mm in twin turrets as *Duquesne*, but with only 120 rounds per gun (the magazines would, however, have a capacity equivalent to 150rpg, which would be embarked only in time of war);[2]
– an anti-aircraft armament comprising eight single 75mm (500rpg), eight 40mm (1000rpg), and twelve 8mm MG;
– a torpedo armament of at least two triple 550mm mountings with six reloads;
– an endurance of 5000nm at 15 knots.

Apart from the reduction in the number of rounds provided for the main guns, these characteristics were identical to those adopted for *Duquesne* and *Tourville* at the time the orders were placed with the Naval Dockyards of Brest and Lorient. While the first two ships were under construction the 40mm AA would be replaced by the 37mm Mle 1925, and the number of torpedo reloads would be reduced to three, and these modifications would be extended to the third ship.

However, the other characteristics demanded by the General Staff reflected a new emphasis on survivability at the expense of speed. They were:

– a hull with sufficient buoyancy and stability to survive the effects of a direct hit from a 550mm torpedo or a near miss by a 100kg bomb, enabling the ship to proceed under its own power at reduced speed;
– protection over the ship's vitals sufficient to resist a direct hit by a 14cm shell[3] or a 100kg bomb;
– the maximum shaft horsepower compatible with the above requirements, ideally for 33 knots.

The initial studies by the STCN suggested that this level of protection was attainable only at the cost of 2 knots in speed, and that the simplest and most cost-effective way of achieving it was to reduce propulsive power by a quarter. Two boilers and one set of turbines would have to be sacrificed, leaving a three-shaft installation producing 90,000CV for 31.6 knots at full load.[4]

DESIGN AND CONSTRUCTION

In order to minimise changes to the overall layout of the ship the engineers adopted 'slimmed-down'

---

[1] What the French did not – and could not – know at the time was that this level of protection had been achieved by exceeding Treaty limits.

[2] This represented an effective saving of about 42 tonnes on the Washington standard displacement, although continued provision for 150rpg meant that no equivalent savings could be made in hull weight or protection. The Royal Navy constructors considered a similar subterfuge for their second series of Treaty cruisers of the *London* class, reducing provision to 100rpg but with space for 150rpg; when during the course of construction it became apparent that 100 tons had been saved, peacetime stowage was increased to 150rpg and the additional rounds were 'declared'.

[3] It was standard practice to specify a gun calibre in service with one's own navy, as this made it easier to verify performance in testing against armour plate. The 14cm calibre appears at first sight to be an odd choice as the Marine Nationale's most obvious potential opponents, the German and Italian Navies, had no intermediate weapon between 12cm and 15cm. Apart from the French, who favoured the 138.6mm calibre for its *contre-torpilleurs* (a non-standard type of ship developed only within the Marine Nationale), only the Japanese and the British had guns of this calibre. It therefore seems likely that deployment to the Far East in defence of French colonial interests, with the IJN's 5000-ton light cruisers as potential opponents, was a primary consideration. Protection against 14cm shell would give immunity against Italian destroyer shell, but not against the 152mm shell which the Regia Marina would adopt in its fast light cruisers of the 'Condottieri' type.

[4] The anticipated maximum speed of *Duquesne* and *Tourville* at full load was 33.2 knots.

machinery spaces aft, with single boilers in separate boiler rooms – each of the after boiler rooms in the *Duquesne*s housed two boilers side by side – and a single set of turbines to drive the centre-line shaft in an engine room located abaft the boiler rooms (see drawings). Topside changes were kept to the minimum by adopting this arrangement, which also had the advantage of ensuring that the after machinery spaces were well inboard of the outer hull, and therefore less vulnerable to penetration by shell and splinters. (The primary disadvantage was the break in the continuity of the longitudinal protective bulkheads outboard of the machinery spaces.) Locating the after boiler and engine rooms well inboard also offered the possibility of providing some sort of protective 'filler' abeam these spaces. Coal had been widely used for this purpose during the early dreadnought era, and tests were conducted by the Marine Nationale using a caisson at the gunnery proving ground at Gâvres to assess the effectiveness of such a filler in a cruiser hull-form.

The problem was that if coal were used solely for protection, under the Washington Treaty it would count towards the standard displacement of the ship. The French constructors therefore opted for two small additional boilers capable of burning either oil or coal in a space immediately abaft the forward engine room. This enabled the protective coal (which weighed 640 tonnes) to be classified as 'fuel' for the purpose of Treaty definitions; it could therefore be omitted altogether from the standard displacement figures. A further benefit of the lateral coal bunkers was that, if used to fire the small central boilers, cruising radius was boosted by 2000nm, albeit at the expense of the ship's protection system.

In January 1925, when the decision was made to replace the original 40mm AA by the 37mm Mle 1925, the General Staff also requested an increase in the number of embarked floatplanes from two to four. The design was duly amended to incorporate two catapults, located on the outer edge of the shelter deck between the second funnel and the mainmast. The General Staff was by now generally satisfied with the proposed

design, but wanted better protection against shell splinters, so as in *Duquesne* certain key transverse and longitudinal bulkheads were reinforced. It also wanted a trim/list compensation system with remote control, to mitigate the effects of flooding in the event of action damage. The system adopted involved flooding certain fuel bunkers with seawater, and was effective provided the fuel in the designated 'ballast tanks' was used first.

Following basin trials with a model of the new hull-form, concern was expressed regarding the excessive turning circle of the ship (estimated to be 1000m at 11 knots). The slim skeg for the single centre-line shaft extending aft from the keel was identified as the cause, and this was duly eliminated. It would be reinstated in the fourth and last ship of the series, *Dupleix* (q.v.).

The additional splinter protection requested was worked in as a result of careful detail design, and the new ship, to be named *Suffren*, was duly approved as part of the 1925 *tranche* and ordered on 1st November of that year. She was laid down at Brest Naval Dockyard in April 1926, and entered service some four years later.

Above: *Suffren* in the early stages of fitting out beneath the *Grande grue*, Brest 1927. On the left: the 8000-tonne cruiser *Primauguet*, with one of the new 1500-tonne *torpilleurs d'escadre* alongside. In the foreground two of the Japanese-built torpedo boats of the *Arabe* class can be seen, and in the background, beneath the arm of the crane, is the cruiser *Metz* (ex-German *Königsberg*).

SUFFREN

NAME

Regarded by many as the French equivalent of de Ruyter and Nelson, Pierre André de **Suffren** de Saint Tropez (1729–88) was France's most famous seaman. Born the third son of a French nobleman, he entered the Navy as a cadet in 1743 and quickly saw action against the English during the Seven Years' War. He became a knight of the order of Malta 1749–51. In 1778 and 1779 Suffren formed part of the squadron of Vice-Admiral D'Estaing, operating off the coast of North America and in the West Indies. His most famous campaign was against the English admiral Sir Edward Hughes in the Indian Ocean in 1782–3 which ended with the battle of Cuddalore.

HULL AND GENERAL CONFIGURATION

As completed *Suffren* resembled the *Duquesne*s in her overall layout. She had the same sturdy tripod forward, a heavy pole mainmast, and widely-spaced funnels. The layout of the main armament, the 75mm and 37mm AA guns, and the torpedo tubes was also

virtually identical, and although there were two catapults these occupied a similar position between the second funnel and the mainmast. However, a closer examination reveals some important differences, the most remarkable being the position of the compass platform, which was raised between the legs of the tripod so that it overlooked the conning tower, and which was connected with the upper bridge deck only by an open ladder.

The other major external means of identification was the configuration of the stern, which was optimised to suit the three-shaft propulsion installation, and was intended to reduce drag. The *cul de poule* (or 'hen's arse') stern was subsequently adopted not only for later ships of this class, but also for the *contre-torpilleurs* of the *Vauquelin* and *Le Fantasque* classes, and was regarded as particularly successful.[5]

---

[5] The traditional 'cruiser' stern of the earlier cruisers and *contre-torpilleurs* tended to bury itself in the wake of the ship at higher speeds, thereby adversely affecting trim.

Suffren: Profile & Plan views

Profile and plan views of *Suffren* as first completed, based on the official plans produced by Brest Naval Dockyard and dated 29 December 1930. It shows the position reserved for future installation of the HA directors abeam the fore-funnel. The aircraft atop the single catapult is the CAMS 37A reconnaissance seaplane. It would never be embarked; *Suffren* operated the GL 810 float monoplane from the outset.

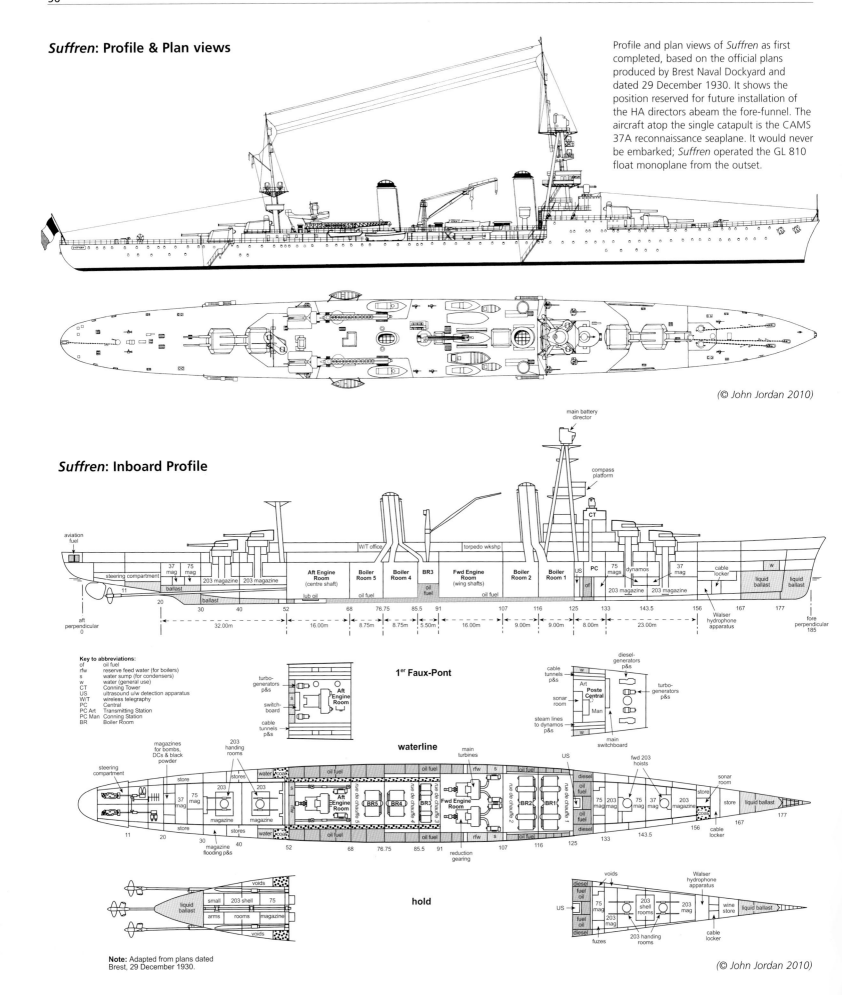

(© *John Jordan 2010*)

Suffren: Inboard Profile

Note: Adapted from plans dated Brest, 29 December 1930.

(© *John Jordan 2010*)

Suffren: Hull Sections

Frame 4.5 (from aft):
Twin Rudders

junior officers' wardroom
stores | steering gear | stores

Frame 44.8 (from aft):
Turret III

203mm turret
junior officer's cabin | p/w | p/w | Medical Officer
mechanicians' workshop | cooling plant | lub oil | p/w
water | 203 mag. | 203 mag. | water
void | shell room | shell room | void
shaft tunnel | void | shaft tunnels

Frame 78 (from aft):
Boiler Room 4

radio antennae
converters
10m steam pinnace | 10m steam pinnace
seamen's mess | drying rooms | seamen's mess
expansion tanks | cable tunnel
oil fuel | void | oil fuel
coal | Boiler Room 4 | coal

Frame 96.35 (from aft):
Fwd Engine Room

9m motor boat | 11m pulling pinnace | 10m pulling cutter | 11m motor launch | 9m motor boat
Secretary to Master at Arms | starboard 550mm TT
seamen's mess | shop | seamen's mess
expansion tanks | Postman
Fwd Engine Room
oil fuel | main gearing | oil fuel
o.f. | void | o.f. | void | voids p&s

Note: Adapted from plans dated Brest, 29 December 1930.

Frame 114 (from aft):
Boiler Room 2

HA director | HA director
upper deck
senior officers' galley | POs' galley
seamen's washplace | p/w | p/w | seamen's washplace
expansion tanks | cable tunnel
Boiler Room 2
o.f. | oil fuel | o.f. | voids p&s

Frame 129.5 (from aft):
Conning Tower

5m RF
transmissions centre
Conning Tower
Passerelle intermédiaire
laundry | encryption
Passerelle inférieure
p/w | p/w | WC.
Pont passerelle
infirmary | sickbay | sickbay | p/w | POs' showers
Premier pont
seamen's mess | seamen's mess
Pont principal
PC Art. | **Poste Central** | PC Man. | cable tunnel
Faux-pont
void | voids p&s
diesel fuel | void | diesel fuel
oil fuel

Frame 148 (from aft):
Turret I

203mm turret
POs' mess | CPO's cabin
seamen's mess | seamen's mess
compressed air bottles | cooling machinery (munitions)
voids p&s | 37 mag. | 37 mag. | 203 handing room
switch-board | voids

Frame 177 (from aft):
Bow Section

POs' mess
PO mechs' mess
drinking water
ballast

(© John Jordan 2010)

The most radical features of the design, however, were not visible to the naked eye, as they concerned the internal layout of the machinery and the protection applied over the machinery spaces and the ship's vitals.

MACHINERY

Although the machinery spaces on *Suffren* occupied less internal volume than those of *Duquesne*, they were longer, which meant that there could be no reduction in hull length (length between perpendiculars was identical: 185m). The after boiler rooms, which now contained only a single boiler, could be made slightly shorter, but this was more than compensated for by an increase in the length of the engine rooms from 15m to 16m. Moreover, an additional 5.5-metre section had to be inserted between the two main machinery units in order to accommodate the two small 'cruising' boilers (see inboard profile). The exhaust uptakes for these were led into the after funnel, which therefore remained of similar cross-section to the fore-funnel.[6] With the exception of the two small boilers with mixed firing, the components of the main and auxiliary machinery were virtually identical to those of the *Duquesne*,

---
[6] This would become a distinguishing feature between the first two ships of the class and the second pair; in *Foch* and *Dupleix* the small boilers were suppressed, so these ships had a slimmer second funnel.

The forward machinery 'unit' was arranged as in *Duquesne*, with the four boilers in pairs serving a full-width engine room housing the turbines for the wing shafts. However, the after pair of main boilers and the after turbines were all on the centre-line, with the latter serving the third (central) shaft. As in the *Duquesne* the after turbo-generators were located on a raised platform above the after turbines at the level of the First Platform Deck, while the forward pair were grouped with the diesel generators in a large, well-

Below: An early photo of *Suffren* in the anchorage at Les Vignettes on 26 January 1931. Note the twin catapults, each with a GL 810 reconnaissance floatplane. The three white bands mark her out as the third ship of the 1st Light Division. *(Marius Bar)*

Suffren & *Colbert*: Protection

Profile & 1st Platform Deck

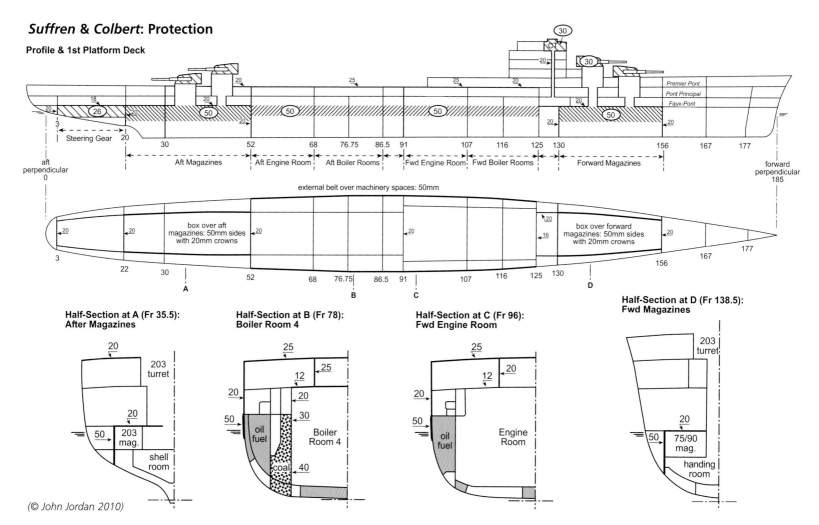

(© John Jordan 2010)

Half-Section at A (Fr 35.5):
After Magazines

Half-Section at B (Fr 78):
Boiler Room 4

Half-Section at C (Fr 96):
Fwd Engine Room

Half-Section at D (Fr 138.5):
Fwd Magazines

MACHINERY TRIALS

Full Power Trial (6 hours)

	Suffren	Colbert
	15 Jan 1929	5 Sep 1929
Displacement:	11,621t	11,426t
Draught:	5.38m	5.87m
Maximum speed:	31.33kts	31.73kts
Maximum power:	98,126CV	100,319CV
Average speed:	31.08ts	31.72kts
Average power:	95,970CV	99,575CV
Endurance (600t oil fuel)	–	475nm

Forcing Trial (1 hour)

	Suffren	Colbert
	1 Mar 1929	20 Sep 1929
Displacement:	10,531t	9830t
Draught:	5.44m	5.22m
Maximum speed:	31.82kts	33.01kts
Maximum power:	106,280CV	105,722CV
Endurance (600t oil fuel)	414.5nm	451.26nm

Fuel Consumption Trial at Cruising Speed (8 hours at 15 knots)

	Suffren
	31 Jan 1929
Displacement:	11,500t
Draught:	5.89m
Average speed:	14.98kts
Average power (2 boilers):	8890CV
Consumption/nm:	284.04kg
Endurance (600t oil fuel)	1320nm

Source: Garier, *op. cit.*

ventilated compartment forward at the same level just below turret II (see drawings).

GROUND TACKLE AND NAVIGATION

Anchors and cables were as for the *Duquesne*, except that there were two kedge anchors of 1400kg and 1140kg respectively.

The change from four shafts to three was reflected in the provision of twin rudders located side by side abaft and between the shafts.[7] *Suffren* was considered to be a good sea-boat, able to maintain high speed even in heavy seas. Response to the helm was good at speeds above 10 knots.

PROTECTION

A narrow belt of non-cemented (NC) armour 50mm thick was applied to the outer hull abeam the machinery spaces. It was 2.6m high,[8] and extended 1m below the waterline.[9] The belt, like the armour over

---

[7] The *Duquesne*s had two axial rudders of unequal size (see Chapter 2).

[8] The side belts of other French cruisers and battleships normally extended to the Main Deck, with a height of around 3.5m.

[9] As weight increased with age and additions, the ship sat deeper in the water. In 1941 the upper edge of the belt of *Suffren*'s half-sister *Colbert* is reported to have declined in height to only 80cm above the waterline, although it is not clear whether this was at normal displacement.

BUILDING DATA AND GENERAL CHARACTERISTICS: *SUFFREN* AND *COLBERT*

Name	Builder	Laid down	Launched	In service
1925 Programme				
Suffren	Arsenal de Brest	17 Apr 1926	3 May 1927	8 Mar 1930
1926 Programme				
Colbert	Arsenal de Brest	12 Jun 1927	20 Apr 1928	1 Apr 1931

Displacement:	10,000 tons standard
	11,769 tonnes (*Colbert* 11,757t) normal
	13,135 tonnes (*Colbert* 13,313t) full load
Length:	185m pp, 194m oa
Beam:	19.26m
Draught:	6.51m max. (normal displacement)
Machinery:	Six Guyot du Temple boilers, 20kg/cm^2 (215°) plus two small coal/oil-fired boilers;
	three-shaft Rateau-Bretagne geared steam turbines for 90,000CV; speed 32kts (designed)
Oil fuel:	1876t oil + 500t coal; radius 4600nm at 15kts (2000nm at 11kts on 'cruise' boilers), 3700nm at 20kts
Armament:	Eight 203mm/50 Mle 1924 in twin mountings Mle 1924 (150rpg);
	Suffren eight 76mm/50 Mle 1924 HA in single mountings Mle 1922 (500rpg);
	eight 37mm/50 Mle 1925 AA in single mountings (1000rpg);
	Colbert eight 90mm/50 Mle 1926 HA in single mountings Mle 1926 (500rpg);
	six 37mm/50 Mle 1925 AA in single mountings (1000rpg);
	both six tubes for 550mm torpedoes Mle 1923D in triple mountings Mle 1925T (3 reloads)
Aircraft:	Three GL 810 HY seaplanes
Protection:	*Belt*: 50mm
	Magazines: 50mm sides, 20mm crowns
	CT: 30mm
	Turrets: 30mm
Complement:	647 (731 as flagship)

Weights

	Duquesne	Suffren	Colbert		Duquesne	Suffren	Colbert
Hull:	4783t	4647t	4967t	Oil Fuel:	900t	n/a	1089t*
Protection (hull):	368t	554t	671t	Reserve feed water:	240t	n/a	175t
Protection (armament):	91t	91t	91t	Miscellaneous:	104t	n/a	333t
Armament:	1224t	n/a	1235t	Normal Displ.	11,404t	11,769t	11,757t
Propulsion:	2271t	n/a	1810t	Oil fuel:	941t	n/a	1258t
Torpedoes/Aircraft:	111t	111t	111t	Combustibles:	–	n/a	28t
Fittings/Provisions:	1242t	n/a	1205t	Ammunition:	78t	n/a	58t
Miscellaneous:	70t	70t	70t	Miscellaneous:	12t	n/a	12t
Washington Displ.	10,160t	10,160t	10,160t	Full Load Displ.	12,435t	13,135t	13,313t

* Includes 640t coal

Source: Official *devis d'armement* (via Robert Dumas).

Notes:
Incomplete figures are available for *Suffren*. It can be reasonably assumed that the weight of armament was as *Duquesne*, machinery as *Colbert*.

Although these figures come from the official legends for the respective ships, there are some odd anomalies, notably the lower figures for hull and hull protection of *Suffren*, which had essentially the same hull and protection system as her half-sister *Colbert*, and the weight allocated to torpedoes and aircraft, which was 111 tonnes in all the French treaty designs, regardless of the fact that some of the later ships had twin catapults .

the magazines, was of 60kg steel, and together with its fixings weighed approximately 150 tonnes.

The upper deck was 25mm thick amidships, and a longitudinal bulkhead of similar thickness ran outboard of the funnel uptakes and ventilation trunking 3.18m from the sides of the ship between the Main Deck and the First Deck. As in the *Duquesne*s, the magazines in the forward and after parts of the ship were inside armoured boxes; these had 50mm (20mm + 30mm) sides and 20mm crowns. There was 30mm plating (15mm + 15mm) on the turrets and the conning tower, and the turret and rangefinder hoods were generally of 35mm cast nickel steel.

Abeam the after machinery spaces there was a continuous longitudinal torpedo bulkhead outboard of the machinery bulkhead with a stand-off of about 2m,

the space being filled with coal from the inner bottom up to the main deck. The bulkhead itself was 30-40mm thick (20mm + 10/20mm) and was lined on its outboard side by a double thickness of 80mm teak planking. Outboard of this bulkhead, protected by the armoured belt, there were bunkers for oil fuel with void compartments beneath them (see drawings). The wider forward machinery spaces were protected only by oil fuel bunkers with a single holding bulkhead (doubled abeam the boilers as in the *Duquesne*). The steering compartment was protected by a box with 26mm sides and an 18mm ceiling. The key transverse bulkheads, principally those enclosing the machinery spaces and the magazines (Frames 20, 52, 91, 107, 125, 143 bis, and 167) were of 60kg steel 20mm thick.

The total weight of the hull protection was 670

Suffren & Colbert: Master Frames

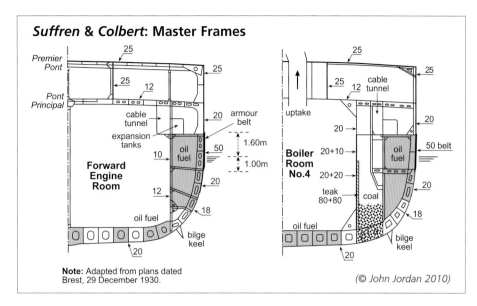

Note: Adapted from plans dated Brest, 29 December 1930.

(© John Jordan 2010)

Suffren: Torpedo Maintenance & Reloading

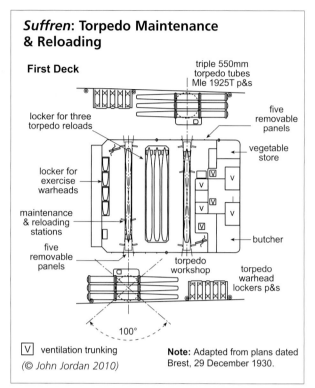

V ventilation trunking

(© John Jordan 2010)

Note: Adapted from plans dated Brest, 29 December 1930.

tonnes,[10] as compared with only 370 tonnes in the *Duquesne*s; the protection accorded to the 203mm turrets remained at 90 tonnes. This was an undoubted improvement, and gave the ships a degree of immunity to destroyer shell, but was still a long way short of the 1025 tons of armour achieved by the Royal Navy constructors with the *Kent*s. Nevertheless, whereas the official plans of *Duquesne* and *Tourville* drawn up at

---

[10] French sources are inconsistent on this point. The official *devis d'armement* gives 554 tonnes for *Suffren* but 671 tonnes for her half-sister *Colbert*, which had the essentially the same hull and protection system. The latter figure seems closer to the mark, particularly if the reinforced bulkheads are taken into account.

the Arsenal de Brest are inscribed simply 'Croiseur de 10 000t W', those of *Suffren* and her successors have the heading: 'Croiseur protégé de 10 000t W', thereby reviving the 'Protected Cruiser' classification of the pre-dreadnought era.

ARMAMENT

The main, secondary and anti-aircraft armament was as in the *Duquesne* class, but there were two small differences resulting from the changed layout of the ship. The floor of the after magazines had to be raised and the magazines extended aft in order to accommodate the centre-line shaft, and the four 37mm Mle 1925 AA guns which in the *Duquesne* had been fitted on the shelter deck abeam the fore funnel were relocated aft to a position abeam the boat/aircraft crane in order to make space for the projected HA directors (see the original plans).

Suffren: Bridge Decks & Platforms

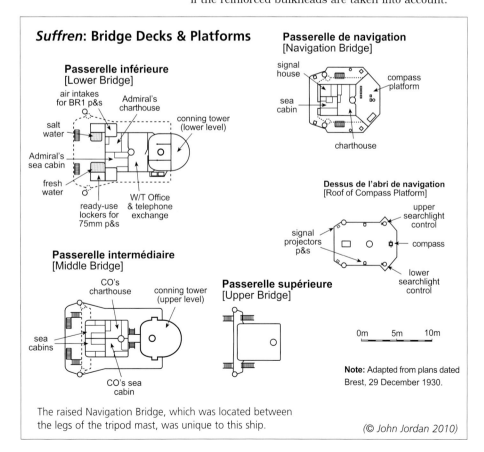

The raised Navigation Bridge, which was located between the legs of the tripod mast, was unique to this ship.

(© John Jordan 2010)

Suffren: Conning Tower

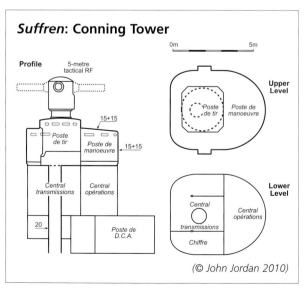

(© John Jordan 2010)

Suffren: Aircraft/Boat Crane

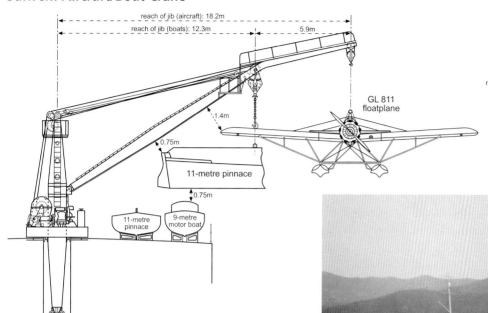

Note: Adapted from plans dated Brest, 29 December 1930.

GL 811 floatplane

Plan of Control Platform

(© John Jordan 2010)

Below: *Suffren* moored off the Côte d'Azur in early 1938, with the tricolore identification markings on turrets II and III which she carried during the Spanish Civil War. The funnel bands mark her out as the third ship of the 2nd Cruiser Division. *(Philippe Caresse collection)*

Fire control

Due to production delays *Suffren* ran her sea trials without any of the fire control directors aboard. The director control tower atop the tripod foremast for the main guns was fitted during 1929, together with the 75mm HA guns and the twin catapults. The HA directors would not be ready for some time, so in the interim small (6ft/2-metre?) Barr & Stroud rangefinders were fitted in tubs atop an extension of the forecastle deck on either side of the fore-funnel.

Torpedoes

The torpedo armament, maintenance and onboard reload arrangements were identical to those of the *Duquesne*.

Aviation Installations

The twin catapults were the same model installed in the *Duquesne* class. In theory the ship was to have a maximum capacity of four aircraft, two of which were to have been carried (off-set) atop the catapults with a further two stowed between the funnels. In practice *Suffren* would never carry more than two, of which one would normally be carried atop a catapult while the second was stowed in a 'rest position' atop the ventilation housing just abaft the fore-funnel. Although the original plans show a CAMS 37A biplane, *Suffren* operated the brand-new Gourdou-Leseurre GL 810 float monoplane from the outset. She ran catapult trials with a single aircraft (No.8) during the Spring of 1930 before having a second aircraft (No.10) permanently assigned from September. From then until her major refit in 1937 at Lorient she operated two GL 810/811 aircraft.

The single centre-line crane was located just forward of the second funnel, as in the *Duquesne*, but the bases of the twin catapults were moved farther forward so that the catapult beams overlapped the second funnel. This made it easier for the crane to move aircraft from the rest position to either of the cata-

pults. Once it was extended in 1929, the crane had a maximum reach of 18.2m and a capacity of 2500kg, enabling it to handle comfortably a GL 810 with sufficient clearance of the ship's sides (see drawing).

BOATS

The outfit when the ship was first completed was as follows:

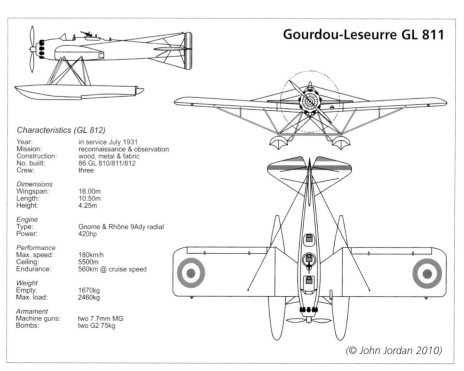

Gourdou-Leseurre GL 811

Characteristics (GL 812)

Year: in service July 1931
Mission: reconnaissance & observation
Construction: wood, metal & fabric
No. buiilt: 86 GL 810/811/812
Crew: three

Dimensions
Wingspan: 16.00m
Length: 10.50m
Height: 4.25m

Engine
Type: Gnome & Rhône 9Ady radial
Power: 420hp

Performance
Max. speed: 180km/h
Ceiling: 5500m
Endurance: 560km @ cruise speed

Weight
Empty: 1670kg
Max. load: 2460kg

Armament
Machine guns: two 7.7mm MG
Bombs: two G2 75kg

(© John Jordan 2010)

Suffren September 1939

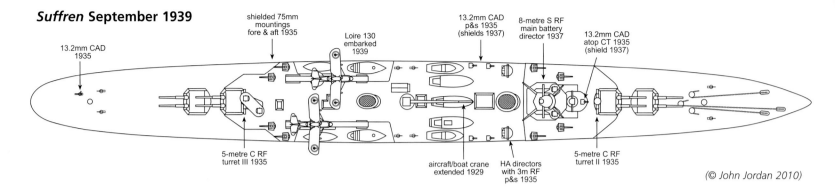

shielded 75mm mountings fore & aft 1935

Loire 130 embarked 1939

13.2mm CAD p&s 1935 (shields 1937)

8-metre S RF main battery director 1937

13.2mm CAD atop CT 1935 (shield 1937)

13.2mm CAD 1935

5-metre C RF turret III 1935

aircraft/boat crane extended 1929

HA directors with 3m RF p&s 1935

5-metre C RF turret II 1935

(© John Jordan 2010)

Below: *Suffren* in June 1939, shortly before her departure for Saigon on the 26th. Modifications include a shortened foretopmast, and the installation of HA directors abeam the fore-funnel. The GL 810/811/812 series of floatplanes has been superseded by the heavier and more capable Loire 130. Note the unusual elevated bridge, which was unique to *Suffren*. (Marius Bar)

– one 11-metre pulling pinnace
– one 11-metre motor launch
– two 10-metre steam pinnaces
– one 10-metre cutter
– two 9-metre motor boats
– two 8.5-metre whalers
– two 5-metre dinghies

The boats were stowed on the shelter deck between the two funnels, and abeam and abaft the second funnel, the steam pinnaces and whalers being located in cutaways on the upper deck so as not to obstruct the training arcs of the catapults. With the exception of the two whalers, which were on davits, the boats were handled by a single crane located on the centre-line just forward of the second funnel. Built by Schneider to an STCN design, the latter was a modified version of the crane fitted in the *Duquesne* class. It was intended from the outset to handle both boats and aircraft, making the mainmast derrick of the earlier class redundant. As modified in 1930 it had a reach of 12.3m for boats up to 12 tonnes, and 18.2m for aircraft.

MODIFICATIONS 1930 TO 1942

Suffren underwent a major refit at Lorient which began on 9 January 1934 and completed on 16 November of the following year, during which her anti-aircraft capabilities were considerably modified and upgraded.

Spray/splinter shields were fitted to the eight 75mm HA guns, and the projected HA directors, each equipped with a 3-metre OPL stereo rangefinder, were finally fitted abeam the fore-funnel. Associated fire control positions with plotting tables were installed on either side of the ship, and RPC was installed (training only).

The eight 37mm Mle 1925 AA guns were left in place, and these were now complemented by six twin 13.2mm Hotchkiss MG mountings for point defence. One of these was located atop the forward end of the conning tower, another on the quarterdeck to port, just abaft the 37mm mountings, and the remaining four were grouped on the boat deck abaft the new HA directors.

At the same time the foretopmast was reduced in height, and new 5-metre rangefinders with 15-degree independent traverse were fitted in place of the original fixed rangefinder on turrets II and III. The refit had to be extended when subsequent trials showed up problems with the turbines, and it appears that work on the latter had to be completed following the ship's return to Toulon in the summer of 1935.

In a subsequent refit at Toulon which took place in 1937, the original 5-metre coincidence model in the main DCT was replaced by a new 8-metre OPL stereo rangefinder. The catapults were modified to enable them to handle the heavier Loire 130 seaplane, and five of the six twin 13.2mm Hotchkiss MG – all except the quarterdeck mounting – were fitted with shields.

COLBERT (C 1)[11]

THE NEXT CRUISER OF THE SERIES, *COLBERT*, WAS virtually identical to *Suffren* in terms of her hull, propulsion, internal general arrangement and protection, but had a radically different topsides layout amidships which reflected some dissatisfaction with the first three French Treaty cruisers. With the increasing importance accorded to aircraft for reconnaissance, it was proving difficult to find a satisfactory arrangement of the aircraft catapults and cranes. In particular, it was difficult to find an arrangement of the boats and catapults which enabled both to be served by a single centre-line crane. Moreover, the adoption of twin catapults for *Suffren* had resulted in a cramped and unsatisfactory arrangement of the boats and the after HA guns between the second funnel and the

---

[11] Beginning with the 1926 Estimates, each new cruiser design was given a 'C' designation with numbers in sequence.

mainmast, together with a wide separation between the catapults and the rest position for the spare aircraft, which was stowed just abaft the fore-funnel.

The logical solution was to provide twin cranes capable of handling both boats and aircraft abeam the second funnel, with the catapults moved to a position between the funnels and the boats grouped fore and aft of the funnel. This change affected not only the position of the catapults, cranes and boats, but also the positioning of the torpedo tubes, the fore-funnel and mainmast, resulting in a very different silhouette which would establish a template for the remaining two cruisers of the series, *Foch* and *Dupleix*.

The only other change requested by the General Staff was the substitution of the newly-developed 90mm/50 Mle 1926 for the 75mm/50 fitted in *Suffren* and the *Duquesne*s. This modification cost an additional 40 tonnes, and as the new ship would essentially be a repeat of *Suffren*, there was no possibility of

Below: Midships view of *Colbert* during fitting out, showing the twin catapults between the funnels and the base of the port-side crane abeam the second funnel. *(CAA)*

Colbert: Profile & Plan views

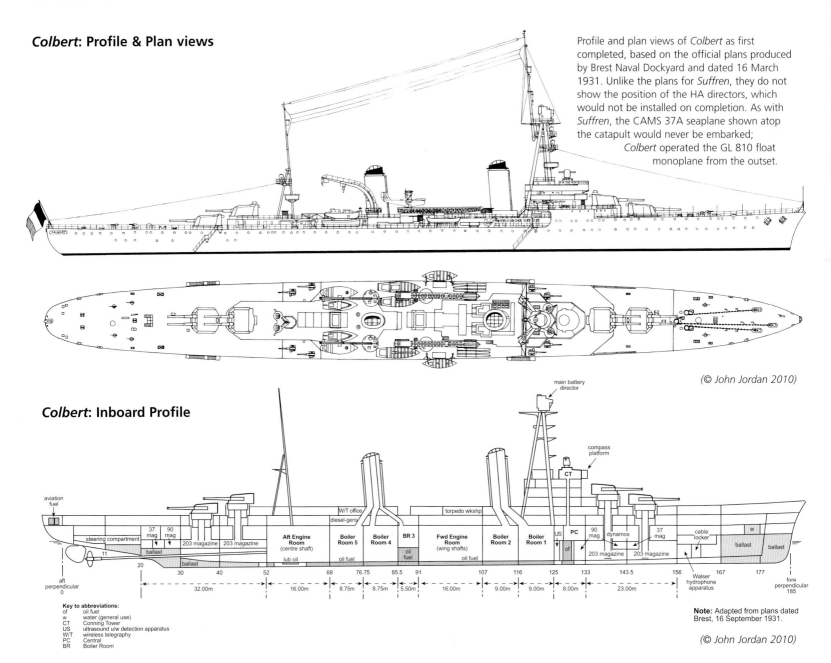

Profile and plan views of *Colbert* as first completed, based on the official plans produced by Brest Naval Dockyard and dated 16 March 1931. Unlike the plans for *Suffren*, they do not show the position of the HA directors, which would not be installed on completion. As with *Suffren*, the CAMS 37A seaplane shown atop the catapult would never be embarked; *Colbert* operated the GL 810 float monoplane from the outset.

(© *John Jordan 2010*)

Colbert: Inboard Profile

Note: Adapted from plans dated Brest, 16 September 1931.

(© *John Jordan 2010*)

Key to abbreviations:
of   oil fuel
w   water (general use)
CT   Conning Tower
US   ultrasound u/w detection apparatus
W/T   wireless telegraphy
PC   Central
BR   Boiler Room

making equivalent savings on the hull or the fittings, so again recourse was made to 'interpreting' Treaty rules. Only nine-tenths of the 90mm munitions were counted in the standard displacement, and only two thirds of provisions, drinking water and boiler feed-water. This saved the required 40 tonnes.

Colbert was approved as part of the 1926 *tranche*, the order again being placed with Brest Naval Dockyard. *Colbert* was laid down in June 1927 following the launch of her near-sister *Suffren*, and took four years to build.

NAME

Jean-Baptiste **Colbert** (1619–83) was Louis XIV's most famous minister. As Controller-General of Finances 1665–83 he brought about major improvements in French manufacturing and pulled the economy back from the brink of bankruptcy, despite Louis' excessive spending on wars. He worked to ensure that the French East India Company had access to foreign markets, and founded the merchant marine. Colbert laid the foundations for the organisation of the Navy, putting in

place an administration of which elements remain to the present day, and training for both officers and crews; the ports and the fleet were also developed.

GENERAL CONFIGURATION AND LAYOUT

Colbert reverted to a conventional bridge structure, with the compass platform extending from the forward face of the conning tower. The fore-funnel was moved 3m farther aft, and angled funnel cowlings were fitted.[12]

The twin catapults were moved forward, between the funnels, and the area of the shelter deck between the second funnel and the mainmast became the boat deck. Aircraft and boats were served by twin gooseneck cranes abeam the second funnel; these had the customary dual-lift arrangements, the outer length of 5.25m giving the necessary clearance beyond the hull

---

12 Trials with the Marine Nationale's first post-war cruisers, *Primauguet* and *Duguay-Trouin*, would have taken place around this time, and almost certainly revealed problems with smoke being drawn into the foretop and bridge.

sides for a 3000kg aircraft with fully-deployed wings. A further advantage of moving the catapults forward was that the mainmast, now a light tripod, could be stepped well clear of turret III. The effect on the eye of these modifications was particularly pleasing; *Colbert* and her two later near-sisters were elegant ships, with a more harmonious appearance than their predecessors.

The only problem with the new arrangement was that there was no obvious position for the midships 37mm, four of which were sited abeam the centre-line boat crane on *Suffren*. Consequently *Colbert* and the two later ships had only six of the single Mle 1925 mountings: four on the quarterdeck with two on the forecastle.

MACHINERY AND PROTECTION
As *Suffren* – see above.

ARMAMENT
The only major change was the substitution of the newly-developed 90mm/50 Mle 1926 for the 75mm/50 fitted in *Suffren* and the *Duquesnes*. During the 1920s all the major foreign navies had moved from the 3in/75mm HA calibre standard during the First World War to heavier weapons, which were variously of 4in/102mm (Britain, Italy), 4.7in/12cm (Britain, Japan) or 5in calibre (USA). The larger-calibre guns, which it was envisaged would be used to put up a fleet barrage through which formations of level bombers and torpedo planes would have to fly, had the advantage of longer range, and as their HE shells were time-fused rather than contact-fused they would have a larger lethal envelope. The French 90mm/50 gun fired a shell weighing 9.5kg compared with the 6kg of the 75mm Mle 1922/1924, and had a theoretical ceiling of

10,500m versus 8000m. Despite its greater power, its firing cycle more than matched that of the earlier gun, and it came to be highly regarded in the fleet. A twin mounting would subsequently be developed and fitted in the last ship of the series, *Dupleix*, in the minelaying cruiser *Emile Bertin* and in the 7600-ton cruisers of the *La Galissonnière* class.

The eight single mountings replaced the 75mm mountings on a one-for-one basis. The location of the forward group of four mountings was identical, but the after group were located on a low platform on the upper deck abeam the mainmast rather than at the after end of the shelter deck, with a consequent reduction in topweight.

It was apparently planned to compensate for the reduction from eight to six 37mm AA guns by fitting two of the projected quadruple 13.2mm Hotchkiss MG forward of the 90mm guns on the lower bridge deck,

Above: *Colbert* moored in the Toulon anchorage; she has the four white bands on the fore-funnel which she wore until 1 April 1931. Note the early-pattern 5-metre rangefinders on turrets II and III.

90/50 MLE 1926

Gun Data

Construction:	Monobloc autofretted barrel with liner
Breech mechanism:	Schneider semi-automatic concentric ring
Weight of gun:	1.57t
Ammunition type:	Fixed
Projectiles:	OEA Mle 1925 (9.51kg)
	OI Mle 1927
	OEcl Mle 1926
Propellant:	OEA/OI: BM5 (3.1kg)
Complete round:	
Weight:	18.1kg (OEA)
Dimensions:	1000.3mm x 130.25mm
Muzzle velocity:	850m/s
Max. range:	15,440m (40°)
Ceiling:	10,600m (80°)

Mounting Data

Designation:	CAS Mle 1926/CAD Mle 1930
Weight of mounting:	7t/13.7t
Loading angle:	-10° / +60°
Elevation of guns:	-10° / +80°
Firing cycle (per gun):	12–15rpm theoretical
	10rpm practical

Notes:

CAS	*Contre-Avions Simple*	AA single mounting
CAD	*Contre-Avions Double*	AA twin mounting
OEA	*Obus Explosif en Acier*	High Explosive (HE)
OI	*Obus Incendiaire*	Incendiary round
OEcl	*Obus Eclairant*	Starshell

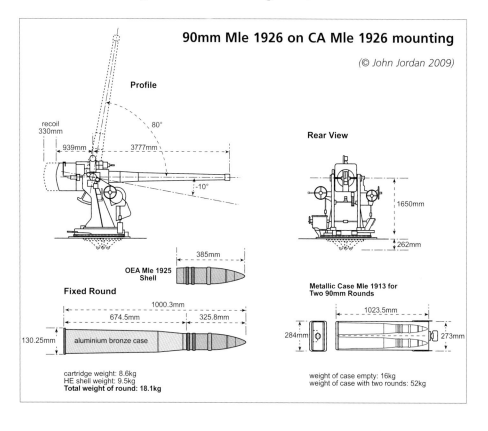

90mm Mle 1926 on CA Mle 1926 mounting

(© John Jordan 2009)

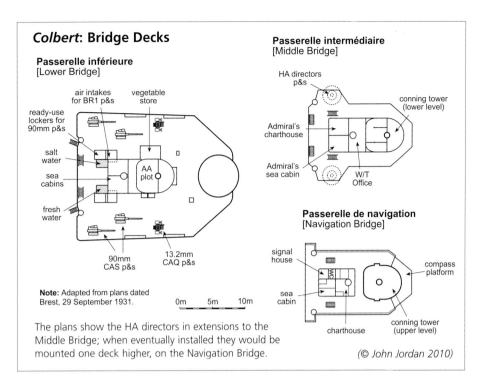

Colbert: Bridge Decks

Passerelle inférieure [Lower Bridge]

ready-use lockers for 90mm p&s

air intakes for BR1 p&s

vegetable store

salt water

sea cabins

AA plot

fresh water

90mm CAS p&s

13.2mm CAQ p&s

Note: Adapted from plans dated Brest, 29 September 1931.

0m 5m 10m

Passerelle intermédiaire [Middle Bridge]

HA directors p&s

conning tower (lower level)

Admiral's charthouse

Admiral's sea cabin

W/T Office

Passerelle de navigation [Navigation Bridge]

signal house

sea cabin

charthouse

conning tower (upper level)

compass platform

The plans show the HA directors in extensions to the Middle Bridge; when eventually installed they would be mounted one deck higher, on the Navigation Bridge.

(© John Jordan 2010)

Colbert: Conning Tower

0m 5m

Profile

5-metre tactical RF

15+15

15+15

Poste de tir

Poste de manoeuvre

Central trans-missions

Central opérations

Central torpilles

20

Upper Level

Poste de tir

Poste de manoeuvre

Lower Level

Central trans-missions

Central opérations

Chiffre

(© John Jordan 2010)

Colbert in the Bizerte Canal on 10 April 1931. On board was the President of the Republic, Gaston Doumergue, who was on an official visit to Tunisia from 10 to 16 April. *(Philippe Caresse collection)*

and a further two mountings outboard of the cranes. Deck plans dated Brest 29 September 1931 show the positions of these (see bridge deck drawings). In the event production of the quad mounting was delayed – the first installations did not take place until the mid-1930s, and the mounting did not become available in numbers until 1939–40. It would be fitted in *Colbert* only in 1941 (see Modifications).

Fire control

Completed some fourteen months after her half-sister *Suffren*, *Colbert* entered service with the director control tower for the main guns in place. However, the projected HA directors, originally to have been mounted in side extensions to the middle bridge deck, were not yet ready and would not be mounted until the mid-1930s (see Modifications). As a temporary measure *Colbert* received two 3-metre rangefinders, which were located not on the middle bridge but one deck higher, on the navigation bridge. This seems to have proved a superior arrangement, as when the HA directors were eventually fitted they were installed in the same location.

Torpedoes

A further consequence of moving the catapult bases forward of the second funnel was that the torpedo tubes could not be offset to the extent they were in *Suffren* and the *Duquesne*s. This resulted in a slight compression of the torpedo maintenance shop. Three reloads were housed in a locker at the after end, and there was now only a single maintenance bed which was, however, given sufficient traverse to enable any of the six tubes in the trainable mountings to be reloaded (see drawing).

AVIATION INSTALLATIONS

The twin catapults were mounted at the deck edge between the funnels, and were served by twin gooseneck cranes with a reach of 13m and a lift capacity of 3000kg. For her trials in 1930 *Colbert* embarked a single GL 810 floatplane, but in September she

Colbert:
Aircraft/
Boat Crane

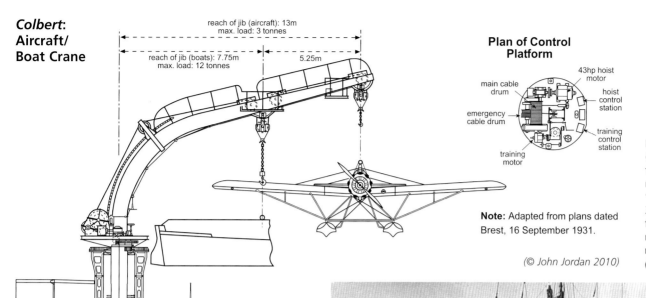

reach of jib (aircraft): 13m
max. load: 3 tonnes

reach of jib (boats): 7.75m
max. load: 12 tonnes

5.25m

0m   5m

Plan of Control Platform

43hp hoist motor

main cable drum

hoist control station

emergency cable drum

training control station

training motor

Note: Adapted from plans dated Brest, 16 September 1931.

(© John Jordan 2010)

Below: The quarterdeck of *Colbert* in April 1931, with the 90mm single HA mountings Mle 1926 on their 'bandstand' to port, and the 37mm CAS Mle 1925 in the foreground. Note the older-model 5-metre coincidence rangefinder atop turret III.
(Philippe Caresse collection)

received her full service complement of two, and would operate either the GL 810 or its folding-wing successor, the GL 811, until 1938. In 1939 the Gourdou-Leseurre monoplane was superseded by the larger and more capable Loire 130 (see Modifications below).

BOATS

The outfit when the ship was first completed was as follows:

– one 11-metre motor pinnace
– one 11-metre pulling pinnace
– two 10-metre steam pinnaces

Colbert: Torpedo Maintenance & Reloading

First Deck

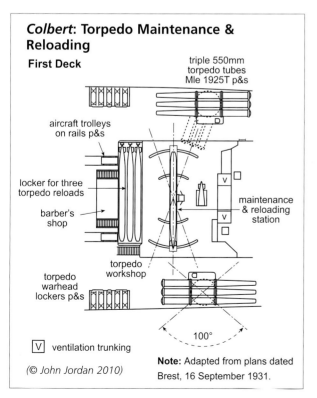

triple 550mm torpedo tubes Mle 1925T p&s

aircraft trolleys on rails p&s

locker for three torpedo reloads

barber's shop

maintenance & reloading station

torpedo workshop

torpedo warhead lockers p&s

100°

V ventilation trunking

(© John Jordan 2010)

Note: Adapted from plans dated Brest, 16 September 1931.

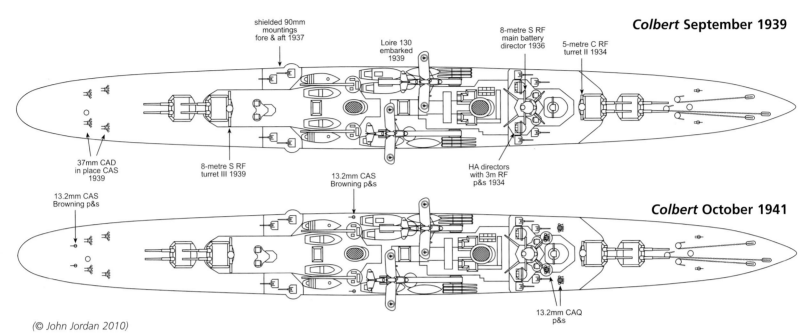

shielded 90mm
mountings
fore & aft 1937

Loire 130
embarked
1939

8-metre S RF
main battery
director 1936

5-metre C RF
turret II 1934

Colbert September 1939

37mm CAD
in place CAS
1939

8-metre S RF
turret III 1939

13.2mm CAS
Browning p&s

HA directors
with 3m RF
p&s 1934

Colbert October 1941

13.2mm CAS
Browning p&s

13.2mm CAQ
p&s

(© John Jordan 2010)

– one 10-metre cutter
– two 9-metre motor boats
– two 8.5-metre whalers
– two 5-metre dinghies

The two steam pinnaces were stowed on crutches outboard of the two 9-metre motor boats immediately abaft the second funnel. The two 11-metre pinnaces and the 10-metre cutter were stowed beneath the after end of the catapults just forward of the second funnel. All could be comfortably handled by the twin cranes. The two whalers, which were on davits, were outboard of the catapults.

The gooseneck cranes, which were to an STCN design, had a reach of 7.75m for boats (capacity: 12 tonnes) and 13m for aircraft (see drawing).

MODIFICATIONS 1931 TO 1942
In a short refit which took place between 1 November 1933 and 1 March 1934 at Toulon, *Colbert* received the

now-standard trainable 5-metre rangefinders on turrets II and III. At the same time the two upper bridge decks were extended to the sides at their after end, and 3-metre rangefinders were fitted as a temporary measure to provide fire control data for the 90mm HA guns.

A major refit at Lorient followed on 1 March 1935 and was completed during early January 1936. RPC (training only) was provided for the main and secondary guns, and the HA directors were finally fitted in the upper bridge wings, together with their associated fire control computers. The machinery also received a major overhaul.

Further planned upgrades of *Colbert*'s equipment were progressively postponed. During 1936–7 the original 5-metre coincidence rangefinder in the main DCT was replaced by an OPL 8-metre stereo model, the fore-topmast was suppressed altogether, and spray/splinter shields were added to the 90mm guns. In 1939, shortly before the outbreak of war in Europe, the catapults were modified to launch the Loire 130 seaplane, and

Colbert November 1942

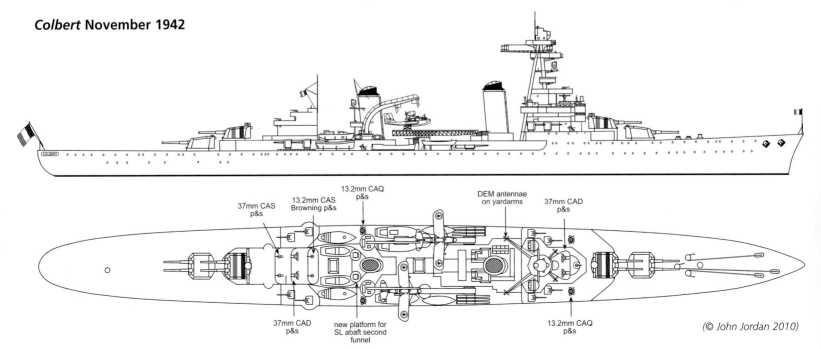

37mm CAS
p&s

13.2mm CAS
Browning p&s

13.2mm CAQ
p&s

DEM antennae
on yardarms

37mm CAD
p&s

37mm CAD
p&s

new platform for
SL abaft second
funnel

13.2mm CAQ
p&s

(© John Jordan 2010)

the four original quarterdeck 37mm single mountings were replaced by the new twin Mle 1933. *Colbert* also received a second 8-metre stereo rangefinder, fitted in place of the 5-metre model on turret III.

In a 1941 refit, while serving with the *Forces de Haute Mer* at Toulon, *Colbert* had her existing light AA boosted by four quad 13.2mm Hotchkiss MG, located on the lower bridge deck as in the original plans and in tubs in the wings of the navigation bridge abeam the conning tower (see drawing). She also received four single 13.2mm Browning MG: two outboard of the cranes and two on the quarterdeck.

It was subsequently decided that *Colbert* should undergo an even more radical refit similar to that extended to *Algérie* (q.v.), in which the mainmast was to be replaced by a three tiered 'pergola' and the existing light AA guns regrouped to achieve greater symmetry fore and aft, the after searchlights being relocated to a platform built around the after end of the second funnel. The remaining two single 37mm Mle 1925 guns were relocated on the lower tier of the *pergola* aft. Two of the four twin 37mm Mle 1933 mountings occupied the second tier, and the other two were relocated to a new platform extending from the foremast over the conning tower. The two lower 13.2mm quad mountings were left in place forward, and the other two moved to the position outboard of

the cranes formerly occupied by two single Browning MG. The latter were relocated to the upper tier of the *pergola*. Finally, two transmitting and two receiving antennae for the DEM radar were fitted to the outer yards of the foremast (see drawing p.191).

The refit probably began in the Spring/Summer of 1942 and appears to have been completed shortly before *Colbert* was scuttled at Toulon on 27 November.

Above: This superb view of *Colbert* dating from 2 March 1937 shows the ship with her original foretopmast suppressed and the new-model 8-metre rangefinder in the director control tower. The original 5-metre coincidence rangefinders atop turrets II and III have been replaced by the new trainable model, and HA directors have been fitted in the upper bridge wings. *(Marius Bar)*

FOCH (C2)

IN JUNE 1927 THE STCN SUBMITTED A NOTE TO the General Staff regarding methods of calculating standard displacement in the light of information concerning practices thought to be employed by foreign navies. The French constructors concluded that by adopting a less rigid interpretation of Washington Treaty definitions, overall savings of 250 tonnes could be made on a ship of 10,160 tonnes. These economies were essentially in the area of 'consumables': washing and drinking water, provisions and munitions.

They further concluded that if this figure were reinvested in the propulsion plant a further 10,000CV would be obtained, thereby restoring the maximum speed to the 34 knots achieved in *Duquesne* and *Tourville*. The General Staff quickly rejected this proposal, as it would have required a new propulsion plant, which in turn would have involved major internal redesign; the inevitable consequence would be a considerable delay in laying down the next ship in the series. Instead it requested that the weight savings be invested in additional protection.

The STCN came up with a radically new proposal. In place of the external armour belt of *Suffren* and *Colbert*, which protected the integrity of the waterline but which was so shallow that shells striking above its upper edge could easily penetrate to the machinery spaces, there was to be an internal armoured box which completely enclosed the latter. The height of the plating on the longitudinal bulkheads outboard of the machinery spaces varied between 5.5m and 6.1m, as compared with only 2.6m for the shallow waterline belt of the earlier ships, and the thickness of the plating was increased by 4mm to 54mm, as was the plating on the sides of the magazines.

The STCN considered that the level of protection

provided for the new ship was sufficient to provide immunity to 138mm shell beyond 14,000m. It was envisaged that HE shell of this calibre would be broken up on impact with the 20mm side plating, and that the 54mm internal protection on the machinery bulkheads would keep out any resulting splinters.

The disadvantage of the internal armoured *caisson* adopted for *Foch* was that protection for the waterline itself was significantly reduced, making it more likely that shell hits on or just above the waterline would result in extensive flooding between the outer hull and the internal armoured bulkheads. However calculations showed that, given a metacentric height of 50cm and the counterflooding system introduced in *Suffren*, the ship could survive the flooding of four compartments on the same side without capsizing.

Below: *Foch* at anchor shortly after completion. Note the experimental 3-metre open rangefinder atop the conning tower. The rangefinders atop turrets II and III have yet to be fitted.

Foch: Profile & Plan views

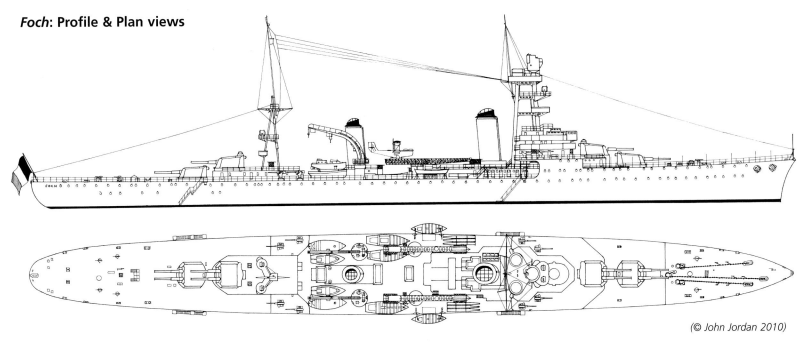

(© John Jordan 2010)

Profile and plan views of *Foch* as first completed, based on the official plans produced by Brest Naval Dockyard and dated 13 January 1933. Note the absence of a turreted rangefinder atop the conning tower; *Foch* would initially trial a new open 3-metre rangefinder which would be fitted in *Algérie* and the 7600-ton cruisers. As with *Suffren* and *Colbert*, *Foch* operated the GL 810 float monoplane rather than the CAMS 37A shown here..

Foch: Inboard Profile

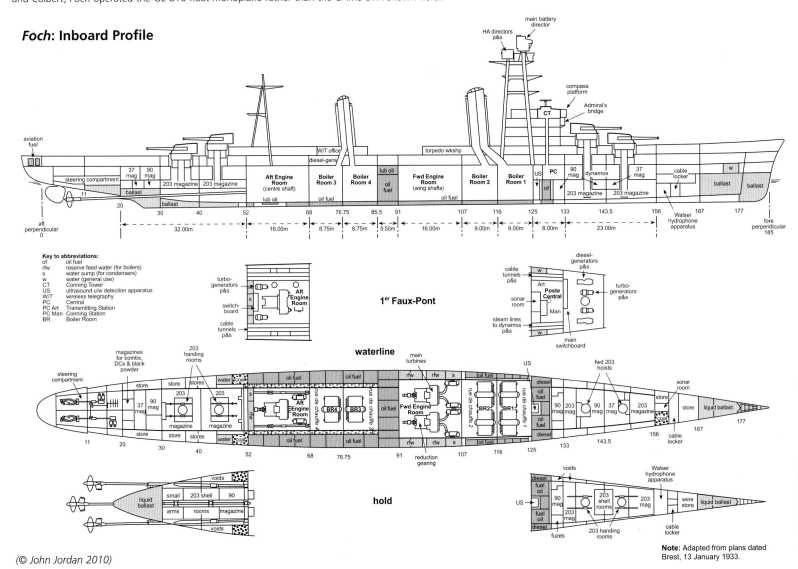

Key to abbreviations:
of	oil fuel
rfw	reserve feed water (for boilers)
s	water sump (for condensers)
w	water (general use)
CT	Conning Tower
US	ultrasound u/w detection apparatus
W/T	wireless telegraphy
PC	Central
PC Art	Transmitting Station
PC Man	Conning Station
BR	Boiler Room

(© John Jordan 2010)

Note: Adapted from plans dated Brest, 13 January 1933.

Foch: Protection

Profile & 1st Platform Deck

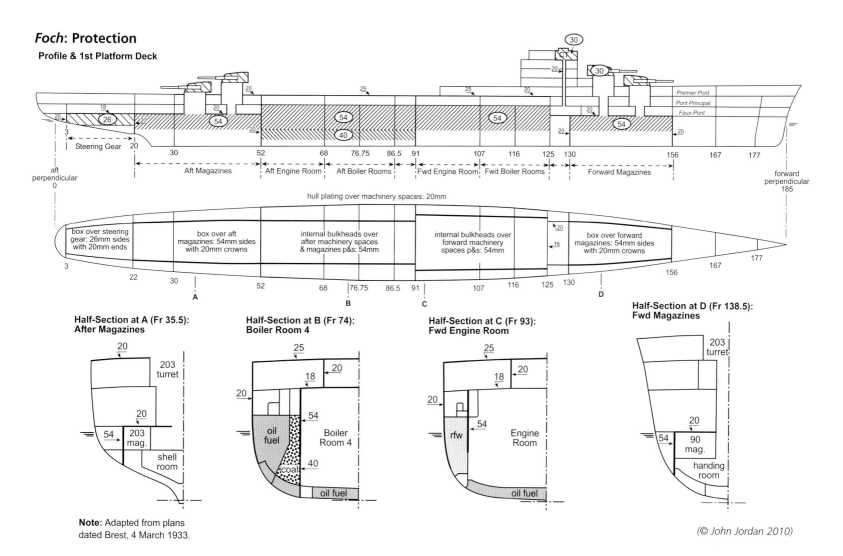

hull plating over machinery spaces: 20mm

Note: Adapted from plans dated Brest, 4 March 1933.

(© John Jordan 2010)

The General Staff was satisfied by these assurances, and approved the final design, which was submitted as part of the 1927 *tranche*. The contract was duly signed on 1 March 1927, and the ship laid down in June of the following year. The first keel plate for *Foch* was laid the day after the launch of *Colbert* at Brest Naval Dockyard. Construction then proceeded relatively smoothly, and *Foch* was completed in only three a half years, as compared with an average construction time of almost four years for the other three ships of the series.

NAME

As we have already seen, *Colbert* was named after the renowned Minister of Finance under Louis XIV, and the next cruiser in the series was originally to be named after the latter's outstanding Minister of War, the Marquis de Louvois. However, on 20 March 1929 Marshal Ferdinand **Foch**, France's most famous soldier of the First World War, died, and the new cruiser, which was due to be launched a month later, was renamed in his honour.

GENERAL CONFIGURATION AND LAYOUT

When finally completed in December 1931, *Foch* was easily distinguished from her half-sisters by her distinctive tripod foremast. The two support legs were moved aft and outwards to support an enlarged foretop platform which had HA directors for the 90mm guns to

port and to starboard, the director control tower for the main guns being slightly raised to clear them. She was also fitted with an experimental lightweight 3-metre open rangefinder atop the conning tower, although this would later be replaced by the standard 5-metre model in an enclosed housing.

Her external appearance was otherwise similar to *Colbert*, except that the second funnel, which no longer needed to accommodate the uptakes for the small boilers with mixed firing of the first two ships, was slimmer than the fore-funnel – a feature repeated in the *Dupleix*.

Above: *Foch* towards the end of 1931, trialling the seaplane landing mat which would be fitted in the 7600-ton cruisers. *(Henri Landais collection)*

Opposite: Bow view of *Foch*
in dry dock. Note the spread
of the supports of the tripod
foremast, which served to
distinguish her from her half-
sisters *Colbert* and *Dupleix*.
The photo dates from the late
1930s, evidenced by the
installation of the 5-metre
rangefinder 'turret' atop the
conning tower and the new
8-metre rangefinder in the
main battery director. *(Henri
Landais collection)*

BUILDING DATA AND GENERAL CHARACTERISTICS: *FOCH* AND *DUPLEIX*

Name	Builder	Laid down	Launched	In service
1927 Programme				
Foch	Arsenal de Brest	21 Jun 1928	24 Apr 1929	20 Dec 1931
1928–9 Programme				
Dupleix	Arsenal de Brest	14 Nov 1929	9 Oct 1930	15 Nov 1933

Displacement: 10,000 tons standard
11,504 tonnes (*Dupleix* 11,516t) normal
13,644 tonnes (*Dupleix* 13,621t) full load
Length: 185m pp, 194m oa
Beam: 19.26m
Draught: 6.57m max. (normal displacement)
Machinery: Six Guyot du Temple boilers, 20kg/cm^2 (215°); three-shaft Rateau-Bretagne geared steam turbines for
90,000CV; speed 32kts (designed)
Oil fuel: 2600t; radius 5300nm at 15kts
Armament: Eight 203mm/50 Mle 1924 in twin mountings Mle 1924 (150rpg);
Foch eight 90mm/50 Mle 1926 HA in single mountings Mle 1926 (500rpg);
six 37mm/50 Mle 1925 AA in single mountings (1000rpg);
Dupleix eight 90mm/50 Mle 1926 HA in twin mountings Mle 1930;
six 37mm/50 Mle 1925 AA in single mountings;
sixteen 13.2mm/76 Mle 1929 Hotchkiss MG in quad mountings Mle 1931;
both six tubes for 550mm torpedoes Mle 1923D in triple mountings Mle 1925T (3 reloads)
Aircraft: Two GL 810 HY seaplanes
Protection: *Caisson*: 54mm (*Dupleix* 60mm) sides, 18mm (*Dupleix* 30mm) deck
Magazines: 54mm (*Dupleix* 60mm) sides, 20mm (*Dupleix* 30mm) crowns
Steering gear: 26mm sides, 18mm roof
CT: 30mm
Turrets: 30mm
Complement: 605 peace, 752 war

Weights: A Comparison

	Colbert	Foch	Dupleix
Hull:	4967t	4126t	4000t
Protection (hull):	671t	1283t	1462t
Protection (armament):	91t	91t	91t
Armament:	1235t	1479t	1435t
Propulsion:	1810t	1763t	1763t
Torpedoes/Aircraft:	111t	111t	111t
Fittings/Provisions:	1205t	1240t	1225t
Miscellaneous:	70t	67t	73t
Washington Displ.	10,160t	10,160t	10,160t

	Colbert	Foch	Dupleix
Oil fuel:	1089t*	600t	600t
Reserve feed water:	175t	180t	180t
Miscellaneous:	333t	564t	576t
Normal Displ.	11,757t	11,504t	11,516t
Oil fuel:	1258t	2020t*	1985t*
Combustibles:	28t	53t	53t
Ammunition:	58t	53t	53t
Miscellaneous:	12t	14t	14t
Full Load Displ.	13,313t	13,644t	13,621t

* Includes 640t coal

Source: Official *devis d'armement* (via Robert Dumas).

MACHINERY
The only major change in the propulsion machinery
was the suppression of the two small boilers with
mixed firing amidships. This saved weight and simplified steam lines and other pipework. The boilers were
replaced by a larger fuel oil bunker and lubrication oil
stowage. This had the effect of increasing bunker
capacity by some 700 tonnes, which helped to
compensate for the loss of additional cruising radius.

PROTECTION
The bulkheads outboard of the machinery spaces were
of HT steel 54mm thick. Since this represented a 4mm
increase in thickness over the 50mm belt of *Suffren*
and *Colbert*, and since the height of this plating varied
between 5.5m and 6.1m, the total weight would have
been around 360–370 tonnes, as compared to an estimated 150 tonnes for the waterline belt of the earlier
ships. Abeam the after machinery spaces the plating
was continued down to the inner bottom at a reduced
thickness of 40mm (see drawings).

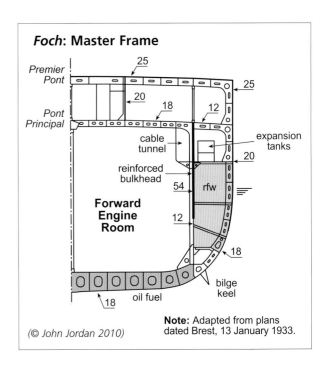

Foch: Master Frame

(© John Jordan 2010)

Note: Adapted from plans
dated Brest, 13 January 1933.

Foch: Bridge Decks

Passerelle inférieure
[Lower Bridge]

The plans show two quad 13.2mm Hotchkiss MG mountings *en echelon* forward of the bridge. Due to delays in the production of these weapons they were not fitted on completion.

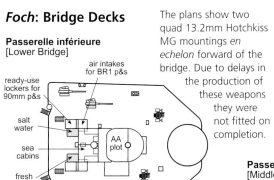

ready-use lockers for 90mm p&s

air intakes for BR1 p&s

salt water

sea cabins

fresh water

AA plot

90mm CAS p&s

13.2mm CAQ p&s

Note: Adapted from plans dated Brest, 13 January 1933.

0m   5m   10m

(© John Jordan 2010)

Passerelle intermédiaire
[Middle Bridge]

Admiral's charthouse

Admiral's sea cabin

W/T Office

conning tower (lower level)

Admiral's bridge

Passerelle de navigation
[Navigation Bridge]

signal house

CO's sea cabin

charthouse

conning tower (upper level)

compass platform

Above: *Foch* comes alongside during the late 1930s. Note the tricolore recognition bands on turret III, which has also now been fitted with a 5-metre rangefinder in a trainable hood.

Above: The distinctive heavy tripod foremast of *Foch*, in which the two outer legs are used to support the HA fire control directors, is prominent in this onboard photo taken on 1 March 1937. The main rangefinder in the director control tower is the new 8-metre stereo model. Note the black concentration dial beneath with its numbers 1–12. The turrets are named after the campaigns with which General Foch was identified, and the name-plates for the individual guns relate to particular actions or place-names associated with those campaigns. The plate for turret I reads LA MARNE, with the guns named FERE-CHAMPENOISE and MONDEMENT; that for turret II reads L'YSER; the port-side gun is named DIXMUDE, but the name-plate for the starboard gun is obscured. *(Marius Bar)*

Box protection for the magazines was on the same pattern as the earlier ships, albeit with an increase in the thickness of the longitudinal bulkheads, again to 54mm. The horizontal protection was slightly reinforced, with the thickness of the plating of the main deck above the machinery spaces being increased from 12mm to 18mm. Protection for the steering gear, the gunhouses and the conning tower remained the same as in the earlier two ships.

This represented a substantial improvement in hull protection; the total weight came to 1283 tonnes, nearly twice that of *Colbert*. This was achieved only in part by interpreting Treaty definitions. It appears from an examination of the breakdown of weights that the major savings came from the weight of the hull, which was down from 4967 tonnes in *Colbert* (49 per cent of standard displacement) to 4126 tonnes (41 per cent of displacement) for the new ship. Even allowing for the notoriously thin dividing line between hull steel and protective plating, this is a substantial saving by any standard, and probably reflects an extensive use of duralumin alloy for internal partitions and fittings as in the *contre-torpilleurs* of the period.[13]

The retention of coal protection over the after machinery spaces, despite a decision to suppress the two small coal-burning boilers (for a saving of approximately 50 tonnes), inevitably raises the question of whether this was in contravention of Treaty regulations. Certainly the coal protection was not counted in the standard displacement, nor could it any longer be justified as 'fuel'. It is possible that the French were aware, following their study of foreign practices, that neither the British (water protection in the *Nelsons*) nor the Japanese (steel tubes in the *Myokos*) counted these items under standard displacement, claiming them as 'optional' defensive supplements to be embarked only in time of war. The official plans of *Foch* show these compartments labelled either '*vide pétrole ou charbon*' ('void, oil fuel or coal') or '*vide ou*

---

[13] French shipyards continued to use riveting for steel structures, whereas contemporary foreign yards were increasingly using welding to reduce hull weight. The first recorded use of welding (for superstructures) was in *Foch*'s successor, *Dupleix*.

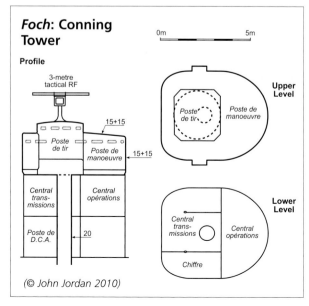

Foch: **Conning Tower**

Profile

(© *John Jordan 2010*)

Foch end 1939

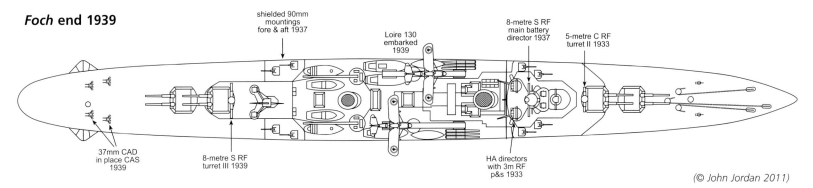

shielded 90mm mountings fore & aft 1937

Loire 130 embarked 1939

8-metre S RF main battery director 1937

5-metre C RF turret II 1933

37mm CAD in place CAS 1939

8-metre S RF turret III 1939

HA directors with 3m RF p&s 1933

(© John Jordan 2011)

charbon' ('void or coal'),[14] making it clear that these fillings were considered optional by the French, and suggesting that coal was not embarked during peacetime.

ARMAMENT

The armament of *Foch* as completed was identical to that of *Colbert*, except that the after 90mm mountings were installed directly on the weather deck, not on a raised platform. The ship was completed without 5-metre rangefinders on turrets II and III in anticipation

---

[14] In the plans for *Suffren* and *Colbert*, all these compartments are simply labelled '*charbon*' (= 'coal').

of the delivery of the new trainable model, which would be fitted in early 1933 (see Modifications). As the projected HA directors were not yet ready, 3-metre open rangefinders were fitted on either side of the foretop as a temporary measure.

Like her half-sister, *Foch* was to have received four quad 13.2mm Hotchkiss MG mountings in addition to her six single 37mm Mle 1925 AA guns. The official plans dated Brest 13 January 1933 show the four mountings fitted as in *Colbert*, except that the forward pair of mountings would have been mounted farther inboard and offset to port and to starboard (see bridge deck drawings). Again, these were not fitted prior to the outbreak of war due to production delays.

Below: The quarterdeck of *Foch* during a visit to Casablanca in 1937, showing the after group of single 37mm Mle 1925 guns. Above can be seen the wing of a GL 810-series floatplane. *(Henri Landais collection)*

AIRCRAFT AND BOATS

The handling arrangements for boats and aircraft were the same as for *Colbert*. The outfit of boats carried by *Foch* as first completed differed from that of *Colbert* only in the provision of an additional 7-metre motor boat, which was stowed forward of the second funnel inboard of the 11-metre motor pinnace.

MODIFICATIONS 1931 TO 1942

Foch appears to have been fitted with propeller guards on completion. The new-model 5-metre rangefinders were fitted to turrets II and III in early 1933, when the HA directors were installed. The original 3-metre open rangefinder atop the conning tower was replaced by the standard 5-metre model in an enclosed housing during the mid-1930s.

During 1936–7 *Foch* received shields for her single 90mm guns, and the original 5-metre coincidence rangefinder in the main director control tower was replaced by an 8-metre stereo model. Shortly before the outbreak of war the catapults were modified to enable them to launch the Loire 130, and the four original quarterdeck 37mm single mountings were replaced by the new twin Mle 1933. *Foch* also received a second 8-metre stereo rangefinder, fitted in place of the 5-metre model on turret III.

Records of subsequent modifications to the AA

Right: The starboard after single 90mm Mle 1926 HA guns of *Foch*, during a visit to Casablanca in 1937. *(Henri Landais collection)*

Below: The after 203mm turrets of *Foch*, seen here at Casablanca in 1937. *(Henri Landais collection)*

outfit have been lost. These were relatively modest in comparison to *Colbert*. *Foch* spent the last few months of her life in care and maintenance (*en gardiennage*) at Toulon. Photographs of the ship following her scut-

tling appear to show single 13.2mm Browning MG mountings atop the bridge structure; other additions were probably limited to two 13.2mm Browning MG amidships.

DUPLEIX (C3)

IN 1927–8 THE ITALIAN PARLIAMENT APPROVED the first four of a series of fast light cruisers intended to counter the French *contre-torpilleurs*. Armed with eight 152mm guns in twin power-operated turrets the new ships (subsequently designated the 'Condottieri' class) packed a considerable punch, and their 152mm shell could theoretically penetrate the armour of French Treaty cruisers up to *Colbert* at virtually any range. Even *Foch* would not be immune to penetration of her vitals by some shells.

These considerations clearly influenced the Staff requirements for the fourth ship, *Dupleix*. In their next submission to the STCN the General Staff requested an increase in the thickness of armour over magazines and machinery sufficient to defeat 155mm shell

beyond 18,000m.[15] The only other change of note requested was an increase in the calibre of the secondary HA guns to 100mm. In the event, although the development of a French 100mm-calibre weapon was in progress, the gun would not be ready in time for installation aboard *Dupleix*, so the 90mm would be retained, albeit in a new twin mounting.

In order to minimise redesign, the constructors opted to retain the armoured *caisson* system introduced in *Foch*, but to make incremental increases in

---

[15] This reflected the view current at the time that engagements between cruisers of these types would take place at long range using increasingly sophisticated director control systems.

Dupleix: Profile & Plan views

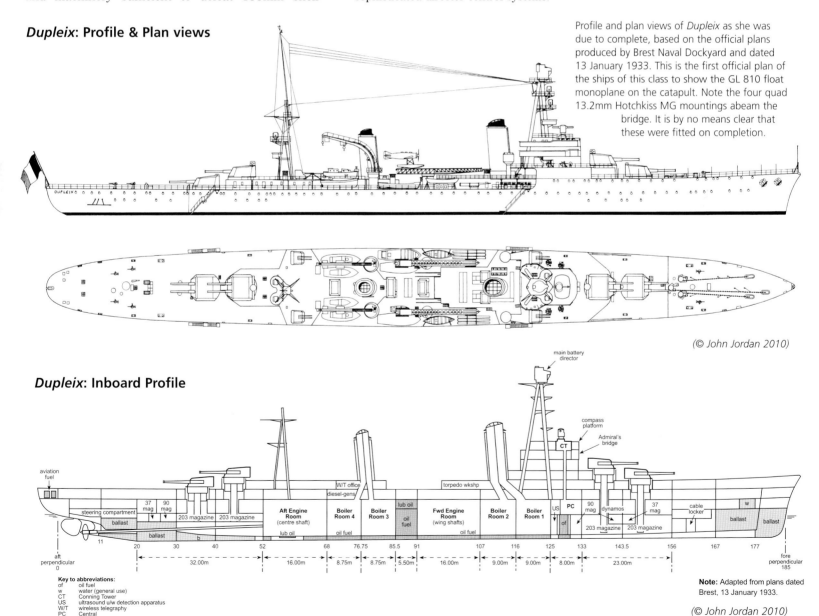

Profile and plan views of *Dupleix* as she was due to complete, based on the official plans produced by Brest Naval Dockyard and dated 13 January 1933. This is the first official plan of the ships of this class to show the GL 810 float monoplane on the catapult. Note the four quad 13.2mm Hotchkiss MG mountings abeam the bridge. It is by no means clear that these were fitted on completion.

(© John Jordan 2010)

Dupleix: Inboard Profile

Key to abbreviations:
of   oil fuel
w   water (general use)
CT   Conning Tower
US   ultrasound u/w detection apparatus
W/T   wireless telegraphy
PC   Central

Note: Adapted from plans dated Brest, 13 January 1933.

(© John Jordan 2010)

Dupleix; Protection

Profile & 1st Platform Deck

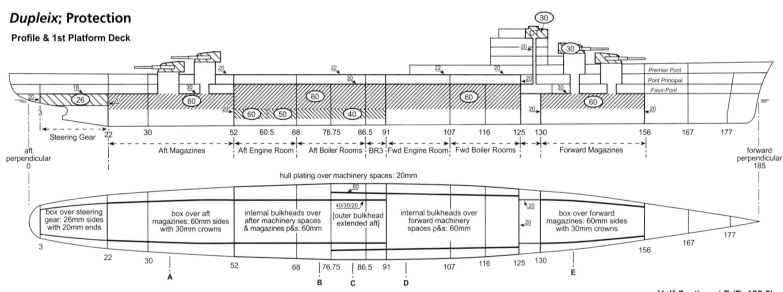

hull plating over machinery spaces: 20mm

| box over steering gear: 26mm sides with 20mm ends | box over aft magazines: 60mm sides with 30mm crowns | internal bulkheads over after machinery spaces & magazines p&s: 60mm | 40/30/20 [outer bulkhead extended aft] | internal bulkheads over forward machinery spaces p&s: 60mm | box over forward magazines: 60mm sides with 30mm crowns |

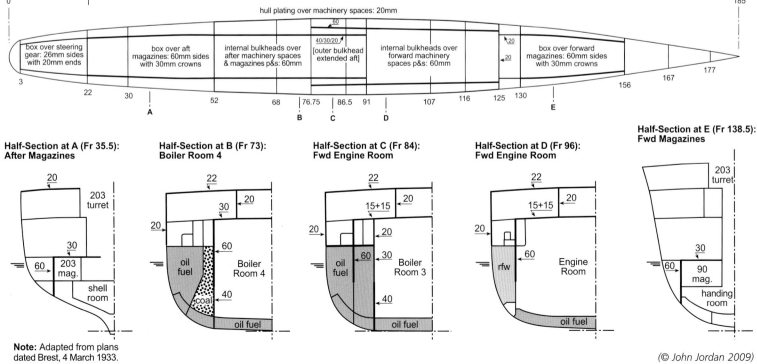

Half-Section at A (Fr 35.5):
After Magazines

Half-Section at B (Fr 73):
Boiler Room 4

Half-Section at C (Fr 84):
Fwd Engine Room

Half-Section at D (Fr 96):
Fwd Engine Room

Half-Section at E (Fr 138.5):
Fwd Magazines

Note: Adapted from plans dated Brest, 4 March 1933.

(© John Jordan 2009)

the thickness of the vertical and horizontal protection throughout. These modifications cost 180 tonnes, the total weight of the hull protection in *Dupleix* being 1462 tonnes. Savings of 185 tonnes were made on the weight of the hull by adopting welding for the super-structures. It was thought that this measure would also provide increased strength and prevent the blast damage currently being experienced with the earlier ships, which during gunnery trials had suffered sheared rivets, and the deformation of doors and superstructure panels when firing their powerful 203mm guns. A further 44 tonnes were saved by adopting a twin mounting for the 90mm HA guns.

The measures taken to 'interpret' Treaty definitions had the effect of shunting the weights of water, provisions and coal protection subtracted from the artificial 'standard' displacement into the normal and full load displacements. Thus the full load displacement showed a steady increase from 12,435 tonnes in *Duquesne*, through 13,300 tonnes in *Suffren* and *Colbert*, to more than 13,600 tonnes in *Foch* and *Dupleix*. From *Suffren* to *Dupleix* there had been no increase in horsepower, so designed speeds would inevitably be more difficult to achieve at deep load, hence the continuing need for careful hull design.

Dupleix was to have been laid down as part of the 1928 *tranche*. However, construction bottlenecks in the French naval dockyards effectively led to the merging of the 1928 and 1929 *tranches*, and she was approved under the latter. The contract was signed on 1 April 1929. Although *Dupleix* was due to follow *Foch* onto the slipway at Brest Naval Dockyard, the delay in ordering the ship meant that it would be almost seven months after the launch of the latter before her keel plates were laid. Construction also proceeded at a slower pace, with the result that *Dupleix* entered service some two years after her half-sister, on 15 November 1933.

NAME

Joseph-François, Marquis **Dupleix** (1697–1763) was a trader in the service of the Compagnie des Indes who made many voyages to America and India. In 1742, having worked to extend the influence of France in the Indies, he became Governor-General of the French establishment in India and the rival of the British Major-General Robert Clive.

GENERAL CONFIGURATION AND LAYOUT

Dupleix reverted to the standard tripod foremast fitted in *Suffren* and *Colbert*, although without the topmast, and the 5-metre rangefinder in an enclosed housing above the conning tower was reinstated, although it was not fitted on completion (see photo p.78)

The HA fire control systems were fitted from the outset, but in contrast to *Foch* the directors were on low-level pedestals abeam the fore-funnel. The adoption of the twin 90mm Mle 1930 enabled the after mountings to be raised one level to the boat deck, and left sufficient deck space abeam the forward super-structure to accommodate all four of the planned quad 13.2mm Hotchkiss MG mountings. However, the delivery of these mountings was delayed and none was fitted before the outbreak of war.

Opposite: *Dupleix* shortly after her completion in November 1933. She had no foretopmast, and HA directors were fitted abreast the fore-funnel from the outset, as was the new-model 5-metre rangefinder in its trainable hood atop turrets II and III. Note the 3-metre open rangefinder fitted as a temporary measure atop the conning tower. It would later be replaced by the standard 5-metre rangefinder 'turret'. *(Courtesy of Robert Dumas)*

Left: *Dupleix* at anchor. Note the white-painted face of the forward concentration dial, which was a feature of many of the cruisers based in the Mediterranean during the mid-1930s. In the background: the 10,000-ton cruiser *Tourville* and one of the older battleships.

Opposite, top: The 1st Division in heavy weather. The photo is taken from the foretop of *Dupleix*; note the twin 90mm HA mountings abreast the mainmast. In her wake is the *Foch*, followed by another unidentifiable 10,000-ton cruiser – possibly the *Colbert*. *(Philippe Caresse collection)*

Opposite, bottom: Dupleix leaving Toulon in 1941. The main topmast has been suppressed. Note the longer-base 8-metre stereo rangefinder on turret III fitted in the late 1930s.

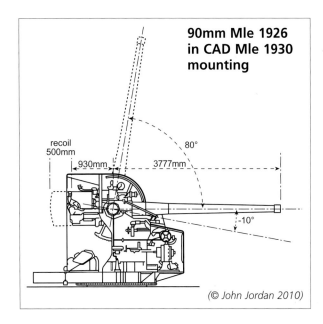

90mm Mle 1926 in CAD Mle 1930 mounting

recoil 500mm 930mm 3777mm 80° -10°

(© John Jordan 2010)

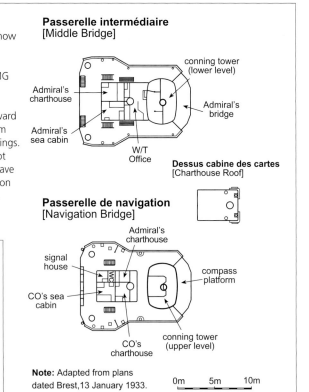

Dupleix: Conning Tower

Profile   5-metre tactical RF   15+15   15+15

Poste de tir — Poste de manoeuvre
Central transmissions — Central opérations
Poste de D.C.A. — 20

Upper Level Poste de manoeuvre Poste de tir

Lower Level Central opérations Central transmissions Chiffre

(© John Jordan 2010)

Dupleix was the first of the inter-war French cruisers to have the revised conning tower configuration.

Dupleix: Bridge Decks & Platforms

Passerelle inférieure [Lower Bridge]

air intakes for BR1 p&s   ventilator for pneumatic network
salt water   sea cabins   AA plot   ready-use lockers for 90mm   fresh water
90mm CAD p&s   13.2mm CAQ p&s

(© John Jordan 2010)

The plans show four quad 13.2mm Hotchkiss MG mountings abreast the bridge, forward of the 90mm twin mountings. These do not appear to have been fitted on completion.

Passerelle intermédiaire [Middle Bridge]

conning tower (lower level)   Admiral's charthouse   Admiral's bridge   Admiral's sea cabin   W/T Office

Dessus cabine des cartes [Charthouse Roof]

Passerelle de navigation [Navigation Bridge]

signal house   Admiral's charthouse   compass platform   CO's sea cabin   CO's charthouse   conning tower (upper level)

Note: Adapted from plans dated Brest, 13 January 1933.   0m 5m 10m

Below: Dupleix moored in the Toulon anchorage in 1935. She has the three white bands on the fore-funnel which she wore from 1 November 1934 to 1st February 1936. Note the GL 810-series floatplanes on the catapults.

MACHINERY

The propulsion machinery layout duplicated that of *Foch*. However, the skeg for the centre-line propeller shaft, eliminated from the original *Suffren* design following basin trials with a model, was reinstated in *Dupleix*. Tank testing had revealed that although it adversely affected the turning circle it also reduced hull resistance at higher speeds, and this was increasingly a consideration with the later ships of the series, the increases in weight not being matched by any increase in horsepower.

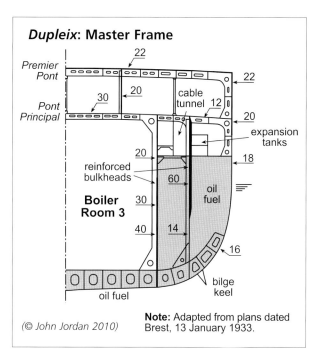

Dupleix: Master Frame

Premier Pont
22
22
20
cable tunnel 12
30
Pont Principal
20
expansion tanks
20
reinforced bulkheads
18
Boiler Room 3
60
oil fuel
30
40
14
16
bilge keel
oil fuel

(© John Jordan 2010)

Note: Adapted from plans dated Brest, 13 January 1933.

PROTECTION

The protection system adopted for *Dupleix* was essentially the same as for *Foch*, but with incremental increases in the thickness of both the vertical and the horizontal protection over the machinery and magazines.

The thickness of the longitudinal bulkheads protecting the machinery spaces and the magazines was increased from 54mm to 60mm. For structural reasons – to compensate for the discontinuity between the forward and after machinery spaces – the forward bulkhead had been extended aft by some 14m to overlap the inner bulkhead in this class. In *Dupleix* this overlapping bulkhead was now reinforced to the full 60mm, with the inboard bulkhead being increasingly thinned from 40mm to 20mm behind it (see Protection drawing).

Horizontal protection was significantly increased. The main deck over the machinery was increased from 18mm to 30mm (15mm + 15mm), albeit at the cost of a slight reduction in the thickness of the plating on the upper deck from 25mm to 22mm. The magazine crowns were also increased from 20mm to a single thickness of 30mm.

ARMAMENT

The only significant difference from *Foch* as completed was that *Dupleix* had her eight 90mm HA guns in the new twin mounting (CAD Mle 1930 – see drawing). The mounting was well-liked, and would be adopted for the minelaying cruiser *Emile Bertin* and for the 7600-ton cruisers built following the London Treaty of 1930. The after pair of mountings was mounted higher, at the after end of the shelter deck, which improved arcs.

AIRCRAFT AND BOATS

Like her immediate predecessors *Dupleix* normally carried two GL 810/811 float monoplanes until 1939, when they were superseded by the Loire 130 (see Modifications below). Her boat outfit as completed was similar to that of her half-sister *Foch*, except that

Dupleix end 1939

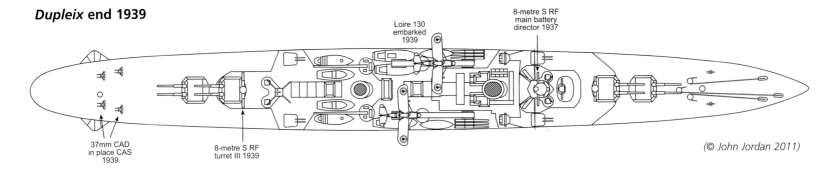

Loire 130
embarked
1939

8-metre S RF
main battery
director 1937

37mm CAD
in place CAS
1939

8-metre S RF
turret III 1939

(© John Jordan 2011)

the 7-metre motor boat of the latter was replaced by one of the two 5-metre dinghies.

Above: *Dupleix* moored alongside one of the Milhaud finger piers 1941–2. In the background is the fleet flagship *Strasbourg*, as yet without her radar installation. Note the port forward twin 90mm mounting abreast the bridge and the HA director abeam the funnel. Some minor modifications have been made to the upper bridge. *(ECPAD)*

CRUISER C4

THE CRUISER WHICH WAS TO FOLLOW *DUPLEIX*, provisionally designated 'C4', continued the quest for more effective protection. The General Staff, following the contemporary example of the US Navy, for the first time specified an 'immune zone' against 155mm shellfire: the vertical armour over the magazines and machinery spaces should not be able to be penetrated beyond 15,000m, and the horizontal armour below 20,000m. Given that the range of engagement ideally envisaged for these ships was around 18,000m, this would ensure that the new generation of Italian light cruisers could be engaged with every prospect of complete success (it was accepted that immunity from 203mm shell was out of the question on a displacement of 10,000 tons standard).

The implications of this new requirement were a thickening of the vertical armour from 60mm to 80mm. This would cost an estimated 400 tonnes in weight, which would be difficult to achieve without reducing the weight of the hull (already less than 40 per cent of displacement in the *Dupleix*), the armament (a non-starter, as the General Staff was pushing for 100mm HA guns to replace the 90mm), or the machinery. The constructors toyed with a reduction in propulsive power to 84,000CV on two shafts for a

MODIFICATIONS 1933 TO 1942

Early photos of *Dupleix* taken during her trials show her without the 90mm twin HA mountings, and with a small open (duplex?) 3-metre rangefinder atop the conning tower. Propeller guards appear to have been fitted from the outset. By the Spring of 1934, when the ship was in service, all the planned items of equipment were in place.

During the late 1930s the original 5-metre coincidence rangefinder in the main director control tower was replaced by an 8-metre stereo model. Shortly before the outbreak of war the catapults were modified to enable them to launch the Loire 130, and the four original quarterdeck 37mm single mountings were replaced by the new twin Mle 1933, as in *Colbert* and *Foch* (these mountings are clearly visible in photographs of the scuttling). *Dupleix* also received a second 8-metre stereo rangefinder, fitted in place of the 5-metre model on turret III.

Records of subsequent modifications to the AA outfit have been lost. As with *Foch*, these were relatively modest. Photographs show that by 1941 a new platform for two 13.2mm Browning MG had replaced the controls for the forward searchlights, and that the forecastle 37mm had been removed. There may have been additional 13.2mm Browning MG amidships.

speed of 31 knots at normal displacement, but this saved only 150 tonnes. Moreover there were increasing concerns regarding the wisdom of persisting with the internal armoured *caisson*. All contemporary foreign cruiser construction featured heavier and more extensive 'external' belt armour, which had the advantage of protecting buoyancy as well as the ship's vitals. The internal armour of *Foch* and *Dupleix* would undoubtedly prove effective against destroyer shell, but the Marine Nationale was now opposed by a navy with growing numbers of cruisers armed with larger-calibre weapons. The Italian 203mm and 152mm SAP and HE shells would make much larger holes in the French cruisers' light shell plating than the 120mm guns aboard their destroyers, and this posed a major threat to the ships' buoyancy and stability in the event of action damage.

It was finally recognised that *Dupleix* was effectively the end of the line, and that a completely new design was needed. The result of these studies was the radically-different *Algérie* which had a 110mm external armour belt, an 80mm armoured deck, and lightweight superheated boilers with four-shaft geared turbines. (The development of the latter ship is detailed in Chapter 5.)

CHAPTER 4:
PLUTON, JEANNE D'ARC AND *EMILE BERTIN*

PLUTON

INTRODUCTION

During the First World War, extensive minefields were laid in the North Sea off Belgium and the Netherlands to restrict the operations of the German High Seas Fleet. Post-war naval planning by both the French and the British continued to envisage minelaying by cruisers and submarines as an important element in their strategy for containing future German naval operations.

For the Marine Nationale the programme of specialist minelaying vessels began in 1925, which saw the authorisation of both the minelaying cruiser *Pluton* and the first two submarines of the *Saphir* class, a further four boats being authorised in successive programmes in 1926–9. The submarines, which carried thirty-two Sautter-Harlé mines in saddle tanks, were intended for covert mining off ports and in river estuaries. However, the French strategy envisaged the laying of larger minefields, probably in conjunction with the British Royal Navy, farther out into the North Sea.

The design of *Pluton* was heavily influenced by the British *Adventure*, laid down in November 1922. With a displacement of 6740 tons, a moderate speed of 28 knots – uncontested night-time operations were contemplated – and a main armament of four single 4.7in (120mm) guns, *Adventure* had a capacity of 300 mines, stowed on four tracks at main deck level and discharged from four traps in a transom stern.

Although authorised under the 1925 *tranche* of the naval programme, *Pluton* could not be laid down for a further three years because of production bottlenecks in the French naval dockyards. In the interim it was decided to convert two ex-Russian 14-knot icebreakers at Lorient in 1927–8 as *Castor* and *Pollux*. These ships would trial the new high-speed minelaying system developed by Sautter-Harlé from the end of 1929. The trials were a complete success, and influenced the design of the system which would be installed in *Pluton*.

DESIGN AND CONSTRUCTION

The general characteristics of the ship were quickly agreed but there was much discussion regarding the gun armament to be installed. It was known that the Royal Navy considered *Adventure*, which was armed only with 4.7in guns for self-defence against enemy torpedo craft, to be under-gunned. In 1925 it was being proposed that *Pluton* be armed with two single 203mm guns in a lightweight mounting developed after the war, with 115 rounds per gun in the maga-

PRINCIPAL CHARACTERISTICS OF *PLUTON* AND HMS *ADVENTURE*		
	Adventure	*Pluton*
Displacement:	6740tW	5300tW
Length oa:	158.5m	152.5m
Beam:	18m	15.55m
Horsepower:	40,000CV	57,000CV
Trial speed:	27.75kts	31kts
Armament:	Four 120mm (4 x I)	Four 138mm (4 x I)
Mines:	300	220/250
Complement:	400	424
Laid down:	Nov 1922	Apr 1928
In service:	May 1927	Jan 1932

zines. The remaining armament was to comprise four single 75mm Mle 1922 HA guns and four single 37mm Mle 1925. By the end of the year two single 138.6mm low-angle guns – the same weapon fitted in the latest *contre-torpilleurs* – had been added, and in 1926 the single 203mm guns were abandoned in favour of a uniform main armament of four single 138.6mm Mle 1923.

Besides the primary minelaying mission, it was envisaged that the ship would also be used as a fast troop transport, 1000 troops being accommodated on the mine deck, which although at upper-deck level was covered by a shelter deck amidships.

Ordered from Lorient Naval Dockyard, *Pluton* was laid down only in April 1928 and took almost four years to complete, entering service in January 1932.

Below: *Pluton* on her full power trials in 1931.

Pluton: Profile & Plan views

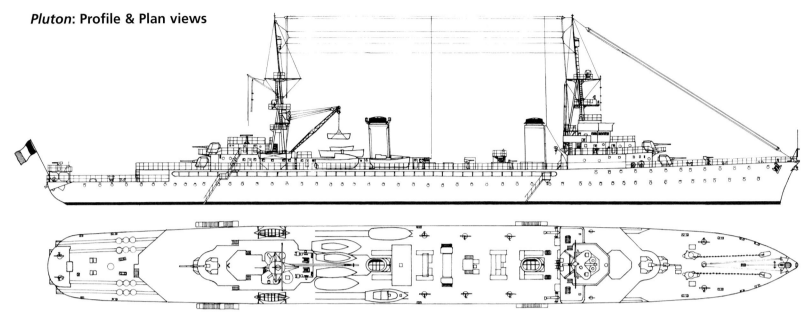

Profile and plan views of *Pluton*, based on the official plans produced by Lorient Naval Dockyard and dated 22 September 1932. They show the cruiser as first completed, with six single 37mm mountings Mle 1925 amidships in place of the four 75mm HA of the original design. The platform for the two stern 37mm mountings straddles the inner pair of mine rails.

(© John Jordan 2010)

Pluton: Inboard Profile

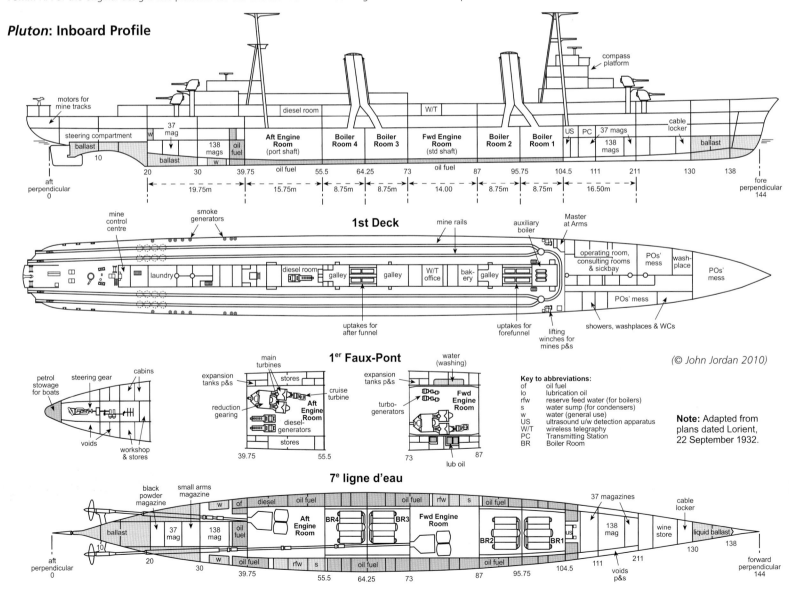

(© John Jordan 2010)

Key to abbreviations:

of	oil fuel
lo	lubrication oil
rfw	reserve feed water (for boilers)
s	water sump (for condensers)
w	water (general use)
US	ultrasound u/w detection apparatus
W/T	wireless telegraphy
PC	Transmitting Station
BR	Boiler Room

Note: Adapted from plans dated Lorient, 22 September 1932.

BUILDING DATA AND GENERAL CHARACTERISTICS: *PLUTON*

Name	Builder	Laid down	Launched	In service
1925 Programme				
Pluton	Arsenal de Lorient	16 Apr 1928	10 Apr 1929	25 Jan 1932

Characteristics (as completed)
Displacement:	5300 tons standard
	5321 tonnes normal
	6214 tonnes full load
Length:	144m pp, 152.5m oa
Beam:	15.55m
Draught:	5.2m max. (normal)
Machinery:	Four du Temple small-tube boilers, 20kg/cm^2; two-shaft Breguet geared steam turbines for 57,000CV; speed 30kts (designed)
Oil fuel:	1150 tonnes; radius 4500nm at 14kts, 2200nm at 24kts
Armament:	Four 138mm/40 Mle 1923 in four single mountings Mle 1924 (600 rounds); ten 37mm/50 Mle 1925 AA in single mountings (10,000 rounds); 220/250 Sautter-Harlé H5 or 270 Breguet B4 mines.
Protection:	None
Complement:	424 peace; 513 war

Weights
Hull:	860.5t
Protection:	nil
Armament (incl. ammunition):	1259.5t
Propulsion:	1346.6t
Fittings:	1754.5t
Misc.:	3.6t
Displ.	5224.7t

The ship was initially typed *mouilleur de mines de surface* but was subsequently reclassified as *croiseur mouilleur de mines*.

NAME

Pluton was the seventh ship of the name to serve with the French Navy. Pluto was the god of the underworld in Roman mythology, and this was considered an appropriate name for a ship associated with underwater warfare. Her immediate predecessor was likewise a minelayer and served during the First World War, being stricken in 1923.

During the Spring of 1939 it was envisaged that *Pluton* would be seconded to the *Ecole d'application* as consort to the training cruiser *Jeanne d'Arc* from the summer of 1940. In this new role her name would have been changed to *La Tour d'Auvergne*. Although the ship was subsequently referred to under this name in a number of reference sources, *Pluton* remained in service as a minelayer on the outbreak of war and due to her early loss at Casablanca carried her original name up to the date of her loss.

HULL AND GENERAL CONFIGURATION

The hull of *Pluton* was of longitudinal construction with fifteen watertight transverse bulkheads. Like that of the *contre-torpilleurs* on which her hull-form and machinery layout was based, it was totally unprotected, and relied on tight subdivision for survival in the event of action damage. In order to save weight extensive use was made of duralumin alloy for the superstructures and accessories (ladders, boat booms, etc.), and this was to result both in structural weaknesses and corrosion problems.

The silhouette of the ship was broadly similar to that of the contemporary Treaty cruiser *Suffren*, with twin tripod masts inclined at 5 degrees and the characteristic widely-spaced funnels which reflected the unit arrangement of the machinery. *Pluton* could, however, easily be distinguished from the early Treaty cruisers by the comparatively small gunhouses superimposed fore and aft, by the absence of a catapult for reconnaissance floatplanes, and by the raised platform for AA guns above the stern.

There was pine planking on the forecastle and on the First Deck outboard of the mine rails. From the bow to just forward of the gun mountings the deck was of painted steel, and the bridge decks were covered with red-brown linoleum.

MACHINERY

Pluton had a unit layout for her machinery, with the two forward boilers and the forward set of turbines offset to starboard, and the after boilers and turbines offset to port (see drawing). Two of the four small-tube boilers, rated at 20kg/cm^2, were manufactured by FC de la Gironde, the other two by the Chantiers Normand (Le Havre). The boilers, which were in separate boiler rooms, were paired back-to-back, with the exhausts from each pair being led up into a canted funnel. There was also an auxiliary boiler on the First Deck forward of the fore-funnel to provide steam for the on-board services.

The two shafts were powered by two groups of Breguet single-reduction impulse turbines, the forward group powering the starboard shaft and the after group powering the port shaft. Each turbine group comprised two identical turbines working in

MACHINERY TRIALS (SELECTED)

	Full Power (10 hours) 24 Apr 1931	Forcing (1 hour) 11 Sep 1931
Displacement:	5587t	5634t
Speed:	30.62kts	31.37kts
Horsepower:	55,850CV	63,907CV

parallel, with a separate cruise turbine; the latter could be disengaged when no longer receiving steam, but could only be clutched to the shaft when the ship was at rest. The reversing turbine was in the housing for the main turbines. The propulsion machinery could operate as two completely independent units, thereby making the ship more resistant to machinery breakdown or action damage. The three-bladed propellers had a diameter of 4.08m.

The designed power of the propulsion machinery was 57,000CV for 30 knots. On trials *Pluton* largely exceeded this figure, sustaining 31.3 knots on 64,705CV over three hours on 29 April 1931. It subsequently proved possible to sustain 28 knots even with a full load of mines. Endurance was calculated to be 7700nm at 14 knots and 4900nm at 20 knots. However, once the ship entered service with a full complement aboard these figures were revised downwards to 4510nm at 14 knots and 2235nm at 24 knots. The problem, as with all French surface ships of the period, was the heavy demands made by the auxiliary machinery which provided on-board services for the crew, and generated electrical power for the ship's weapon systems and other electro-mechanical systems such as boat cranes, the ship's rudder, etc. When the auxiliary machinery was operating in service, the ship's fuel consumption increased by a massive 50 per cent.

Power generation when underway was provided by two 200kW (266kW max.) turbo-generators located in the forward engine room (to port of the turbines), which served a 235V 'cruiser' electrical circuit. There were also two 100kW (120kW max.) diesel generators for use when alongside, powering a 220V circuit and located in the after engine room to starboard of the turbines; a third (emergency) diesel was located in a special compartment on the First Deck.

GROUND TACKLE AND NAVIGATION

Pluton was fitted with three Byers type 4000kg anchors in hawsepipes forward; the bower anchors were to port

and to starboard with the sheet anchor – unusually – in the bow. There was a single 1400kg Byers type stern anchor on the centre-line, and two kedge anchors of 1020kg and 760kg respectively were provided.

The single rudder was of the counter-balanced type with a surface area of 19.87m², and was powered by two electric servo-motors. The latter proved to be underpowered, as in other French ships of the period. At 27 knots with 25 degrees of rudder the turning circle was 875m (greater than the 8000-tonne cruiser *Duguay-Trouin*, which was 30m longer).

ARMAMENT

Main battery

The 138mm/40 Mle 1923, in four single mountings Mod.1924, was the same weapon installed in the second group of *contre-torpilleurs*, the *Guépard/Valmy* classes. It had a traditional Welin screw breech, unlike later guns of this calibre, and the theoretical rate of fire was 8–9rpm; in practice it proved to be less. Elevation was between -10 degrees and +35 degrees; at maximum elevation range was 18,200m with a muzzle velocity of 700m/sec. The mounting weighed 13 tonnes.

The 138mm Mle1923 fired the standard OPf Mle1924 SAP and OEA Mle 1924 HE shells, which weighed approximately 40kg. A total of 150 rounds per gun was provided. Guns II and III each had thirty starshell plus twenty exercise rounds; guns I and IV each had sixty exercise rounds. Separate hoists for shells and charges served an ammunition lobby behind each of the four guns; each lobby had racks for twenty-four (2 x 12) ready-use mixed rounds. As on the *contre-torpilleurs* shells were moved to the guns via brass guttering which surrounded the mounting, enabling rapid loading to take place at all angles of training.

Anti-aircraft weapons

Pluton was completed without the four 75mm HA guns she was designed for, although the deck seatings were

Below: *Pluton* arrives at Toulon on 23 January 1932, following her work-up cruise (*croisière d'endurance*) via Cherbourg and Oran. (*Marius Bar*)

138.6/40 MLE 1923

Gun Data

Construction:	Autofretted 'A' tube with shrunk jacket and liner
Breech mechanism	Upward-opening Welin screw
Weight of gun:	4.1t (incl. breech)
Ammunition type:	Separate
projectiles	OPf Mle 1924 (39.9kg)
	OEA Mle 1924 (40.4kg)
Propellant:	BM7 (9kg)
Muzzle velocity:	700m/s
Max. range	18,200m (35°) :

Mounting Data

Designation:	Single Mle 1924
Weight of turret:	13.1t
Elevation of guns:	−10° / +35°
Firing cycle (per gun):	5–6rpm

Notes:

OPf	*Obus de Perforation*	Armour Piercing (AP)
OEA	*Obus Explosif en Acier*	High Explosive (HE)

retained (shelter deck amidships) with a view to future installation. In their place, as a temporary measure, there were an additional six 37mm/50 Mle 1925, for a total of ten: two on the forecastle, six to port and starboard of the shelter deck between the funnels, and two on a raised platform above the stern (to clear the mine tracks). One thousand rounds per gun were provided, with 144 rounds in ready-use lockers close to each gun. There was also provision for twelve elderly Hotchkiss 8mm MG Mle 1914 in six twin mountings: two atop the bridge, two atop the ventilation housing for the after boiler room, and two just forward of the tripod mainmast.

Fire control

Fire control for the main guns was provided by two SOM 3-metre coincidence rangefinders, which fed data into a mechanical computer Mle 1923 located on the lower bridge deck, just behind the upper ammunition lobby. One of the rangefinders was atop the bridge, the second abaft the mainmast. There were also four 0.75-metre searchlight projectors for night fire: two on the

upper platform of the tripod foremast, and two on the upper platform of the mainmast, with remote control positions on platforms directly beneath them.

Mines

Pluton was designed for a normal deckload of 220 Sautter-Harlé H5 mines (250 maximum load). The H5 mine was a traditional tethered mine with a spherical body 1.04m in diameter, a cable and a sinker; all-up weight was 1160kg, and there was a 220kg TNT bursting charge. The sinker, which served as a trolley on board ship, was provided with four hooks which were secured to the upper part of the U-shaped rail when underway and released for laying.

There were four sets of rails (two to port, two to starboard), which ran on either side of the superstructures at First Deck level. They terminated in ramps angled down at 30 degrees to the stern to reduce the height above water (and therefore the impact) of the mines when laid. Each of the mine tracks had a gauge of 0.5m, and the mines were linked together by continuous 192m chains powered by electric motors located beneath the mine deck at the stern. A minelaying control station at the end of the after deckhouse overlooked the after end of the ship.

At their forward end each pair of rail tracks converged on circular turntables linked by a single athwartships set of rails. This permitted all four tracks to be used for minelaying even when mines were embarked on only one side. The mines were embarked close to the turntables using two electrically-powered cranes installed on the Second Deck, and were laid alternately from the port and starboard tracks over the stern. The mine deck openings along the sides of the ship could be closed in by steel panels with watertight leather seals to enable the ship to be used for transporting troops (capacity 1000).[1]

The minelaying system was designed by Sautter-Harlé with its own mines in view, and when the later Breguet B4 mine was embarked it proved less secure.

---

[1] During *Pluton*'s service as a gunnery training ship the mine deck openings were progressively closed off as more trainees were embarked.

Pluton: Bridge Decks

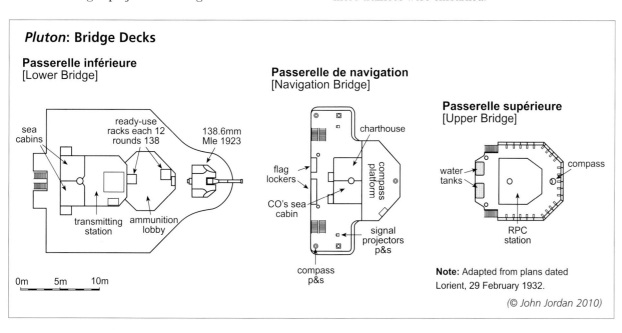

Passerelle inférieure [Lower Bridge]

Passerelle de navigation [Navigation Bridge]

Passerelle supérieure [Upper Bridge]

Note: Adapted from plans dated Lorient, 29 February 1932.

(© John Jordan 2010)

RANGEFINDER OUTFIT AS EATM SHIP 1933–1939

	Apr 1933	Feb 1936
Bridge structure:	2 OPL (S) 3-metre	4 OPL (S) 3-metre (Mle 1927/32)
	2 Zeiss (S) 3-metre	2 Zeiss (S) 3-metre
	2 Barr & Stroud (C)* 2-metre	2 SOM (C) 3-metre (Mle 1926)
	2 Zeiss (S) 1.5-metre	1 Barr& Stroud (C) 2-metre
Amidships:	1 Barr & Stroud (C) 4.57-metre	none
	1 OPL (S) 3-metre	
After deckhouse:	1 OPL (S) 4-metre	1 SOM (C) 5-metre
	1 OPL (S) 3-metre	2 OPL (S) 4-metre (Mle 1933)
		4 OPL (S) 3-metre (Mle 1924/27)
		3 SOM (S) 3-metre (Mle 1932)
		1 SOM (C) 3-metre (Mle 1931)
HA director:	none	1 OPL (S) 3-metre (Mle 1926)
Searchlight command platform:	none	2 OPL (S) 3-metre (Mle 1926/27)
For light AA:	none	8 OPL (S) 1-metre Mle J.30

Notes:
(C) = coincidence; (S) = stereoscopic

This was to be cited by the Board of Inquiry as a factor in the eventual loss of the ship. The Breguet B4 mine, which proved to be less robust than its predecessor, had smaller dimensions and a maximum of 270 could be accommodated.

BOATS
The outfit when *Pluton* was first completed was as follows:

– one 10-metre pulling pinnace
– two 9-metre steam pinnaces
– one 9-metre motor boats
– one 9-metre motor launch
– one 9-metre pulling cutter
– two 8-metre whalers
– two 5-metre dinghies

The boat deck was located between the second funnel and the mainmast, and was served by a duralumin lifting derrick with an 800kg capacity and a reach of 10.5m, the controls being located at the foot of the mainmast. This had to be replaced within two years of the ship's entry into service due to serious corrosion.

The larger boats were on crutches with the exception of the CO's motor boat and one of the two steam pinnaces, which were stowed outboard of the second funnel on rails which extended aft so that they could be moved in reach of the crane. The two 8-metre whalers were mounted on davits outboard of the mainmast.

MODIFICATIONS 1934 TO 1939
Pluton entered service on 25 January 1932; on her arrival at Toulon she was attached to the Training Squadron of the *1re Escadre*. Her trials had revealed various problems, some of which would continue to plague the ship throughout her active service. In particular there were numerous machinery breakdowns: the turbo-pumps were prone to serious oil leaks even when tested in the factory prior to installation; the reduction gearing tended to overheat, and there was excessive play in both cruise and one of the main turbines.

The *Commission Permanente des Essais* (CPE – Trials Commission), which was responsible for the initial evaluation of *Pluton*, considered her to be well-adapted to the mission intended. However, there was concern regarding the military value of the ship, and especially the relatively feeble main armament, given her size and cost.

On 27 April 1932, when *Pluton* had been in service barely four months, it was decided to convert her to a gunnery school ship (EATM: Ecole d'application du tir à la mer) as a replacement for the elderly armoured cruiser *Gueydon*. It was stipulated that this conversion should in no way impair the ship's primary mission as a minelaying cruiser, and that the statutory annual minelaying exercises should continue. Conversion involved the installation of:

Right: *Pluton* in March 1934, showing the modifications made to fit her out for the gunnery training school (EATM). Note the HA director atop the tripod foremast, and the multiple rangefinders atop the deckhouse at the foot of the mainmast. This photo gives an excellent view of the minelaying arrangements and 37mm AA gun platform at the stern. *(Marius Bar)*

- a transmitting station of the type fitted in the 10,000-tonne cruisers;
- the 138mm director control system from *Gueydon* (the director was located atop the enlarged bridge structure);
- fire simulation equipment;
- four single 75mm/50 Mle1922 HA guns from *Gueydon*;
- an HA director control system for the 75mm guns;
- two twin 13.2mm/76 Hotchkiss MG from *Gueydon*, plus a further four to replace the elderly 8mm Hotchkiss MG
- additional rangefinders atop the bridge, between the funnels and on the stern platform (see table).

It also involved the conversion of two after crew spaces to accept eight dismountable cabins for trainee midshipmen (to be removed in four days), and temporary spaces for forty men on the port-side mine deck (the openings were permanently closed with steel panels).

These additions resulted in some modifications to the bridge structure and mast platforms. The deckhouse atop the upper bridge deck was removed and the director for the 138mm guns installed in its place. New, heavier support legs were fitted to the tripod foremast to enable it to take the weight of the HA director, the topmast being reduced to a stump. One of the forward searchlight projectors was disembarked, the other moved to a platform beneath the director. The new rangefinders were installed in two main groupings atop the fore and after superstructures, with two longer-base models between the funnels.

The armament was now: four single 138mm/40, four single 75mm/50, two single 37mm/50 (stern platform), and six twin 13.2mm/76 Hotchkiss MG (two on the forecastle, and two on either side of the upper deck amidships). There was a slight reduction in the ship's stability because of the additional topweight.

In 1933–4 full RPC was provided for the 75mm HA guns, a concentration dial was installed just below the control top, and the after gangway, which was made of duralumin and had badly corroded, was replaced by a steel model. The following year the forward gangway was replaced, together with the boat crane and boat booms, which had suffered similar corrosion. Temporary spaces were provided for a further forty men on the starboard-side mine deck, the 75mm guns were fitted with shields, and eight (later sixteen) Brest-type life rafts were fitted. In 1936 the foretopmast was suppressed and a further ten range-finders fitted (the total was by now thirty-one!). The boilers and condensers were overhauled and the turbines inspected.

During a major refit in 1937–8 the turbines and reduction gearing were refurbished, and a massive DCT *type croiseur de 8,000t* was fitted atop the bridge structure in place of the original. Remote power control (training only) was provided for the main guns, and the two forecastle 13.2mm mountings, which had proved to be too exposed to the elements, were relocated to the bridge structure.

In 1938–9 the boilers were retubed, the HA director was completely enclosed, and the 13.2mm MG received protective shields. The original lifting derrick was replaced by a new model with greater reach and almost twice the lift capability (1500kg); it could now also handle mines. Outriggers were fitted to the second funnel to handle a revised communications outfit.

Following a short refit at Lorient in July 1939, *Pluton* was again converted to serve as a minelayer, and it was in this configuration that she was lost on 13 September.

JEANNE D'ARC

INTRODUCTION
French naval officer cadets and those entering the engineering branch had traditionally trained for two years at specialised schools ashore before embarking on a cruiser for a world tour which enabled them to further their education and hone their skills. During the early 1920s the school ship was the elderly armoured cruiser *Jeanne d'Arc*, which had been refitted specially for the purpose in 1912. However, by the mid-1920s she was on her last legs, and it was decided to replace her with a new, purpose-built ship with a modern armament. Such a vessel would not only provide the cadets with access to the latest naval hardware, but could function as a fighting vessel in time of war.

The new ship, designated *croiseur école d'application des enseignes de vaisseau*, was authorised under the 1926 Estimates, and would bear the same illustrious name as her predecessor. There was a two-year delay in placing the order, and the new *Jeanne d'Arc* would be completed only in October 1931. In the interim the role of School Ship was taken on first by the armoured cruiser *Edgar Quinet*, and from 1930 to 1931[2] by the three new Treaty cruisers of the 1st Light Division.

Designed to provide accommodation and training facilities for 156 midshipmen, *Jeanne d'Arc* would have a secondary role of showing the flag in the remote islands and territories of the French Empire and the major foreign ports of the world.

DESIGN AND CONSTRUCTION
Early proposals included the conversion of an older cruiser and the conversion of a liner. Both were rejected on grounds of the cost of conversion and their lack of suitability to prepare officer cadets for the command in a modern, technologically advanced navy.

The first proposal for a purpose-built ship was for a cruiser of 5000 tonnes. This was not liked by the French Senate, which cited its inadequate armament, its mixed-fired boilers, and in particular its maximum speed of 20 knots and low endurance. It would accommodate only 125 officer cadets, yet would cost as much as two fleet submarines or two *contre-torpilleurs*. The Senate Commission felt the money would be better spent on a ship which would have real military value in time of war.

The Navy Ministry responded with a new proposal for a ship of 6500 tonnes with a main armament comparable to that of the *Duguay-Trouins*. The overall layout of the ship precluded more than two single

---

[2] *Edgar Quinet* foundered on a rock west of Oran in January 1930.

Jeanne d'Arc: Profile & Plan views

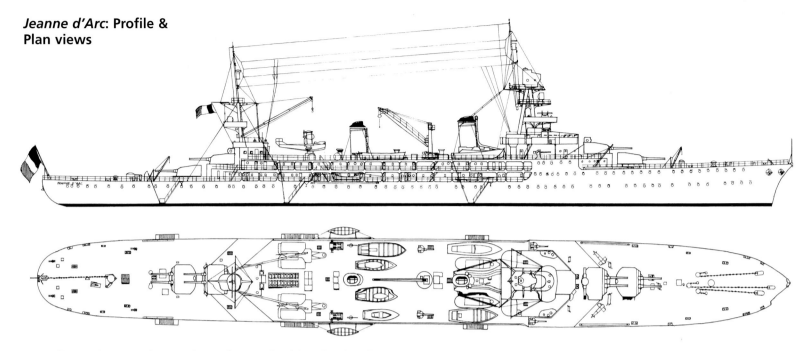

Profile and plan views of *Jeanne d'Arc* as first completed, based on the official plans produced at Saint-Nazaire and dated 15 September 1932. The aircraft atop the pedestal is the CAMS 37A

(© John Jordan 2010)

torpedo tubes,[3] but two catapults would be fitted, and the oil-fired propulsion plant would give a designed speed of 25 knots and an endurance of 6000nm. There would be accommodation for 150 officer cadets and 20 instructors. This was the design authorised under the 1926 Estimates. The contract for Jeanne d'Arc was placed with AC St.Nazaire-Penhoët in

---

[3] The midship section occupied by the multiple torpedo tubes and their reload lockers in the *Duguay-Trouin*s had to support the built-up accommodation for the officer cadets.

September 1928. Construction of the ship took just over three years.

NAME

Joan of Arc (**Jeanne d'Arc**, c.1412–31) is a national heroine of France and a Catholic saint. A peasant girl born in eastern France who claimed divine guidance, she led the French army to several important victories during the Hundred Years' War, which paved the way for the coronation of Charles VII as King of France. Tried by the English and condemned by an ecclesiastical court, she was burned as a witch at the stake

Right: *Jeanne d'Arc* on the slipway at Saint-Nazaire, shortly before her launch.

Left: The launch of *Jeanne d'Arc* from the Penhoët slipway at Saint-Nazaire on 14 February 1930.

when she was 19 years old. The name *Jeanne d'Arc* had been borne by four previous French warships, and from 1912 until the present day has been associated with school ships.

HULL AND GENERAL CONFIGURATION

With the hull and armament of a cruiser, the stern of a yacht, and a midship superstructure resembling that of an ocean liner, *Jeanne d'Arc* had a distinctive appearance. The built-up superstructure amidships housed the accommodation and associated facilities for the officer cadets. There were two slim funnels, the standard cruiser tripod foremast topped by a director, and a pole mainmast, all inclined at an angle of 5 degrees. The boat deck and aviation facilities were atop the officer cadet accommodation (i.e. one deck higher than in regular cruisers), and there was a single crane to handle the boats between the funnels.

MACHINERY

Jeanne d'Arc had a two-shaft propulsion system similar to that of the minelayer *Pluton*, but with horse-

power reduced from 57,000CV in the latter ship to 32,500CV. This made for much more spacious machinery rooms. The forward boiler room housed two boilers in tandem, offset to starboard to permit a small auxiliary boiler to be located to port. The latter was used to fire the main propulsion boilers, to provide steam for auxiliary machinery such as the windlass and the after capstan, for services for the crew, and for heating of the living spaces.

Directly abaft the forward boiler room was the forward engine room with the turbine set for the starboard shaft, comprising Parsons HP and LP geared turbines, two Rateau impulse cruise turbines, and a reverse turbine (housed in the exhaust casing of the LP turbine). The after machinery unit comprised the after boiler room, which housed the other two main boilers in tandem, offset to port, and the after engine room, with a second set of turbines driving the port shaft. The three-bladed propellers had a diameter of 3.65m.

The designed speed of 25 knots was comfortably attained on trials. In a one-hour forcing trial 43,000CV was achieved, for a maximum speed of 27.86 knots.

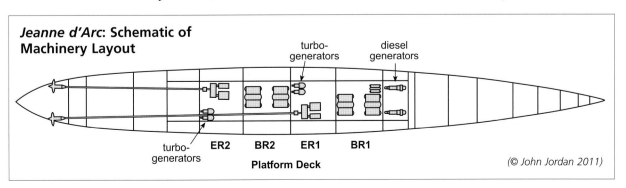

Jeanne d'Arc: Schematic of Machinery Layout

turbo-generators

diesel generators

turbo-generators   ER2   BR2   ER1   BR1

Platform Deck

(© *John Jordan 2011*)

Right: *Jeanne d'Arc at the end of her trials in 1931. (Chantiers de l'Atlantique)*

Endurance was estimated at 6670nm at 11 knots and 2300nm at 27 knots. Vibration was experienced between 13.5kts and 15kts, and again at higher speeds. This phenomenon was undoubtedly aggravated by the light construction of the hull, and it made rangefinding and optical observation difficult – the bridge and conning tower appear to have been more seriously affected than the DCT atop the tripod foremast.

The electrical generating machinery was exceptionally powerful for a ship of this size, reflecting the demands of accommodating the large number of personnel, particularly when the ship was in port. There were two turbo-generators each rated at 200kW in each of the engine rooms to provide power for electrical systems while underway, and two 120kW diesel generators in a separate dynamo room forward of the main machinery spaces (see drawing) for use when alongside. A third 120kW diesel generator was located above the level of the Main Deck for use in emergency.

GROUND TACKLE AND NAVIGATION
There were two bower anchors and one sheet anchor in hawsepipes forward, each of the Marrel-Byers type and weighing 5300kg. The stern anchor was 1700kg, and there were no fewer than six sheet anchors ranging from 1140kg to 85kg. The single counterbalanced rudder was 5.14m by 6.95m and weighed 8 tonnes.

PROTECTION
Compartmentation on *Jeanne d'Arc* was on a par with contemporary French cruisers, with sixteen watertight transverse bulkheads from the double bottom to the main deck. There were void spaces outboard of the magazines, around the diesel tanks, and between the boiler rooms and the oil fuel bunkers. Protection was limited to the reinforcement of certain key bulkheads. The magazines fore and aft had 20mm sides, and the conning tower was protected by 30mm of layered plating (15mm + 15mm); the communications tube was 20mm. There was no horizontal protection.

ARMAMENT
Main battery
The main gun of the *Jeanne d'Arc*, the 155/50 Mle 1920, was the same model as that fitted in the three *Duguay-Trouin*s. The turrets, however, were modified for the ship's role as a School Ship. Essentially this meant a significant enlargement of the gunhouse to permit groups of officer cadets to observe the loading

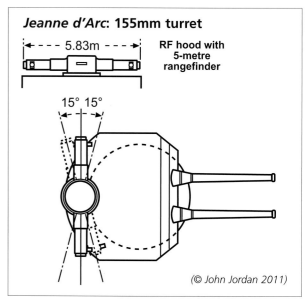

Jeanne d'Arc: 155mm turret
5.83m
RF hood with 5-metre rangefinder
15° 15°
(© John Jordan 2011)

and firing of the guns (see drawing); the loading mechanisms were unchanged.

The same 56.5kg SAP shell was fired; provision was 150 rounds per gun. Of the 150 charges provided (in bagged half-charges), 25 per cent were for night firing, with 2400kg of KCl in 15 per cent paraffin wax added to the standard charge.

Anti-aircraft weapons
There were four 75mm Mle 1924 guns on Mle 1922 mountings, which were located on either side of the boat deck. The two forward mountings were abeam the conning tower and the two after mountings amidships, outboard of the boat crane. The guns could be used against surface or aerial targets. There were 400 rounds per gun, together with 50 starshell, and 400 time fuses and 200 percussion fuses were provided. The two hoists were in the bridge structure.

There were also two 37mm Mle 1925 AA guns located on the boat deck, on either side of the second funnel, firing through open sights. Ready-use lockers close to the mountings each held eighteen cases of six rounds to enable fire to be opened quickly.

Fire control
Jeanne d'Arc received a fire control outfit on a par with contemporary Treaty cruisers; indeed, because of the ship's primary role of training future naval officers fire

BUILDING DATA AND GENERAL CHARACTERISTICS: *JEANNE D'ARC*

Name	Builder	Laid down	Launched	In service
1926 Programme				
Jeanne d'Arc	AC St Nazaire-Penhoët	31 Aug 1928	14 Feb 1930	6 Oct 1931

Displacement:	6496 tons standard
	7894 tonnes normal
	8928 tonnes full load
Length:	160.0m pp, 170.0m oa
Beam:	17.5m wl
Draught:	5.7m max. (normal)
Machinery:	Four du Temple small-tube boilers, 20kg/cm^2; two-shaft Parsons geared steam turbines for 32,500CV;
	speed 25kts (designed)
Oil fuel:	1450 tonnes; radius 6670nm at 11kts, 2900nm at 24kts
Armament:	Eight 155mm/50 Mle 1920-26 in twin mountings Mle 1926 (1200 rounds);
	four 75mm/50 Mle 1924 HA in single mountings Mle 1922 (1600 rounds + 20 starshell);
	two 37mm/50 Mle 1925 AA in single mountings (1800 rounds);
	two tubes for 550mm torpedoes Mle 1923D in two single mountings Mle 1926S (+4 reloads)
Protection:	*Magazines*: 20mm
	CT: 30mm
Complement:	482 + 156 officer cadets

Weights

Hull:	3531t
Protection:	69t
Armament (incl. torpedoes):	647t
Propulsion:	1562t
Fittings:	1203t
Munitions:	171t
OF, RFW:	711t
Normal Displ.	**7894t**

control provision was not only exceptionally complete but was regularly upgraded to ensure that officer cadets had access to the latest equipment. The director control tower atop the tripod foremast was the *type croiseur de 10,000 tonnes* model, and was initially fitted with the standard 5-metre SOM coincidence rangefinder and a 4-metre Zeiss stereo model for scartometry. The director provided data for a Mle 1923 fire control computer housed in the transmitting station (*PC Artillerie*) below decks, and for the fire control station in the conning tower. The fire control computer generated an angle of train for the turrets, taking into account parallax, and an angle of elevation for the guns; these were then transmitted to the turrets via a Granat follow-the-pointer system (or, in the event of a systems failure, a special telephone network designated '*telephone* 17')

The *Poste de tir* in the conning tower was equipped with periscopic glasses. These enabled it to generate an angle of train which was then transmitted to the *Poste central artillerie*. Both the director control tower and the conning tower were equipped for remote firing of the guns (taking into account movement of the platform), although the required systems were installed only in September 1933.

The emergency fire control position was at the rear end of turret III, which was equipped for the purpose with a second 5-metre SOM coincidence rangefinder. There was a third 5-metre rangefinder atop turret II. Both turrets could send range and bearing data to the transmitting station (ranging was reliable out to 15,000m), but only turret III had a control position which enabled it to coordinate the firing of all four turrets.

Like other French cruisers *Jeanne d'Arc* was

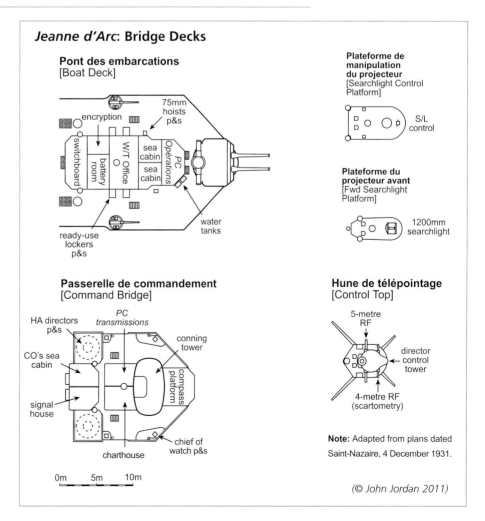

Jeanne d'Arc: Bridge Decks

Pont des embarcations
[Boat Deck]

Passerelle de commandement
[Command Bridge]

Plateforme de manipulation du projecteur
[Searchlight Control Platform]

Plateforme du projecteur avant
[Fwd Searchlight Platform]

Hune de télépointage
[Control Top]

Note: Adapted from plans dated Saint-Nazaire, 4 December 1931.

(© John Jordan 2011)

equipped with a tactical rangefinder which could be employed as a secondary rangefinder for the main guns and also provided data for torpedo firing. It was an open 3-metre model, as in *Algérie* and the new light cruisers, and was located on the searchlight control platform above the conning tower.

The two HA directors, each with a 3-metre OPL stereo rangefinder, were fitted in the upper bridge wings shortly after completion. The associated fire control table, Mle 1930, was not installed until September 1934. There was a free-standing 1-metre OPL stereo rangefinder to provide firing data for the two 37mm AA guns.

Torpedoes

Jeanne d'Arc was fitted with two single trainable 550mm torpedo tubes Mle 1926S, located on the First Deck outboard of the fore-funnel (see drawing of Accommodation for Officer Cadets). There was provision for six Mle 1923D torpedoes, two in the tubes and the remaining four stowed in deck-edge lockers abaft the tubes; the six warheads were stowed in hinged deck-edge lockers, as in the *Duguay-Trouins*. There was a large torpedo workshop between the tubes.

In peacetime only four Mle 1923D were embarked, and the other were stored ashore. They were replaced by two exercise torpedoes Mle 1924M. The latter had a range of 12,000m at 25 knots and 7000m at 32 knots and were fitted with dummy warheads (*cônes de choc*).

AVIATION INSTALLATIONS

As designed, *Jeanne d'Arc* was to have been fitted with two catapults for CAMS 37 reconnaissance seaplanes. However, the catapults were never ordered, the pedestals being modified as rest positions for the aircraft, which were launched from the water. Two 17.7-metre handling derricks, powered by two 22hp winches, were fitted to the base of the mainmast, and there were two 15-metre booms for handling the aircraft when in harbour. Two stern tanks held 6000 litres of aviation fuel, and there was a special trolley with a capacity of 300 litres to move the fuel from the tanks to the aircraft.

The inability to launch aircraft from catapults was recognised as unsatisfactory, as it restricted operations in higher sea states.[4] From October 1936 to July 1938 *Jeanne d'Arc* embarked a special training version of the CAMS 37, the 37-11. It was unarmed, but in addition to the pilot could accommodate a trainee pilot plus two passengers. From October 1938 to May 1940 the ship operated two Loire 130 in place of the CAMS 37. These proved better suited to the instruction of officer cadets.

ACCOMMODATION FOR THE OFFICER CADETS

The accommodation, services and instruction facilities for the officer cadets were kept separate from the crew spaces, and were distributed between the First Deck and the Forecastle Deck between the bridge and the after 155mm turrets. The messes and instruction rooms were flanked by broad promenade decks, as on an ocean liner (see drawing). The First Deck had four messes disposed on either side of the centre-line, each for twelve midshipmen with washplaces and heads between them. Every mess had a central table, with bookcases and lockers to the sides. In accordance with tradition the officer cadets slung hammocks from the deck beams and stowed them in the morning. Abaft

---

[4] It was generally easier to land in moderate sea states than it was to take off.

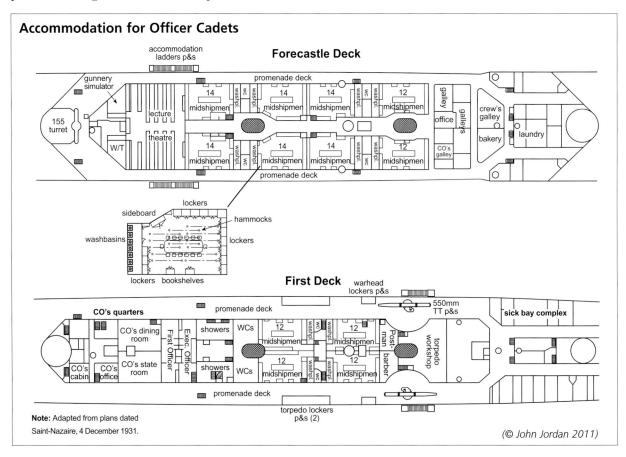

Accommodation for Officer Cadets

Note: Adapted from plans dated Saint-Nazaire, 4 December 1931.

(© John Jordan 2011)

the messes were showers and heads, followed by the accommodation for the First Officer, Executive Officer and the CO. The quarters for the ship's captain were unusually well-appointed because of his important role in representing France during port visits. At the forecastle end there were well-equipped medical facilities including a sick bay, a consulting room, an isolation ward – many of the ship's port visits were to the tropics – and an operating theatre.

Most of the accommodation and the main instruction spaces for the officer cadets were located on the deck above, the Forecastle Deck. There were eight messes, each for twelve to fourteen officer cadets, on either side of a broad passageway. The messes were laid out in similar fashion to those on the First Deck, with washplaces and heads between each pair. At the forward end were the galleys for the officer cadets, the officers and the ship's crew, and the laundry. At the after end there was a lecture theatre able to accommodate all 156 midshipmen and their instructors, with a dais and chart lockers at its after end; this could be converted to a cinema, or to a dance hall for receptions given on board. There was a space abaft the lecture theatre which was used specifically for gunnery instruction.

BOATS
The outfit when the ship was first completed was as follows:

– one 12.6-metre motor boat
– one 11-metre motor pinnace
– one 11-metre pulling pinnace
– two 10-metre steam pinnaces
– one 10-metre motor launch
– one 10-metre pulling cutter
– one 9-metre motor boat
– two 7-metre whalers
– one 5-metre dinghy

The number of 10/11-metre boats reflected the need for increased capacity to get the officer cadets ashore on visits to distant anchorages.

In 1932 the two steam pinnaces were replaced by 10.8-metre motor boats, and the 10-metre motor launch by a second 11-metre motor pinnace. With the exception of the whalers, which were on davits, the

boats were on crutches and were handled by a centreline crane similar to the model embarked on the *Duguay-Trouin*s. It had a reach of 11.7m and a capacity of 12 tonnes.

MODIFICATIONS 1931 TO 1942
During 1933 the 5-metre SOM coincidence rangefinders in the DCT and in turret III were replaced by OPL stereoscopic models, and the HA directors were fitted. The associated Mle 1930 fire control computer was installed the following year, but the single HA plotting room permitted the engagement of only a single target to port or to starboard.

The year 1935 saw the installation of four twin 13.2mm Hotchkiss MG Mle 1929. Two were mounted in the bridge wings, and two at the after end of the boat deck. At the same time splinter shields were fitted to the four 75mm HA guns. A direction-finding station was installed to monitor transmissions in the 200–3000m waveband, and a new 'pinger'-type active sonar with a range of 60m to 2000m replaced the existing ultrasonic apparatus. During 1935–6 the radio outfit was completely renewed.

In 1938 light splinter shields were fitted to the twin 13.2mm MG, the other AA weapons were refurbished, and defective electrical cabling – a common problem in French warships of the period – was replaced. The 3-metre rangefinder was raised, and Loire 130 aircraft embarked for the first time.

With the deterioration of the international situation in the late 1930s there was a requirement to increase the number of officers being trained. The torpedo maintenance shop was converted to become a thirteenth mess for officer cadets; the maximum number which could be embarked now rose from 156 to 172. An improvised depth-charge rack built by the ship's crew was installed on the quarterdeck, and fifteen 35kg depth charges were embarked.

Immobilisation in the West Indies from June 1940 meant that few further modifications could be carried out. The foretopmast was shortened by 5m, and the crow's nest disembarked together with the lower yard. This entailed some modifications to the radio antennae. A degaussing cable was installed, and waterproof blast bags fitted to the main guns. The Loire 130 aircraft were disembarked.

Above, left: On 5 October 1935 François Piétri, the current Navy Minister, gives the traditional address to the officers under training on the quarterdeck of *Jeanne d'Arc*, prior to her departure for the 1935–6 world cruise. *(Philippe Caresse collection)*

Above, right: *Jeanne d'Arc* sailing from Portsmouth, UK, on 5 May 1937, with the two CAMS 37-11 seaplanes embarked from October 1936 to April 1938. *(Stephen Dent collection)*

EMILE BERTIN

INTRODUCTION

By 1925, the year that *Pluton* was authorised, the French minelaying strategy had been further refined, and the length of the proposed off-shore minefields established at 7.5nm. At the maximum spacing of 40m this implied a field of 350 mines. These estimates led to a request by the *Conseil Supérieur* for an enlarged *Pluton* (an STCN study indicated a displacement of 7500 tonnes), which was considered in committee on 10 March 1925. However, there was much discussion regarding the practical utility of such a vessel, and this line of thinking was eventually to be overtaken by other considerations.

In the interim the Marine Nationale had conducted its first major review of cruiser construction since 1922. It had become apparent to the French, as well as to the British, that the acquisition of costly 10,000-ton Treaty cruisers in the requisite numbers to support the fleet and to police the empire was essentially unsustainable. Despite the failure of the Geneva Conference of 1927 to secure lower 'qualitative' limits for future cruisers, it was clear that the British would be pushing hard at the next scheduled naval arms limitation conference[5] for ships with a maximum displacement of 7500 tons standard and a maximum gun calibre of 6in (152mm).

The other new factor was that France's main rival in the Mediterranean, the Italian Regia Marina, was about to embark on the construction of a series of fast 5000-ton cruisers armed with eight 6in guns. Intended as a counter the French *contre-torpilleurs*, the Italian ships (the 'Condottieri' class) had a designed speed of 36.5 knots and minimal protection. They were also capable of minelaying: 78–169 mines could be embarked, depending on type.

In 1928 the Naval General Staff established three criteria for the new ships: they were to be essentially unprotected, with a maximum standard displacement of 6000 tonnes; they would be fast, powered by a propulsion plant using high-pressure, superheated steam; and they would be armed with 152mm guns both in order to conform to the anticipated future treaty restrictions and to match the armament of the Italian ships.

In the same year it was decided to abandon the construction of specialised surface minelayers. Instead, all light ships – cruisers, *contre-torpilleurs* and colonial sloops – would be fitted with removable mine-rails. The first step was the redesign of the last eight *contre-torpilleurs* of the *2400 tonnes* series (*Milan*, *Epervier* and the six *Vauquelins*), which were given a reconfigured stern to enable them to carry fifty Breguet mines on quarterdeck rails. The second was to incorporate this latter feature into the prototype for the new 152mm gun cruiser, which by 1929 was being referred to as a *croiseur mouilleur de mines* (the same designation as *Pluton*, despite the fundamental differences in conception).

DESIGN AND CONSTRUCTION

The first studies for the new cruiser were commissioned from the STCN in December 1928. Characteristics were quickly established as follows: displacement 5980tW, length overall 177m, propulsive power 102,000CV for 34kts, and range 3000nm at 18kts.[6] These characteristics were to remain essentially unchanged between the drawing board and the slipway.

The ship was authorised under the 1930 Programme with the number CL1, and on completion was designated *croiseur de 2e classe* in accordance with the classification system adopted by the Marine Nationale following the London Treaty.[7] The contract for *Emile Bertin* was accorded not to one of the major French

---

[5] Under the Washington Treaty provisions this had to take place before 1932. In the event it would be convened in London in early 1930.

[6] A figure which strongly suggests that the new 152mm-gun cruisers would be 'fleet' units rather than for trade protection.

[7] The treaty designated these ships 'category (b)' cruisers; the original French 'CL' number suggests that the ship was originally typed '*croiseur léger*' (light cruiser).

Right: *Emile Bertin* on 6 August 1934, during her full power trials on the Penmarc'h range in southern Brittany. Turret II is still without its guns, and the main and HA directors, the 90mm HA guns and the catapult have yet to be embarked. *(Philippe Caresse collection)*

Emile Bertin: Profile & Plan views

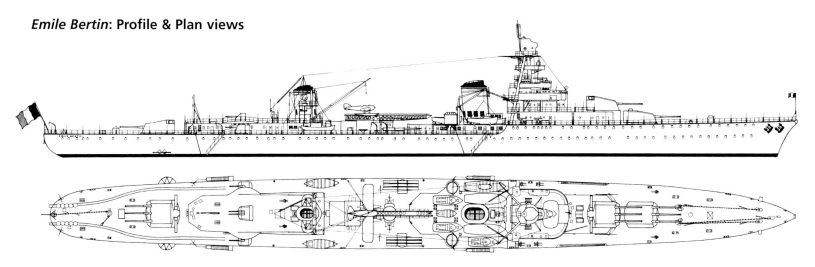

Profile and plan views of *Emile Bertin*, based on the official plans produced at Saint-Nazaire and dated 20 September 1935. These show the projected 37mm Mle 1933 twin mountings in place abreast the bridge structure, not the four Mle 1925 single mountings fitted on completion. The aircraft atop the single catapult is the GL 832 floatplane embarked on *Emile Bertin* and the three older 8000-tonne cruisers.

(© John Jordan 2010)

Emile Bertin: Inboard Profile

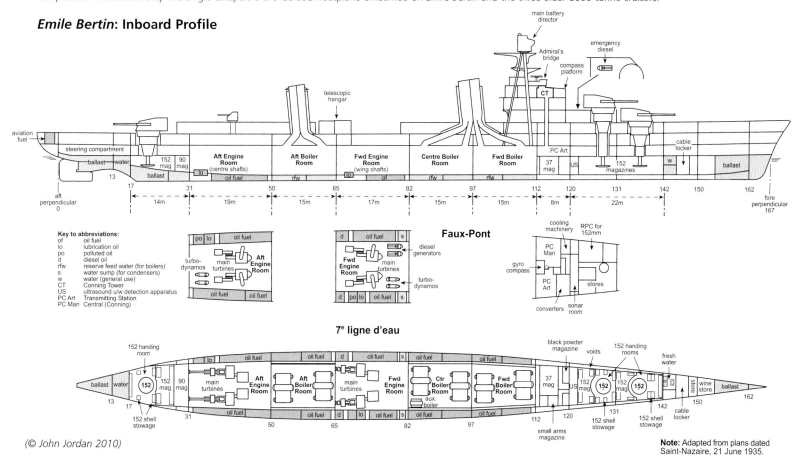

(© John Jordan 2010)

Note: Adapted from plans dated Saint-Nazaire, 21 June 1935.

naval dockyards, but to the AC St Nazaire-Penhoët. The contract, signed on 26 August 1931, specified acceptance of the completed ship at Brest on 30 June 1934. In the event the ship was delivered two days early, a performance which reflects great credit on the shipbuilders given the radical innovations in the construction of the ship's hull and the design of the propulsion machinery. Only the late delivery and installation of the main and secondary guns and their related control systems, all of which were newly developed, delayed the ship's entry into service until 17 May of the following year. In the interim, as the prototype of a new generation of cruisers, *Emile Bertin* underwent extensive sea trials to assess the performance of the new superheated propulsion machinery, achieving remarkable results in the process.

NAME

The name *Emile Bertin* honoured one of France's greatest naval constructors, who had recently died. **Emile**-Louis **Bertin** (1840–1924) had been closely associated with the design of innovative but powerfully armed warships such as armoured cruisers; allocating his name to a light but powerfully-armed cruiser with innovative propulsion machinery was therefore particularly appropriate.

Emile Bertin: Hull Sections

Frame 4 (from fwd):
Rudder

mines   mines

junior officers' wardroom

rope store · steering gear · rope store

Frame 21 (from fwd):
Turret III

152 turret

mines   mines

junior officers' bathroom   p/w   p/w   p/w   junior officers' WCs

armourer's workshop & store   junior officers' store

handing room

Frame 41 (from fwd):
Aft Engine Room

90mm CAD

90mm ready-use ammunition

90mm CAS   90mm CAS

senior officer's cabin   p/w   archives & codes   p/w   Chief of Staff's cabin

oil fuel   **Aft Engine Room**   oil fuel

Frame 56 (from fwd):
Aft Boiler Room

aerial spreaders

1.2m searchlight projectors p&s

aircraft cranes p&s   searchlight controls p&s

W/T Office   conver-ters

cells   p/w   engine room workshop

cable tunnels p&s   oil fuel   oil fuel   voids p&s

Aft Boiler Room

rfw   rfw

Note: Adapted from plans dated Saint-Nazaire, 21 June 1935.

Frame 75 (from aft):
Fwd Engine Room

GL832 floatplane

catapult   torpedo warhead lockers p&s

550mm triple TT p&s

CPO's cabin   p/w   written orders   POs' store   p/w   CPO's cabin

oil fuel   **Fwd Engine Room**   oil fuel

Frame 114 (from fwd):
Command Spaces

3-metre rangefinder

Conning Tower

Passerelle de navigation

Adm's day cabin   p/w

Passerelle inférieure

p/w   p/w   37mm p&s

Teugue

CPO's cabin   p/w   shop   p/w   infirmary

Premier pont

seamen's mess   seamen's mess

Pont principal

PC 152mm   **Poste Central**   PC Man.

Faux-pont

small arms mag.   37mm magazine

void   void

Frame 128 (from aft):
Turret II

152 turret

emergency diesel   dirty linen

sickbay   p/w   seamen's washplace

seamen's mess   seamen's mess

provisions store   p/w   store room

void   handing room   void

Frame 147 (from aft):
Capstan

capstan

seamen's mess

seamen's mess

cable locker

(© John Jordan 2010)

Emile Bertin: Master Frame

Premier Pont   18   16   18   20   18

Pont Principal   12   9   12   16

cable tunnel

Fwd Engine Room   6   oil fuel   14

5   14

oil fuel   10

bilge keel

16

Note: Adapted from plans dated Saint-Nazaire, 1934.

(© John Jordan 2010)

HULL AND GENERAL CONFIGURATION

The requirement for high speed necessitated careful design of the hull. A relatively high length to beam ratio of 10.5:1 was adopted. The raised forecastle combined gentle sheer with a pronounced flare at the bow, so that the fore-deck was dry in a moderate sea. The cruiser stern, '*en cul de poule*', was similar to that of the three-shaft Treaty cruisers of the *Suffren* class, and had been adopted for the contemporary *contre-torpilleurs* of the *Vauquelin* class to ensure that mines were laid well clear of the ship's hull. It had the additional effect of conserving the trim of the ship at high speed, when the four propellers exerted powerful downward forces on the stern.

Major efforts were made to minimise the weight of the hull and superstructures. Longitudinal construction was again employed, and extensive use was made of welding as in the Treaty cruiser *Algérie* (see Chapter 5). The hull was of standard 50kg steel, riveting being employed only for the 'strength' elements of the ship's framing. Duralumin was used extensively for external and internal fittings. The total weight of the hull, including protection, accounted for only 46.3 per cent of Washington displacement. In a departure from previous practice, wood deck planking was abandoned in favour of a red-brown linoleum, the forecastle deck forward of turret II being bare steel painted with a dark grey non-slip paint. This would be repeated in

BUILDING DATA AND GENERAL CHARACTERISTICS: *EMILE BERTIN*

Name	Builder	Laid down	Launched	In service
1930 Programme				
Emile Bertin	AC St Nazaire-Penhoët	18 Aug 1931	9 May 1933	17 May 1934

Displacement:	5886 tons standard
	6530 tonnes normal
	8480 tonnes full load
Length:	167m pp, 177m oa
Beam:	15.84m
Draught:	5.33m max. (normal)
Machinery:	Six Penhoët small-tube boilers, 27kg/cm^2 (325°); four-shaft Parsons geared steam turbines for 102,000CV; speed 34kts (designed)
Oil fuel:	1360 tonnes; radius 6000nm at 15kts, 1100nm at 33kts
Armament:	Nine 152mm/55 Mle 1930 in triple mountings Mle 1930 (1300 rounds); four 90mm/50 Mle 1926 HA in one twin mounting Mle 1930 and two single mountings Mle 1926 (1000 rounds + 200 starshell); four 37mm/50 Mle 1925 AA in single mountings (2500 rounds per gun); eight 13.2mm/76 Mle 1929 Hotchkiss MG in twin mountings Mle 1931 (2500 rounds per gun); six tubes for 550mm torpedoes Mle 1923D in two triple 1928T mountings; 84 Breguet B4 mines
Aircraft:	Two GL 832 floatplanes
Protection:	*Magazines*: 30mm
	Deck: 20mm
	CT: 30mm sides, 20mm roof
	Turrets: none
Complement:	543 peace (+24 as flagship), 675 war

Weights

Hull:	2646t
Protection:	124t
Turrets:	338t
Propulsion:	1374t
Fittings:	809t
Catapult/mine tracks:	37t
Consumables:	537t
Washington Displ.	**5984t**

the early 7600-ton cruisers, although wood planking would be reinstated for later units of the class (see Chapter 6).

Protection was minimal. However, particular care was taken over the compartmentation of the ship. There were thirteen transverse bulkheads extending from the keel to the upper deck, and these were fully watertight with no penetrations other than for cables and pipework below the main deck. The fourteen watertight compartments thereby created were served by nine 30-tonne pumps, one of which was located in each of the five main machinery spaces.

The external appearance and layout of *Emile Bertin* was a cross between the contemporary Treaty cruiser *Dupleix* and the *contre-torpilleurs* of the *Le Fantasque* class. The 'cruiser' aspects of her design are evidence by the heavy turrets fore and aft, and the capacious bridge structure with its tripod mast topped by the fire control director for the main guns. However, the tripod was lower than in the 10,000-ton cruisers, and the low, raked funnels were reminiscent of the *Le Fantasque*s and gave the ship a 'racy' appearance which matched her high speed. As in the *contre-torpilleurs* the machinery spaces took up a considerable proportion of the hull,[8] pushing the main turrets and their magazines farther towards the ends of the ship.

---

[8] The three boiler rooms and two engine rooms occupied 81m – 43.5 per cent of the length between perpendiculars. The corresponding figure for *Dupleix* was 36.5 per cent.

MACHINERY

The advanced propulsion plant occupied more than 43 per cent of the ship's length, yet accounted for only 23 per cent of the ship's displacement. It comprised six Penhoët boilers with superheating, and four sets of Parsons single-reduction turbines, disposed in a unit arrangement. The six Penhoët boilers were offset from the ship's axis in three boiler rooms, two of which (compartments G and H) had their uptakes combined into the broad fore funnel, with the narrower after funnel combining the uptakes from the third (compartment J). The boilers operated at a pressure of 27kg/cm^2, with superheated steam at 330°.

The forward machinery room (compartment I), which housed the two sets of turbines driving the wing shafts, was located between the second and third boiler rooms. The after machinery room (compartment K), housing the turbines driving the inner shafts, was located abaft the third boiler room (see inboard profile). Each set of turbines comprised HP, MP and LP turbines operating in series, with the reversing turbine in the casing for the LP turbine and a separate cruise turbine. The four three-bladed Brard propellers were 3.6m in diameter, and rotated outwards with the engines running ahead.

Four turbo-generators each of 200kW, distributed between the fore and after engine rooms and located on platforms at the level of the First Platform Deck, provided the ship's electrical power while underway. The forward engine room also housed two of the three 100kW diesel generators for use when alongside; the third (emergency) diesel was at forecastle deck level in the deckhouse immediately abaft turret II.

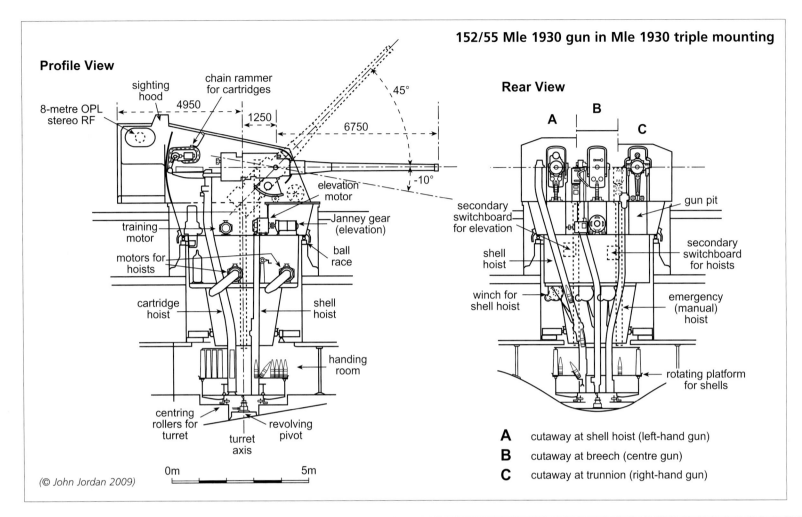

152/55 Mle 1930 gun in Mle 1930 triple mounting

Profile View

8-metre OPL stereo RF

sighting hood

chain rammer for cartridges

4950

1250

6750

45°

-10°

elevation motor

Janney gear (elevation)

training motor

ball race

motors for hoists

cartridge hoist

shell hoist

handing room

centring rollers for turret

turret axis

revolving pivot

(© John Jordan 2009)

0m   5m

Rear View

A   B   C

secondary switchboard for elevation

gun pit

shell hoist

secondary switchboard for hoists

winch for shell hoist

emergency (manual) hoist

rotating platform for shells

A   cutaway at shell hoist (left-hand gun)
B   cutaway at breech (centre gun)
C   cutaway at trunnion (right-hand gun)

Remarkable figures were achieved on trials. During her eight-hour 'normal power' trial on 1 August 1934, *Emile Bertin* averaged 36.33 knots with 108,026CV. Much of her heavy equipment, including the main guns and fire control directors, had yet to be embarked; on the other hand these trials were conducted in difficult sea conditions, with 3–4-metre waves. On 8 August, at Washington displacement, a one-hour 'forcing' trial gave an average of 39.67 knots with 137,908CV. In service *Emile Bertin* could comfortably sustain 33 knots. Fuel consumption was in line with expectations, giving a projected range of 6000nm at 15kts on cruise turbines alone, and 2800nm at 20kts/1100nm at 33kts on the main turbines.

High performance was not without its cost, however. The ship's first post-trials docking at Brest on 15 August revealed serious erosion and deformation of the Brard propellers, which were returned to the manufacturer for repair. At a further docking in Brest the following January similar damage was found, and a new set of propellers was subsequently ordered. These were installed in July 1936 but on 13 August, during a 35-knot sortie, there were severe vibrations aft which caused a breakdown in turret III. A further inspection in dry dock revealed that the propellers had again suffered serious deformations and erosion from cavitation. In order to minimise disruption to the ship's programme, a major refit was brought forward during which the propellers were repaired. Meanwhile, a new set of propellers with a modified configuration were ordered from Brard. These were fitted in 1938–9, after which the ship appears to have suffered no serious problems.

GROUND TACKLE AND NAVIGATION

The three main anchors (two bower, one sheet) were in hawsepipes forward: two to starboard and the third to port. They were of the Byers type and each weighed 4900kg. The single stern anchor weighed 1400kg. Two kedge anchors of 1140kg and 890kg were initially provided. The larger of these was subsequently replaced by two anchors of 600kg and 200kg respectively, which were stowed below decks. There was a single counter-balanced rudder with a surface area of 24.5m².

Emile Bertin proved to be a remarkably seaworthy ship in service, although the light construction of the hull resulted in some problems. There was some working of the bow section in a heavy head sea, enforcing a reduction in speed, and the hull structure beneath the turrets had to be reinforced following trials in order to permit salvo firing. On the other hand, *Emile Bertin* was a good seaboat, and the roll period of 12 seconds coincided almost exactly with the rate of fire of the main artillery, making her a remarkably steady gunnery platform. The only significant negative feature was her large turning circle (800m with the single axial rudder at 32 degrees); this was a common defect with other contemporary French warships with a high length/beam ratio, particularly the *contre-torpilleurs*.

PROTECTION

Emile Bertin had only light protection on a par with the earlier *Duguay-Trouins*. Only the conning tower and the sides of the magazines were armoured; the plating comprised two layers of 60kg steel each 15mm thick.

The turrets were virtually unprotected – the weight of each triple turret was 112 tonnes, as compared with 172 tonnes for the same turret when installed in the *La Galissonnière* class (see Chapter 6). The total weight of armour was a mere 123.8 tonnes, representing 4.5 per cent of the displacement.

ARMAMENT
Main battery
The 152mm/55 Mle 1930 was specially developed for the second generation of inter-war cruisers. Derived from the 138.6mm/50 Mle 1929 fitted in the *contre-torpilleurs* of the *Le Fantasque* class, it had the same semi-automatic sliding breech mechanism as the latter in place of the traditional Welin interrupted screw breech of earlier medium guns. It was also the first cruiser gun to use 'cased' ammunition, the propellant charge being in a single cartridge rather than separate bags. All of these features were adopted to secure more rapid fire than was possible with the 155mm guns of the *Duguay-Trouins*, which had a firing cycle little better than the 203mm gun of the Treaty cruisers.

A completely new turret and replenishment system was required to ensure that the above features delivered on their promise. The Marine-Homécourt turret was the first multi-gun turret to enter service with the Marine Nationale.[9] It was constructed of riveted steel, and weighed 112 tonnes. The guns were in individual cradles, and training and elevation were each powered by a 60hp Léonard electric motor with hydraulic drive. Full remote power control was planned, but was not installed until the ship's refit in 1938 due to delays in development. The guns were driven together by the elevating gear with differentials for individual correction between the hydraulic drive and the elevating worms. Although maximum elevation for firing was 45 degrees, the guns could be loaded only between –5 degrees and +15 degrees.

Shell rooms and magazines were separate but on the same level, and shared a common handing room. There were three shell hoists and two double cartridge hoists for each turret, all of the pusher type. This meant that the shells and cartridges were delivered directly to the gunhouse – the earlier cruiser turrets had two-stage hoists with transfer from the lower hoists to the upper cage hoists in the working chamber. On arrival in the gunhouse the shells were tipped by hand into a slide which transferred them to the power-operated loading gear. The breech mechanism was arranged to open automatically, and there was a catapult rammer for shells with a chain rammer for cartridges, both of which were on arms which extended from the gun and elevated with it.

The two standard projectiles were the OPf Mle 1931 SAP shell, and the OEA Mle 1936 HE shell, which could be fired against either surface or aerial targets (a Schneider time fuse was fitted in the latter role). Both weighed approximately 55–56kg. Using a C1 combat charge and the OPf Mle 1931, maximum range was 26,500m against surface targets with a muzzle velocity

---

9 The *Normandie* and *Lyon* classes of battleship designed in 1913–14 would have had quadruple 34cm turrets, but the ships were never completed. Although nominally multi-gun turrets, the quads were actually two twins side by side, with a bulkhead dividing the gunhouses.

152/55 MLE 1930

Gun Data

Construction:	Autofretted jacket and 'A' tube with loose liner
Breech mechanism:	Vertical sliding block
Weight of gun:	7.78t
Ammunition type:	Separate
Projectiles:	OPf(K) Mle 1931 (54.50kg/56.03kg) OEA Mle 1936 (55.09kg)
Propellant:	BM11 (17.1kg)
Muzzle velocity:	870m/s
Max. range:	26,500m (45°)

Mounting Data

Designation:	Triple Mle 1930
Weight of turret:	112t
Distance apart gun axes:	1.65m
Loading angle:	-5° / +15°
Elevation of guns:	-10° / +45°
Max. training speed:	12°/sec
Max. elevating speed:	8°/sec
Firing cycle (per gun):	8rpm theoretical 4–5rpm practical

Notes:

OPf	*Obus de Perforation*	Semi Armour Piercing (SAP)
OEA	*Obus Explosif en Acier*	High Explosive (HE)

The OPf 1931 and OPfK 1937 shells were SAP with a burster of 1.7kg picric acid; the K extension denoted a shell with colorant.

of 870m/s. There was ready-use stowage in each of the three handing rooms for seven full rounds. Total magazine capacity was 1315 rounds – the equivalent of 145 rounds per gun.

There were significant teething problems when the 152mm mounting first entered service. It proved impossible to obtain the high designed firing cycle of 8rpm, and numerous jams related to the complex loading system and the safety locks were experienced. *Emile Bertin* executed no fewer than twenty-four gunnery trials between 1934 and 1938, and many more trials were also conducted with the first three units of the *La Galissonnière* class (see Chapter 8). The problems were largely resolved by the outbreak of war, but 4-5 rounds per minute per gun was generally the maximum practical figure.

ANTI-AIRCRAFT WEAPONS

The secondary armament, based on the 90mm/50 Mle 1926 gun about to enter service on the 'Treaty'

cruisers *Colbert*, *Foch* and *Dupleix*, was intended to provide defence against torpedo boats as well as aircraft. Like the 152mm Mle 1930, it was a modern semi-automatic weapon with a sliding breech. Maximum elevation in the anti-aircraft rôle was 80 degrees, and the use of fixed ammunition resulted in a high rate of fire (theoretically 13/14rpm, although the gun proved difficult to load above 60 degrees). The standard OEA Mle 1925 HE shell was fitted with an impact fuse for surface targets and a time fuse for aerial targets; starshell Mle 1926 and incendiary Mle 1927 could also be fired.

According to the original design plans *Emile Bertin* was to have had only a single centre-line twin mounting (Mle 1930) atop the after deckhouse, but in November 1930 it was decided to fit additional single mountings (Mle 1926) on either side of the twin mounting at upper-deck level. The reason for this unusual disposition was that all three mountings had to be served by the single centre-line magazine originally provided for the twin mounting. Although this magazine had a capacity of 1422 rounds (the standard combat loading was 1000 plus 200 starshell for the twin mounting), and was therefore just about adequate for the task, the capacity of the single Sautter-Harlé electric hoist was unaltered. This provided ten cases each with two rounds per minute – insufficient even to supply the axial twin mounting at its maximum rate of fire! Moreover, the hoist exited onto the upper deck, whence the rounds had to be distributed to the mountings by hand.

The centre-line mounting enjoyed excellent all-round arcs (320 degrees), while those of the single mountings were inevitably more restricted (75 degrees fore and aft of either beam). Both single and twin mountings were provided with 5mm splinter shields.

It was originally envisaged that the *Emile Bertin* would be fitted with the new twin 37mm mounting (Mle 1933) currently under development. Four were to be installed at forecastle deck level abeam the bridge structure. In the event development of this weapon was delayed, and on completion the ship was given a temporary outfit of four single 37mm Mle 1925, a

37/50 MLE 1933

Gun Data

Weight of gun:	300kg
Ammunition type:	Fixed
Projectiles:	OEA Mle 1925 (0.73kg) OI Mle 1924 (0.73kg)
Propellant:	BM2 in cartridge (0.2kg)
Complete round:	
Weight:	2.8kg
Dimensions:	408mm x 61mm
Muzzle velocity:	810m/s
Max. range:	8000m theoretical 5000m effective

Mounting Data

Mounting designation:	CAD Mle 1933
Weight of mounting:	??t
Elevation of guns:	-15° / +80°
Firing cycle (per gun):	30rpm theoretical 15–21rpm practical

Notes:

CAD	*Contre-Avions Double*	AA twin mounting
OEA	*Obus Explosif en Acier*	High Explosive (HE)
OI	*Obus Incendiaire*	Incendiary

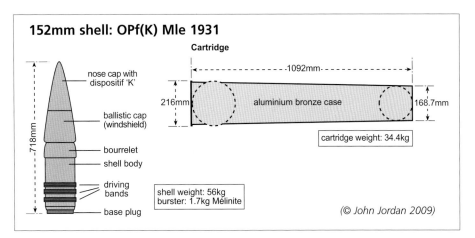

152mm shell: OPf(K) Mle 1931

- nose cap with dispositif 'K'
- ballistic cap (windshield)
- bourrelet
- shell body
- driving bands
- base plug

718mm

Cartridge

1092mm
216mm   aluminium bronze case   168.7mm

cartridge weight: 34.4kg

shell weight: 56kg
burster: 1.7kg Mélinite

(© John Jordan 2009)

Above: The forecastle of *Emile Bertin*, with her turrets trained to starboard, 1936.

robust and reliable weapon which nevertheless suffered from an inadequate rate of fire (20rpm). The twin mountings Mle 1933 were fitted in their place only in late 1939. The magazine, which had a capacity of 2500 rounds per gun, was located immediately forward of boiler room 1, beneath the mountings. Single Sautter-Harlé hoists were provided port and starboard, each with a capacity of ten seven-round cases per minute, and there were ready-use lockers close to the mountings.

The 37mm mountings were complemented by four of the new twin 13.2mm Hotchkiss MG Mle 1929, of which two were mounted abeam turret I on the forecastle deck, and the other pair on the after deckhouse. These had a high rate of fire (450rpm) but insufficient range to be truly effective.

Fire control

The main DCT, located atop the tripod foremast, was similar to the ones fitted in the Treaty cruisers, and was associated with a similar Mle 1924 fire control computer in the transmitting station. It was initially fitted with a 5-metre base coincidence rangefinder (SOM 50 Mle 1926) for ranging and a 3-metre stereo RF for scartometry. It housed positions for:

– the Gunnery Control Officer (equipped with periscopic binoculars);

Left: The director for the main guns is prominent in this photo of *Emile Bertin* taken in Martinique some time between 1940 and 1943. Note the long-base 8-metre stereo rangefinder fitted in the late 1930s, and the smaller 3-metre stereo model in the forward lower compartment of the director, which was used to measure the distance between the shell splashes and the target – a technique called scartometry. *(US Navy)*

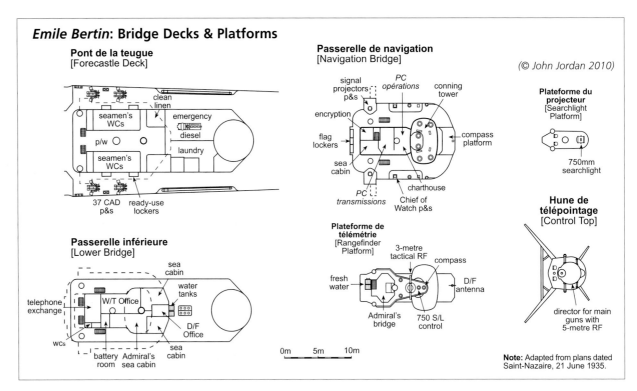

Emile Bertin: Bridge Decks & Platforms

(© John Jordan 2010)

Note: Adapted from plans dated Saint-Nazaire, 21 June 1935.

– the Rate Officer;
– the Cross-Leveller;
– the Spotting Officer;
– the director trainer and layer (equipped with stereoscopic binoculars);
– the two rangetakers (lower level).

The DCT proved to be the weak link in the fire control system. It was incapable of making successive turns in the same direction, and its training rate was significantly slower than that of the turrets (a full turn took 70 seconds). In rapid combat manoeuvres the director was often temporarily 'disconnected' by the Gunnery Control Officer, and fire control was exercised from the conning tower or from the auxiliary *Poste de tir* in turret III. The latter was equipped from the outset with the excellent OPL 8-metre stereoscopic rangefinder Mle 1932, and a similar RF was also fitted in turret II.

The 90mm mountings had full RPC using Janney electric motors. Fire control was provided by two HA directors located at the edge of the shelter deck immediately abaft the fore-funnel. Each incorporated a 3-metre stereoscopic range-finder (SOM Mle 1932), replaced in late 1939 by the 4-metre OPL Mle 1933. The fire control table Mle 1930, which was located on the main deck to starboard, just forward of the mountings, proved to be the weak link in the system. Intended to operate in conjunction with the twin mounting originally envisaged, it could handle only one target at a time. A target on the opposite beam could be engaged only by using the local control sights fitted on the mountings.

Fire control for the 37mm guns was provided by two 1-metre rangefinders (OPL Mle 1930) on light pedestals, which were located immediately abaft turret II to port and to starboard. Target data was transmitted by telephone to the individual mountings. Similar local rangefinders were provided for the forward and after 13.2mm mountings.

For night firing three searchlight projectors were provided, of which one was located on the tripod foremast and the other two atop platforms on either side of the second funnel. Originally all were to have been Breguet 75cm models similar to those in the *contre-torpilleurs*, but it was subsequently decided (May 1930) to fit the more powerful Sautter-Harlé 1.2-metre projector abeam the second funnel. The six tonnes of additional topweight implicit in this decision had to be compensated for by the suppression of the original mainmast, thereby contributing to the ship's distinctive, racy appearance. The radio antennae were attached to outriggers on the second funnel – a solution adopted for a number of *contre-torpilleurs* following the Armistice.

Torpedoes

Triple 550mm tubes Mle 1928T were mounted port and starboard between the funnels at upper deck level. The tubes had arcs of 20–160 degrees on either beam, and fired the powerful Type 1923D torpedo. There was no torpedo workshop between them and no reloads were provided. The lockers for the six warheads were on either side of the base of the catapult.

The primary torpedo fire control position, equipped with a Mle 1933 plotting table, was located in the armoured conning tower, with data being provided using periscopic binoculars and the 3-metre 'tactical' rangefinder on the admiral's bridge. Two auxiliary torpedo fire control positions, also with Mle 1933 fire control computers, were installed in the bridge wings. Fire was normally exercised remotely from the *PC torpilles*, but there were local on-mount sights (Mle 1935) for use in the event of a breakdown in centralised control.

Mines

The mine rails, manufactured by Decauville, were 50m long and were removable. When fitted they extended from the stern to the 90mm single mountings. The sections of track were normally stowed below decks, and could be assembled by the ship's crew when required. The Breguet Type B4 mine, which was specifically designed to be carried by the *contre-torpilleurs*, had an all-up weight of 535kg – half that of the Sautter-Harlé H5 carried by *Pluton* – and an 80kg TNT charge. The mines were embarked using special davits fitted on either side of the stern. Maximum combat load was eighty-four mines, and the additional 45 tonnes of topweight had to be compensated by the disembarkation of the catapult and floatplanes.

During her entire career, the only occasion on which *Emile Bertin* laid mines was during her acceptance trials in 1934, eight exercise mines being embarked for the purpose.

AVIATION INSTALLATIONS

A single trainable 20m catapult – a Penhoët compressed-air model similar to the one fitted in the *Duguay-Trouin*s and capable of launching aircraft with a take-off weight of two tonnes – was located on the ship's axis between the funnels. The catapult imparted a speed of 95km/h on launch. Practical training arcs were restricted to 30 degrees on either side of the beam.

Two electrically-powered derricks were installed abeam the second funnel; they were stowed flat on the deck, facing aft, when not in use. The derrick arms were 16.1m long and each had a maximum lift of four tonnes. One of the two aircraft carried was carried atop the catapult while the other was stowed, partially broken down, in a telescoping hangar of corrugated steel located beneath the after end of the catapult. There was a fully-fitted workshop, and 2400 litres of aviation fuel were provided in tanks located in the upper part of the stern.

The floatplane embarked was the Gourdou-Leseurre Type 832 two-seat float monoplane, a smaller version of the GL 810/811/812 series which equipped the 10,000-ton cruisers. It entered service in 1934, and was also carried by the *Duguay-Trouin*s. It proved to be of limited value, being capable of landing only in the

Above: *Emile Bertin* followed by a *contre-torpilleur* of the *Le Fantasque* class. In the foreground is the port HA director, with integral 3-metre stereo rangefinder; on the centre-line catapult is a GL 832 floatplane.

Left: The 90mm twin mounting on the after deckhouse of *Emile Bertin*.

most favourable sea conditions. A report dated 15 October 1938 by Capitaine de Vaisseau Battet, the ship's CO, states that he would have preferred the extensive aircraft-handling facilities to be removed in favour of enhanced anti-aircraft provision – a sentiment not uncommon among cruiser captains of the period.

BOATS

The outfit when the ship was first completed was as follows:

– two 10-metre motor launches
– one 10-metre pulling cutter
– three 7-metre motor boats (Admiral/CO/officers)
– two 8-metre whalers
– one 5-metre dinghy

The larger boats and the 7-metre admiral's barge were stowed on crutches abeam the fore-funnel, with the other two motor boats and the dinghy abaft the funnel. All of these boats could be handled by one of the two boat cranes, which had a reach of 5.9m. The two whalers were on davits on the First Deck outboard of the second funnel.

MODIFICATIONS 1934 TO 1942

During a refit at Brest August to November 1936 the new propellers ordered in 1935 were fitted; they were not a success and were replaced with the original propellers as a temporary measure. Modifications were made to the loading arms of the 152mm guns and installation of RPC was begun.

The first major refit of the ship was brought forward to 1938, so that propellers of new design could be fitted. An 8-metre OPL stereoscopic rangefinder Mle

1937 was delivered, and on the initiative of the ship's officers was installed atop turret II; the 8-metre Mle 1932 it replaced, being considered superior, was installed in the main DCT. The forward 13.2mm Hotchkiss mountings were moved from their exposed position on the forecastle deck to the after end of the bridge wings. At the same time all four mountings were fitted with splinter-proof shields, the local control position on the torpedo mountings were fitted with spray deflectors, and the radio equipment was upgraded.

In 1939 the final pair of Brard propellers was fitted. Other upgrades included the fitting of VHF short-range tactical radio and improved direction-finding equipment. Repairs at Toulon at the end of 1939 presented the opportunity to install a G-32 passive acoustic array comprising sixteen hydrophones, and the original C4 paravanes were replaced by the latest D6 model, which could be towed at 30 knots. The 3-metre stereo rangefinders in the HA directors were replaced by the OPL 4-metre Mle 1933. The 37mm twin mounting Mle 1933 was now becoming available in numbers; the single Mle 1925 mountings abeam the bridge were replaced, and a new transmitting system linking the 1-metre rangefinders with the mountings provided simultaneous bearing and elevation data.

In April/May 1940, during repairs of the damage sustained during the Norwegian Campaign, a breakwater was installed on the forecastle and waterproof blast bags were fitted to the 152mm guns. Steel plating 8mm thick was welded to the sides of the bridge for protection against strafing. Following her immobilisation at Fort-de France, Martinique, in mid-1940, *Emile Bertin* remained essentially unmodified until her modernisation in the United States in 1943.

Below: *Emile Bertin* leaving Toulon on 28 October 1938. Note the tricolore identification bands painted on turrets II and III during the Spanish Civil War.

CHAPTER 5
ALGÉRIE

INTRODUCTION

By the late 1920s the naval situation had evolved in ways which few had anticipated. In the absence of new capital ship construction the naval 'arms race' – such as it was in a time of great financial stringency – was becoming increasingly focused on 10,000-ton cruiser construction. The ageing battle fleets of the major powers, for the most part capable of barely 20 knots, were being fast left behind by technology, and some navies now envisaged that their cruiser squadrons would be the first major forces engaged in any large-scale naval action, with the battle fleet plodding along some distance in the rear. This was certainly true of the two Pacific powers, the United States and Japan, and these ideas were gaining currency in the Mediterranean, where the French Marine Nationale would be opposed by the fast, powerful Treaty cruisers being built for the Italian Navy. When in the late 1920s the Italian and French navies contemplated using the limited new battleship tonnage permitted to them under the Washington Treaty, both drew up designs for fast, battlecruiser-type ships intended to hunt down and destroy Treaty cruisers.

Moreover, the destroyers of the post-war generation were no longer the feebly-armed 800-ton ships of the First World War. The standard post-war destroyer guns were 120mm (4.7in), 127mm (5in) or even 130mm (5.1in), firing shells nearly twice as heavy as their predecessors (25–32kg as compared with 15kg for the 100/105mm gun). The latest ships of the French *contre-torpilleur* type were armed with 138.6mm guns firing a 40kg shell, and these ships would soon be opposed by the small Italian cruisers of the 'Condottieri' type, armed with eight 152mm (6in) guns each firing a 55kg shell.

Thus the choice was no longer between building ships which could be protected against 8in shell at all ranges (an impossibility on the permitted displacement), and ships with splinter protection against small-calibre shell. The Treaty cruisers could now be opposed by a whole plethora of intermediate weapons mounted in nominally inferior vessels, all of which were capable of disabling a lightly-armoured warship.

In 1928 the Italians authorised the first two cruisers of the *Zara* class, heavily (and conventionally) armoured ships with lightweight machinery which gave a designed speed of 32 knots. These clearly outclassed France's latest Treaty cruisers, *Foch* and *Dupleix*,[1] and would need to be matched by any new French construction.

THE DESIGN PROCESS

Having accepted that the *Suffren* design had been progressed as far as it could, and that the incremental improvements to the protection of the *Foch/Dupleix* type exemplified by the C4 proposal (see Chapter 3)

were insufficient to meet the new challenge, the French constructors were compelled to start with a blank sheet of paper, taking into account advances in propulsion technology to buy additional weight for protection within the maximum 10,000 tons permitted by the Washington Treaty. This would prove to be a productive avenue by which to advance.

By the time *Algérie* was designed, high-pressure steam conditions were becoming technological feasible and increasingly widely adopted. It had been proposed in the C4 design to reduce horsepower from 90,000CV with three shafts in the *Suffren*s to 84,000CV with two shafts, which it was estimated would deliver a speed of 31 knots, thereby saving 400 tonnes in weight. However, by adopting superheated boilers with a working pressure of 25kg/cm^2 (vs. 20kg/cm^2 in the earlier ships), the weight of the propulsion machinery could be reduced by a further 300 tonnes without any reduction in horsepower.

Two shafts, as in the C4 proposal, would make for significant space and weight gains. This solution also made possible a slimmer, faster hull. However, there were concerns about shaft loading at 42,000+CV per shaft.[2] The three-shaft solution of the *Suffren* design had a number of disadvantages with regard to the layout of the machinery and the after magazines, and was not popular; in effect it had been adopted for the earlier ships as a simple expedient which delivered three-quarters of the power of the *Duquesne*s using the same boilers and turbines.

In the end, despite the weight/space disadvantages of four shafts, this was the solution adopted. It implied a broader hull-form with greater resistance and therefore inferior powering characteristics, but four shafts provided greater redundancy and the broader beam could be utilised to increase the depth of the underwater protection system.

With the adoption of traditional hull protection, comprising a thick waterline belt topped by a substantial armoured deck, together with an air/liquid-layer 'sandwich' beneath the waterline to absorb the explosion of a torpedo against the outer skin, a unit propulsion arrangement was less crucial to survivability. This made possible a more compact layout of the machinery, with only three in-line boiler rooms followed by the two engine rooms.[3] This reduced the

---

[1] It was not, of course, known at the time that the designed standard displacement of the Italian ships exceeded Treaty limits by around 1700 tonnes.

[2] 'Forcing' was not only considered acceptable in the Marine Nationale but was actively encouraged for short periods in certain tactical situations. A ship designed for 42,000CV per shaft would therefore be expected to deliver up to 50,000CV with forcing.

[3] A parallel can be found with the US Navy's cruisers of the *New Orleans* class, which were designed at around the same time as *Algérie*. Earlier US Navy cruisers of the *Pensacola* and *Louisville* classes, which had only light protection, had the unit machinery layout, while the heavily-armoured *New Orleans* had the traditional 'in-line' arrangement of boiler and engine rooms.

Algérie: Profile & Plan views

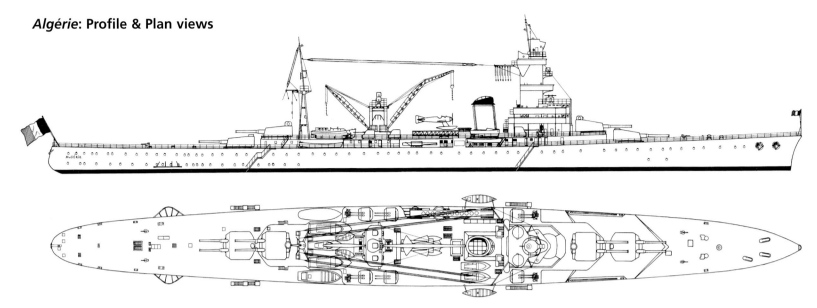

Profile and plan views of *Algérie* as first completed, based on the official plans produced by Brest Naval Dockyard and dated
1 August 1935. The quad 13.2mm Hotchkiss MG are mounted on the shelter deck at the four 'corners' of the ship. In 1939
the original funnel cap would be given a prominent curved cowling to take the funnel gases clear of the forward tower.

(© John Jordan 2010)

Algérie: Inboard Profile

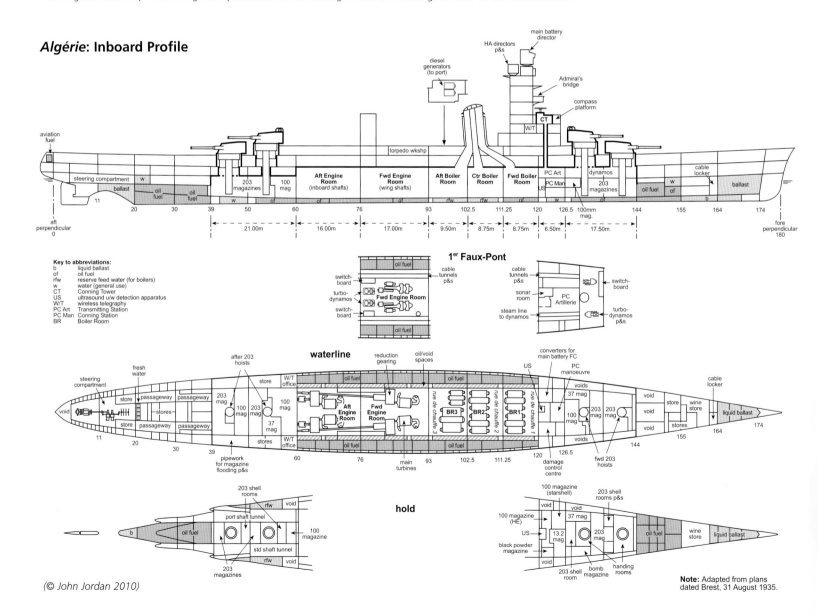

Key to abbreviations:
b	liquid ballast
of	oil fuel
rfw	reserve feed water (for boilers)
w	water (general use)
CT	Conning Tower
US	ultrasound u/w detection apparatus
W/T	wireless telegraphy
PC Art	Transmitting Station
PC Man	Conning Station
BR	Boiler Room

Note: Adapted from plans
dated Brest, 31 August 1935.

(© John Jordan 2010)

length of the machinery spaces by 7.5m (a reduction from 36.5 per cent of length between perpendiculars to 33 per cent). An additional benefit of this arrangement was that all the uptakes from the boilers could be led up into a single broad funnel, which in turn freed up centre-line space amidships for boats, aircraft and a more powerful battery of HA guns.

The traditional external belt of the new design, more than a metre deeper than that of *Suffren* and *Colbert* – it extended up to the main deck – was nevertheless less than two thirds the height of the internal longitudinal bulkhead plating of *Foch* and *Dupleix*. This saved some 370 tonnes, which could then be invested in a thicker belt, a main armoured deck capable of resisting 152mm shells, and protection for the main gun turrets and barbettes. Further weight savings were made by abandoning the raised forecastle (80 tonnes) and the suppression of one of the catapults.

NAME AND CONSTRUCTION
The new cruiser departed from earlier practice in yet another important respect. Whereas all previous post-war cruisers had borne the names of famous French seamen or statesmen, *Algérie* was named in celebration of 100 years of French colonisation of that North African country, the centenary being marked by a naval review off Algiers on 10 May 1930.

The ship was again ordered from Brest Naval Dockyard. Like her predecessors she was laid down on the Point du Jour slipway, six months after the launch of *Dupleix*, and began her official trials almost four years later, on 4 January 1934.

HULL AND GENERAL CONFIGURATION
In appearance *Algérie* differed radically from her predecessors. She had a flush-deck hull, partially compensated by marked sheer and flare at the bow, and she reverted to a traditional cruiser stern, suggesting that the stern of the *Suffren* class was adopted primarily because of the unusual three-shaft machinery arrangement. Arguably the most unusual feature of the hull-form was the pronounced tumble-home amid-

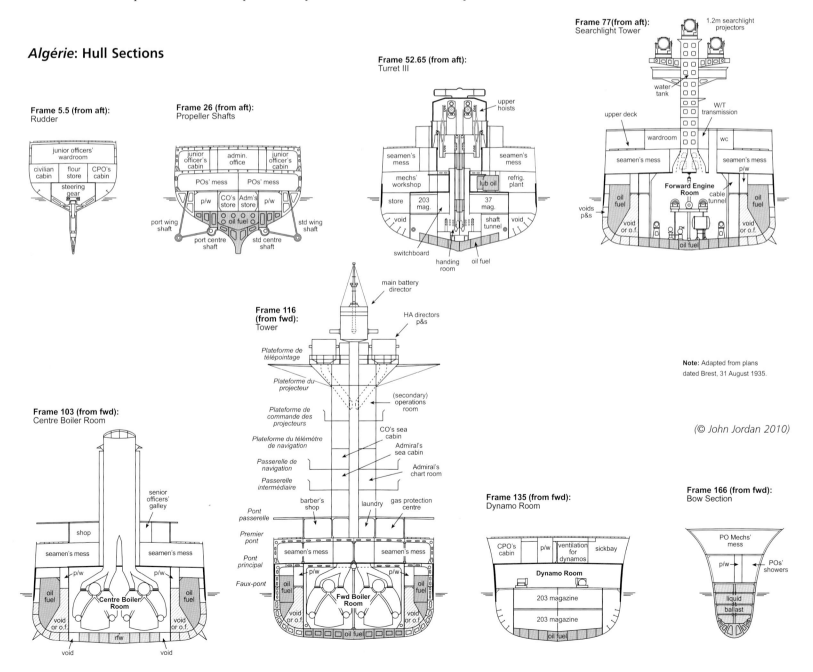

Algérie: Hull Sections

Frame 5.5 (from aft): Rudder

Frame 26 (from aft): Propeller Shafts

Frame 52.65 (from aft): Turret III

Frame 77 (from aft): Searchlight Tower

Frame 116 (from fwd): Tower

Frame 103 (from fwd): Centre Boiler Room

Frame 135 (from fwd): Dynamo Room

Frame 166 (from fwd): Bow Section

Note: Adapted from plans dated Brest, 31 August 1935.

(© John Jordan 2010)

BUILDING DATA AND GENERAL CHARACTERISTICS

Name	Builder	Laid down	Launched	In service
1930 Programme				
Algérie	Arsenal de Brest	19 Mar 1931	21 May 1932	19 Oct 1934

Displacement:	10,000 tons standard
	10,950 tonnes normal
	13,677 tonnes full load
Length:	180m pp, 186.2m oa
Beam:	20m
Draught:	6.3m max. (normal)
Machinery:	Five Indret small-tube boilers, 27kg/cm² (325°);
	four-shaft Rateau-Bretagne geared steam turbines for 84,000CV; speed 31kts (designed)
Oil fuel:	3190 tonnes; radius 8000nm at 15kts, 4000nm at 27kts
Armament:	Eight 203mm/50 Mle 1924 in twin mountings Mle 1931;
	twelve 100mm/45 Mle 1930 HA in twin mountings Mle 1931;
	four 37mm/50 Mle 1925 AA in single mountings;
	sixteen 13.2mm/76 Mle 1929 Hotchkiss MG in quad mountings Mle 1931;
	six tubes for 550mm Mle 1923D torpedoes in Mle 1929T triple mountings (three reloads)
Aircraft:	Two GL 812 HY seaplanes
Protection:	*Belt*: 110mm
	Deck: 30–80mm
	CT: 100mm sides, 70mm roof
	Turrets: 100mm face, 70mm sides, 50–85mm rear, 70mm roof
Complement:	746 as flagship

Weights: A Comparison

	C4	Algérie			C4	Algérie
Hull:	3784t	3800t				
Protection (hull):	1820t	1720t			C4	Algérie
Protection (armament):	140t	315t		OF + RFW:	n/a	750t
Armament:	1435t	1415t		Miscellaneous:	n/a	40t
Propulsion:	1614t	1335t		Normal Displ.	n/a	10,950t
Torpedoes/Aircraft:	111t	111t				
Fittings/Provisions:	1202t	1427t		OF + Combustibles		
Miscellaneous:	62t	37t		+ Ammunition + Misc.:	n/a	2727t
Washington Displ.	10,160t	10,160t		Full Load Displ.	n/a	13,677t

Note: C4 was the design derived from the *Dupleix*, and was abandoned in favour of a radical new design which became the *Algérie*.

ships. All of *Algérie*'s predecessors had conventional, vertical sides to the hull, and the reversion to a hull-form not seen since the early 1900s was almost certainly prompted by a desire to maximise the depth of the underwater protection and possibly also to create a steady gunnery platform.

The heavy tripod foremast of the earlier designs was replaced by a modern tower structure, and there was a light tripod mainmast similar to that of the later *Suffren*s. The single broad funnel was angled at 5 degrees and located just abaft the forward tower.

The shelter deck between the funnel and the mainmast was divided into two broad areas by a tall centre-line structure housing the ventilation intakes and uptakes for the engine rooms. Atop this structure was a broad athwartships platform for the three main 1.2-metre searchlight projectors for target illumination, the centre projector being elevated on a housing to clear the outboard projectors. A fourth, smaller 75cm projector (for navigation) was located on the forward side of the tower. The midship structure served as the base for two centre-line cranes: an aircraft crane on its forward face and a boat crane on its after face, the controls and winches being located directly below on the shelter deck. Outboard of the searchlight tower were paired 100mm HA gun mountings, the remaining pair of mountings being located abreast the forward tower.

This arrangement effectively divided the shelter deck

into two. Between the funnel and the searchlight tower there was stowage space for two aircraft, with a third on the catapult itself, to port. To starboard of the funnel were two 7-metre motor boats. The remainder of the ship's boats, with the exception of the two whalers, were stowed on crutches abaft the searchlight tower, where they were in easy reach of the shorter boat crane.

COMMAND SPACES

It was envisaged from the outset that *Algérie*, as the seventh (and last) of France's Treaty cruisers, would serve as a squadron flagship, the remaining six ships being grouped in two broadly homogeneous divisions of three.[4] During her construction the internal layout of the forward tower was redesigned to provide enhanced command spaces for a senior admiral and his staff. The middle platform of the tower was originally termed *Plateforme de commande des projecteurs*, and was to have been fitted with the remote control station for the after centre-line projector and lookout positions. It was remodelled as a pentagonal flag bridge, with an open platform equipped with a compass and the remote

---

[4] When completed *Suffren* was grouped with the two *Duquesne*s, which she superficially resembled, while the three later ships of the class were likewise grouped together. This pattern was broken only when one or other of the ships was in refit.

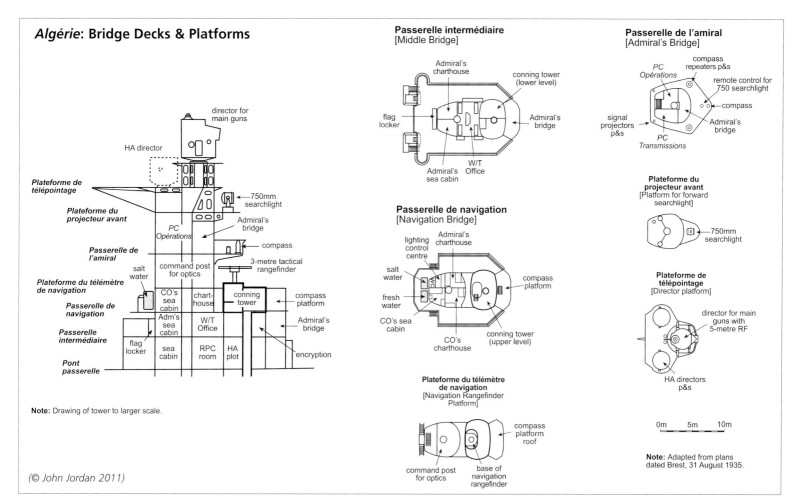

Algérie: Bridge Decks & Platforms

director for main guns

HA director

Plateforme de télépointage

Plateforme du projecteur avant

PC Opérations

750mm searchlight

Admiral's bridge

compass

Passerelle de l'amiral

salt water

command post for optics

3-metre tactical rangefinder

Plateforme du télémètre de navigation

CO's sea cabin

chart-house

conning tower

compass platform

Passerelle de navigation

Adm's sea cabin

W/T Office

Admiral's bridge

Passerelle intermédiaire

flag locker

sea cabin

RPC room

HA plot

encryption

Pont passerelle

Note: Drawing of tower to larger scale.

(© John Jordan 2011)

Passerelle intermédiaire
[Middle Bridge]

Admiral's charthouse

conning tower (lower level)

flag locker

Admiral's bridge

Admiral's sea cabin

W/T Office

Passerelle de navigation
[Navigation Bridge]

lighting control centre

Admiral's charthouse

salt water

fresh water

compass platform

CO's sea cabin

CO's charthouse

conning tower (upper level)

Plateforme du télémètre de navigation
[Navigation Rangefinder Platform]

compass platform roof

command post for optics

base of navigation rangefinder

Passerelle de l'amiral
[Admiral's Bridge]

PC Opérations

compass repeaters p&s

remote control for 750 searchlight

signal projectors p&s

compass

PC Transmissions

Admiral's bridge

Plateforme du projecteur avant
[Platform for forward searchlight]

750mm searchlight

Plateforme de télépointage
[Director platform]

director for main guns with 5-metre RF

HA directors p&s

0m   5m   10m

Note: Adapted from plans dated Brest, 31 August 1935.

control position for the 75cm projector at its forward end; a glazed wind-proof screen was fitted in 1937, and a roof the following year. Behind it, housed in the tower itself, was an admiral's bridge, with auxiliary plotting and transmissions centres. There were gyro-compass repeaters in the forward corners of the open platform, and signal projectors in the after corners (see drawing).

This position gave the admiral a commanding view of his own force during the cruising and approach phases. When the ship was closed up for combat he moved with his key staff to the middle bridge, which had the primary *Postes centraux* (housed in the lower level of the conning tower) and an enclosed admiral's bridge at its forward end.

MACHINERY

The boilers adopted for *Algérie* were vertical small-tube boilers with superheating designed and built by Indret and rated at $27kg/cm^2$ ($325°$ C). No. 1 and No. 2 boiler rooms each housed two identical boilers with a heating surface of $885m^2$; boiler room No. 3 had a larger model with a heating surface of $1515m^2$ to starboard and a small auxiliary boiler of $300m^2$, which provided steam for the windlass and services for the crew, to port.

There were four sets of geared turbines, each powering one of the four shafts. Each of the four turbine sets was constituted by a HP turbine, a medium pressure (MP) turbine and a LP turbine working in series via single reduction gearing, and was completely independent in operation, with its own condensers and lubricating pumps. The reverse turbines were incorporated in the exhaust housing of the LP turbines, which

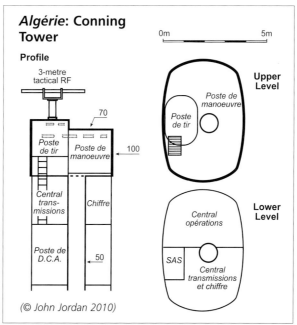

Algérie: Conning Tower

0m   5m

Profile

3-metre tactical RF

70

Poste de tir

Poste de manoeuvre

100

Central trans-missions

Chiffre

Poste de D.C.A.

50

Upper Level

Poste de manoeuvre

Poste de tir

Lower Level

Central opérations

SAS

Central transmissions et chiffre

(© John Jordan 2010)

were Parsons reaction turbines designed by Brown Boveri. The HP and MP turbines were of the Rateau-Bretagne impulse type and were built by Indret.

The turbine machinery was distributed between two engine rooms immediately abaft the after boiler room. The forward pair of turbine sets powered the wing shafts and the after pair the inner shafts. The three-bladed propellers were 3.6m in diameter.

Electrical power when the ship was underway was provided by four turbo-dynamos each rated at 300kW (400kW overload for one hour). They were grouped in pairs which could be coupled together: one pair was located in the forward engine room, the other in its own compartment forward. Power when alongside was provided by two diesel generators rated at 100kW (120kW max.). These could also be coupled together, and were located in their own compartment forward at First Deck level to port just abaft the funnel (see inboard profile drawing). A standard 'cruiser' voltage of 230–235V was employed throughout the ship.

GROUND TACKLE AND NAVIGATION

Anchors and cables were as for the *Suffren* series. In contrast to earlier French Treaty cruisers, there was a single large counter-balanced rudder with a surface area of 24.76m². Maximum helm was 32 degrees to port or to starboard.

PROTECTION

As with the earlier French Treaty cruisers, the hull of *Algérie* was of longitudinal construction, the continuous 105-metre bulkheads outboard of the propulsion machinery and magazines constituting a key element in the hull girder to give the necessary rigidity. External armour also contributed to longitudinal strength; the ship thereby avoided the structural prob-

lems which became apparent when the first French Treaty cruisers entered service.

For the first time in a major French warship extensive use of electric welding was made. Welding was employed for the inner bottom, the platform decks, the primary and secondary transverse bulkheads and the web-frames. Riveting was however retained for the vertical and horizontal armour, the first platform deck and the main strength elements of the hull girder. Welding was also employed for the internal partitions, which were of light duralumin alloy, while the double bottom, the shell and the weather deck were partially welded, partially riveted. The weight saved by the adoption of modern construction techniques could be put into hull armour.

Sixteen main transverse bulkheads extending from the ship's bottom to the upper deck contributed further to hull strength and divided the hull into seventeen watertight compartments, with no penetrations other than pipework and electrical cabling below main deck level. Each compartment had its own pumps, the larger machinery compartments being equipped with pumps of greater capacity than the outer ones.

The main armour belt was of 80kg special steel[5] with

---

[5] In the earlier French Treaty cruisers 60kg steel was employed for all protective plating, including the reinforced transverse bulkheads.

Below: A superb view of *Algérie* on March 1935 in the anchorage at Villefranche, near Nice, on 4 March 1935. In the foreground: a Breguet Short Calcutta long-range maritime patrol aircraft belonging to Squadron 3E1 (left) and a Farman F 168 Goliath bomber of Squadron 3B1 on the right. *(Patrick Maurand collection)*

Algérie: Protection

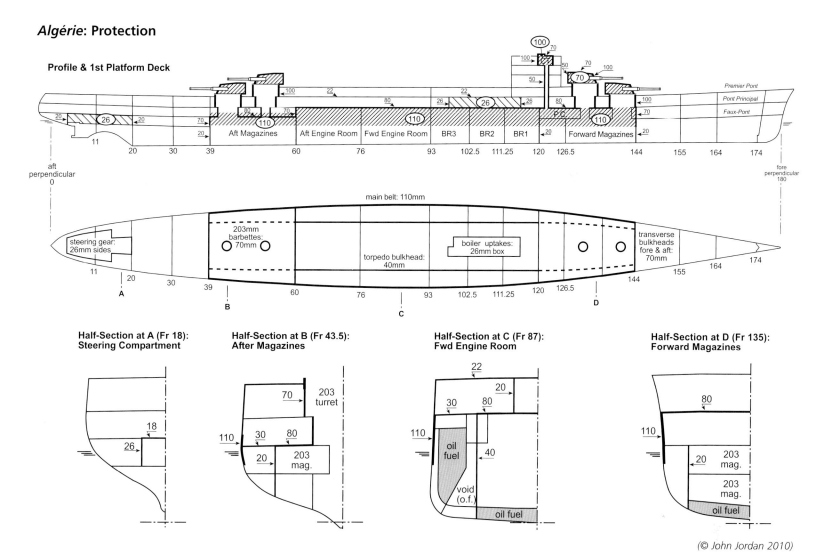

Profile & 1st Platform Deck

Aft Magazines | Aft Engine Room | Fwd Engine Room | BR3 | BR2 | BR1 | Forward Magazines

main belt: 110mm

steering gear: 26mm sides

203mm barbettes: 70mm

torpedo bulkhead: 40mm

boiler uptakes: 26mm box

transverse bulkheads fore & aft: 70mm

Half-Section at A (Fr 18): Steering Compartment

Half-Section at B (Fr 43.5): After Magazines

203 turret

203 mag.

Half-Section at C (Fr 87): Fwd Engine Room

oil fuel

void (o.f.)

oil fuel

Half-Section at D (Fr 135): Forward Magazines

203 mag.

203 mag.

oil fuel

(© John Jordan 2010)

a uniform thickness of 110mm. It comprised a single strake of plates with a height which varied between 3.76m and 4.45m – the maximum possible with current production capabilities – and a maximum length compatible with the lift capacity of the standard docking cranes: 25 tonnes. It extended from the forward end of the 203mm magazines (frame 144) to the after end of

the machinery spaces (frame 60), the lower edge being 1m below the waterline at normal displacement. It then continued at a reduced height of 2.45m abreast the after magazines, terminating at frame 39 (see Protection drawing). The belt was closed by armoured transverse bulkheads 70mm thick, also of 80kg steel, at frames 39, 60 and 144. The two outer bulkheads were of 20mm steel plate of the same quality.

The main armoured deck was of 80kg special steel, and covered the machinery spaces and the magazines. Over the forward magazines (frames 120 to 144) it extended over the full breadth of the hull and rested on the upper edge of the 110mm armoured belt. Over the machinery spaces (frames 60 to 120), however, it extended only to the 40mm torpedo bulkheads, the outer section of deck being reduced to 30mm.[6] This arrangement was repeated over the after magazines (frames 39 to 60); the side belt in this area extended above the level of the armoured deck, so that plunging shell passing over it would strike the main 80mm section of the armoured deck rather than the reduced (30mm) thickness outboard.

The steering gear was protected, as in the earlier French Treaty cruisers, by a box with 26mm sides and 20mm end bulkheads, the tensile strength of the

Algérie: Master Frame (FR89)

Premier Pont

Pont Principal

cable tunnel

Forward Engine Room

torpedo bulkhead

oil fuel

oil fuel

void *or* oil fuel

armour belt

2.76m

1.00m

bilge keel

(© John Jordan 2010)

Note: Adapted from plans dated Brest, 31 August 1935.

---

[6] It was assumed that plunging shell which penetrated this 30mm plating would be stopped by the torpedo bulkhead itself.

Right: *Algérie* on a visit to Venice which took place from 29 May to 3 June 1935. Part of the 1st Squadron (*Algérie, Dupleix, Tourville* and six *contre-torpilleurs*) sortied from Naples into the Adriatic in May before rejoining the rest of the squadron at Oran in early June. *(Philippe Caresse collection)*

plating again being increased from 60kg to 80kg. There was 26mm vertical plating of similar thickness for the funnel uptakes between the main deck and the upper deck, and 20mm plating on the access tubes for the machinery spaces; this plating was of standard 50kg construction steel.

The main gun turrets and the conning tower were armoured to a level unprecedented in earlier French Treaty cruiser construction. The turret plates were of 80kg (or 100kg) nickel-chrome steel, and were assembled without backing plates, as in French battleships. The 100mm faces were angled at 41 degrees to the vertical, the roofs and sides had 70mm plating and the turret rears 50mm. The floor of the turret was 40mm, with a 30mm reinforcing plate of 80kg steel at its forward end forming a glacis. There were sighting hoods of 60mm cast nickel steel for for turret I, and cast steel housings for the 5-metre rangefinders atop turrets II, III and IV. The ring bulkheads were protected by 100mm armour on a 50kg steel backing above the main deck, reducing to 70mm over the turret trunks. The total weight of armour allocated to the main armament was 315 tonnes, as compared with only 91 tonnes for the previous ships.

Similar protection was extended to the conning tower, which had 100mm walls, a 70mm roof and a 50mm communications tube connecting with the control spaces beneath the armoured deck.

Underwater protection

Algérie was the only French Treaty cruiser – arguably the only Treaty cruiser in the world – to have a fully-developed underwater protection system. This was based on the combination of free-flooding spaces and fuel bunkers which were a feature of contemporary capital ships. It was designed to resist a 300kg torpedo warhead.[7]

In order to minimise flooding in the event of armour plates being displaced by shell hits, the inner bottom was extended up to main deck level, giving a free-flooding space 1m across. Inboard of this was a fuel bunker 2.2m wide at its upper end, the containing bulkhead being angled out towards the bilge keel at its lower end. This was followed by a free-flooding space just over 1m in width at its upper end between the inner wall of the fuel bunker and the engine room bulkhead (see drawings). This gave a maximum depth of 4.2m amidships – an impressive figure for a ship of this size.[8]

The longitudinal bulkhead which formed the outer wall of the machinery compartments was of 60kg non-cemented steel plating 40mm thick, and extended from the ship's bottom to the main deck. Thickness was increased to 50/60mm at its outer ends to compensate for the reduction in depth of the underwater protection. This bulkhead served both as splinter protection for shells which passed through or above the belt and penetrated the thin outer section of the armoured deck, and as a torpedo bulkhead. The magazines and control spaces were outside the liquid-loaded underwater protection system, and were given side splinter protection of 80kg steel with a thickness of 20mm as an extension of the torpedo bulkhead.

ARMAMENT
Main battery
Despite what has been written in some sources, the main gun of *Algérie* was the same 203mm/50 cal Mle 1924 gun fitted in the earlier Treaty cruisers. The twin gun mounting was slightly modified to cope with the

---

[7] Italian surface ship and submarine torpedo warheads of the period were generally armed with 270kg of explosive.

[8] The British had abandoned bulges after the *Kent*s. The IJN, which persisted with them, adopted an early British-style 'dry' system with an outer void space and an inner space filled with sealed steel tubes for their Treaty cruisers of the *Myoko* and *Atago* classes; this had a depth of only 2.5m.

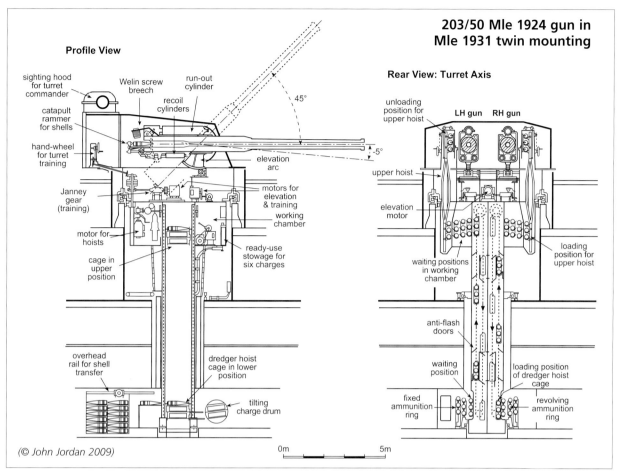

Profile View

sighting hood for turret commander

Welin screw breech

run-out cylinder

recoil cylinders

45°

catapult rammer for shells

hand-wheel for turret training

-5°

elevation arc

Janney gear (training)

motors for elevation & training

working chamber

motor for hoists

cage in upper position

ready-use stowage for six charges

overhead rail for shell transfer

dredger hoist cage in lower position

tilting charge drum

(© John Jordan 2009)

0m   5m

203/50 Mle 1924 gun in Mle 1931 twin mounting

Rear View: Turret Axis

unloading position for upper hoist

LH gun   RH gun

upper hoist

elevation motor

loading position for upper hoist

waiting positions in working chamber

anti-flash doors

waiting position

loading position of dredger hoist cage

fixed ammunition ring

revolving ammunition ring

additional weight of armour, but was otherwise similar in configuration; it may have been designated Mle 1931. The magazines and shell rooms fed twin dredger hoists each with four/six three-tier cages (each holding one shell and two half-charges); shells and charges arriving at the working chamber were then transferred to the two upper cage hoists (see drawing). These came up outside each gun, and the shells were transferred to swinging arms which locked to the guns for loading.

Anti-aircraft weapons

The secondary armament of twelve 100mm guns in open-backed twin mountings was a marked improvement on the HA armament of earlier French Treaty cruisers. The adoption of the 100mm calibre served to bring the Marine Nationale into line with the other major European navies, while the six twin mountings matched the secondary armament of the Italian Treaty cruisers and the British 'Improved Towns' of the late 1930s..

The 100mm/45 Mle 1930 had originally been intended for *Dupleix*, but delays in development meant that it was only ready in time for *Algérie*. The guns in the twin Mle 1931 mounting were in a common cradle which allowed an elevation of +80 degrees to –10 degrees, and loading was by spring rammers. In the anti-aircraft role the 100mm Mle 1930 fired a time-fused 13.5kg shell (OEA Mle 1928) with an initial velocity of 780m/s. The weight of the fixed ammunition was 22.7kg, so manual loading was relatively straightforward. There was an SAP shell (OPf Mle 1928) with a contact fuse for use against surface

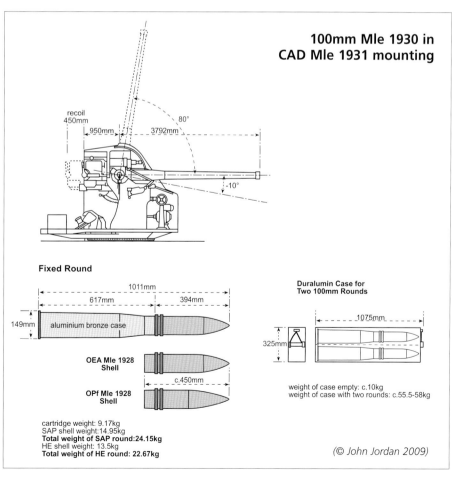

100mm Mle 1930 in CAD Mle 1931 mounting

recoil 450mm

80°

950mm   3792mm

–10°

Fixed Round

1011mm

617mm   394mm

149mm

aluminium bronze case

OEA Mle 1928 Shell

c.450mm

OPf Mle 1928 Shell

cartridge weight: 9.17kg
SAP shell weight:14.95kg
Total weight of SAP round:24.15kg
HE shell weight: 13.5kg
Total weight of HE round: 22.67kg

Duralumin Case for Two 100mm Rounds

1075mm

325mm

weight of case empty: c.10kg
weight of case with two rounds: c.55.5-58kg

(© John Jordan 2009)

100/45 MLE 1930

Gun Data
Construction: Monobloc autofretted barrel with liner
Breech mechanism: Schneider semi-automatic concentric ring
Weight of gun: 1670kg
Ammunition type: Fixed
Projectiles: OPf Mle 1928 (14.95kg)
OEA Mle 1928 (13.47kg)
OEcl Mle 1921/31
Propellant: OPf/OEA: BM7 (3.9kg)
OEcl: BM5 (3kg)
Complete round:
Weight: 24.15kg (OPf), 22.67kg (OEA), 21.8kg (OEcl)
Dimensions: 1.01m x 0.15m
Muzzle velocity: 765m/s (OPf)
780m/s (OEA)
Max. range: 15,800m
Ceiling: 10,000m

Mounting Data
Mounting designation: CAD Mle 1931
Weight of mounting: 13.5t
Loading angle: -10° / +60°?
Elevation of guns: -10° / +80°
Firing cycle (per gun): 10rpm

Notes:
CAD   *Contre-Avions Double*   AA twin mounting
OPf   *Obus de Perforation*   Semi Armour Piercing (SAP)
OEA   *Obus Explosif en Acier*   High Explosive (HE)
OEcl *Obus Eclairant*   Starshell

targets, and starshell (*Obus Eclairant* Mle 1921/31) was also provided. The ammunition was stowed in double cases of either duralumin or brass, depending on the type of round, in the forward magazines. The mounting had a 5mm shield and was equipped with an optical sight, and aiming and correction systems designed to follow aircraft with a maximum speed of 250km/h – a figure considered adequate at the time. It weighed 13.5 tonnes.

Algérie was also to have been equipped with the new

Below: A bow view of *Algérie* at her moorings dating from 1937 or 1938.

13.2/76 MLE 1929

Gun Data
Weight of gun: 30kg
Ammunition type: Fixed
Projectiles: AP & HE (50g)
Tracer
Propellant: 52g
Complete round:
Weight: 122g
Dimensions: 135mm x ??mm
Muzzle velocity: 800m/s
Max. range: 3500m theoretical
2500m effective

Mounting Data
Mounting designation: CAD and CAQ Mle 1929
Weight of mounting: 1.16t
Elevation of guns: -15° / +90°
Firing cycle (per gun): 450rpm theoretical
250rpm practical

Notes:
CAD   *Contre-Avions Double*   AA twin mounting
CAQ   *Contre-Avions Quadruple*   AA quad mounting

automatic 37mm Mle 1935, but this weapon was subject to numerous development problems and its introduction into service was delayed (it was eventually to be cancelled). Four single 37mm Mle 1925 guns were therefore fitted as a temporary measure, two being installed on the forecastle and two on the quarterdeck. They were complemented by Hotchkiss 13.2mm/76 MG Mle 1929, in the new Mle 1931 quadruple mounting. There were four mountings, disposed at the four corners of the shelter deck fore and aft of the secondary 100mm mountings. Like the machine guns of other navies they were to prove too lightweight to be effective against modern aircraft.

Fire control
The adoption of a tower superstructure in place of the tripod foremast of the earlier ships allowed the three principal fire control directors (main armament plus two secondary) to be carried high above the waterline, permitting accurate ranging at the maximum distance. The upper platform of the tower was 25m above the waterline, with the main director control tower at its summit, topped by a short topmast, and the HA directors on platforms extending directly beneath it to port and starboard. The DCT was the standard *type 10,000-tonnes* model, equipped with a SOM coincidence rangefinder with a 5-metre base for target ranging and a stereoscopic rangefinder with a 3-metre base for scartometry. The secondary directors were fitted with the standard 3-metre stereoscopic OPL rangefinder Mle 1926. Access to the directors was via ladders in a central tube, which divided into three at its upper end and which also contained the cabling for the directors.

The principal drawback to this arrangement was the concentration of weights high in the ship. The main DCT weighed 10.5 tonnes (including personnel), and each of the secondary directors 5.5 tonnes. This was presumably deemed acceptable because of the improvement in stability due to the heavy armouring of the hull and the reduced freeboard resulting from the suppression of the forecastle deck. Nevertheless every effort was made to ensure that the tower structure was as light as possible. Its outer structure was of light steel plating on a framework of T-bars, and all access ladders were constructed of lightweight duralumin alloy.

In addition to the 5-metre rangefinder in the main DCT there were 5-metre range-finders in trainable hoods atop three of the four 203mm turrets. Turrets II and IV had the standard SOM coincidence rangefinder, while turret III, which served as the auxiliary gunnery control position, had the new OPL stereoscopic model. Data from these instruments was coordinated by a Mle 1924 fire control computer located in the main transmitting station low in the hull, with fire control being exercised either from the DCT or from the conning tower.

The HA plotting room was located directly beneath the conning tower, with the RPC for the 100mm mountings below. Fire control for the small-calibre AA weapons was limited to four 1-metre range-finders, two of which were located fore and aft at upper-deck level in close proximity to the 37mm guns, the other two being located on the shelter deck to port and starboard of the searchlight tower.

There was a 3-metre tactical rangefinder in a lightweight open mounting on the roof of the conning tower. The outer 1.2-metre searchlight projectors were controlled via RPC from the HA directors, the centre-line projector from special sights located at the after corners of the lower platform of the tower. The 75cm 'navigation' projector on the forward side of the tower was trained and elevated remotely from a sight-equipped position immediately beneath it, at the forward end of the admiral's bridge.

Concentration dials continued to be fitted. The forward dial was high on the face of the tower, just above the forward projector; the after dial was fitted to the after side of the mainmast.

Top: *Algérie* in one of the Vauban *Grands Bassins* at Toulon some time before November 1937. *(Francis Dousset collection)*

Above: The upper deck of *Algérie* on the starboard side aft, around October 1939. Above, on the left, 203mm turret III; in the background the starboard torpedo tubes. All the early French inter-war cruisers had wooden planking on their upper decks as far as turret I. *(Alain Marchand)*

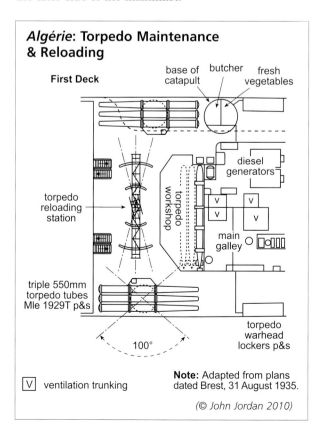

Algérie: Torpedo Maintenance & Reloading

First Deck

base of catapult — butcher — fresh vegetables

diesel generators

torpedo reloading station

torpedo workshop

main galley

triple 550mm torpedo tubes Mle 1929T p&s

torpedo warhead lockers p&s

100°

V ventilation trunking

Note: Adapted from plans dated Brest, 31 August 1935.

(© John Jordan 2010)

Torpedoes

The torpedo armament of *Algérie* was comparable to that of the earlier French Treaty cruisers. There were two triple Mle 1929T torpedo tube mountings mounted at First Deck level amidships, firing the standard 550mm Mle 1923D torpedo. A total of nine torpedoes was carried: six in the tubes and a further three reserve torpedoes in a steel-plated locker at the forward end of the torpedo workshop, which was located between the tubes. When embarked by crane, torpedoes were transferred to an athwartships trolley on rails between the tubes (see drawing). The trolley could either deliver the torpedoes to the reserve locker, or could be turned using a winch, as in previous ships, to line up with the tubes for reloading. In wartime the torpedo warheads were fitted but not fused; in peacetime they were stowed in the standard hinged deck-edge lockers, to facilitate rapid disposal in the event of an on-board fire.

AVIATION INSTALLATIONS

The single trainable catapult was located to port, its broad cylindrical pedestal being located between the funnel and the searchlight tower, immediately forward of the port-side torpedo tubes. The base of the catapult was seated on the upper deck, so that the beam barely protruded above the shelter deck. As in earlier French Treaty cruisers there was no hangar to protect the aircraft from the elements, so the second floatplane carried was stowed on the shelter deck abaft the funnel.

The catapult, ordered in May 1933, was a compressed-air model designed to launch seaplanes with a take-off weight up to 3000kg at 97km/h. It had an overall length of 22.3m, the launch beam itself being 21.0m long. The aircraft crane had a reach of 19.7m, and had the same capacity: 3000kg.

When *Algérie* entered service she operated two of the

then-standard GL 811/812 floatplanes. Both models had folding wings, and a span of 16m. They had a maximum speed of 200km/h, and a range of 560km. They were soon to be replaced by the Loire 130, which began development in 1933 as a replacement for the GL 810–812 series. The Loire 130, which had an identical wing-span to the GL 812, was nevertheless a heavier, more substantial aircraft similar to the British Walrus. It had a higher maximum speed of 225km/h, and a substantially improved range of 800km. The original catapult had to be strengthened and lengthened, the work being undertaken during a refit between 1 November 1938 and 1 January 1939. Capacity after modification was a 3300kg aircraft with a launch speed of 103km/h. The first Loire 130 was embarked on *Algérie* in October 1938, and a second was embarked following modifications to the aviation facilities in January 1939.

BOATS

The outfit when *Algérie* was first completed was as follows:

– one 11-metre motor pinnace
– one 11-metre pulling pinnace
– two 10.8-metre motor boats
– two 9-metre motor boats (admiral/officers)
– two 7-metre motor boats
– two 8.5-metre whalers
– two 5-metre dinghies

The two 7-metre motor boats were stowed on rails to starboard of the funnel; the rails extended aft almost to the searchlight tower to enable them to be handled by the aircraft crane. The two 8.5-metre whalers were on davits outboard of the funnel.

The remaining boats were on crutches on the shelter deck between the searchlight tower and the tripod mainmast. The largest of these, the two 11-metre pinnaces, were stowed outboard at First Deck level, the shelter deck being cut away at this point in order to secure good arcs astern for the after 100mm and 13.2mm AA guns. These boats were handled by a boat crane which, like the aircraft crane, had its machinery located at the base of the searchlight tower – a neat, practical solution which economised on deck space.

MODIFICATIONS 1934 TO 1942

During a refit at Toulon from 3 August 1936 to 1 March 1937, occasioned by the need for repairs following *Algérie*'s collision with *Colbert*, the 5-metre coincidence rangefinder in the main DCT was replaced by an 8-metre stereoscopic model. A new funnel cap was fitted and the boiler superheaters replaced. Remote power control was provided for the main turrets (training only) and for the centre-line searchlight projector. At the same time the admiral's bridge at the forward edge of the tower was given a glass windscreen – a roof was added the following year. The bridge wings on the forward superstructure were also extended.

In a short refit from 20 November 1937 to 1 April 1938 the RPC installation for the HA guns was completed, and the light AA guns were regrouped. The 37mm guns originally installed on the forecastle were re-located to a less exposed position on the quarterdeck, abaft the other two 37mm. In compensation one

Algérie July 1941

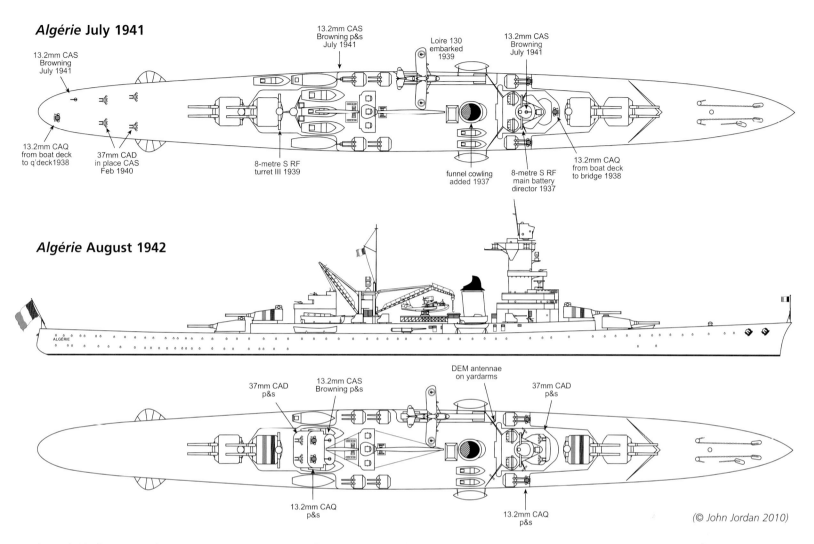

13.2mm CAS Browning July 1941

13.2mm CAS Browning p&s July 1941

Loire 130 embarked 1939

13.2mm CAS Browning July 1941

13.2mm CAQ from boat deck to q'deck 1938

37mm CAD in place CAS Feb 1940

8-metre S RF turret III 1939

funnel cowling added 1937

8-metre S RF main battery director 1937

13.2mm CAQ from boat deck to bridge 1938

Algérie August 1942

37mm CAD p&s

13.2mm CAS Browning p&s

DEM antennae on yardarms

37mm CAD p&s

13.2mm CAQ p&s

13.2mm CAQ p&s

(© John Jordan 2010)

Below: *Algérie* departing Toulon in August 1941. The distinctive funnel cowling was fitted during the winter of 1939-40. In an earlier refit, which took place November 1938 to January 1939, the HA directors were enclosed and the original 5-metre stereo rangefinder in the main battery DCT replaced by an 8-metre model. Two Loire 130 seaplanes are in evidence: one on the catapult to port and another in the rest position to starboard. There are tricolore neutrality markings on turrets II and III, and *Algérie* is flying the flag of Squadron Vice-Admiral (VAE) Lacroix, commanding the First Cruiser Group (1st and 3rd Cruiser Divisions). *(Marius Bar)*

of the after 13.2mm quads was moved to the roof of the conning tower, the other being relocated above the stern to starboard.

In a further refit from 1 November 1938 to 1 January 1939 the 5-metre stereoscopic rangefinder on turret III was replaced by an 8-metre model, and the HA directors were given a roof to protect the crew from the elements. At the same time modifications were made to the catapult to enable it to handle the larger Loire 130 reconnaissance seaplane.

Following two months of war service, *Algérie* underwent a short refit from 1 December 1939 to 1 February 1940. A taller, more rounded funnel cowling was fitted to keep smoke clear of the bridge. The four single 37mm Mle 1925 mountings on the quarterdeck were replaced by four twin Mle 1933 mountings, and a protective screen was constructed around the 13.2mm quad mounted on the bridge.

From 1 May to 1 July 1941 watertight blast bags were fitted to the main guns, and the close-range AA armament was reinforced by the installation of four single 13.2mm Browning MG: one on the DCT, one on the quarterdeck, and two in the shelter deck positions formerly occupied by the after 13.2mm quads. These *ad hoc* installations were clearly less than satisfactory; the AA positions forward were badly exposed to the elements, while those amidships had poor arcs obstructed by boats, cranes, the catapult and the secondary gun mountings – hence the preference for the quarterdeck location. A more permanent solution was proposed, involving the construction of a new deckhouse with tiered platforms (designated *pergola*) in place of the tripod mainmast, which was replaced by a simple pole mast seated at the forward end of the

searchlight tower. In order to cover forward arcs the admiral's bridge was replaced by an AA platform. Most of the existing AA weapons were relocated to one or other of these two positions.

The necessary modifications were made during a refit from 1 May to 1 August 1942 at Toulon. The four 37mm Mle 1933 were redistributed fore and aft, two mountings being relocated to the AA platform which replaced the former admiral's bridge, the other two occupying the after (lower) platform of the *pergola* (see drawing). The forward 13.2mm Hotchkiss quad mountings were retained in their original position at the forward end of the shelter deck, while the other pair was relocated to the middle platform of the *pergola*. Two of the four 13.2mm Browning MG were installed immediately forward of the Hotchkiss quads at the top of the *pergola*, and it was envisaged that the remaining two would be fitted forward atop the DCT. During the same refit *Algérie* received the D.E.M. radar, the two transmitting and two receiving antennae being fitted to the yards of the forward tower – an arrangement similar to that on *Colbert* (see drawing page 191).

The new arrangement of the light AA was more symmetrical, and was clearly superior to the previous layout. However, the weapons themselves were of three different types, were markedly inferior in capabilities to the 20mm Oerlikons and 40mm Bofors being installed in Allied cruisers during the same period, and fire control was unsatisfactory. It was the best that could be done in very difficult circumstances, with the bulk of the French military-industrial complex in occupied territory and political constraints imposed by the crippling conditions of the Armistice.

Below: Stern quarter view of *Algérie* on 24 August 1942, shortly after the completion of the major refit in which her AA armament was reorganised. Note the distinctive *pergola*, with its stepped structure for the after light AA weapons, located in the position of the former tripod mainmast. The latter was replaced by a simple pole mast fixed to the forward face of the searchlight tower. *(Marius Bar)*

CHAPTER 6

THE *LA GALISSONNIÈRE* CLASS

INTRODUCTION

The London Treaty of 1930 effectively put an end to the construction of 10,000-ton cruisers armed with 8in guns. Although France and Italy were not bound by Part III of the treaty, which divided cruisers into subcategories (a) and (b), armed with 8in/203mm and 6.1in/155mm guns respectively, and established strict quantitative limits for each of the three major powers, both countries informally agreed that *Algérie* and *Pola* respectively would be their last ships of the subcategory (a) type. A failure to honour this informal agreement would have sabotaged the bilateral negotiations which were now scheduled to take place and would have risked the British Government invoking the 'escalation' clause written into Part V of the treaty.

The French were already committed to building a smaller, less expensive type of cruiser for the same reason as the British: the larger 10,000-ton type was simply unaffordable in the numbers required to police their respective empires. Hence the review of cruiser construction which took place in 1927–8 and the construction of a 6000-ton prototype, *Emile Bertin* (see Chapter 4). However, whereas the latter ship was virtually unarmoured, like the Italian 'Condottieris' she was intended to face, the new British 6in gun cruiser which was being offered up as a template for future construction, HMS *Leander*, was better protected than the early British 10,000-ton cruisers, with a 3in (76mm) belt and a 1.25in (32mm) deck over the machinery as well as substantial box protection for the magazines. Indeed, the displacement of *Leander* had grown to more than 7000tW during development as a consequence of this search for a level of protection which would mean that the ship was virtually immune to 6in shell at probable engagement ranges.

The views aired by the various delegations during the London Conference made it clear that the Americans would never agree to a qualitative limit on cruiser displacement as low as 7000 tons, as the British had hoped, but a future treaty limit of 7500–8000 tons remained a strong possibility.[1] This would permit a cruiser design marginally superior to the British *Leander*, and this was the route which the French Naval General Staff would take in the wake of London 1930.

It appears that the French always saw the new cruisers as 'fleet' units, fighting in divisions of three ships in support of the modern battleships currently

being designed. And with the perceived threat from a resurgent Germany increasing, it made sense to have two divisions: one for the Atlantic, the other for the Mediterranean.

DESIGN AND CONSTRUCTION

Design work on the new cruisers began shortly after the conference concluded in April 1930 but was not completed until early 1932. Following a series of meetings which took place between 30 June 1930 and July 1931 the principal characteristics were agreed:

- displacement: 7720 tonnes (7600 tons) standard;
- length: 172m between perpendiculars;
- propulsion: four boilers rated at $27kg/cm^2$, four sets of geared turbines driving four shafts; 84,000CV = 31 knots at normal displacement;
- endurance: 3000nm at 18 knots (4000nm with a full load of oil fuel);
- armament: nine 152mm (3 x III), four 90mm (2 x II), eight 37mm (4 x II), eight 13.2mm MG (4 x II), six 550mm TT (2 x III);
- aircraft: four 1600kg floatplanes (two in hangar, one on catapult, one on deck);
- protection: 105mm belt; 38mm deck.

The comparatively heavy protection system was modelled on that of *Algérie*, but had to be scaled down

Below: The stern of *La Galissonnière* on 18 November 1933, the day before her launch from the *Point du Jour* slipway at Brest. *(Jean Labayle Couhat collection)*

---

[1] The London Conference of 1936 would finally agree to limit future cruiser displacement to 8000 tons; by this time the US Navy had laid down all the large cruisers it required for scouting, and was again interested in smaller cruisers to accompany the battle fleet.

La Galissonnière: Profile & Plan views

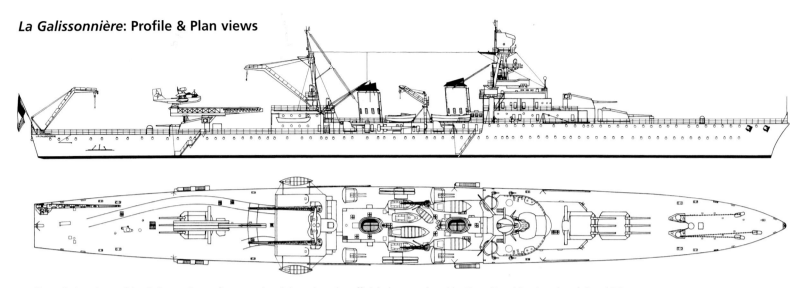

Profile and plan views of *La Galissonnière* as first completed, based on the official plans produced by Brest Naval Dockyard and dated 20 May 1937. Only the forward four twin 13.2mm Hotchkiss mountings are in place abreast the bridge structure, and the turntable atop the hangar (see Aviation Installations) has yet to be installed.

(© John Jordan 2010)

La Galissonnière: Inboard Profile

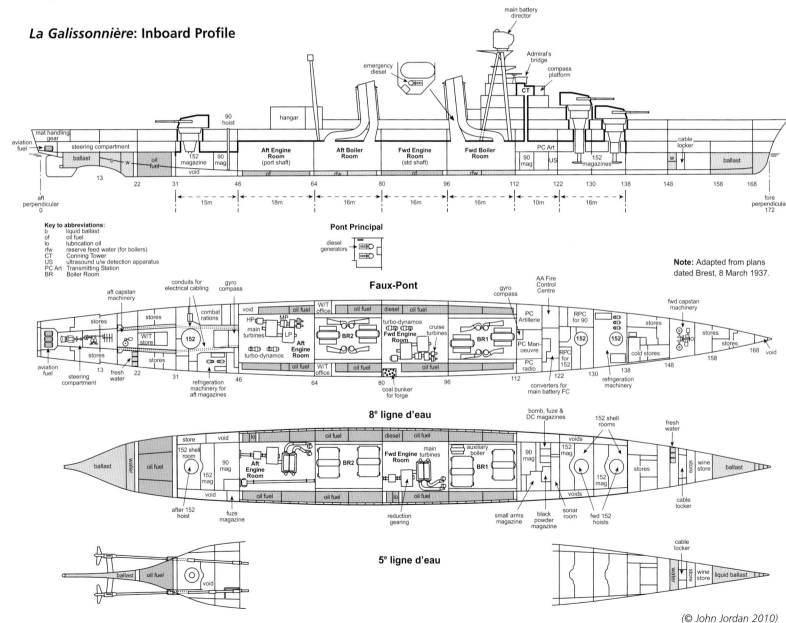

Key to abbreviations:
b	liquid ballast
of	oil fuel
lo	lubrication oil
rfw	reserve feed water (for boilers)
CT	Conning Tower
US	ultrasound u/w detection apparatus
PC Art	Transmitting Station
BR	Boiler Room

Note: Adapted from plans dated Brest, 8 March 1937.

(© John Jordan 2010)

La Galissonnière: Hull Sections

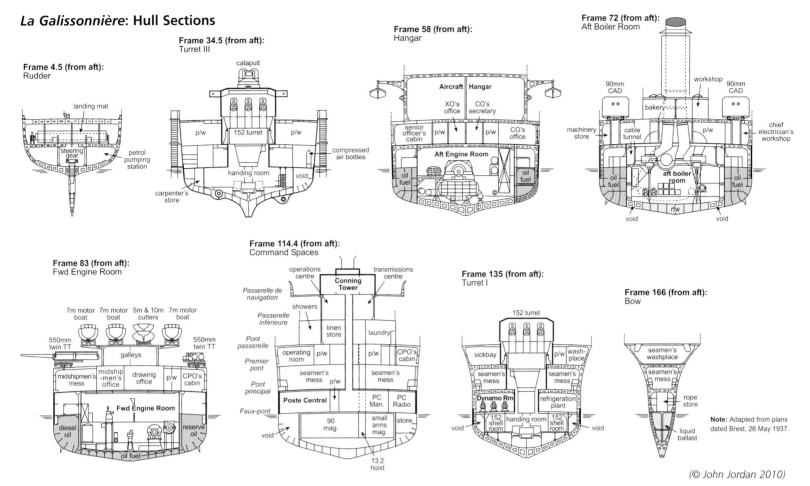

(© John Jordan 2010)

because of weight considerations. The 80mm main armoured deck of the latter was considered the minimum thickness necessary to protect against bombs, but it would have cost 1120 tonnes. An underwater protection system similar to that of *Algérie* was also considered, but was costed at 300 tonnes. Adopting these two features would have resulted in a displacement of 9000 tonnes for the new ships. Even so, the weight of protection in the final design was 1884 tonnes, much greater than in the earlier Treaty cruisers.

Discussion continued on two issues. The General Staff was unhappy with the multiplicity of AA gun calibres and the disposition of the mountings. It was finally decided that the secondary armament would be doubled, the four additional 90mm guns (also in twin mountings) replacing the four twin 37mm mountings. As weight compensation the triple torpedo tubes became twins. The four twin 13.2mm Hotchkiss MG were moved to the positions originally projected for the 37mm, on the forecastle abeam the bridge.

The other issue was the propulsion machinery, which was the subject of a meeting of the *Comité technique* on 29 September 1931. The original design stipulated four shafts, but it was recognised that a two-shaft solution would save 80 tonnes in weight and increase endurance by 500nm at 18 knots. The four-shaft solution was preferred from both a technical and a military point of view. As a compromise, Eng.-Gen. Parent proposed a third (emergency) centre-line shaft powered by a 1000kW electric motor which would be capable of getting a damaged ship home at 7 knots. However, a centre-line shaft would have complicated

the layout of the after magazines, as it had in the *Suffren* class. In the end the committee opted for two shafts, and this was subsequently approved.

All post-war French cruisers except the *Emile Bertin* and the training cruiser *Jeanne d'Arc* (both built by Ateliers et Chantiers de St Nazaire-Penhoët) had been constructed by one or other of the two naval dockyards at Brest and Lorient. However, the naval dockyards would not have the capacity for a cruiser programme of the proposed scale (six ships authorised within two years), and it was decided that *La Galissonnière* would be allocated to Brest, *Jean de Vienne* to Lorient, and that the four ships of the 1932 programme would be put out to tender to private shipbuilders. The result was that each of the six ships was built in a different shipyard. In order to ensure uniformity of construction Brest was again designated as the lead yard, and was responsible for supplying detailed plans to the other shipyards. The first ship, *La Galissonnière*, was launched some eighteen months before the second, the construction of all subsequent units being delayed to accommodate any modifications found to be necessary; this was to result in a number of detail differences between the name ship of the class and her sisters.

The French were particularly anxious to get the first two ships on the slipway prior to the first League of Nations general *Conference* for the Limitation and Reduction of Armaments at Geneva, which was scheduled for February 1932. However, because of the heavy workload in the two naval dockyards construction was not begun in earnest until much later, so that a period of three years and eight months elapsed between the laying down and the launch of *Jean de Vienne*. The ships built in the naval dockyards took some five years to complete, those built by the private shipyards just over four.[2]

NAMES

Roland-Michel Barrin, marquis de **La Galissonnière**, (1693–1756), was the son of a naval lieutenant-general and studied at the College of Beauvais in Paris. He subsequently became Commandant Général of New France, the French colonies of continental North America. He was the victor of the battle of Minorca in 1756.

Jean de Vienne (1341–96) was a French knight, general and admiral during the Hundred Years War. In 1373, Charles V made him Admiral of France. Working with determination, de Vienne reorganised the navy, started an important programme of construction, created an effective coast guard and navigation police, and attributed licences for the building and selling of ships.

La **Marseillaise** was a marching song written and composed by Claude Joseph Rouget de Lisle in 1792. It was adopted in 1795 as the national anthem of the French Republic.

Gloire means 'Glory' and is one of the tenets of the French Navy. The new cruiser *Gloire* was the fifth ship of the name; her most illustrious predecessor was the world's first ironclad battleship, 1858–83.

Louis-Joseph de **Montcalm**-Gozon, Marquis de Saint-Veran (1712–59) was the commander of French forces in North America during the Seven Years War. In 1756 Louis XV sent him to New France to lead its defence against the British. He met with notable successes in 1756, 1757 and 1758, but British mobilisation of large numbers of troops against New France led to military setbacks in 1758 and 1759, culminating in Montcalm's defeat and death at the battle of Quebec and the French surrender at Montreal.

The cruiser *Georges-Leygues* was originally to have been named *Châteaurenault*.[3] Born in 1857, **Georges Leygues** was the outstanding Navy Minister of the inter-war period, promoting the interests of the Marine Nationale at home and abroad and super-

---

[2] Construction times for the contemporary British *Leanders* averaged 26–30 months.

[3] The name was subsequently allocated to one of the three cruisers of the *De Grasse* class (see Chapter 7).

BUILDING DATA AND GENERAL CHARACTERISTICS

Name	Builder	Laid down	Launched	In service
1931 Programme				
La Galissonnière	Arsenal de Brest	15 Dec 1931	18 Nov 1933	29 Oct 1936
Jean de Vienne	Arsenal de Lorient	20 Dec 1931	31 Jul 1935	9 Oct 1937
1932 Programme				
Marseillaise	A C de la Loire	23 Oct 1933	17 Jul 1935	26 Oct 1937
Georges Leygues (ex-*Châteaurenault*)	Penhoët	21 Sep 1933	24 Mar 1936	4 Dec 1937
Gloire	F C de la Gironde	13 Nov 1933	28 Sep 1935	4 Dec 1937
Montcalm	F C de la Méditerrannée	15 Nov 1933	26 Oct 1935	4 Dec 1937

Displacement:	7600 tons standard
	8360 tonnes normal
	9460 tonnes full load
Length:	172m pp, 179.5m oa
Beam:	17.48m
Draught:	5.28m max. (normal)
Machinery:	Four Indret boilers, 27kg/cm^2 (325°); two-shaft Parsons (Rateau in *La Galissonnière*, *Jean de Vienne*, *Gloire*) geared steam turbines for 84,000CV; speed 31kts (designed)
Oil fuel:	1569 tonnes; radius 7000nm at 12kts, 1600nm at 34kts
Armament:	Nine 152mm/55 Mle 1930 in triple mountings Mle 1930 (1850 rounds); eight 90mm/50 Mle 1926 HA in twin mountings Mle 1930 (2400 rounds + 200 starshell); eight 13.2mm/76 Mle 1929 Hotchkiss MG in twin mountings Mle 1931; four tubes for 550mm Mle 1923D torpedoes in two twin mountings
Aircraft:	Two/three Loire 130 seaplanes
Protection:	*Belt*: 105mm
	Deck: 38mm
	CT: 95mm sides, 50mm roof
	Turrets: 100mm face, 50mm sides, 40mm rear, 45mm roof
Complement:	557 peacetime, 612 wartime

La Galissonnière: Weights

Hull:	2681t
Protection (hull):	1081t
Protection (armament):	380t
Armament (incl. torpedoes):	1279t
Propulsion (incl. RFW):	1370t
Fittings:	1081t
OF:	380t
Normal Displ.	8250t

vising the building of a modern navy which could rank with the navies of the major powers. Following his death on 2 September 1933 the hull due to be laid down during the same month at St Nazaire was renamed in his honour.

HULL AND GENERAL CONFIGURATION

The starting point for the design of the new light cruisers was the *Emile Bertin*. The hull-form was similar in profile, with a raised forecastle. However, it was significantly broader with less of the fining at the bow essential to high speed, and there was a transom stern intended to accommodate a canvas landing mat for the embarked aircraft. It was initially proposed that the ship would have reduced superstructures on the model of *Emile Bertin* to minimise the silhouette, but the decision to incorporate a large double hangar aft effectively reversed this.

The reduction to four boilers in two boiler rooms enabled the turrets and their associated magazines to be moved farther away from the ends of the ship. The machinery spaces were 66m long (equivalent to 38 per cent of the length between perpendiculars), whereas in *Emile Bertin* the corresponding figure was 81m (43.5 per cent). This effectively reduced the length and weight of the citadel protection. There were two equal, evenly-spaced funnels, and the superstructures were altogether more compact. This created a problem regarding the best location for the single catapult, for which there was insufficient centre-line space amidships. In the end it was decided to locate the catapult, which was an extending type, atop turret III and to turn the hangar so that it was facing aft. This freed up the midship section for boats and the twin HA mountings, and moved the focus of aircraft operations to the quarterdeck. A specialised aircraft crane of new design was located on the port corner of the stern to recover aircraft from the canvas landing mat, and the latter were then transferred to the twin hangar via a set of rails which circumvented the after 152mm turret. In theory this was a neat solution, but the weight of the catapult atop the turret was considerable, and there would be vibration problems.

MACHINERY

Considerable thought was given to the propulsion system of these ships. The required horsepower (84,000CV) was identical to that of *Algérie*. However, in the latter ship power had been provided by five superheated boilers, four of which had been arranged side by side in two boiler rooms with the fifth, larger boiler in a third. It would have been difficult to fit boilers side by side into the smaller hull, so the designers opted for four larger boilers providing steam for two sets of turbines in a unit arrangement. Each of the two boiler rooms had two boilers in tandem, offset slightly from the ship's axis. The turbines in the forward engine room drove the starboard shaft, those in the after engine room the port shaft.

The boilers were of a new model, an Indret vertical small-tube type with double superheaters rated at 27kg/cm². The superheaters were responsible for a number of problems on trials, notably on the *Jean de Vienne*, requiring a strengthening of the supports. A small auxiliary boiler for ship's services rated at 20kg/cm² was fitted to port of boiler no. 2 in the forward boiler room.

MACHINERY TRIALS

Full Power Trial (8 hours)

	Jean de Vienne	Montcalm
	30 Apr 1936	8 Mar 1937
Displacement:	8164t	8231t
Maximum speed:	34.78kts	34.62kts
Maximum power:	97,801CV	101,384CV
Consumption:	n/a	34.76t/h

Forcing Trial (1 hour)

	La Galissonnière	Montcalm	Gloire
	26 Jun 1936	8 Mar 1937	28 Apr 1937
Displacement:	7735t	8020t	8008t
Maximum speed:	35.42kts	36.13kts	36.80kts
Maximum power:	108,615CV	115,000CV	116,174CV
Consumption:	n/a	39.17t/h	n/a

Fuel Consumption Trial at Cruising Speed (8 hours at 18 knots)

	Montcalm
	?? Mar 1937
Displacement:	8242t
Average speed:	18.06kts
Average power (2 boilers):	4069CV
Consumption:	3.54t/h

Source: Jean Moulin, *op. cit.*

Notes:
The trials of all six cruisers were run on the Penmarch-Lesconil range, which was 11.03km long and 90m deep.
The forcing trial of the lead ship, *La Galissonnière*, was deliberately run at an average theoretical displacement which corresponded to Washington standard displacement, 7720 tonnes.

The turbines were Rateau-Bretagne impulse or Parsons reaction models with single-reduction gearing. The Rateau turbines were built by Indret (*La Galissonnière*, *Jean de Vienne*) and Schneider (*Gloire*), the Parsons turbines by AC Loire (*Marseillaise*, *Georges Leygues*) and FC Méditerranée (*Montcalm*). Each set of turbines had a maximum rating of 55,000CV, and comprised HP, MP and LP turbines working in series, with the reverse turbine in the exhaust housing of the LP turbines. The Parsons ships had one, the Rateau ships two impulse cruise turbines on each shaft; these had a combined rating of 10,500–11,000CV, and were

Below: *Jean de Vienne* under tow, probably prior to one of her first trials sorties between April and June 1936. She is still lacking her main battery director, the 90mm HA guns and the catapult atop turret III. *(Philippe Caresse collection)*

Right: An overhead of *Georges Leygues* at sea in late 1938. *(Pradignac & Léo)*

Far right: The controls for the turbines on the *Montcalm*. The photo was taken at the end of 1944; it is clearly posed, as the rpm counter is at zero. *(ECPA)*.

Below: The starboard propeller of the *Montcalm*; the photo was taken following the ship's decommissioning. *(Jean Guiglini collection)*.

capable of driving the ship at an economical speed of 18–19 knots. The Parsons turbines proved to be more reliable than the Rateau-Bretagne turbines. The *Gloire*, which was fitted with the latter, suffered from numerous problems, sometimes at embarrassing moments, as when she suffered a complete engine breakdown while being shadowed by the heavy cruisers *Cumberland* and *Australia* off French Guinea in September 1940 (see Chapter 10).

There were small differences in the propellers fitted in each ship. Those fitted in *Marseillaise* were of a three-bladed type with a diameter of 4.6m.

All ships of the class exceeded 35 knots on the standard nine-hour speed trial, the fastest being *Gloire*, which attained 36.9 knots with about 118,000CV. In service they comfortably maintained their designed speed of 31 knots in formation. Endurance, although inferior to that of contemporary Royal Navy light cruisers, was adequate given their intended theatre of operations, and was superior to that of their most likely opponents, the 'Condottieri' of the Regia Marina.

Electrical power when underway was provided by four turbo-generators each rated at 200kW. The two-shaft arrangement greatly facilitated their accommodation in the two engine rooms; the pair in the forward engine room was to port of the turbines, the after pair to starboard. Power when alongside was provided by a pair of 100kW diesel-generators in a compartment to port on the main deck (see drawing), and a third diesel, for use in emergency, was located high in the ship, to starboard of the fore-funnel on the First Deck. When refitted in the United States in 1943 these generators were generally replaced by uprated models of US design and manufacture.

La Galissonnière: Protection

Profile & 1st Platform Deck

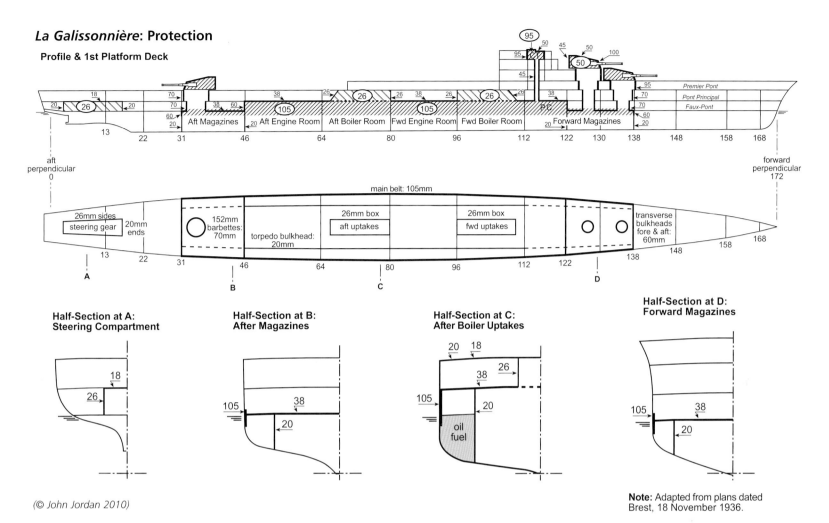

(© John Jordan 2010)

Note: Adapted from plans dated Brest, 18 November 1936.

GROUND TACKLE AND NAVIGATION

The three main anchors (two bower, one sheet) were in hawsepipes forward: two to starboard and the third to port. They were of the Byers type and each weighed 4900kg. The single stern anchor weighed 1400kg. Two kedge anchors of 1140kg and 890kg were initially provided. The larger of these was subsequently replaced by two anchors of 600kg and 200kg respectively, which were stowed below decks.

There were two Sperry-Sagem Mark V gyro-compasses (one forward, one aft), and four magnetic compasses, with eighteen strategically-placed repeaters. The ships were also fitted with a Warluzel Bianchetti W31 ultrasonic depth sounder.

As in *Emile Bertin* there was a single counter-balanced rudder, with a surface area of 23.70m². A breakwater, trialled on the *Jean de Vienne*, was fitted to the forecastle of the other five ships during 1937.

The 7600-ton cruisers were much praised for their sea-keeping qualities. No vibration was experienced at the highest speeds of 30–33 knots, and there was little spray over the forecastle and bridge even in a head sea. They steered well above 9 knots, and heel was only 5 degrees in a cross-wind. The roll period of 12–13.4 seconds coincided almost exactly with the average firing cycle of 4–5rpm, making them excellent gunnery platforms.

PROTECTION

The hull was of longitudinal construction with a double bottom between frames 13 and 158, and was divided into fifteen watertight compartments. The double boiler rooms were 16m long, but tight subdivision was less of a concern in these ships because of the level of protection. The hull plates and frames were of 50kg steel, the armour plating of 80kg special steel.

The protection scheme was necessarily a compromise, as it was for most foreign cruisers of the period. It was officially stated that the 105mm main armour belt, which was closed at either end by 60mm bulkheads, was effective beyond 9000m against 140mm shell, and beyond 14,000m for 152mm shell. The horizontal armour, which comprised a 38mm main protective deck resting on the upper edges of the side armour belt, was stated to be effective up to 19,000m against 140mm shell and up to 15,000m against 152mm shell. This gave a substantial immune zone against destroyer fire, and a relatively small immune zone against the Italian 'Condottieri' (although sources do not state the angle of fire on which these figures are based). There was no question of providing immunity against 8in (203mm) shellfire, although this was also true for the 8in Treaty cruisers of the period.

The turrets had 100mm faces with 50mm on the roofs and the sides, and fixed protection comprised 95mm on the ring bulkheads and 70mm on the ammunition trunks. The conning tower was armoured to the same standard: 95mm on the vertical walls with a 50mm roof. The communications tube had 50mm protection. These figures were again only slightly reduced from *Algérie*. As in the latter ship there was 26mm box protection for the funnel uptakes, and a

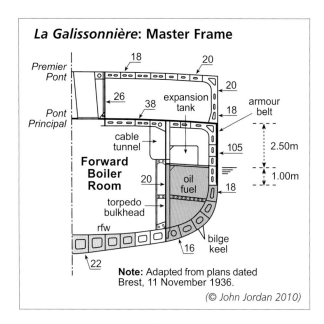

La Galissonnière: Master Frame

Premier Pont — 18, 20, 20, 26, 38, expansion tank, armour belt, 18
Pont Principal — cable tunnel, 105, 2.50m, 1.00m
Forward Boiler Room — 20, oil fuel, 18
torpedo bulkhead, rfw, 16, bilge keel, 22

Note: Adapted from plans dated Brest, 11 November 1936.

(© John Jordan 2010)

Below: *Georges Leygues* at speed off Toulon on 24 July 1940. The photo was taken one month after the Armistice, and the ship already has her tricolore recognition markings on turrets II and III. One of her Loire 130 seaplanes is atop the catapult, which is fully extended. The single green band on the forefunnel marks her out as the first ship of the 4th Cruiser Division; the flag of Rear-Admiral Bourragué is flying from the mainmast. *(Marius Bar)*

similar level of protection for the steering compartment.

Although it proved impossible to provide underwater protection on the scale of *Algérie*, considerable attention was given to counterflooding arrangements. An initial list of up to 22 degrees could be corrected within five minutes by flooding designated tanks on the opposite side of the ship. Flooding the two ballast tanks in the bow would provide 0.55m trim compensation. The two liquid ballast tanks aft affected trim by 0.60m, while flooding the after magazines would provide a further correction of 0.47m.

ARMAMENT
Main battery
The 152mm/55 Mle 1930 triple mounting was essentially the same model trialled in the *Emile Bertin* (see Chapter 4). It was heavier (178 tonnes vs. 112 tonnes) because of the weight of armour plating; it therefore

required an increase in the power of the motors used for training the turret. However, internal arrangements, including replenishment and loading, were otherwise identical.

The mounting, which was built like those fitted in *Emile Bertin* by FAM Homécourt, incorporated a high level of automation. Unfortunately it was plagued by the customary problems associated with technological complexity, and numerous modifications were necessary before the Marine Nationale was satisfied with its performance. During firing trials there were frequent breakdowns in the firing mechanism, the breech safety mechanism and the shell and cartridge hoists. Low standards of manufacture, incorrect settings and even poor maintenance were blamed. As a result the rate of fire averaged only three rounds per minute per gun, half the figure anticipated. Simplification of the turret mechanisms aboard *Gloire* in 1938 eventually yielded a rate of fire of nine rounds per minute at an elevation of +8 degrees. However, these modifications were not extended to all ships of the class, and the maximum rate of fire sustained in service remained at around 5rpm – although *Montcalm* claims to have attained 8rpm for a short period at Dakar (see Chapter 10).

There were initial problems with ingress of water into the mounting. In 1938 *Marseillaise* received some minor modifications, including a reduction in the gap between the fixed and mobile turret armour by 25mm, and the fitting of light leather blast bags. Further measures were taken after the winter of 1939–40 (see modifications).

Barrel life was 300–350 rounds, which became a problem for the surviving units after the bombardments of 1944. By the end of April 1945 *Georges Leygues* had fired 580 rounds per gun! The urgency of the problem resulted in the order of replacement barrels from Canada. These were of a different construction to the original model, being of modern monobloc design.

Continued on p.137

THE ART OF JEAN BLADÉ

Surgeon General Jean Bladé, now in his eighty-first year, was formerly *Directeur Central du Service de santé des Armées*. Previously he served in the Marine Nationale as Medical Officer aboard the frigate *La Confiance*, the fast escorts *Le Béarnais*, *Le Basque* and *Le Lorrain*, the escort sloop *Commandant Bourdais*, the cruiser *Colbert* and the helicopter carrier *Jeanne d'Arc*. His passion for the sea, and in particular for the Marine Nationale, is expressed in the many superlative paintings, both watercolours and oils, which he has produced over the years; these currently total 3600 and cover the period 1922 to 1965. In this eight-page colour section we reproduce a small sample of his watercolours of the inter-war cruisers and their aircraft. Jean Bladé's painting of the *Emile Bertin* graces the jacket of this book.

Left: *Duquesne* leading the 1st Light Division to sea in 1932. In her wake are *Suffren* and the recently-commisioned *Foch*.

Left: *Suffren* during 1931, with one of her two embarked Gourdou-Leseurre 810 reconnaissance floatplanes taxiing on the water. The three white rings on the fore-funnel mark her out as the third ship of the 1st Light Division.

Right: *Colbert* during the period 1931–2, when she was not assigned to a division – hence the absence of funnel bands. Note the goose-necked crane abeam the second funnel, which handled boats and aircraft.

Right: *Foch* in 1934–5, with one of her two embarked GL.810 floatplanes overhead. The distinctive heavy tripod foremast, with its supporting legs spread, is much in evidence; note also the white-painted concentration dial, a feature of the Mediterranean-based cruisers of the period. The single white band on the second funnel marks out *Foch* as the flagship of the newly-formed 3rd Light Division (Rear-Admiral Gensoul).

Left: A Loire 130 reconnaissance seaplane being readied for catapult launch aboard the cruiser *Colbert* in 1942. The aircraft is painted in the distinctive 'Vichy' colours of the period, with prominent red and yellow stripes on the tail surfaces.

Right: The fore turrets and bridge of *Jeanne d'Arc* in December 1944, by which time she had been incorporated into the cruiser group providing fire support on the Italian front. The extensive accommodation provided for officer cadets was put to good use during the later phase of the war in the Mediterranean; *Jeanne d'Arc* was regularly employed as a fast troop transport between North Africa and newly-liberated metropolitan France.

Left: The School Ship *Jeanne d'Arc* leaves Brest for her third training cruise on 5 October 1933. She would serve in this role until 1964, when she was replaced by the helicopter carrier of the same name.

Left: The minelayer *Pluton* at anchor off the coast of Britanny shortly after her completion in 1931, and prior to her entry into service. Note the twin minelaying tracks angled down at the stern, and the platform for two single 37mm AA guns straddling the tracks.

Right: *La Galissonnière* in October 1938, with the two Loire 130 reconnaissance seaplanes she had recently acquired. The neutrality colours tell us that the Spanish Civil War was still in progress.

Right: *Marseillaise* in late 1940 (post-Armistice), again wearing neutrality colours on turrets II and III. The single yellow band on the first funnel marks her out as the flagship of the 3rd Cruiser Division (Rear-Admiral Barnaud), now incorporated into the *Forces de Haute Mer* (FHM).

Right: A Loire 130 seaplane being hoisted from the catapult to the rest position atop the hangar roof on a cruiser of the 7600-ton type. The admiral's flag suggests that this is either *Georges Leygues* or *Marseillaise*.

Right: A Loire 130 seaplane is readied for catapult launch aboard the cruiser *Marseillaise* in August 1940. The telescopic catapult of these ships was mounted atop turret III.

Left: An aerial view of *Marseillaise* in December 1940 during a general sortie by the *Forces de Haute Mer*. From that same month *Marseillaise* no longer carried a single yellow band on the fore-funnel.

Right: *Georges Leygues* in 1944 following her major modernisation in the United States at the Philadelphia Navy Yard. Note the six prominent quadruple 40mm mountings: in the bridge wings, atop the after deckhouse and on the stern. She is wearing the standard US Navy Measure 22 paint scheme of Navy Blue hull and Haze Gray upperworks with Deck Blue horizontal surfaces, which was applied to all the modern French cruisers except *Gloire*.

Right: The ceremonial entry into Toulon 13 September 1944. In the foreground is *Emile Bertin*, flagship of Rear-Admiral Philippe Auboyneau commanding the recently-formed 3rd Cruiser Division (*Emile Bertin*, *Jeanne d'Arc* and *Duguay-Trouin*). Ahead of her, and leading the French line, is the 7600-ton cruiser *Georges Leygues*, in which the French C-in-C, Vice-Admiral André Lemonnier, was embarked. In the distance and to the right of the picture is the US Command Ship *Catoctin*.

Left: *Emile Bertin* in Ha Long Bay, French Indochina, 23 March 1946 following the operations at Hai Phong (see Chapter 12). Alongside is one of the junks the French used to patrol the Gulf of Tonkin.

Continued from p.128

The ships fired the same range of ammunition as *Emile Bertin* (q.v.). By the time they entered service the 'K' shell, which used a coloured dye to distinguish the shell splashes of ships firing in formation, was becoming available. During a visit to Rosyth in mid-June 1939 the 4th Cruiser Division (4ᵉ DC) demonstrated these shells to the Royal Navy, which subsequently adopted the technology. *Georges Leygues*, as lead ship of the division, fired red, the other two ships green and yellow.

Anti-aircraft weapons

The 90mm/50 Mle 1926 HA gun was already in service aboard the heavy cruisers *Colbert* and *Foch*, and the twin mounting Mle 1930 was currently being installed in the latest of the series, *Dupleix*, and the *Emile Bertin*. The twin mountings on the *La Galissonnière* class weighed 13.7 tonnes and were fitted with remote power control; maximum elevation was 80 degrees and rate of fire was 6rpm per gun, but loading proved difficult above 60 degrees. There were sixty ready-use rounds in lockers adjacent to each mounting. The original autofretted barrels were replaced by monobloc barrels ordered from Canada in 1945.

The four twin 13.2mm Hotchkiss MG were fitted on the forecastle deck abeam the bridge – the same position adopted for the twin 37mm mountings in *Emile Bertin*. From July 1937 the crews were given some protection against splinters and spray when shields were added to the mountings. Even before the ships entered service there was concern about the inadequacy of the close-range AA provision. In January 1937 it was proposed to fit a quad 13.2mm Hotchkiss mounting initially to starboard on the quarterdeck, and subsequently at the starboard after corner of the hangar. A shortage of quad mountings precluded this installation (the only ship so fitted was *La Galissonnière*, which trialled the mounting atop the hangar from January to April 1938), and the final solution adopted in 1938 was to install two twin mountings at the after corners of the hangar, together with a one-metre rangefinder on the after searchlight platform. The mountings installed in *Montcalm* and *Georges Leygues* would be fitted with protective shields in 1940.

Fire control

The main fire control director in the 7600-ton cruisers had a different configuration to that of earlier ships; it was fitted from the outset with an 8-metre OPL stereoscopic rangefinder for ranging but not the customary 3-metre stereo rangefinder for scartometry, and weighed 12 tonnes. It provided data for a 'mixed' Mle 1934 fire control computer, which as originally projected was to have been capable of handling both surface and aerial targets Difficulties in training the director were resolved in the first ship, *La Galissonnière*, by fitting larger ball bearings, but this modification was not extended to the three ships which survived the scuttling until 1945. As in *Emile Bertin* there were further 8-metre stereo rangefinders integrated into the rear compartments of turrets II and III. Remote power control was provided for training.

The two HA fire control directors were on circular platforms extending from the after end of the navigation bridge. Those of the first two ships had 3m stereoscopic rangefinders, while the later ships had a 4m

model. Two calculating positions Mle 1930 were provided to enable aerial targets on both sides of the ship to be engaged. The mountings had full RPC. Although the performance of the 90mm gun proved generally satisfactory, the fire control system was considered unreliable, to the extent that under combat conditions the guns were often operated in local control, as was the case with *Montcalm* off Norway in April 1940. Each pair of twin 13.2mm Hotchkiss mountings was provided with a one-metre rangefinder located in the wings of the bridge.

All ships had the now-standard open 3-metre

Above: The starboard 90mm mountings with the twin torpedo tubes between on *La Galissonnière*. *(Bousquet collection)*

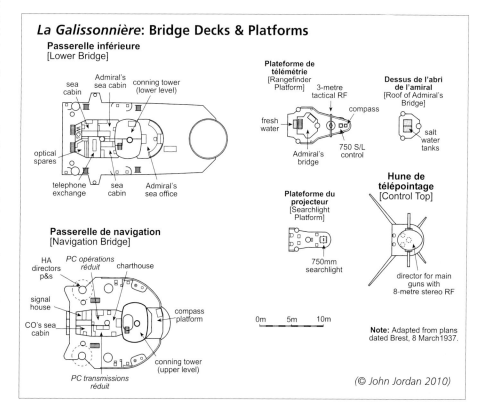

La Galissonnière: Bridge Decks & Platforms

Passerelle inférieure
[Lower Bridge]

- sea cabin
- Admiral's sea cabin
- conning tower (lower level)
- optical spares
- telephone exchange
- sea cabin
- Admiral's sea office

Plateforme de télémétrie
[Rangefinder Platform]

- 3-metre tactical RF
- fresh water
- compass
- Admiral's bridge
- 750 S/L control

Dessus de l'abri de l'amiral
[Roof of Admiral's Bridge]

- salt water tanks

Passerelle de navigation
[Navigation Bridge]

- HA directors p&s
- PC opérations réduit
- charthouse
- signal house
- CO's sea cabin
- compass platform
- conning tower (upper level)
- PC transmissions réduit

Plateforme du projecteur
[Searchlight Platform]

- 750mm searchlight

0m   5m   10m

Hune de télépointage
[Control Top]

- director for main guns with 8-metre stereo RF

Note: Adapted from plans dated Brest, 8 March 1937.

(© John Jordan 2010)

Above: A torpedo is launched from *Montcalm*. *(Philippe Caresse collection)*

Right: Photo taken on board *Georges Leygues* in 1938 or 1939. In the foreground: the port-side torpedo tubes. *Georges Leygues* had a single green funnel band from March 1939 until late 1942; throughout that period she was flagship of the 4th Cruiser Division. *(Pradignac & Léo)*

Below: Recovery of a Loire 130 reconnaissance seaplane on the stern ramp. *(SHAA)*

tactical coincidence rangefinder atop the conning tower (used also to provide torpedo fire control solutions). There were also three 1.2-metre Sautter-Harlé searchlight projectors, with full RPC, at the base of the mainmast, and a 75cm 'navigation' searchlight on a platform which projected from the tripod foremast.

Torpedoes
Only four 550mm Mle 23D torpedoes were embarked, and these were launched from the twin tubes amidships. As in previous ships, the main fire control panel for the torpedoes (Mle 1933) was located in the conning tower, target data being provided by the 3-metre tactical rangefinder, and there were similarly-equipped fire control positions with remote firing in the bridge wings. The local sights on the mountings themselves were fitted with shields from late 1937 to protect them from spray.

AVIATION INSTALLATIONS
The aircraft arrangements on the light cruisers of the *La Galissonnière* class were the most elaborate yet. A

capacious double hangar for two seaplanes with folding wings was fitted between the second funnel and turret III. The single catapult, powered by compressed air, was initially to have been located between the hangar and the gun mounting, but was finally mounted atop the turret itself in order to clear the quarterdeck and improve launching arcs. Unusually, it was telescopic, having a length of 14.6m when

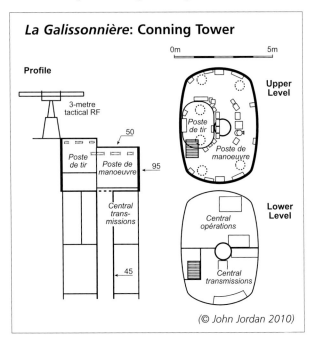

La Galissonnière: Conning Tower

(© John Jordan 2010)

La Galissonnière: Aviation Facilities

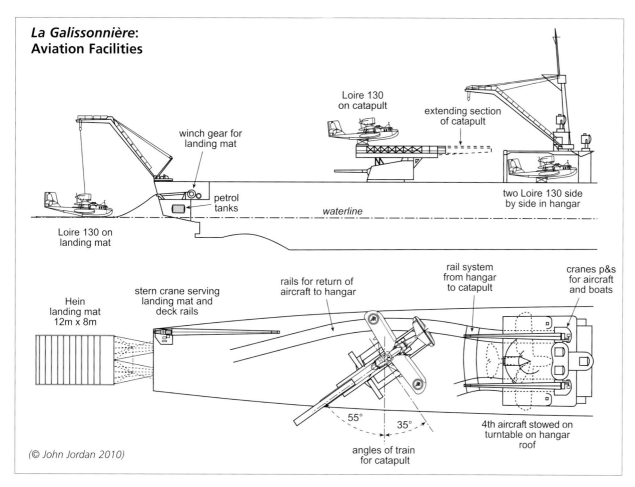

(© John Jordan 2010)

retracted and a length of 22.15m when fully extended. It trained with the turret (see drawing), and aircraft could be launched between 55 degrees and 145 degrees to starboard, and between 215 degrees and 305 degrees to port. By 1935 it was envisaged that four aircraft would be carried: two in the hangar, one atop the catapult itself and a fourth atop the hangar. However, it was found that aircraft stowed atop the catapult were subject to vibration and blast damage, and the final aircraft complement was three.

The most interesting feature of the aircraft handling arrangements was the landing mat deployed to enable the ships to recover aircraft while steaming at speeds of 10–15 knots. This comprised a sheet of ribbed canvas measuring approximately 12m by 8m which was deployed from a narrow aperture in the transom stern; the floatplane or seaplane approached the mother-ship from the stern, and once safely aboard the mat could be lifted via a stern crane onto the quarterdeck. The models installed were of German design and manufacture and comprised two different types, both of which were subject to modification as trials proceeded. Those fitted in the *Jean de Vienne* and the *Georges Leygues* were manufactured by Kiwull, those in the remaining four ships by Hein. The first was installed in February 1937, and extensive trials took place the following year.

It took some 15 minutes to deploy the mat, and the recovery operation, which included hoisting the aircraft aboard and ramp stowage, took a further 23–30 minutes. The stern aperture was relatively close to the waterline, and operations in heavy seas often resulted in the flooding of the mat handling room. It also proved

La Galissonnière: Aircraft Crane (Stern)

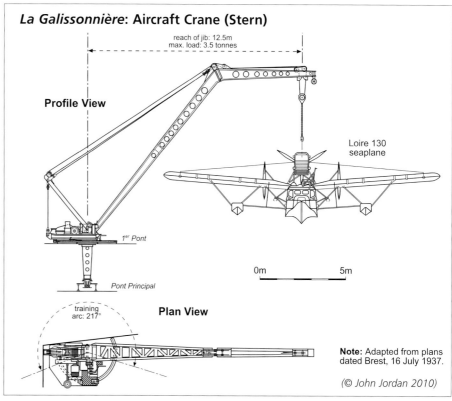

Note: Adapted from plans dated Brest, 16 July 1937.

(© John Jordan 2010)

difficult to dry out the ramps after use, and after two years they had deteriorated to such an extent that it was decided to abandon them and to plate-in the stern aperture. They were finally removed in 1941–2.

140   FRENCH CRUISERS 1922-1956

Three cranes, each with a 3300kg capacity, were provided to serve the aircraft (there were separate, smaller cranes between the funnels to handle the ships' boats). The cranes located atop the hangar to port and starboard, which had a reach of 15.7m, served to transfer the aircraft between the quarterdeck, the catapult and the hangar roof, while the stern crane (12.5m reach) was necessary to recover the seaplanes from the landing mat. It took about 40 minutes to transfer a floatplane from the hangar to the catapult. A set of quarterdeck rails linked the stern with the hangar. Following a decision in July 1936 to install a stowage position for a fourth aircraft atop the hangar, turntables were fitted from September 1937.

By 1935 it was envisaged that these ships would operate two of the Loire 130 reconnaissance seaplanes currently under development, together with two float fighters of an unspecified type. The first two ships completed, *La Galissonnière* and *Jean de Vienne*, embarked two GL 812 (the successor to the 810) and a single Potez 452 light reconnaissance seaplane as an interim measure; the latter aircraft could not be catapulted. The Loire 130 began to reach service squadrons in late 1937. Its floatplane fighter

Above: A Loire 130 reconnaissance seaplane on the extending catapult mounted on turret III; the photo is of *Gloire* in 1939. Note the concentration dial fixed to the after side of the mainmast. *(ECPA)*

Loire 130

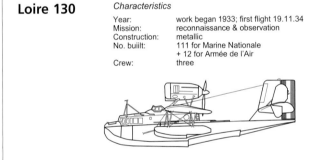

Characteristics

Year:	work began 1933; first flight 19.11.34
Mission:	reconnaissance & observation
Construction:	metallic
No. buiilt:	111 for Marine Nationale + 12 for Armée de l'Air
Crew:	three

Dimensions

Wingspan:	16m (4.69m wings folded)
Length:	11.25m
Height:	3.85m

Engine

Type:	Hispano-Suiza 12-cylinder ('X' config.) liquid-cooled
Power:	720hp

Performance

Max. speed:	210km/h @ 2100m
Cruise speed:	165km/h @ 1300m
Climb:	12 minutes to 3000m
Ceiling:	6000m
Endurance:	7h30 at 150km/h and 500m altitude

Weight

Empty:	2050kg
At catapult load:	3260kg
Max. load:	3500kg

Armament

Machine guns:	two Darne 7.5mm (one in nose, one dorsal aft-facing)
Bombs:	two 75kg G2 type

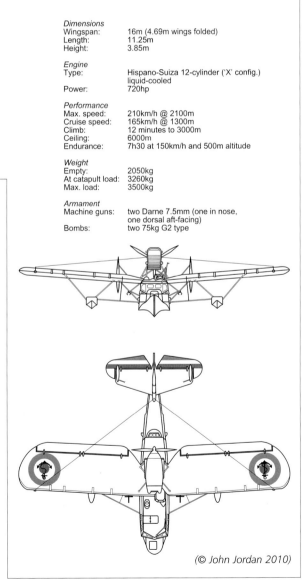

Loire 210

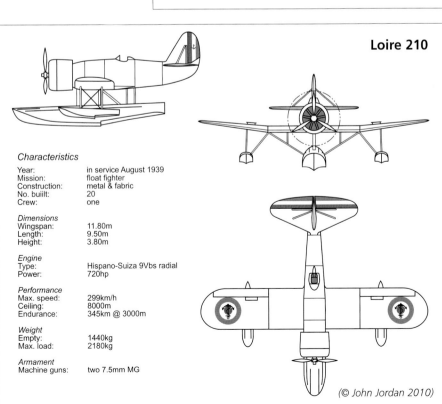

Characteristics

Year:	in service August 1939
Mission:	float fighter
Construction:	metal & fabric
No. buiilt:	20
Crew:	one

Dimensions

Wingspan:	11.80m
Length:	9.50m
Height:	3.80m

Engine

Type:	Hispano-Suiza 9Vbs radial
Power:	720hp

Performance

Max. speed:	299km/h
Ceiling:	8000m
Endurance:	345km @ 3000m

Weight

Empty:	1440kg
Max. load:	2180kg

Armament

Machine guns:	two 7.5mm MG

(© John Jordan 2010)

(© John Jordan 2010)

Left: The prototype of the Loire 210 floatplane fighter on the catapult of *La Galissonnière* for trials which took place 29–30 April 1937.

counterpart, the Loire 210, was duly ordered in March 1937, and deliveries began in late 1938. The Loire 130 proved successful, but the Loire 210 experienced power/weight and structural problems throughout its development, and although twenty production aircraft were completed, the float fighter concept was abandoned and the two squadrons dissolved in November 1939. From that point onwards the cruisers generally operated three Loire 130, two being accommodated within and one atop the hangar. On occasions these were disembarked and operated from shore bases.

BOATS

The boat outfit as designed (*La Galissonnière*) was as follows:

– one 10-metre pulling cutter
– three 9-metre motor launches
– one 9-metre pulling cutter

Below: *Marseillaise* on 28 July 1941. Twin 13.2mm Hotchkiss AA mountings can be seen atop the hangar roof. The Loire 130 seaplane on the catapult has the distinctive red and yellow striped markings of Vichy aircraft applied to its tail surfaces. *(Marius Bar)*

Above: The after section of *Gloire* seen from the top of the tripod foremast. There is a Loire 130 on the catapult. Note the angled bar painted (in black?) across the mainmast yard, typical of the *Gloire* during the early war period. *(ECPA)*

– four 7-metre motor boats
– two 8-metre whalers
– one 5-metre dinghy

Two of the 9-metre motor launches were abreast the second funnel. The other boats were stowed on crutches abaft the funnel. There were two boat cranes,

each with a reach of 6m and a lift capacity of four tonnes, also abaft the second funnel. The two 8-metre whalers were on davits outboard of the hangar. The subsequent outfit of boats varied considerably, depending on the ship and its affiliation.

MODIFICATIONS 1935 TO 1942

Following the outbreak of war the cruisers of the *La Galissonnière* class were fitted with a depth charge rack conceived by a naval lieutenant called Krant. The rack held a total of twelve 35kg depth charges, which were deployed over the stern in groups of three. There were three reloads. The depth charges were used by the *La Galissonnière* against the Italian submarine *Dandolo* on 13 June 1940.

Following experience of operations in the North Atlantic during the winter of 1939–40 it was decided that waterproofing of the 152mm turrets would need to be improved (Note of 15 January 1940), and thick waterproof blast bags were fitted. The three Atlantic ships of the 4th Cruiser Division were prioritised; the Mediterranean ships were not modified until 1941.

Further improvements in the ships' anti-submarine capabilities were planned in the form of G32 hydrophone systems, trialled by *La Galissonnière* and *Marseillaise* in January 1941. The results were poor; the equipment proved useless above 15 knots and was subsequently removed from all ships.

In December 1940 it was decided to improve the anti-aircraft capabilities of the ships by installing additional close-range AA guns. Given the proven inadequacy of the models then in service and a limited capacity for the manufacture of more advanced models, the modifications were necessarily of a piecemeal nature. A twin 37mm/50 Mle 1933 was installed atop the conning tower, and two single 25mm/60 Hotchkiss Mle 1939 were located atop the hangar in mid-1941. The three cruisers based in West Africa received further additions in the form of single Browning 13.2mm MG; *Georges Leygues* received four (two in the bridge wings, two atop the hangar), *Montcalm* three (two in the bridge wings, one in reserve), and *Gloire* four (two on the lower bridge deck abaft turret II, one on the after searchlight platform, and a fourth in reserve).

These measures were of limited effectiveness given the inadequate number of guns, their lack of uniformity, and the primitive nature of the fire control arrangements (generally an associated 1-metre rangefinder with a telephone communication with the mounting(s). The entire close-range AA armament would be removed and replaced by a powerful combination of 40mm Bofors quads and 20mm Oerlikon singles when the cruisers of the 4th Division entered US Naval Dockyards for reconstruction in 1943 (see Chapter 11).

CHAPTER 7

THE *DE GRASSE* CLASS

INTRODUCTION

France not only took part in the London Conference which took place in 1935, but was happy to sign and ratify the subsequent treaty. Following the withdrawal of the Japanese from the Treaty System and Germany's renunciation of the Treaty of Versailles it was clear that no agreement could be reached on quantitative limits to naval construction, and this effectively removed the obstacles to French signature on a new agreement. Unrestricted building programmes both in Europe and in the Pacific would result. However, one of the key clauses of the London Treaty of 1936 was the restriction of cruiser displacement to 8000 tons (8127 tonnes) standard.

When in early 1936 the French Navy sat down to consider the design of the next generation of cruisers it found that the new limit permitted an increase in standard displacement of only 400 tons (406 tonnes) over the *La Galissonnière* type. The Naval General Staff therefore requested that the STCN look at how best to use this additional 406 tonnes in order to secure improvements with a focus on (i) speed, (ii) armament and (iii) protection.

THE DESIGN PROCESS

In a note dated 25 June 1936[1] the STCN first of all focused on the cost of general improvements which were now considered desirable in the light of trials with *La Galissonnière*, which had been proceeding since the Spring of 1935. These would comprise hardwood planking on the quarterdeck from the stern to abeam the hangar, an increase in the size and number of boats (to be matched by a corresponding increase in the capacity of the twin handling cranes), and replacement of the single extending catapult by twin catapults mounted either atop the hangar or in place of the hangar (see below).

Two further modifications would need to be taken into account before considering radical improvements in the performance of the ships. The 152mm triple turrets of the 7600-ton type were capable of a maximum elevation of 45 degrees but could be loaded only at elevations of 15 degrees or below, which reduced the firing cycle considerably at longer ranges. It was therefore proposed that the guns on the new ships should be capable of being loaded up to their maximum angle of elevation of 45 degrees. The new cruisers would also need an increase in horsepower simply to cope with the increase in displacement. The 7600-ton cruisers had an overload power rating of 100,000CV to deliver 35 knots on their eight-hour

1 The NGS request is in Note 477 EMG.3 of 25 May; the STCN response is Note No.29888 C.N.4.

FRENCH AND ITALIAN CRUISERS OF THE EARLY 1930s

	La Galissonnière	Montecuccoli	Duca d'Aosta	Abruzzi
Built:	Six ships 1931–7	Two ships 1931–5	Two ships 1932–6	Two ships 1933–7
Displacement:	7720tW	7524tW	8450tW	9592tW
Speed:	31–32kts	37kts	36kts	34kts
Armament:	Nine 152mm	Eight 152mm	Eight 152mm	Ten 152mm
	Eight 90mm	Six 100mm	Six 100mm	Eight 100mm
	Four TT	Four TT	Six TT	Six TT
	Three aircraft	Two aircraft	Two aircraft	Four aircraft
Protection: (vert)	105mm	60mm	70mm	100mm
(hor)	38mm	30mm	35mm	40mm

speed trial, and it was calculated that this figure would need to be increased to a minimum of 105,000CV in the 8000-ton cruisers. The STCN recommended going to 110,000CV, considering this to be the maximum figure possible with a two-shaft installation; four shafts would have an unacceptable cost in machinery weight.

In summary, the STCN pointed out that even assuming that armament and protection remained unchanged the above modifications would leave 170 tonnes available, of which only 120 tonnes was usable. It was thus already been clear that dramatic improvements in speed, armament and protection would not be forthcoming, and that any further modifications to the baseline 7600-ton type would have to be subject to the usual process of compromise. Despite this, the STCN note went on to suggest possibilities which in due course would result in a distinctive cruiser design.

First the STCN looked at possible changes in the main armament of the ships. There were three possibilities:

(i) to retain the current turret (albeit with loading at 45 degrees) but to increase the number of guns to ten, the after turret becoming a quad (two twins and two triples as in the Italian *Abruzzi*s were considered, but this would have had too great an impact on length and displacement);
(ii) to adopt the new Model 1936 DP turret of the *Richelieu* class, in which the guns could elevate to 90 degrees;
(iii) to adopt a modified *Richelieu* turret with elevation restricted to 70 degrees.

Option (i) had the advantage of superior distribution of the main armament (six guns forward, four aft), but a new quad turret would have to be developed. There would also be training and fire control issues, and access to the aircraft hangar (if fitted) from the quarterdeck would be impossible due to the greater width of the turret.

Option (ii) was found to be only partially realisable. The *Richelieu* turret was 70 tonnes heavier even without allowing for ammunition (magazine stowage would need to be greater for a DP gun due to the high expenditure of rounds in the anti-aircraft mode). Installation of such a turret would have to be restricted to the after gun mounting; this would greatly complicate fire control and would again preclude access to the hangar because of the greater width of the turret.

Option (iii) was much more promising. Each turret would be 22 tonnes heavier – i.e. three could be had for the additional weight cost of a single *Richelieu* turret – and this would still leave 50 tonnes available for improvements to the anti-aircraft weaponry. This option was therefore the one favoured by the STCN.

Attention then turned to AA capabilities. It was not possible to increase the number of 90mm twin mountings beyond the four provided in the 7600-ton type, as even these four mountings had proved difficult to accommodate. It was possible to increase gun calibre by adopting the 100mm CAD Mle 1930 mounting installed in the 10,000-ton cruiser *Algérie* in their place, and this would still leave 70 tonnes available for the favoured 70 degrees option for the main guns. However, this failed to meet two concerns regarding the existing arrangements: the relatively poor arcs of the side-mounted 90mm mountings, which on forward bearings were constrained by the superstructures and

on after bearings by the aircraft hangar; and the distance of the mountings from their magazines, which effectively limited them to rapid bursts of AA fire using the ready-use rounds available.

The STCN now proposed its most radical solution: the adoption of the new fully-enclosed 100mm CAD Mle 1933 to be installed in the new series of *avisos-dragueurs*. This promised to be a much more effective weapon in the anti-aircraft role than either the 90mm Mle 1926 or the 100mm Mle 1930. The enclosed mounting was significantly heavier (30 tonnes as opposed to 13.5 tonnes for the open-backed mountings) and had to be replenished from a magazine located directly beneath with hoists on the axis of the mounting, but it provided much-enhanced protection for the gun crews and could be fitted with RPC, thereby facilitating centralised fire control. Installation of either two or three of these mountings (see preliminary study drawings) would mean suppressing the aircraft hangar so that the guns could be placed directly above their respective magazines, which would be adjacent to the after 152mm magazine. However, this location offered infinitely superior AA arcs, as all mountings could be fired on after bearings and the centre-line mounting, which was raised on its own deckhouse, was capable of firing even on forward bearings against aerial targets at high altitude.

Two alternative plans (614/615 ST – see drawings) were provided to illustrate this option. In both cases the catapults were moved forward and the number of aircraft was reduced from four to three, the third being stowed, wings folded, between the catapults. Adoption of either of these proposals in conjunction with the 70 degrees option for the main guns would give the following ammunition stowage: 1602 rounds of 152mm (178rpg), and either 1280 rounds (two mountings) or 1920 rounds (three) of 100mm (320rpg). Both types of ammunition would include contact- and time-fused rounds.

The STCN study also investigated the possibility of investing the additional 120 tonnes available in protection. Variant 4 had increases in horizontal protection only, Variant 5 increases in vertical protection only, and Variant 6 a mix; all three variants assumed that the original armament – i.e. that of the 7600-ton type – was unchanged. Detailed tables of thicknesses and weights were drawn up for comparison with Variants 1–3, but although there was seen to be some benefit in increasing the protection over the steering gear, the overall increase in protection was found to be insignificant, and would certainly have added less to the ship's capabilities than the proposed modifications to the main and secondary guns.

Having considered all the possible options the STCN therefore expressed a strong preference for a ship with the 70 degrees main gun mounting, two or three 100mm *type avisos-dragueurs*, twin catapults on the shelter deck and three aircraft, with protection similar to the *La Galissonnière*. This was accepted by the Naval General Staff.

The 1936 design

By late 1936 detailed drawings for the new ship had been produced. There was one important modification: by adopting a broad single funnel in place of the twin funnels of the 7600-ton type sufficient space was created for twin hangars, Royal Navy-style, abreast the

De Grasse: Preliminary Studies, 1936

Variant 1a with 152mm Mle 1930 (593 ST)

4 aircraft

Variant 1b with 152mm CA Mle 1936 (594 ST)

4 aircraft

Variant 1c with quad. 152mm CA Mle 1930 aft

4 aircraft

Variant 1d with 100mm CAD Mle 1931

4 aircraft

Variant 2 with 2x100mm CAD Mle 1933 (614 ST)

3 aircraft

Variant 3 with 3x100mm CAD Mle 1933 (615 ST)

3 aircraft

(© Bruno Gire, 2007)

De Grasse: Profile & Plan 1936

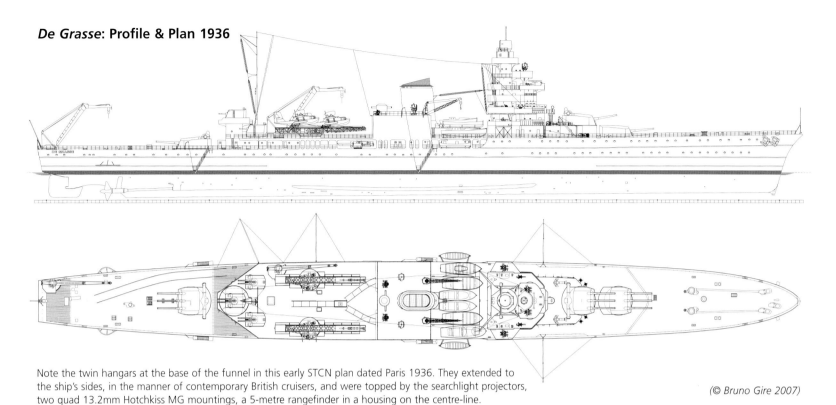

Note the twin hangars at the base of the funnel in this early STCN plan dated Paris 1936. They extended to the ship's sides, in the manner of contemporary British cruisers, and were topped by the searchlight projectors, two quad 13.2mm Hotchkiss MG mountings, a 5-metre rangefinder in a housing on the centre-line.

(© Bruno Gire 2007)

funnel. As with the British ships the roofs of the hangars were used to accommodate fire control directors and light AA guns (see 1936 drawing), and there were tracks leading from each hangar to the centre-line, where they crossed a powered elevating platform similar to that of the new battleships, the function of which was to raise the aircraft to the level of the catapults; they could then be transferred manually without use of the crane.

There was, however, a cost to the new arrangements. Space for the catapults was squeezed to such an extent that the port-side catapult had to be moved inboard in order to accommodate the handling crane. An athwartships catapult similar to that fitted in the latest British battleships and cruisers would have provided a far superior arrangement, but no such model had been developed for the Marine Nationale.

The second problem was that there was a substantial increase in topweight, and the Marine Nationale became concerned that standard displacement might now exceed the 8000-ton treaty maximum. By 1938 the double hangar had again been suppressed, and the reserve aircraft had to be stowed on the centre-line rail between the catapults (see 1938 drawing). The layout of the fire control directors and the light AA needed to be revised in consequence. In part compensation, Vice-Admiral Darlan requested at the last moment that the original twin torpedo tubes become triples. This change was implemented, but it is clear from a note from the Chief of Naval Staff that although officially the new cruiser displaced precisely 8127 tonnes (8000 tons) this figure was likely to be exceeded on completion.[2]

The 1938 design

By January 1938 the official specifications of the *De Grasse* were as follows:

[2] Note 100 EMG.3 dated 29 January 1938.

– main armament: as *La Galissonnière* but with triple mountings derived from the dual-purpose mounts developed for the battleships of the *Richelieu* class; maximum elevation 70 degrees;
– secondary armament: three twin 100mm Mle 1933 dual-purpose guns in pseudo-turrets *type avisos-dragueurs*;
– close-range AA: four twin 37mm Mle 1933 semi-automatic mountings,[3] with one quad and two twin 13.2mm Hotchkiss MG;
– fire control: two directors superimposed (as in the battleships) atop the forward tower, of which the lower was for control of the main and secondary guns against surface targets and the upper for HA fire control; there was also an after auxiliary director for emergency control of the 100mm guns;
– torpedo tubes: two triple 550mm mountings;
– aviation: two aircraft (one reconnaissance, one fighter) accommodated either on the catapult or on rails on the centre-line;
– protection: armour broadly comparable to *La Galissonnière*, but with additional light splinter protection for the command spaces and the directors;
– speed and endurance: a maximum speed of 33.5 knots was specified; endurance was to be 8000nm at 15 knots with a full load of fuel; both these figures were an improvement on the *La Galissonnière* (31kts/5000nm at 15kts).

ORDERS AND CONSTRUCTION

The first of the three cruisers, *De Grasse*, was autho-

[3] The *Directeur général de l'artillerie navale* had pressed for the 37mm automatic mounting then under development (Mle 1935), but this required an ammunition lobby directly beneath the mounting, making it difficult to find suitable locations; in any case this mounting failed to materialise before the Armistice of 1940.

rised on 31 December 1936 under the 1937 *tranche*. The order was placed with the Lorient Naval Dockyard, and the ship was laid down on 28 August 1939, a few days before the outbreak of the Second World War; she was due to enter service in September 1942. The second ship, *Châteaurenault*, was authorised on 31 December 1937 under the 1938 Estimates and ordered from the private shipyard Forges et Chantiers de la Méditerranée, which had recently completed the 7600-ton cruiser *Montcalm*; her entry into service was projected for 1944. A third ship, *Guichen*, was authorised on 2 May 1938 under the supplementary 1938 *bis* Estimates, and was to have been built by Forges et Chantiers de la Gironde at Bordeaux, which had recently completed the *Gloire*.

When war was declared on 3 September 1939, construction of the *De Grasse* was suspended and the orders for her two sisters were cancelled. Work was

resumed on 28 September with the workforce available, but was again suspended on 10 June 1940. The ship was only 28 per cent complete at this time; the boilers and machinery had yet to be installed. On 22 June the Germans occupied Lorient and envisaged continuing construction with a view to clearing the slipway. Work on the hull proceeded slowly, and in August 1942 it was proposed to complete the ship as an aircraft carrier of 11,000 tons, with a complement of thirty-three aircraft. More than a year elapsed before work on this project commenced; there were delays in the delivery of equipment, and little enthusiasm or urgency was displayed by the dockyard workers. Work was further delayed when the ship was struck by two Allied bombs. When Lorient was liberated on 9 May 1945 it was found that that a large quantity of material had been concealed by the workforce in the double bottom of the ship! Construction was again resumed,

De Grasse: Profile & Plan 1938

By 1938 the original aircraft hangar had been suppressed, so the searchlight projectors and the rangefinder were mounted on platforms and a pedestal respectively. Note the position of the port-side catapult, which had to be moved inboard to accommodate the aircraft crane. The plans are dated Paris 22 July 1938; they were approved by the Navy Minister on 13 October of the same year.

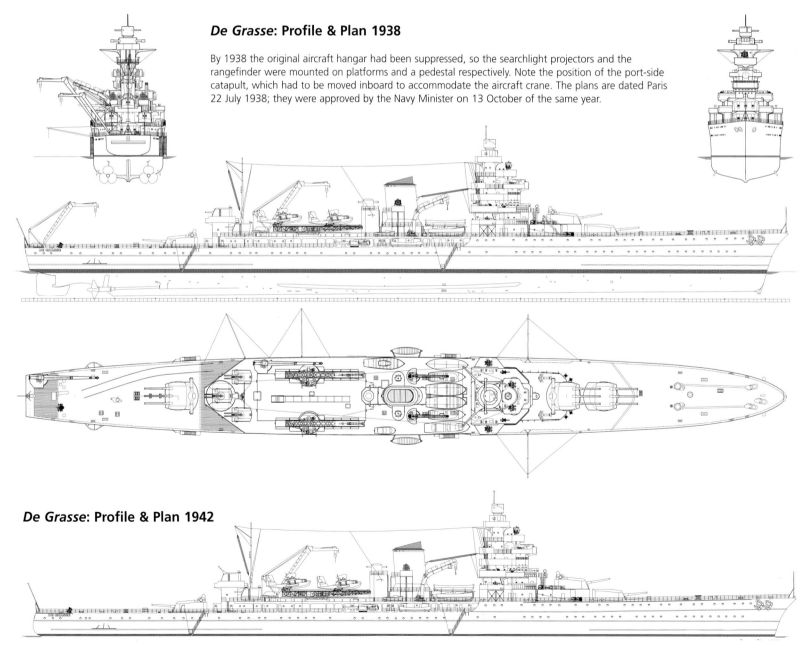

De Grasse: Profile & Plan 1942

The most significant change in the plans dating from 1942 was the configuration of the stern. Following the suppression of the landing mat *De Grasse* would have resorted to a traditional cruiser stern in preference to the earlier transom.

(© Bruno Gire 2007)

BUILDING DATA AND GENERAL CHARACTERISTICS

Name	Builder	Laid down	Launched	In service
1937 Programme				
De Grasse	Arsenal de Lorient	28 Aug 1939	11 Sep 1946	3 Sep 1956
1938 Programme				
Châteaurenault	F C Méditerranée	Cancelled		
1938 bis Programme				
Guichen	F C Gironde	Cancelled		

Displacement:	8000 tons standard
	8948 tonnes light
	10,190 tonnes trial
	11,431 tonnes deep load
Length:	180.4m pp, 188.0m oa
Beam (wl):	18.6m
Draught:	5.5m max. (normal)
Machinery:	Four Indret boilers, 35kg/cm^2 (385°C); two-shaft Rateau A.C.B. geared steam turbines; 110,000CV for 33.5kts
Oil fuel:	2080 tonnes; radius 1760nm at 33kts, 5000nm at 20kts, 8600nm at 15kts
Armament:	Nine 152mm/55 Mle 1930 in triple mountings Mle 1936 (1980 rounds);
	six 100mm/45 Mle 1933 HA in twin mountings Mle 1937 (1840 rounds);
	eight 37mm/50 Mle 1933 (6000 rounds) in twin mountings Mle 1933;
	eight 13.2mm Hotchkiss MG in two twin mountings and one quad mounting Mle 1931 (2000 rpg);
	six tubes for 550mm Mle 1923D torpedoes in two triple mountings Mle 1928T
Aircraft:	One Loire 130 recce, one Loire 210 floatplane fighter
Protection:	*Belt*: 100mm
	Deck: 38mm
	Turrets: 100mm faces, 40mm sides
	CT: 95mm sides, 50mm roof
Complement:	691

De Grasse: Inboard Profile

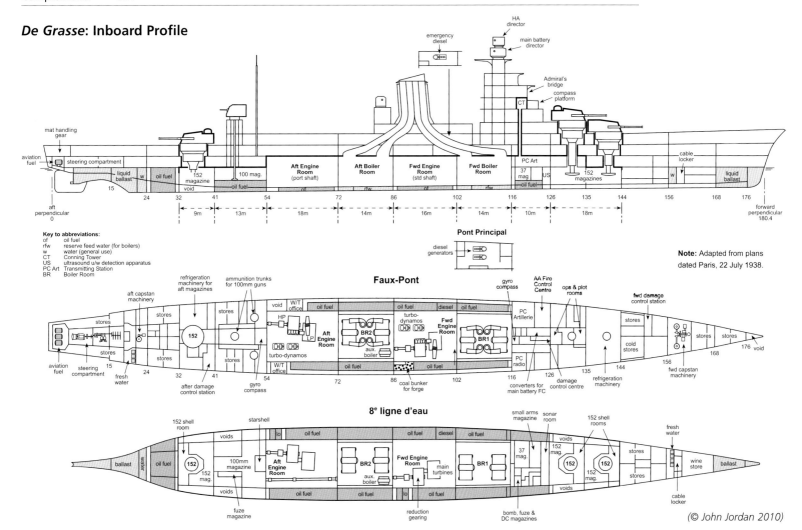

Key to abbreviations:
of   oil fuel
rfw   reserve feed water (for boilers)
w   water (general use)
CT   Conning Tower
US   ultrasound u/w detection apparatus
PC Art Transmitting Station
BR   Boiler Room

Note: Adapted from plans dated Paris, 22 July 1938.

(© *John Jordan 2010*)

De Grasse: Hull Sections

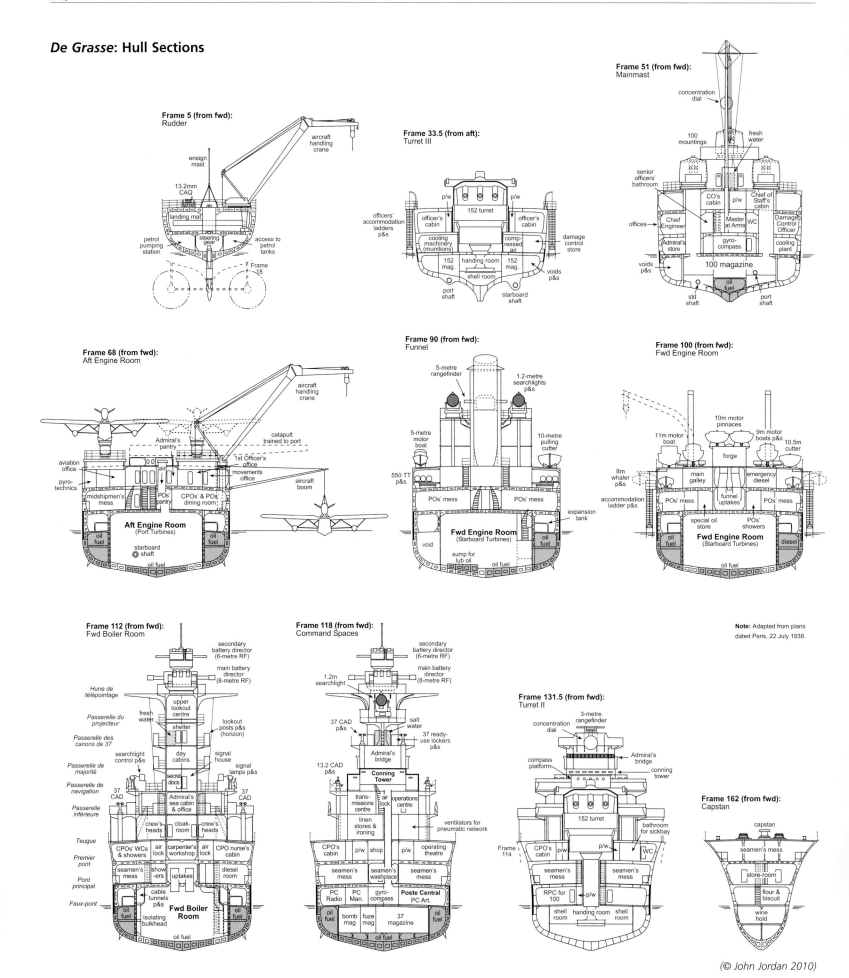

Frame 5 (from fwd): Rudder

Frame 33.5 (from aft): Turret III

Frame 51 (from fwd): Mainmast

Frame 68 (from fwd): Aft Engine Room

Frame 90 (from fwd): Funnel

Frame 100 (from fwd): Fwd Engine Room

Frame 112 (from fwd): Fwd Boiler Room

Frame 118 (from fwd): Command Spaces

Frame 131.5 (from fwd): Turret II

Frame 162 (from fwd): Capstan

Note: Adapted from plans dated Paris, 22 July 1938.

(© *John Jordan 2010*)

and the hull was finally launched on 11 September 1946. The hull would remain alongside while new plans for the ship's completion were considered.

NAMES

François-Joseph Paul, marquis de Grasse Tilly, comte **de Grasse** (1722–88) is best known for his command of the French fleet at the battle of the Chesapeake, which led directly to the British surrender at Yorktown. De Grasse was decisively defeated the following year by Admiral Rodney at the battle of the Saintes (known to the French as the battle of Dominica), where he was captured. A subsequent court martial cleared him of blame. He remains one of France's greatest admirals, and is held in equal esteem by the Americans, who named one of the destroyers of the *Spruance* class after him.

François-Louis Rousselet, marquis de **Châteaurenault** (1637–1716), fought against the Dutch admiral de Ruyter during the 1670s. He subsequently led squadrons at the battles of Pevensey and Lagos, and became commander of the French Fleet in 1694.

Luc Urbain de Bouëxic, comte de **Guichen** (1712–90), was an admiral who served alongside De Grasse during the American Wars of Independence. As C-in-C of the Channel Fleet, he was present at the battle of Ushant 27 July 1778, where his flagship, *Ville de Paris*, took station just abaft the fleet flagship *Bretagne* and several times fought off Keppel, Palliser and other determined English assailants. He subsequently fought against Rodney at the battle of Martinique (1780).

HULL AND GENERAL CONFIGURATION

Length between perpendiculars was increased by 8.5m over the 7600-ton type and beam by just over a metre. Trial displacement, projected at 10,190 tonnes, was almost 1500 tonnes in excess of the 7600-ton cruisers and broadly comparable to that of the latest Italian cruisers of the *Abruzzi* type.

The hull-form was derived from the *La Galissonnière* class, but in order to secure the high speed required it was finer forward with greater flare, and the stem was

WEIGHTS: A COMPARISON

	La Galissonnière	De Grasse
Hull:	2524t	2887t
Wooden deck:	–	50t
Protection:[1]	1505t	1519t
Armament (incl protection):	1155t	1383t
Ammunition:	239t	264t
Torpedoes + TT:	33t	46t
Aviation facilities:	118t	164t
Propulsion:	1238t	1366t
Fittings:	1041t	1269t
Margin:	–	–
Weight equivalent to Light Displacement:	7795t	8948t
Fuel/provisions[2]	1850t	2483t
Full load Displacement:	9645t	11,431t
Trials Displacement:	8720t	10,190t

Note:
Trials displacement = light displacement + one half fuel and provisions.

[1] Breakdown of protection weights:		
Belt	520t	501t
Deck	500t	542t
Transverse b/hds	74t	75t
Splinter b/hds	192t	187t
Steering gear	18t	19t
CT	58t	67t
Bridge, etc.	–	10t
Funnel uptakes,cabling	85t	118t

[2] Breakdown of fuel and provision weights:		
Oil fuel	1530t	2080t
Diesel	55t	54t
Petrol	4.5t	5.3t
Reserve oil	20t	22t
Feed water	120t	165t
Drinking water	10t	14t
Washing water	40t	55t
Food and provisions	34t	41t
Meat	2.8t	6.9t
Wine	10t	14t
Consumables	23t	25t

less curved at the waterline. There were 60-metre bilge keels 0.7m wide. High-tensile 60kg steel was used for the first time in the construction of the hull. Overall hull weight as a proportion of light displacement remained at just over 32 per cent.

Construction was again on the longitudinal principle. There was some welding of joints and decks but riveting continued to be employed for the strength elements of the hull girder and for the hull plating.

Below: De Grasse in the Lanester Building Dock at Lorient on 9 September 1940. Construction of the hull was well-advanced by this time. (ECPA)

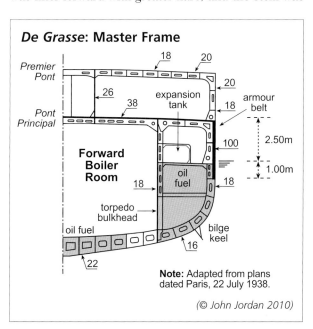

De Grasse: Master Frame

Premier Pont

Pont Principal

18   20
26   expansion tank   20
38   armour belt   18

Forward Boiler Room

100   2.50m
1.00m

oil fuel

18   18

torpedo bulkhead

oil fuel   bilge keel

16

22

Note: Adapted from plans dated Paris, 22 July 1938.

(© John Jordan 2010)

Topweight was reduced, as in other contemporary light French surface units, by the extensive use of duralumin for internal partitions, ladders and other fittings. The upper deck had wood planking from the stern to the catapult pivots. The forecastle was to have a linoleum or rubberised covering as far as turret I, and the same covering was to be applied to the after part of the boat deck. All other exposed parts of decks were to have a special paint being trialled on the *Mogador* class. There was more attention to corrosion issues than in earlier ships; all metal sheets of 5mm thickness or less were to be galvanised, and other parts of the hull were to receive two coats of lead paint or special paint.

The silhouette combined features of both the *La Galissonnière* class and *Algérie*. The forward superstructure was a built-up tower, as in the latter ship, with a broad single funnel combining the uptakes from both boiler rooms stepped well abaft the bridge structure. The main fire control directors were superimposed atop the tower – a feature of the new fast battleships of the *Dunkerque* and *Richelieu* classes. The three twin 100mm mountings were grouped together aft, and anti-aircraft fire on forward bearings was provided by the four twin 37mm Mle 1933 mountings, which were located in the bridge wings. The aviation facilities were located between the single funnel and the after deckhouse for the 100mm guns, and the boat deck was between the funnel and the bridge.

COMMAND SPACES

The forward tower was influenced by *Algérie* and the new battleships of the *Dunkerque* class, and had exceptionally well-developed command spaces. The high tower supported the two superimposed fire control directors for the main and secondary guns and the forward searchlight projector. At its base was an admiral's bridge with good views forward and to port and starboard, for use while cruising and during the approach phase; it was equipped with auxiliary plotting and signal distribution centres, together with sea cabins for the personnel. There was a 3-metre open tactical rangefinder on the level above. During combat the admiral and key staff would operate from the lower bridge deck in the main superstructure, on the same level as the lower conning tower (see Introduction).

There were look-out stations equipped with binoculars on four levels of the tower. These reported to the port and starboard chiefs of the watch, whose stations were in the wings of the navigation bridge. On three of the four levels the lookouts shared the platform with the light 37mm and 13.2mm AA twin mountings (see drawing).

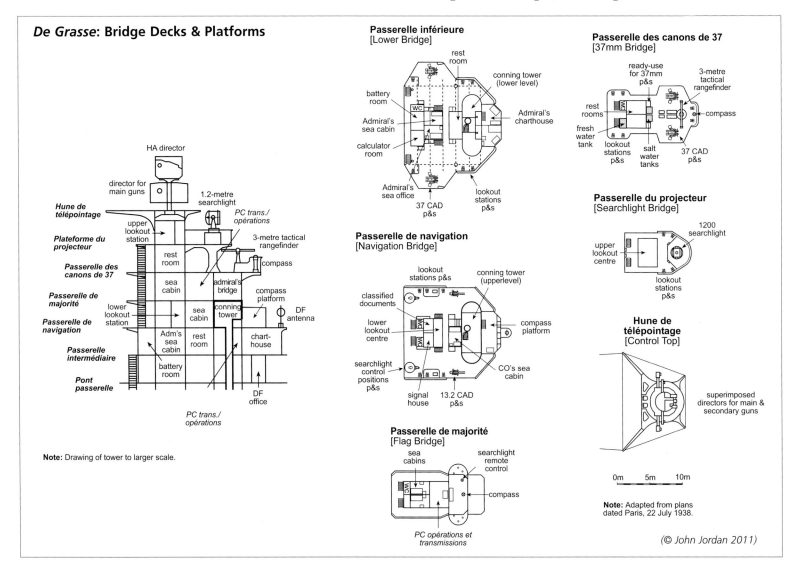

De Grasse: Bridge Decks & Platforms

Note: Drawing of tower to larger scale.

Passerelle inférieure [Lower Bridge]

Passerelle de navigation [Navigation Bridge]

Passerelle de majorité [Flag Bridge]

Passerelle des canons de 37 [37mm Bridge]

Passerelle du projecteur [Searchlight Bridge]

Hune de télépointage [Control Top]

Note: Adapted from plans dated Paris, 22 July 1938.

(© John Jordan 2011)

MACHINERY

Although the layout of the propulsion machinery of the *De Grasse* was identical to that of the *La Galissonnière* class, with two independent propulsion units each comprising a boiler room with two boilers in tandem and an engine room with a single set of geared turbines, power was increased significantly in order to secure the higher speed of 33.5kts stipulated in the staff requirements. Whereas both the *La Galissonnière* type and *Algérie* total horsepower (designed) was 84,000CV, in the *De Grasse* class this figure was to be increased to 110,000CV (121,000CV with forcing), which was close to that of France's first Treaty cruisers of the *Duquesne* class.

The four identical Indret small-tube boilers, which featured four collectors, superheating and air reheating, were similar in principle to those developed for the latest *contre-torpilleurs* of the *Mogador* class; they were rated at 35kg/cm² (385°C) – equivalent to 500psi and 725°F. Each boiler was enclosed in its own containment box and had its own auxiliary ventilators and emergency feed pumps.

Each of the two Rateau-AC Bretagne turbine groups comprised main HP, MP and LP turbines with single-reduction gearing. A cruise turbine, with single reduction gearing and a Vulcan coupling, was located in the housing of the MP turbine. It was decoupled above 15,000shp, equivalent to a speed of 20 knots. The reverse turbines were incorporated in the LP turbine housing. Together the reverse turbines were rated at 23,000CV, and were to be capable of stopping the ship when she was making 18 knots in only two and a half ship lengths. As with the boilers, each of the turbine groups was provided with its own independent auxiliaries.

The number of high-performance systems to be fitted in these ships necessitated a major increase in electrical generating power. The *La Galissonnière* class had been fitted with four paired 200kW turbo-generators located in the two engine rooms; the *De Grasse* class would have the same arrangement, but each of the four turbo-generators was rated at 300kW. The two dynamos in the same group could be coupled together in parallel. The provision for spare capacity was such that three dynamos were sufficient to power all services on board, even for night action; this permitted one dynamo to be closed down for maintenance. When alongside electrical power was provided by one or more of the three 150kW diesel generators, each of which was capable of a 180kW overload for one hour. One diesel generator was normally sufficient, but two or three needed to be on-line in order to train all turrets without the boilers being lit. Two of these three generators were located on the main deck above the forward boiler room; the third – considered to be the 'emergency' generator in the event of major flooding below – was housed in the forward deckhouse on the First Deck (see drawing).

GROUND TACKLE AND NAVIGATION

Cables and anchors were identical to those fitted in the *La Galissonnière* class. The three main anchors (two bower, one sheet) were in hawsepipes forward: two to starboard and the third to port. They were of the Byers type and each weighed 5600kg. The single stern anchor weighed 1600kg. As in the *La Galissonnière* class there was a single counter-balanced

POWER AND ENDURANCE (ESTIMATED)

Power vs speed
Basin trials suggested the following figures (trial displacement):

5710shp	= 15kts
15,290shp	= 20kts
33,320shp	= 25kts
60,170shp	= 30kts
110,000shp	= 34kts
127,460shp	= 35kts

The contract stipulated 33.5kts to be attained on trials.

Endurance
Practical consumption at various speeds (increase of 30% over theoretical consumption to take account of operational conditions):

33kts	1179kg/nm
25kts	593kg/nm
20kts	417kg/nm
15kts	241kg/nm

Bunker capacity 2080t fuel oil, so practical endurance estimated as follows:

33kts	1760nm
25kts	3500nm
20kts	5000nm
15kts	8600nm

[Order for emptying fuel bunkers established: lateral bunkers fwd and abeam turbines first, lateral abeam boiler rooms last.]

rudder, but it was significantly larger with a surface area of 29.98m².

PROTECTION

The protection system of the *De Grasse* class was similar in conception to that of the *La Galissonnière*. The midships section was protected by a 100mm vertical belt of special steel 3.5m high, which extended from the main deck to 1m below the waterline and covered the machinery, transmitting station and other main control spaces, together with the magazines for turret II and the 37mm AA guns. This belt was continued aft at a reduced height of 1.6m to protect the after 152mm and 100mm magazines and shell rooms (Frames 32–54), and forward to cover the magazine for turret I (Frames 135–144). There were 60mm transverse bulkheads at frames 32, 54, 135 and 144 to enclose the armoured citadel, and the thickness of these bulkheads was reduced to 18mm between the lower edge of the armour and the ship's bottom. Eighty-kilogram special steel was preferred to cemented armour because the technology of the period was insufficiently advanced to manufacture plates of the required length, and the number of vertical joints in the armour would have weakened the integrity of the bulkheads. Nevertheless a few plates of cemented armour were ordered for possible installation in these cruisers.

Outboard of the machinery, at a distance of 5.8m from the centre-line, there was a longitudinal (torpedo) bulkhead of 18mm 80kg special steel, and there was a similar bulkhead alongside the magazines up to the level of the magazine crowns. The uptakes for the broad single funnel were protected by longitudinal and transverse bulkheads 26mm thick between the armoured deck and the upper deck.

Horizontal protection was on a par with the *La Galissonnière* class: the main deck above the machinery was of 38mm special steel to protect the machinery

De Grasse: Protection

Profile & 1st Platform Deck

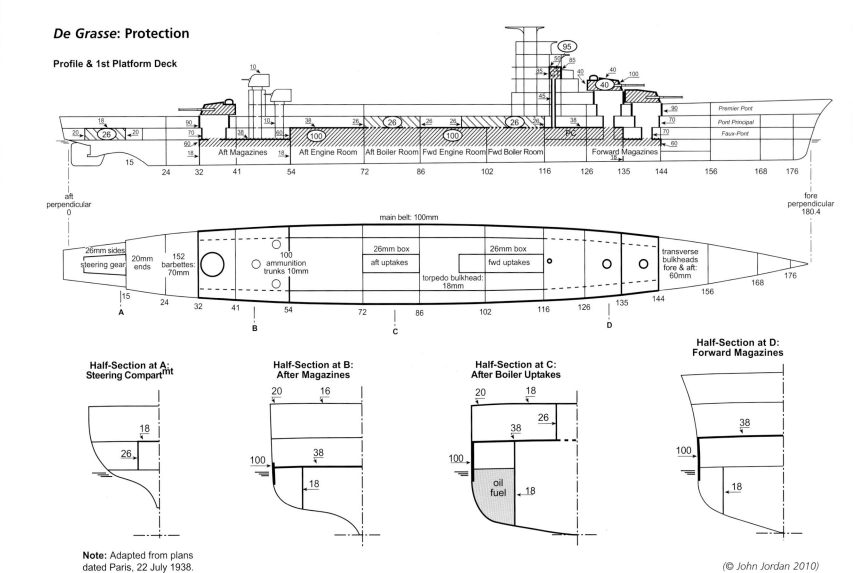

Note: Adapted from plans
dated Paris, 22 July 1938.

(© John Jordan 2010)

and main control spaces, and the decks over the 152mm and 100mm magazines were given the same protection. All penetrations of the armoured deck (funnel uptakes, ventilation trunking, etc.) were covered by fixed or removable gratings of special steel. The steering gear, as in *La Galissonnière*, was protected by an armoured box with 26mm sides, 20mm end bulkheads and an 18mm roof. (For the estimated effectiveness of the main vertical and horizontal plates see the accompanying table.)

The turret and the conning tower armour was again similar to the *La Galissonnière* (see table). In addition, the operations/transmissions centre directly beneath

the conning tower was protected by 20mm splinter plating. Plating of 10mm 80kg steel was applied to the gunhouses of the 100mm DP guns, the forward tower and some of its internal partitions, and the director housings. This was intended to provide protection against strafing and shell splinters.

Much attention was given to the protection of the 152mm and 100mm magazines fore and aft. The magazines were isolated from the hull by two protective 'walls': the 100mm outer armour belt and the 18mm internal 'splinter' bulkhead. There were the customary provisions for ventilation, refrigeration and flooding the magazines, and the space between the

EFFECTIVENESS OF ARMOUR

Values for penetration at normal angles. Armour effective:

		Beyond	
Vertical armour	130 Mle 1932	138 Mle 1927	152mm Mle 1930
(100mm special steel)	7400m	10,200m	13,900m
		Up To	
Armoured deck	130 Mle 1932	138 Mle 1927	152mm Mle 1930
(38mm special steel)	15,700m	16,200m	17,500m

Note: These figures do not take into account:
– the 18mm splinter bulkhead behind the vertical belt;
– the upper deck above the armoured deck.

TURRET AND CONNING TOWER ARMOUR

Turrets:
Fwd faces:	100mm
Sides:	40mm
Roofs:	40mm
Coamings:	90mm
Seatings:	70mm

Conning tower:
Walls:	95mm at sides, 85mm fwd/after faces
Roof:	50mm
Floor:	20mm
Comms. Tube:	45mm

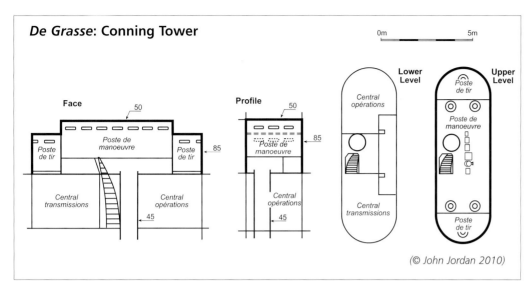

De Grasse: Conning Tower

Face — Poste de tir — Poste de manoeuvre — Poste de tir — Central transmissions — Central opérations

Profile — Poste de manoeuvre — Central opérations

0m 5m

Lower Level — Central opérations — Central transmissions

Upper Level — Poste de tir — Poste de manoeuvre — Poste de tir

(© John Jordan 2010)

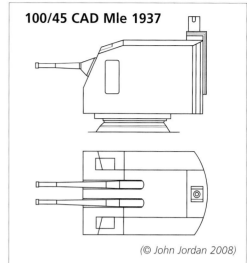

100/45 CAD Mle 1937

(© John Jordan 2008)

magazines and the bulkheads was to be filled with an inert substance called Alfol, which replaced the rock-wool favoured in earlier ships. The 152mm shells stowed in the magazine were protected by aluminium plates and the 100mm fixed ammunition by aluminium sheaths.

Compartmentation was so arranged that all sections of the ship were as far as possible autonomous. The ship was divided into sixteen compartments by fifteen main watertight bulkheads, and the propulsion machinery, as in the *La Galissonnière* class, was arranged as two independent units, each with its own pumps and other auxiliary machinery, in order to minimise the effects of flooding of the machinery spaces.

As in the *La Galissonnière* class there was to be an elaborate gas protection system. The alert system comprised three klaxons plus a network of green lights. There were gas masks for individual protection, all ventilation machinery for the machinery, the magazines and the command spaces could be shut down from the bridge, and there were also remote-controlled gas-tight covers for the ventilation trunking.

ARMAMENT
Main battery
The triple 152mm mountings to be installed in the *De Grasse* were essentially of the same model as the one designed for the battleships of the *Richelieu* class, but with a number of important modifications. Like those of the battleships – and unlike those of the *La Galissonnière* class – they were DP mountings intended to engage aircraft as well as surface targets. However, whereas the mountings in *Richelieu* had a theoretical angle of elevation of 90 degrees, with loading at all angles of elevation, this was reduced to 70 degrees for the mountings in *De Grasse*. This reduced the depth of the gun wells. Moreover, the three hoists which served each of the three guns – one for charges, one for contact-fused shells, the other for time-fused anti-aircraft shells – were disposed longitudinally. This meant that the distance between the guns could be reduced, resulting in a turret ring of smaller diameter, with a consequent saving in armour protection. The all-angle reloading mechanism was virtually identical to that of the *Richelieu*, and given that the battleship mountings were to give trouble at angles of elevation in

excess of 75 degrees, the arrangements adopted for the *De Grasse* would probably have been more satisfactory and just as effective.

There was magazine space for an impressive 1980 rounds (including exercise rounds). However, dual-purpose capability came at a cost. Only 900 rounds (100 per gun) were SAP; the remainder were time-fused HE rounds for anti-aircraft use.

Anti-aircraft weapons
The 100mm Mle 1933 was a 45-calibre weapon which fired a 14.9kg SAP shell or a 13.5kg time-fused HE shell at a muzzle velocity of 760m/s. The twin base-ring mounting, a lighter version of which was also to have been fitted in the *avisos-dragueurs* of the *Elan* and *Chamois* classes, had a gunhouse with 10mm plating, and therefore required more powerful motors for training. The guns, which were in individual cradles, could elevate from -10 degrees to +90 degrees and were supplied by pusher hoists with mechanical loading. Total provision was 1840 rounds, of which 600 were SAP rounds for use against surface targets and 280 were starshell.

The three 100mm mountings were grouped together

100/45 MLE 1933

Gun Data

Construction:	Monobloc autofretted barrel
Breech mechanism:	Horizontal sliding breech
Weight of gun:	1500kg
Type of munitions:	Fixed
Projectiles:	OPf Mle 1928 (14.9kg)
	OEA Mle 1928 (13.5kg)
	OEcl. Mle 1928
Propellant:	BM7 4kg
Complete round:	
Weight:	24.8kg
Dimensions:	1.02m x 0.15m
Muzzle velocity:	765m/s
Max. range:	15,800m
Ceiling:	10,000m

Mounting Data

Mounting designation:	CAD Mle 1937
Weight of mounting:	??t
Elevation of guns:	−10° / +90°
Firing cycle (per gun):	16rpm per gun theoretical
	10rpm practical

aft, the centre-line mounting being raised above the outboard mountings in such a way that all three fired above turret III. This gave them excellent arcs on after bearings but restricted coverage forward of the beam, particularly at low angles of elevation. In order to compensate for this four 37mm Mle 1933 twin AA mountings were mounted forward: two in the wings of the lower bridge deck, and two just above the Admiral's Bridge. The light AA outfit was completed by two twin 13.2mm Hotchkiss MG in the bridge wings and a quadruple 13.2mm Hotchkiss on the quarterdeck; the latter was offset to starboard to clear the aircraft rails.

Fire control

The lower of the two directors atop the forward tower, which was equipped with an OPL 8-metre stereo rangefinder, was specially fitted to control the main guns, and fire against surface targets could also be controlled from the armoured conning tower. The transmitting station was located forward beneath the armoured deck. As in the *Richelieu* full RPC in both elevation and azimuth was to be provided. Turrets II and III were also equipped with 8-metre stereo rangefinders and could act as secondary fire control positions, and turret III was to be fitted for this purpose with a mechanical computer *type Aviso* Mle 1936.

The principal fire control director for the 100mm guns was the upper director on the forward tower, although these guns could also be controlled by the lower director when firing against surface targets. It was fitted with a 6-metre stereoscopic rangefinder. There was also a rangefinder turret on a high pedestal directly abaft the funnel equipped with a 5-metre stereo model. Nothing beyond the standard off-mount 1-metre rangefinders with telephone links to the mountings would have been provided for any of the light AA guns

There were three 1.2-metre searchlight projectors for night action: one on the face of the forward tower, the other two on platforms projecting from the sides of the funnel. Full RPC was provided; all projectors could be controlled from positions in the bridge wings, and the forward projector could also be controlled from the main 152mm director.

Torpedoes

The two triple 550mm torpedo mountings were located on the upper deck amidships, as in the *La Galissonnière* class, and training arcs were 50 degrees either side of the beam. As in the earlier cruisers no reloads were provided. The six Type D5 torpedoes were embarked using the boat cranes.

AVIATION INSTALLATIONS

The twin catapults were located amidships on either side of the shelter deck abaft the single funnel. It was planned to accommodate a single reconnaissance seaplane with a maximum take-off weight of 3300kg (the latest Loire 130 model) and a single floatplane fighter (the Loire 210, due to enter service in 1939). Between the catapults was a lift with a rotating platform, similar to that installed in the *Dunkerque* class, which raised the aircraft to the level of the catapult. The aircraft could be transferred directly onto the catapult beams with the lift in the raised position.

The benefit of fitting a second catapult is not imme-

diately apparent. The *La Galissonnière* class could operate a (theoretical) maximum of four aircraft and yet were equipped with only a single catapult. This was not an entirely satisfactory arrangement, but the cramped arrangements on *De Grasse*, in which the port catapult had to be moved inboard to clear the aircraft crane, meant that they would have operated only two aircraft. The 1936 arrangement with a double hangar abeam the funnel, but with a single catapult to starboard, would seem much the best solution, and would have provided some protection for the aircraft from the elements. An asymmetric arrangement involving a single deck-edge catapult had already been trialled in *Algérie*, and appears to have been successful. The additional weight of the light steel plating used to construct the hangar would probably have been compensated by dispensing with the second catapult.

A canvas recovery mat similar to that fitted in the earlier cruisers and the seaplane carrier *Commandant Teste* was to be installed in the transom stern. This was served by a 4-tonne crane with a 13.5-metre reach located on the port corner of the stern. Once the aircraft was safely on the mat it was lifted aboard by this crane and placed on rails which ran forward along the quarterdeck to port of the after 152mm turret. A second 4-tonne crane, located on the shelter deck close to the port catapult and with a 16-metre reach, then lifted the aircraft onto the centre-line platform. There were 12-metre booms abeam the after turret to handle the aircraft when alongside. The cranes were to be used for recovery only; all aircraft manoeuvres prior to launch were carried out without use of the forward crane, which was normally stowed flat on the shelter deck so as not to obstruct the port catapult.

As in earlier French cruisers the aviation fuel – 5000 litres for the planes and 1800 litres for the boats – was stowed in special tanks located in the stern and isolated from all surrounding bulkheads; the tanks had a heat-resistant coating. The fuel was pumped to the aircraft station amidships using CO_2 under pressure.

BOATS

The boat outfit as designed was as follows:

– one 11-metre motor boat
– one 10.5-metre motor launch ('drakkar')
– two 10-metre motor pinnaces
– one 10-metre pulling cutter
– two 9-metre motor boats
– two 8-metre whalers
– one 5-metre motor boat

With the exception of the 10-metre pulling cutter and the 5-metre boat, which were outboard of the funnel, the boats were stowed abreast on crutches between the bridge structure and the funnel. They were served by two 'goose-necked' electric boat cranes similar in configuration to those of the later units of the *Suffren* class; these had a capacity of 7 tonnes. The two 8-metre whalers were on davits outboard of the funnel on the First Deck.

CONVERSION TO ANTI-AIRCRAFT CRUISER POST-WAR

In late 1946 it was still envisaged that *De Grasse* could be completed quickly without major redesign. It was felt that the 1938 design had been sufficiently

advanced in conceptual terms to be still relevant to the post-war era. Both major Allied navies, Britain and the USA, seemed convinced of the value of the 6in dual-purpose gun. The 100mm calibre of the projected secondary battery guns was still considered effective against aircraft, being intermediate between the 4.5in secondary guns of the British *Neptune* and the 3in weapon adopted post-war by the Americans for their cruisers and destroyers. Although the twin 45-calibre Mle 1933 of the 1930s had never entered service, the Marine Nationale had in 1945 begun the development of a new weapon with even better performance (20–25rpm), the 100mm/55 Mle 1945, which would equip the rebuilt battleship *Jean Bart* from 1952. However, a much heavier secondary battery was now envisaged for *De Grasse*, the aviation facilities being landed in compensation. The original 100mm wing mountings were to be retained, but were to be moved slightly farther forward so that two superimposed mountings could be accommodated on the centre-line aft, firing above the after 152mm turret. A further two twin mountings were to be installed abeam the single funnel, for a total of twelve 100mm Mle 1945 guns in six twin mountings.

The original light AA was now considered hopelessly inadequate by the Marine Nationale, which had been very impressed by the performance of the 40mm Bofors quad mountings installed in the *Richelieu* and the modern cruisers and *contre-torpilleurs* refitted in the USA during 1943–4. It was therefore proposed to fit seven quad Bofors mountings in place of the orig-

inal 37mm and 13.2mm AA. There were to be two mountings in the bridge, two on the shelter deck amidships in place of the catapults, two on the quarterdeck aft, and a seventh superimposed above the after 100mmm mountings.

Had it not been for a chronic shortage of funds and the chaotic state of France's naval dockyards and their associated industries during the late 1940s there can be little doubt that *De Grasse* would have been completed to the revised plans outlined above. A new long-term plan (*Marine Future*) promulgated in November 1947 called for six 152mm cruisers (the three 7600-ton ships plus three new-build) and six smaller AA cruisers. Under this plan the completion of *De Grasse* was to be authorised in 1950, with two new cruisers authorised in 1954 and 1956 respectively. The first five of the AA cruisers, studies for which were to begin immediately, would be authorised in 1949, 1950, 1952, 1954 and 1956.

On 30 January 1948 the Naval General Staff duly requested a formal study of an AA cruiser of 5/6000

Left: The completed hull is towed from Lorient to Brest for reconstruction in February 1951.

Above: The hull of *De Grasse* in the River Penfeld, Brest, shortly after her arrival from Lorient. Facing us, close to the bow, is the entrance to the *Point du Jour* slipway. On the right: the Bouguen plateau, with temporary prefabricated housing for the inhabitants of Brest made homeless by the bombs and demolitions.

Below: *De Grasse* as first completed. The DRBI 10B height-finding radar has yet to be installed. (*Robert Dumas collection*)

The profile and plan views are based on DGA official plans dated Brest 1957.
The light helicopter on the quarterdeck is the SE.3130 Alouette II, which first flew on
12 March 1955 and was used for liaison duties; the helicopter could be refuelled on
board ship but no hangar was provided. The plans show the radar outfit as
completed, with the antenna for the DRBV 22 air surveillance radar
above the DRBV 11 combined surface/air surveillance radar on the
pole foremast, and the DRBI 10 height-finder on its pedestal
abaft the funnel.

De Grasse as an AA Cruiser

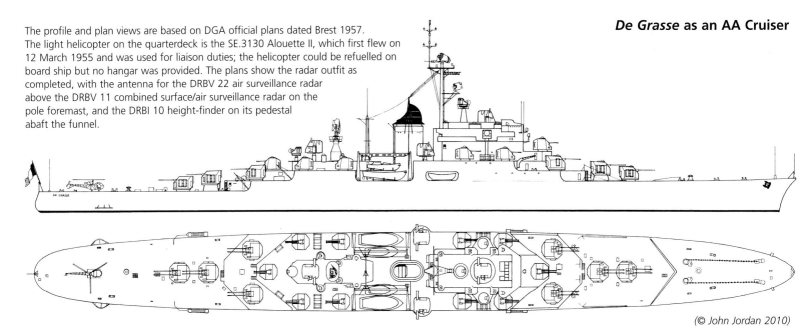

(© John Jordan 2010)

tons standard. It was envisaged that the ship would be armed with the twin 130mm mounting under development after the war, which as a result of a decision of 6 June 1947 would now be modified to accommodate a 127mm/54 gun designed to use US Navy 5in ammunition. However, a new 152mm dual-purpose weapon using proximity-fused shells was not excluded from consideration.

The constructors of the STCN experienced considerable difficulty in designing an effective ship on such a limited displacement, and came up with two basic designs:

CA1: 6150tW (6968 tonnes trials), six twin 127mm, six twin 57mm.

CA2: 6600tW approx. (7400 tonnes trials), two triple 152mm DP, four twin 100mm, four twin 57mm.

Plan 50, adopted 9 April 1948, envisaged the completion of *De Grasse* alongside the first of the AA cruisers in 1952. Three months later the CA1 design was adopted, but with some modifications to allow more space for machinery and accommodation. There were

to be three twin 127mm mountings forward but only two aft, the twin 57mm mountings being paired abeam the forward superstructure, amidships and on the quarterdeck. The first was to be ordered in 1951 or 1952 for completion in 1956, and the second in 1955 for completion in 1959.

The *Projet de statut naval* of 29 August 1949 still envisaged six 7000-tonne AA cruisers – a figure subsequently amended to five cruisers of 8000 tonnes. However, the projects drawn up by the Marine Nationale after the war were becoming increasingly detached from the hard financial realities which faced the French government of the period. French naval priorities in the early post-war years were reconstruction, the consolidation of existing force structures and the integration of ex-German and ex-Italian war prizes, together with the development of a new generation of weapons and sensors of French design and manufacture; new construction would have to wait.

The key factor which was to revitalise naval construction was French membership of NATO in 1949, which was followed by a massive injection of American funding in the form of the Mutual Defense

DE GRASSE AS AN ANTI-AIRCRAFT CRUISER 1956

Displacement:	9380 tons standard
	11,350 tonnes trials
	12,520 tonnes full load
Length:	180.4m pp, 188.0m oa
Beam:	18.6m wl
Draught:	5.5m, 6.3m max.
Machinery:	Four Indret boilers, 35kg/cm^2 (385°C); two-shaft Rateau A.C.B. geared steam turbines; 105,000CV; speed 33kts
Oil fuel:	1850 tonnes; radius 6000nm at 18kts, 2000nm at 31kts
Armament:	Sixteen 127mm/54 Mle 1948 in twin mountings (4800 rounds); twenty 57mm/60 Mle 1951 HA in twin mountings (30,000 rounds)
Electronics:	*Surveillance radars*: DRBV 22A, DRBV 11, DRBI 10B
	Navigation radars: DRBN 31
	FC radars: Four DRBC 11, four DRBC 30,
	ESM: ARBR 10, ARBR 20
	Sonar: DSBV 1
Protection:	*Belt*: 76–100mm
	Deck: 38–68mm
Complement:	950 (980 as flagship)

Left: *De Grasse* at anchor in 1956, shortly after her completion, with all guns pointing skywards. *(Robert Dumas collection)*

Below: The midships section of *De Grasse* following her completion in 1956, with two of the ten 57mm twin mountings at centre. To the right and above them can be seen two of the four directors for the 127mm guns, topped by the dish antenna for the DRBC 11 gunnery fire control radar. *(Robert Dumas collection)*

Assistance Program (MDAP). In January 1951 it was decided that *De Grasse* would be completed as an anti-aircraft cruiser, with 55 per cent of the funding coming from MDAP. At the same time it was decided to modernise the two ex-Italian cruisers *Châteaurenault* and *Guichen*[4] to complement the new 'fleet escorts' of the *Surcouf* class. The latter were to be armed with a combination of the new 127mm Mle 1948 DP gun and the 57mm Mle 1951 AA gun, together with a new generation of air surveillance, target designation and fire control radars of French design and manufacture, and these would also be the main weapons and sensors fitted in the *De Grasse*.

General configuration and layout

When launched on 11 September 1946 at Lorient the hull was complete to the upper deck, and the propulsion machinery and hull protection were in place. All that remained was to build new superstructures and install the new armament. This would involve some important modifications to the existing structure: in particular, the magazine and hoist arrangements would need to be drastically revised. New generators would also be needed to cope with the increased electrical load.

The reduction in topweight resulting from the elimination of the 152mm turrets and conning tower with their heavy armour permitted much more built-up superstructures, which where possible were constructed of light alloy. The forecastle was extended to the quarterdeck, and a broad deckhouse built out to the ship's sides amidships to accommodate the powerful battery of AA guns. There was now a massive bridge block for the command spaces with a heavy pole mast at its after end. The funnel was no longer raked, and was topped by a prominent cowling

---

[4] Note that these were to have been the names of the second and third ships of the *De Grasse* class.

Right: The three after 127mm twin dual-purpose mountings on *De Grasse* shortly after her completion in 1956.
(Henri Landais collection, courtesy of Robert Dumas)

designed to take the exhaust gases clear of the enlarged bridge structure. The after superstructure was kept to a minimum, as in the original design – just sufficient to accommodate the after guns and their fire control directors. Abaft the funnel was a simple pole mast for the ESM antennae and radio communications aerials.

Below: *De Grasse* at sea in 1961, following a refit in 1960 in which four twin 57mm mountings and the two beam directors for the 127mm guns were removed to provide additional accommodation.
(Henri Landais collection, courtesy of Robert Dumas)

The anti-aircraft battery was disposed symmetrically at either end of the ship. There were two superimposed twin 127mm/54 Mle 1948 mountings on the centre-line fore and aft, with two wing mountings at the corners of the deck above, making for a 'lozenge' arrangement. The ten twin 57mm/60 Mle 1951 mountings were grouped around the forward and after superstructures one or two decks above, with one mounting of each group on the centre-line and the remaining four paired at the sides. The four fire control directors for the main armament, which were of the same model installed in the fleet escorts of the *Surcouf* class, were disposed in a 'lozenge' arrangement which reflected the layout of the turrets, the side-mounted directors being mounted directly abaft the forward 57mm guns on either side of the funnel. They were complemented by four smaller fire control directors for the 57mm guns, two of which were on the centre-line fore and aft, and the other two in the bridge wings above the forward group of gun mountings. This layout was intended to optimise all-round coverage for the AA battery at all angles of elevation, with up to eight aerial targets able to be engaged simultaneously.

De Grasse finally entered service in 1956, and served as an anti-aircraft cruiser until 1965, when she underwent conversion to a command ship for the French nuclear tests in the Pacific. A similar but purpose-built ship, *Colbert*, would be completed in 1959 and would subsequently undergo a missile conversion; details of the latter ship can be found in Chapter 12.

CHAPTER 8

THE C5 AND *SAINT LOUIS* DESIGNS

INTRODUCTION

With the completion of the three ships of the *De Grasse* type the cruiser programme on which the Marine Nationale had been embarked since 1922 would essentially be complete. It would have produced seven 'Treaty' cruisers of 10,000 tons standard displacement, armed with 203mm guns, three light cruisers and a training cruiser armed with 155mm guns, a minelaying cruiser armed with 138.6mm guns, and ten light cruisers of modern design armed with 152mm guns.

The current treaties had decreed a life-span of twenty years for cruisers above 3000 tons. That meant that the first of the 8000-tonne cruisers of the 1922 Programme, *Duguay-Trouin*, would be due for replacement in 1946, and her two sisters the following year. Given that it was taking an average of one year to design and 4–5 years to build a cruiser in France, early consideration would need to be given to the ships which would replace them.

Not only would there be no constraints on armament and displacement by 1946, but the Marine

Nationale now found itself in a difficult strategic environment in which the naval threat already posed by Italy was being matched by that of Germany. During the late 1930s the *Kriegsmarine* had laid down five heavy cruisers armed with 20.3cm guns, with a nominal displacement of 10,000 tons.[1] And where Germany led, France would be compelled to follow. Thus in the Spring of 1939 preliminary designs were drawn up by the STCN for a new cruiser design designated 'C5' (ie a successor to C4 *Algérie*).

THE DESIGN PROCESS

The documentation which has survived is fragmentary and incomplete. It appears that two basic variants were the subject of the preliminary studies: one with, and one without aircraft (A – *aviation*; SA – *sans aviation*).

---

[1] They completed at a standard displacement of around 14,250 tons. The French undoubtedly suspected this from the published dimensions, and this probably explains the jump in size between the C5 design of mid-1939 and the *Saint Louis* of May 1940.

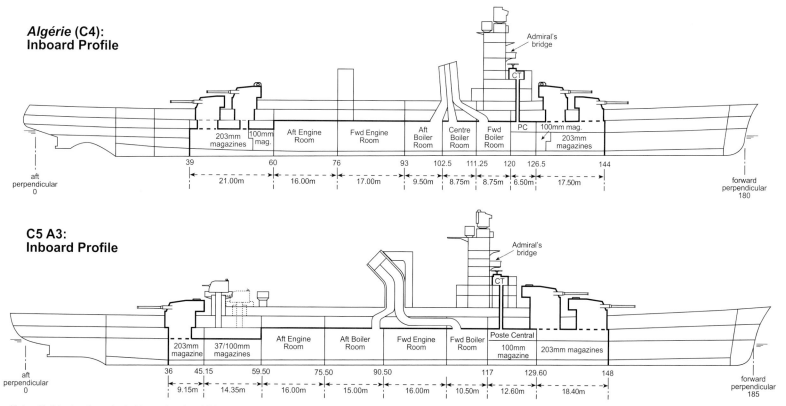

Algérie (C4): Inboard Profile

C5 A3: Inboard Profile

Note: *Algérie* drawing adapted from plan dated 31 Aug. 1935 (Brest); C5 A3 from ST1508 12 May 1939.

A note dated 12 May 1939 has plans and characteristics for two of these variants, which were probably the ones selected for competitive evaluation: A3 and SA1. The designation A3 suggests that there were also A1 and A2 variants; however, SA1 may have been the only variant without aircraft, with the object of demonstrating how much additional anti-aircraft capability could be purchased if the catapults and aircraft were suppressed. The Marine Nationale was still very much committed to aircraft aboard its major surface ships at this time – as is demonstrated by the inclusion of aircraft in the later *Saint Louis* – and the SA1 design was possibly no more than a 'what if...?' demonstrator.

Algérie (C4) was taken as the starting point for the studies, which featured a flush deck, a bridge tower structure, and a similar level of protection. The major difference was the adoption of a main armament of nine guns in three triple turrets. This gave the ships a single gun advantage over contemporary European cruisers, and also reduced the centre-line length occupied by the turrets, in theory freeing up space amidships for anti-aircraft weaponry and – in the case of the 'A' series – for aircraft. This was important because the NGS wished to accommodate not only the bulky twin 100mm Mle 1933 which had been adopted for the *De Grasse* class, but also the fully-automatic 37mm *Automatique Contre-Avions Double* (ACAD – automatic twin AA) mount currently under development, which required an ammunition lobby directly beneath the mounting.[2]

The influence of the *De Grasse* can also be seen in the layout of the main gun turrets, while the central 'mack' (combined mainmast and 'stack'/funnel) was similar to that adopted for the latest French battleships of the *Richelieu* class.

A3

The A3 design incorporated an impressive battery of five twin 100mm and four 37mm CAD mountings. The

---

[2] The first prototype mounting was installed for trials aboard the old sloop *Amiens* in the Spring of 1940.

Opposite, below: The only known photograph of the prototype 37mm ACAD gun mounting aboard the sloop *Amiens*. The photo dates from 1942. Note the twin barrels *en echelon*, and the director amidships covered by a tarpaulin.

WEIGHTS: A COMPARISON

	Algérie	C5
Hull:	3800t	3400t
Protection (hull):	1720t	1860t
Protection (armament):	315t	
Armament:	1415t	1950t
Propulsion:	1335t	1335t
Torpedoes/Aircraft:	111t	
Fittings/Provisions:	1427t	1615t
Miscellaneous:	37t	
Washington Displ.	10,160t	10,160t
OF + RFW:	750t	750t
Miscellaneous:	40t	40t
Normal Displ.	10,950t	10,950t
OF + Combustibles + Ammunition + Misc.:	2727t	2730t
Full Load Displ.	13,677t	13,680t

Note: In the Spring of 1939 preliminary designs were drawn up by the STCN for a new cruiser design designated C5 based on the *Algérie*. The data here reflect the initial staff requirements, which were found to be too 'tight'; weights were subsequently increased and standard displacement rose to 10,410 tonnes (10,246 tons) in the A3 design, and 10,515 tonnes (10,349 tons) in the SA1.

three after 100mm mountings were grouped together with the centre-line mounting atop a deckhouse, as in *De Grasse*. Two further twin mountings abeam the bridge covered the forward arcs. The twin HA directors – one to port, the other to starboard – were disposed atop the tower, as in *Algérie*. The 37mm ACAD mountings were likewise in forward and after groups. The forward mountings were on the forecastle deck abeam turret II, with the associated directors on the deckhouse above; the other two mountings were located at the after end of the shelter deck, with the associated directors between them.

Between the forward and after AA mountings were the twin catapults and a central 'rest' position with rails. Between the catapults there was an aircraft lift with a rotating platform similar to that of the *De*

C5 A3: Profile & Plan

9 - 203mm (3 x III)
10 - 100mm (5 x II)
8 - 37mm ACAD (4 x II)
6 - 533mm TT (2 x III)
3 Loire 130 recce seaplanes

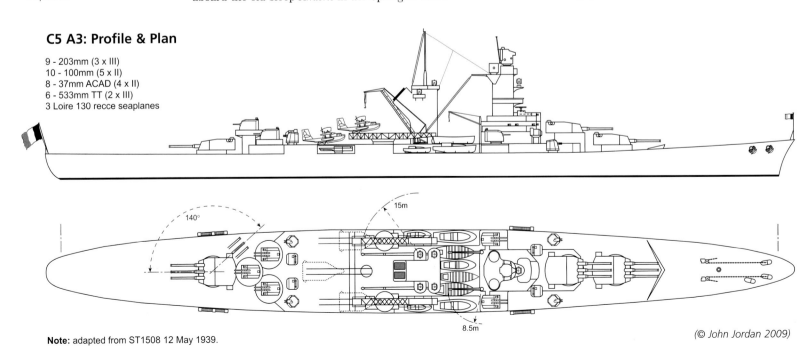

Note: adapted from ST1508 12 May 1939.

(© *John Jordan 2009*)

37mm Mle 1935 ACAD Air Defence System

The French 37mm ACAD mounting was one of the most advanced light AA guns in the world at the time of its conception in 1935. Requirements for the new gun were for a rapid rate of fire, a high-speed projectile to minimise 'dead time' (implying a high muzzle velocity), and a highly-sensitive contact fuse for instant detonation with as powerful a burster as possible to ensure maximum damage to the aircraft. These demanding – and partially conflicting – requirements proved extremely difficult to meet.

For a high sustained rate of fire it was important that the rapid fire possible with a single cartridge box (six rounds) be matched by a fast, reliable continuous replenishment system. This was realised in the Mle 1935 gun by inserting the cartridge box into the breech horizontally via the trunnion axis (see drawing). Continuity was achieved by using a continuous-belt hoist capable of rapid replenishment located beneath the rotating mounting and emerging on either side of the guns. Loaders in the ammunition lobby transferred cartridge boxes from a ready-use rack to a feed which replenished the hoist. Loaders in the gunhouse then transferred the boxes to the horizontal feed for the breech.

A problem experienced with the older-model 37mm guns was that the flash and vibration of rapid firing made aiming using the on-mount sights difficult. For continuous fire against a fast-moving target the mounting ideally needed to be controlled remotely from a separate position in which the personnel were isolated from the effects of firing. This was achieved by locating a director equipped with a 2-metre rangefinder close to the mounting and linking the two by an RPC system driven by Sautter-Harlé electric servo-motors. The director had a five-man crew: the control officer, a director layer, a director trainer, a cross-levelling operator and a rangetaker. The gun mounting itself was power-controlled in training but not in elevation. A complete 37mm ACAD installation, as exemplified in the accompanying drawing, comprised the twin mounting, its ammunition lobby and the director. In some shipboard installations, notably in the SA1 design, a single director controlled two gun mountings.

The 37mm ACAD mounting was built at Ruelle. Very high rates of fire were achieved with the prototype single gun, and a prototype ACAD mounting, designated Mle 1936, was

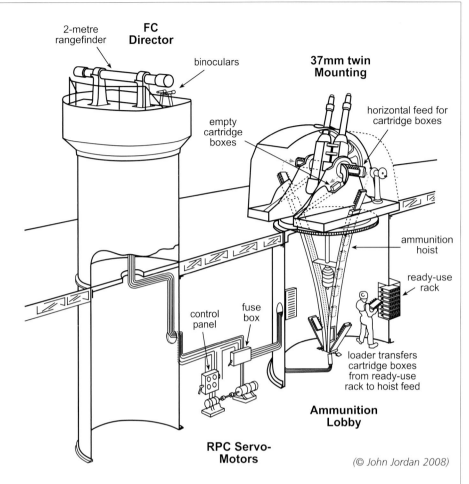

(© John Jordan 2008)

trialled aboard the sloop *Amiens* from 1939; it was used, apparently successfully, during the evacuation of Dunkirk. However, the high muzzle velocity and the comparatively heavy projectile combined to create a firing pressure of around 3000kg/cm^2, and this resulted in rapid barrel wear. The delay in the 37mm ACAD's entry into service was largely attributable to continuing efforts to resolve this problem.

Grasse and the *Dunkerque*; this enabled an aircraft on its trolley to be manoeuvred directly onto either catapult without the use of cranes. Landing mats had clearly been discredited by this time; there was no transom stern, no stern crane to lift the aircraft aboard, and no system of rails on the quarterdeck. There were, however, twin aircraft cranes with a 15-metre reach to lift the aircraft from the water when they landed alongside.

A full outfit of boats, handled by separate boat cranes at the after corners of the bridge structure (as in contemporary French battleships), could be accommodated forward and outboard of the funnel. And although the triple torpedo tubes are not shown on the original sketch drawing (Plan ST 1508), which comprises an inboard profile plus a plan view, these could easily have been located beneath the 'flight deck' section of the shelter deck, at First Deck level.

A3 was a neat, practical design with much to recommend it. There were only two small issues, although these would admittedly have been difficult to resolve. The location of the after 37mm ACAD directors was not ideal, as the directors were 'wooded' on after arcs at lower angles of elevation by the 100mmm

mountings; raising them on a deckhouse would have made them vulnerable to blast from the centre-line 100mm mounting if fired on forward bearings. It was also difficult to find a satisfactory position for the two whalers (on davits), as the obvious position – in the after angle of the shelter deck at First Deck level – would have obstructed the after 203mm guns on forward bearings.

SA1

In the *sans aviation* (SA) design, the deck-space taken up by the catapults and aircraft stowage abaft the funnel became available for the installation of a further two 100mm mountings and six (*vice* four) 37mm ACAD mountings. The sketch plan (ST 1509) also shows four quaduple 13.2mm Hotchkiss MG at the corners of the shelter deck, as in *Algérie*.

The additional 100mm mountings were to be fitted abreast the funnel, the boat deck being relocated to the former 'flight deck' abaft the funnel and served by a single centre-line crane with longer reach. There were now four after 37mm ACAD mountings, grouped in pairs to port and starboard, at the edges of the boat deck, with their two associated directors abaft the funnel. There was space for the two 8-metre whalers on davits outboard of the boat deck. However, there was unused deck space between the funnel and the bridge tower, and it would have been difficult to find sufficient space between the gun mountings for the torpedo tubes.

Arguably the greatest weakness of the SA1 design was that the increase in the number of AA mountings required a significant lengthening of the magazines to accommodate the required ammunition. Plan ST 1509 shows an after 100/37mm magazine section of 17.85m, as compared with 14.35m for ST 1508 (A3) – the compartmentation for the magazines and propulsion spaces is otherwise identical. This would have required an additional 3.5m of vertical and horizontal protection, and would have reduced the internal volume available for stores and accommodation. As the crewing requirements of the additional AA guns and their replenishment systems would almost certainly have exceeded the number of personnel required to

operate the ships' aircraft, this made it a less satisfactory design; in effect SA1 traded internal volume for deck space.

Saint Louis

Following the outbreak of the Second World War, construction of all ships not able to be completed in the short term was suspended, and the naval programme was reviewed. Note 162 FMF 3, dated 23 January 1940, authorised a new study for a cruiser with a standard displacement of 13,000 tons, and three of these ships featured in a decree dated 1 April 1940. Besides the new cruisers, the programme was to comprise two new battleships of 40,000 tons,[3] a light cruiser, six *contre-torpilleurs*, sixteen destroyers (*torpilleurs*) and six submarines. In a later modification to the programme dated 27 May (ie just before the collapse of the French Army which preceded the Armistice) the single light cruiser was deleted in favour of six more *contre-torpilleurs*. In the meantime the displacement of the proposed heavy cruisers had grown to 14,770 tons standard – remarkably close to that of the German *Admiral Hipper* class as completed.[4]

All that survives of the Note describing this project, which was dated 15 April 1940, is a handwritten draft outlining the general characteristics and four protection options (see table below). A further Note dated 15 May offered six possible names for consideration, all but one of which had previously been borne by battleships of the pre-dreadnought era. They were: *Saint Louis*, *Henri IV*, *Charlemagne*, *Brennus*, *Charles Martel* and *Vercingetorix*.[5] None of these names was

[3] The battleships would have had the same main armament layout as the heavy cruisers: two triple turrets forward and one aft (see *French Battleships 1922-1956*).
[4] A contemporary (January 1940) British heavy cruiser proposal, also with nine 8in guns, would have had a standard displacement of 15,000 tons.
[5] The same note proposed four names for the two 40,000-ton battleships: *Alsace*, *Normandie*, *Flandre* and *Bourgogne*.

C5 SA1: Profile & Plan

9 - 203mm (3 x III)
14 - 100mm (7 x II)
12 - 37mm ACAD (6 x II)
16 - 13.2mm MG (4 x IV)
6 - 533mm TT (2 x III)

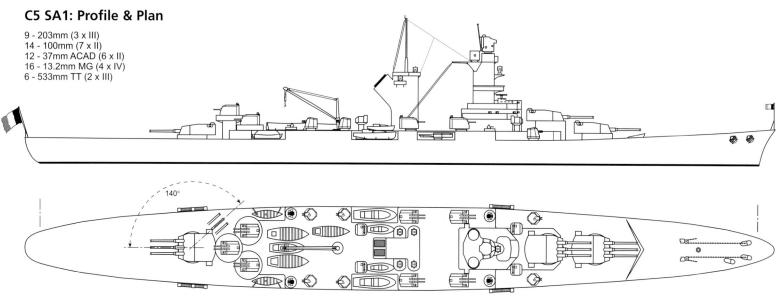

Note: adapted from ST1509 12 May 1939.

(© John Jordan 2009)

CHARACTERISTICS

	C5 A3	C5 SA1	*Saint Louis*
Displacement:	10,246 tons standard 11,970 tonnes normal	10,349 tons standard 12,070 tonnes normal	14,537 tons standard 16,000 tonnes normal
Length:	185m pp		202m pp
Beam (wl):	19.85m wl 21.8m		
Draught:	5.55m		
Machinery:	Four Indret boilers, 35kg/cm^2 (385°C); two-shaft geared steam turbines; 100,000CV for 32.5kts		120,000CV for 33kts
Oil fuel:			4200nm at 20kts + 200nm @ 33 knots
Armament:	Nine 203mm (3 x III) Ten 100mm Mle 1933 (5 x II) Eight 37mm ACAD (4 x II) Six 550mm TT (2 x III)	Nine 203mm (3 x III) Fourteen 100mm Mle 1933 (7 x II) Twelve 37mm ACAD (6 x II) Six 550mm TT (2 x III)	Nine 203mm (3 x III) Twelve 100mm Mle 1933 (6 x II) Twelve 37mm ACAD (6 x II) Six 550mm TT (2 x III)
Aviation:	Two cats / two aircraft	None	Two cats / two aircraft
Protection:		*Belt*: 100mm inclined 20° *Deck*: 80mm / 38mm *Turrets*: [as *Algérie*] *Underwater*: to resist 300kg warhead	[Four schemes under study – see text]
Boats:		11m motor pinnace 11m pulling pinnace 2 x 10.8m motor boats 10m pulling cutter 9m motor motor boat 2 x 7m motor boats 2 x 8m whalers (SA1 only?)	

Note: For the *Saint-Louis* class, endurance was calculated on the basis of a cruising speed of 20 knots + an allowance for combat at full speed.

officially attributed. The only surviving sketch, redrawn and reproduced here, shows a possible arrangement of the anti-aircraft guns.

The four protection options were as follows:

– Plan 1789: vertical side belt with flat armoured deck.
– Plan 1789 *bis*: inclined side belt with bulge; flat armoured deck.
– Plan 1789 *ter*: inclined side belt and bulge; armoured deck inclined (at sides?).
– Plan 1789 *qater*: side belt vertical, then inclined; bulge; flat armoured deck.

Option 4 seems distinctly odd, but may reflect French concerns regarding the tendency for inclined belts to deflect shells downwards into the ship's vitals. Presumably the vertical strake of the belt would have been at the waterline and the inclined strake above. If anything this unusual proposal shows the extent to which the French were still prepared to innovate (as with the *caisson* system of *Foch* and *Dupleix*) in their search for new solutions to perceived problems, even where this meant breaking with established practice abroad.

All discussion of these ships was halted by the German invasion.

St Louis 1940: Arrangement of Main & AA Guns

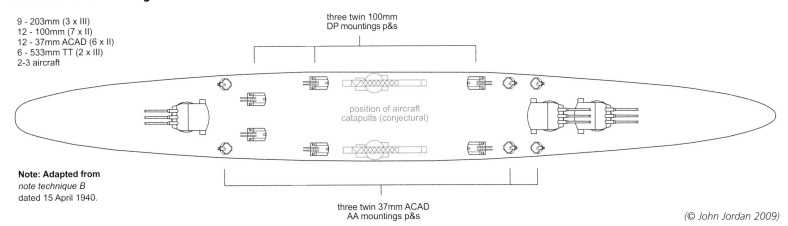

9 - 203mm (3 x III)
12 - 100mm (7 x II)
12 - 37mm ACAD (6 x II)
6 - 533mm TT (2 x III)
2-3 aircraft

three twin 100mm
DP mountings p&s

position of aircraft
catapults (conjectural)

Note: Adapted from
note technique B
dated 15 April 1940.

three twin 37mm ACAD
AA mountings p&s

(© John Jordan 2009)

CHAPTER 9:

THE PERIOD
1926–1939

ORGANISATION

During the period in question, and almost to the outbreak of war in September 1939, the bulk of the French naval forces were distributed between two major formations based respectively at Toulon and Brest. Some vessels, mainly sloops, were permanently stationed overseas, and a single cruiser was deployed to the Far East. Cruisers also undertook occasional long-range deployments which combined endurance trials with 'showing the flag'.

When serving with the fleet, cruisers were organised in divisions, in principle of three ships, initially designated 'light divisions' (*division légère* or DL) then, from 12 April 1937, 'cruiser divisions' (*division de croiseurs*

or DC). Ships which were not attached to a particular division were termed *hors rang*. They could be used as flagship of a group of *contre-torpilleurs* or a 'light squadron' (*escadre légère* or EL), or could be detached for an overseas deployment; they might also be placed *hors rang* if undergoing a major refit or reconstruction.

Training was undertaken according to an annual cycle termed the *année d'instruction*. The latter was derived traditionally from the French school year, and ran from October to July. A proportion of the crew of each ship, in part made up of conscripts, was renewed during the summer, with training recommencing in the Autumn. Training followed a logical progression: work-up with single ships, followed by exercises first with

THE ADMINISTRATIVE STATUS OF SHIPS

AFTER LAUNCH, A SHIP WAS MANNED READY TO RUN HER SEA TRIALS when fitting out was well advanced. The Navy designated an officer – *capitaine de vaisseau* (CV) for a cruiser – to take command of the ship and to supervise her progress to completion. The cruiser was from this point designated *armé pour essais*.[1] The trials period was marked by several administrative stages:

– The ship was accepted from the builder (*présentation en recette*) following the first sea trials of the propulsion machinery, provided the performance criteria outlined in the contract were met.
– The term *armement définitif* in practice corresponded to the physical completion of the ship.[2] The ship would now have her full peacetime complement and would have all consumables embarked.
– The term *clôture d'armement* signified that the ship and all its fittings and equipment had been accepted for service.

The date of *admission au service actif* was the date the ship entered service. She was now in theory complete – although in practice late delivery of equipment meant that this was not always the case – and her crew had reached a certain level of readiness. She was then generally incorporated into a formation (division, squadron).

Once in service, the ship was normally in a condition termed *armé* (in commission). However, even if the ship was operational there would still be periods when she was placed in care and maintenance (*disponibilité armée* or DA)[3] with a reduced crew, or in 'normal' reserve (*réserve normale*). If the ship was not operational, her status was defined as 'major repairs' (*grandes réparations*) or 'special' reserve (*réserve spéciale*).

Although a ship in normal reserve could quickly be returned to service if

assigned a full complement, a ship in special reserve could take a long time to become operational again, as she would require repairs and refurbishment to her equipment. Special reserve was generally followed by striking the ship from the list and then, unless the hull was to be used for accommodation, by sale for scrap.

Cruiser Designations

The designation of the different types of French cruiser is complex, and was subject to various revisions during the period in question. An official publication entitled *Listes de la flotte* is the key document in this respect, but usage often departed from the strict application of the official terminology.

The Washington Treaty of 6 February 1922 played a key role in the history of cruiser development by limiting displacement to 10,000 tons standard (10,160 metric tons) and main gun calibre to 8in (203mm).

In 1927 France had two types of cruiser in service: armoured cruisers and light cruisers. The former were inherited from the beginning of the century, while the latter comprised former enemy cruisers recommissioned to serve in the Marine Nationale, the three new 8000-tonne cruisers (*Duguay-Trouin* class), and the first of the 10,000-ton 'Treaty' cruisers, which were fitting out.

The London Treaty of 22 April 1930 introduced two new sub-classes of cruiser:

– Category 'A' cruisers armed with 8in (203mm) guns: the French would subsequently designate these '1st class' cruisers (*croiseurs de 1re classe*) from 1931; the Americans would classify their own ships as 'heavy' cruisers.
– Category 'B' cruisers armed with guns not exceeding 6.1in (155mm) calibre: for the French these ships would become '2nd class' cruisers (*croiseurs de 2e classe*) from 1931, for the Americans 'light' cruisers.

From 1931 the classification '1st class cruiser' embraced not only the French 'treaty' cruisers but the surviving armoured cruisers. Subsequently the terms 'heavy' and 'light' cruiser, made popular by the Anglo-Saxons, also came to be widely used in France, notably after the Second World War. In 1948 the '1st class' and '2nd class' designations disappeared altogether, and the fleet lists used only the term 'cruiser' for ships which had previously occupied one or other of these sub-categories, and 'light cruiser' for the *contre-torpilleurs* modernised in the United States in 1943.

---

[1] The terms *armé* and *armement* mean 'manned' and 'manning' respectively; this can be confusing to an English reader. The phrase *armé pour essais* literally means 'manned for trials'; *armement définitif* (see below) implies that the ship now had her full complement.
[2] Key items of equipment such as fire control directors were often fitted only after sea trials. If the ship was built at Lorient or in a private shipyard these items were generally installed at Brest.
[3] From 1932 the term *en complément* was used.

FRENCH FLEET: ORGANISATION 11 DECEMBER 1929

1re Escadre
> 1re escadre de ligne
>> 1re DL: *Provence, Bretagne, Paris*
>> 2e DL: *Courbet, Jean Bart, Lorraine*
>> *Béarn*
>> 1re DL: *Duquesne, Suffren, Tourville* (temporarily attached)
> 1re escadre légère:
>> 3e DL: *Lamotte-Picquet, Primauguet, Duguay-Trouin*
>> 5e DL: *Panthère, Tigre, Chacal, Guépard*
> 1re flottille de torpilleurs:
>> 1re escadrille de torpilleurs:
>>> *Amiral Sénès*
>>> 1re DT: *Boulonnais, Tempête, Bourrasque, Ouragan, Brestois, Orage, L'Adroit*
>>> 3e DT: *Tornade, Tramontane, Trombe, Typhon*
>> 3e escadrille de torpilleurs:
>>> *Siroco*
>>> 5e DT: *Cyclone, Mistral, Simoun*
>>> 7e DT: *Le Mars, Le Fortuné, La Railleuse, La Palme*
>> 4e escadrille de torpilleurs:
>>> 8e DT: *Chastang, Mazaré, Deligny, Vesco*
>>> 10e DT: *Delage, Rageot de la Touche, Buino, Pierre Durand*
> 3e escadrille de sous-marins: *Marsouin, Souffleur, Requin, Narval, Dauphin, Espadon, Morse, Phoque, Caïman*
> Train d'escadre: *Vulcain, Champlain, Arroyo, Fraiche, Trident, Dunkerque, Nancy, Aube, Rance*

2e Escadre:
> 2e escadre légère:
>> 2e DL: *Mulhouse, Strasbourg*
>> 4e DL: *Léopard, Lynx*
> 3e division de ligne:
>> *Diderot, Voltaire*
> 2e escadrille de torpilleurs
>> *Mécanicien principal Lestin*
>>> 2e DT: *Touareg, Annamite, Hova, Somali*
>>> 4e DT: *Arabe, Algérien, Bambara, Kabyle*
>>> 6e DT: *Marocain, Tonkinois, Sakalave, Sénégalais*
> 4e escadrille de sous-marins: *Léon Mignot, Jean Roulier, Jean Autric, Pierre Marrast*
> Train d'escadre: *Nièvre, Durance, Ruisseau, Allier*

3e Escadre:
> *Condorcet*
> Ecole des torpilleurs-électriciens:
>> *Torpilleur 349, Torpilleur 369, Chasseur 85*
> CEPLT-EALM:
>> *Thionville*
> Ecole de canonnage:
>> *Ernest Renan, Rhin, Chasseur 79*
> 5e escadrille d'avisos:
>> *Suippe, Yser, Scarpe*
> 13e DT: *Intrépide, Aventurier, Opiniâtre, Téméraire*
> Ecole de tir à la mer:
>> *Gueydon*
> Ecole des mécaniciens de Toulon:
>> *Bisson, Chasseur 103, Chasseur 108, Chasseur 109, Perce-Neige*

FNEO:
> *Waldeck Rousseau*
> *Régulus, Altaïr, Algol, Marne, Craonne*

Division navale du Levant:
> *Diana, Baccarat, Liévin, Montmirail*

Marine au Maroc:
> *Duperré*

Station du Pacifique:
> *Cassiopée*

Station de l'Atlantique:
> *Antarés, Aldebaran*

Station de l'océan Indien:
> *Bellatrix*

Ecole d'Application:
> *Edgar Quinet*

FRENCH FLEET: ORGANISATION 1 AUGUST 1933

1re Escadre:
> 1e DL: *Lorraine*
> 2e DL: *Jean Bart, Béarn, Commandant Teste*
> 1re DL: *Foch, Colbert, Suffren, Tourville*
> Groupe des contre-torpilleurs:
>> 7e DL: *Verdun, Guépard, Albatros*
>> 5e DL: *Gerfaut, Aigle, Vautour, Tartu*
> 1re flottille de torpilleurs:
>> *Jaguar*
>> 1re escadrille de torpilleurs:
>>> 7e DT: *Le Mars, La Railleuse, Le Fortuné*
>>> 5e DT: *Cyclone, Basque, Simoun*
>> 3e escadrille de torpilleurs:
>>> 11e DT: *L'Alcyon, Fougueux, Frondeur*
>>> 9e DT: *Foudroyant, Brestois, Forbin*
> 3e escadrille de sous-marins:
>> *Suippe*
>> *Redoutable, Vengeur, Actéon, Fresnel, Pégase, Phénix*
> Train d'escadre:
>> *Rhône, Fraîche, Nancy*
> Groupe de complément:
>> *Valmy, Tramontane, Boulonnais, La Palme*
> Division d'instruction:
>> *Paris, Courbet, Condorcet*
>> *Pluton, Rhin*
>> 9e DL: *Panthère, Tigre*
>> 5e escadrille d'avisos: *Yser, Scarpe, Engageante*
>> Annexes: *T 349, T 369, Chasseur 79, Chasseur 85*

2e Escadre:
> *Lamotte-Picquet*
> Groupe des contre-torpilleurs:
>> 6e DL: *Bison, Maillé-Brézé, Vauban*
>> 4e DL: *Lion, Léopard, Lynx*
> 1re DT: *L'Adroit, Orage, Bourrasque*
> 4e escadrille de sous-marins:
>> *Jules Verne*
>> *Poncelet, Argo, Pascal, Henri Poincaré*
> Train d'escadre: *Niévre*

Division Navale du Levant:
> *Diana, Vimy, Ypres*

FNEO:
> *Primauguet*
> *Dumont d'Urville, Altair, Régulus, Algol, Marne, Tahure*

the division and then with the fleet. Most of these exercises, both for single ships and for groups, took place between the coast of southern France and Corsica in the Mediterranean, or off Brest and in the Bay of Biscay in the Atlantic. They were interrupted by short stays in the anchorages off the French coast (Villefranche and Hyères or Les Salins in the south of France, Quiberon or Douarnenez Bays in Brittany). Group exercises often took the ships to the coasts of North Africa. In general, the training year ended with a cruise to the eastern Mediterranean or to Dakar (or even the Gulf of Guinea) in West Africa, terminating in major exercises in which the squadrons based at Brest and Toulon were combined, generally during the month of June.

These periods of activity were punctuated by maintenance and docking periods. The latter, termed *petits carénages*, were frequent. Major refits (*grands carénages*) were generally undertaken with reduced crews (DA), and provided an opportunity for reconstruction and modernisation.

THE FRENCH CRUISERS IN 1927

A 3rd Light Division (3e DL) was formed from 19 November 1926 for the three 8000-tonne cruisers. The first cruiser to be laid down since the First World War, *Duguay-Trouin* was also the first of her class to enter service on 15 February 1927.

In 1927 the cruisers currently in service were divided into two groups. The first group comprised the large armoured cruisers built before the war, now largely obsolete:

- *Jeanne d'Arc*, serving as a school ship (*Ecole d'application*)[4] for officer cadets, which would be decommissioned after the 1927–8 world cruise.
- *Gueydon*, which would serve as a gunnery school

---

[4] The principle of the *Ecole d'Application* was that it gave the officers under training the opportunity to 'apply' the skills and knowledge acquired during their two years of theoretical studies at the Naval College (*Ecole Navale*) at Brest.

BUILDING DATES OF FRENCH CRUISERS 1922–1937

8000-tonne Cruisers / Minelayers/School Ship

Name	Duguay-Trouin	Lamotte-Piquet	Primauguet	Pluton	Jeanne d'Arc	Emile Bertin
Programme	1922	1922	1922	1925	1926	1930
Hull no.	1	2	3	71	95	155
Project no.					E1	CL1
Builder	Brest	Lorient	Brest	Lorient	Penhoët	Penhoët
First plates cut	14 Apr 1922	18 Apr 1922	14 Apr 1922	1 Mar 1927	8 Oct 1928	11 Sep 1931
Laid down	4 Aug 1922	17 Jan 1923	16 Aug 1923	16 Apr 1928	31 Aug 1928	18 Aug 1931
Launched	14 Aug 1923	21 Mar 1924	21 May 1924	10 Apr 1929	14 Feb 1930	9 May 1933
Sea trials	1 Aug 1925	1 Feb 1926	1 Feb 1926	15 May 1930	15 Dec 1930	15 May 1933
Acceptance trials	6 May 1926	2 Jul 1926	16 Jun 1926	10 Mar 1931	28 Jan 1931	10 Jul 1934
Commissioned	10 Sep 1926	1 Sep 1926	1 Oct 1926	15 Nov 1931	1 Apr 1931	15 Oct 1934
Completed	2 Nov 1926	5 Mar 1927	1 Apr 1927	1 Oct 1931	14 Sep 1931	28 Jan 1935
Entered service	15 Feb 1927	19 Nov 1927	25 Apr 1927	25 Jan 1932	6 Oct 1931	17 May 1935

10,000-ton Cruisers

Name	Duquesne	Tourville	Suffren	Colbert	Foch	Dupleix	Algérie
Programme	1924	1924	1925	1926	1927	1929	1930
Hull no.	44	45	54	77	100	119	141
Project no.				C1	C2	C3	C4
Builder	Brest	Lorient	Brest	Brest	Brest	Brest	Brest
First plates cut	1 Jul 1924	1 Jul 1924	1 Nov 1925	1 Mar 1927	1 Mar 1928	1 Apr 1929	15 May 1930
Laid down	30 Oct 1924	4 Apr 1925	17 Apr 1926	12 Jun 1927	21 Jun 1928	14 Nov 1929	19 Mar 1931
Launched	17 Dec 1925	24 Aug 1926	3 May 1927	20 Apr 1928	24 Apr 1929	9 Oct 1930	21 May 1932
Sea trials	1 Aug 1927	20 Sep 1927	20 Aug 1928	15 Jun 1929	1 Aug 1930	1 Oct 1931	15 May 1933
Acceptance trials	15 Nov 1927	3 Feb 1928	20 Dec 1928	29 Aug 1929	16 Dec 1930	1 Dec 1931	22 Dec 1933
Commissioned	1 May 1928	5 May 1928	1 May 1929	11 Nov 1929	15 Mar 1931	1 May 1932	15 Jun 1934
Completed	6 Dec 1928	1 Dec 1928	1 Jan 1930	4 Mar 1931	15 Sep 1931	20 Jul 1932	5 Sep 1934
Entered service	25 Jan 1929	12 Mar 1929	8 Mar 1930	1 Apr 1931	20 Dec 1931	15 Nov 1933	19 Oct 1934

7600-ton Cruisers

Name	La Galissonnière	Jean de Vienne	Marseillaise	Gloire	Montcalm	Georges Leygues
Programme	1931	1931	1932	1932	1932	1932
Hull no.	168	169	176	177	178	179
Project no.	CL2	CL3				
Builder	Brest	Lorient	AC Loire	FC Gironde	FC Méditerranée	Penhoët
First plates cut	27 Oct 1931	12 Nov 1931	11 Jul 1933	11 Jul 1933	11 Jul 1933	11 Jul 1933
Laid down	15 Dec 1931	20 Dec 1931	23 Oct 1933	13 Nov 1933	15 Nov 1933	21 Sep 1933
Launched	18 Nov 1935	31 Jul 1935	17 Jul 1935	26 Sep 1935	26 Oct 1935	24 Mar 1936
Sea trials	20 Mar 1935	1 Feb 1936	1 Jun 1936	1 Jan 1937	1 Sep 1936	1 Jan 1937
Acceptance trials	13 Jun 1935	10 Apr 1936	8 Dec 1936	25 Mar 1937	23 Jan 1937	29 Apr 1937
Commissioned	1 Jan 1936	1 Sep 1936	15 Jul 1937	15 Jul 1937	20 May 1937	15 Aug 1937
Completed	1 Apr 1936	10 Feb 1937	11 Oct 1937	15 Nov 1937	1 Nov 1937	15 Nov 1937
Entered service	29 Oct 1936	7 Apr 1937	26 Oct 1937	4 Dec 1937	4 Dec 1937	4 Dec 1937

ship (*Ecole d'application du tir à la mer*, or EATM) from 1927 to 1935, and subsequently as an accommodation ship at Brest.[5]

- *Marseillaise*, which would be attached to the gunnery school (*Ecole de canonnage*) at Toulon until 1929.
- *Condé*, already decommissioned, which would serve as an accommodation ship at Lorient from June 1927 for the school of the *fusiliers marins* (similar to the British Royal Marines).
- *Jules Michelet*, which served in the Far East from July 1925 to May 1929 before paying off.
- *Ernest Renan*, which was attached to the gunnery school 1927–8 and was subsequently stricken.
- *Edgar Quinet*, which following a refit replaced the *Jeanne d'Arc* as training ship for officer cadets; she was lost after running aground on 4 January 1930 on the coast of Algeria.
- *Waldeck Rousseau*, which replaced *Jules Michelet* on the Far East station from June 1929 to May 1932 before being paid off.

The second group comprised the former enemy light cruisers handed over as war reparations in 1920. These were relatively modern ships, of which four remained in service in 1927:[6]

- *Mulhouse* (ex-German *Stralsund*), which remained in service at Brest at the end of 1929.
- *Strasbourg* (ex-German *Regensburg*), which was decommissioned in 1930, subsequently serving as an accommodation ship at Lorient; the wreck of the ship can still be seen in front of the Kéroman submarine base.
- *Metz* (ex-German *Königsberg*), decommissioned in 1929.
- *Thionville* (ex-Austro-Hungarian *Novara*), used for trials and by the torpedo school (*Ecole d'application de lancement à la mer*, or EALM) until 1 May 1932.[7]

THE CRUISERS BASED IN THE ATLANTIC

The official designation of the naval force based at Brest, often referred to as the *Escadre du Ponant* (Western Squadron), was subject to successive changes. From 15 September 1921 it was designated the *Division navale de la Manche et de la Mer du Nord* (Naval Division of the Channel and North Sea), then the *2e Escadre* (Second Squadron) on 1 February 1927, becoming the *Escadre de l'Atlantique* (Atlantic Squadron) on 15 August 1936 and finally the *Flotte de l'Atlantique* (Atlantic Fleet) on 10 June 1939.

During this time the composition of the squadron saw a considerable evolution. At the end of the 1920s it comprised only elderly units, occasionally reinforced

---

[5] She would be modified by the Germans during the Second World War to resemble the cruiser *Prinz Eugen*.
[6] The *Colmar* (ex-*Kolberg*) had recently been stricken.

[7] *Thionville* was specially fitted for the purpose with seven 550mm torpedo tubes.

Below: *Primauguet* on a port visit to Douala, Cameroon, in February 1932 to mark the inauguration of the port. The early inter-war cruisers were employed extensively to 'show the flag' and to represent France on ceremonial occasions. Note the canvas awnings rigged to protect the crew from the intense heat of equatorial Africa; they were stowed in a broad compartment abaft the after magazines. (*Marc Saibène collection*)

by ships running their sea trials before leaving for the Mediterranean.

The three 8000-tonne cruisers made up a 3rd Light Division in the Second Squadron from 19 November 1926, even before they entered service. Their final fitting out was delayed by the late delivery of key items of equipment – the new DCTs were fitted between April 1928 and July 1929 – and they remained in the Atlantic until the departure of the division for the Mediterranean on 21 July 1928. Brest served as the base for cruisers running sea trials. The first three 10,000-ton 'Treaty' cruisers made up a new 1st Light Division from 29 November 1929, and would remain at Brest until October 1930. It would be mid-1932 before the 2nd Squadron had another cruiser attached. *Lamotte-Piquet* returned to Brest from Toulon, and was replaced in August 1933 by her sister *Duguay-Trouin*. The two ships served successively as flagship of the 2nd Squadron while the battleship *Provence* was in refit. Brest would also be the base for the training cruiser *Jeanne d'Arc* when she entered service in October 1931.

The evolution of the international situation, particularly with regard to Germany, led the Marine Nationale to reinforce the squadron at Brest, and from 1935 the three elderly but modernised battleships *Bretagne*, *Provence* and *Lorraine* were based there.

The cruiser *Emile Bertin* remained at Brest following her entry into service, and became the flagship of the 2nd Light Squadron (*2e Escadre légère*) on 1 September 1935. On 5 December of the same year she deployed to the French West Indies, which were celebrating the tricentenary of their attachment to France. She returned to Brest on 27 February having rejoined her *contre-torpilleurs* at Dakar. On 9 August 1938 *Emile Bertin* left the 2nd Light Squadron for the Mediterranean.

Finally, the Atlantic Squadron was boosted in June 1938 by the arrival of the three new 7600-ton cruisers *Georges Leygues*, *Montcalm* and *Gloire*, which made up the 4th Cruiser Division (4e DC).

A step change took place on 1 September 1938 when the new fast battleship *Dunkerque* joined the Atlantic Squadron. The latter was now to comprise two modern battleships (*Strasbourg* would join on 24 April 1939), the three modern cruisers of the 4th Cruiser Division and eight of the latest *contre-torpilleurs* of the *Le Fantasque* and *Mogador* classes.

The level of training now intensified and, in the course of a night exercise on 7/8 February 1939, the *Georges Leygues* collided with the *contre-torpilleur* *Bison*, slicing off her bow. One of the forward 138mm mountings of the *contre-torpilleur*, together with the gun crew, ended up on the forecastle of the cruiser. Eighteen crew members were lost, all from the *contre-torpilleur*. Damage to the cruiser was limited to some

Below: The three ships of the 4th Cruiser Division on a visit to Glasgow between 22 and 30 May 1939. It was during this brief visit to northern Britain that the French gave a demonstration to the Royal Navy of the *dispositif 'K'* shell splash colorant, which was subsequently part of a technology transfer agreement between the two nations.

bent plates, the ship being subsequently docked for repairs at Saint-Nazaire from 14 February to 17 March. The 4th Cruiser Division, once again at full strength, embarked on a final cruise to Scotland from 23 May to 21 June, before leaving for New York.

THE CRUISERS BASED IN THE MEDITERRANEAN

The squadron based at Toulon, often referred to as the *Escadre du Levant* (Eastern Squadron), became the *Escadre de la Méditerranée* (Mediterranean Squadron) on 20 July 1921. It was renamed the *1re Escadre* (First Squadron) on 1 January 1927, reverted to being the Mediterranean Squadron on 30 October 1936, and finally became the *Flotte de la Méditerranée* (Mediterranean Fleet) on 1 July 1939. It was the major French naval formation from the end of the First World War until the mid-1930s. Its most likely adversary was the Italian Regia Marina, and the squadron based at Toulon not only embraced all the operational battleships, but during the period in question all new cruisers (including the seven 10,000-ton 1st class cruisers), *contre-torpilleurs* and fleet torpedo boats were assigned to it when they entered service. On the eve of war the French Mediterranean Fleet was still sufficiently powerful to contain the Italians with British support.

Between July 1928 and July 1932 the 1st Squadron was boosted by the arrival of the 3rd Light Division comprising the three 8000-tonne cruisers, of which two were generally available.

All seven of the 1st class cruisers were assigned to the Mediterranean on completion. The first two, *Duquesne* and *Suffren*, arrived at Toulon on 27 April 1930. They were only fully incorporated into the 1st Squadron, together with *Tourville*, in July 1931, following their round-the-world training cruise for the *Ecole navale*. They then became the 1st Light Division. The division was joined by the *Colbert* on 1st May 1931, by *Foch* on 20 December 1931, and by the *Dupleix* on 1st December 1932.

The last of the 10,000-ton cruisers, *Algérie*, arrived in Toulon on 19 October 1934. She became the flagship of the 1st Squadron. Her arrival saw the reorganisation of the Light Divisions: the 1st Division comprised *Algérie*, *Dupleix* and *Colbert*, and the 3rd Division *Foch*, *Duquesne* and *Tourville*. On 1 May 1936 *Foch* left the 3rd Division, being replaced by *Suffren*. From this point on the 1st Light (subsequently Cruiser) Division comprised the four most modern 10,000-ton cruisers.

In 1937 the squadron at Toulon was reinforced by three of the six 7600-ton cruisers. The first was *La Galissonnière* on 1 November 1936. Temporarily attached to the 3rd Cruiser Division, she was subsequently joined by *Jean de Vienne* on 9 October 1937, then by *Marseillaise* on 26 October, thereby permitting a reorganisation of the divisions on 2 November. The 1st class cruisers were divided between the 1st Cruiser Division (*Algérie*, *Dupleix*, *Foch* and *Colbert*) and a new 2nd Cruiser Division (*Duquesne*, *Tourville* and *Suffren*). The three 2nd class cruisers made up the 3rd Cruiser Division; *Marseillaise* would be the flagship of the division until 1942.

Above: The anchorage at Villefranche, near Nice, on 4 or 5 March 1935. The three cruisers present are *Algérie*, *Foch* and *Tourville*. The *contre-torpilleurs* are the *Chevalier Paul* (No.3) and *Cassard* (no pennant number because not currently attached to a division). There are two seaplanes in the photo: the one beyond the *Chevalier Paul* is a Breguet Short Calcutta long-range maritime patrol aircraft belonging to Squadron 3E1; the one in the distance, beyond *Algérie*, is a Farman F 168 Goliath bomber of Squadron 3B1. The small ship on the right is the former transport *Hamelin*, which had been converted into a seaplane tender. *(Stephen Dent collection)*

The squadron embarked on a cruise to the eastern Mediterranean between 11 May and 1 July 1938. The Munich crisis of late September led to the postponement of a major refit for all three ships of the 3rd Division, which finally took place between October 1938 and January 1939. Between 27 January and 10 March 1939 *Marseillaise* and *La Galissonnière* were deployed to French West Africa (Dakar, Conakry). The threat of war led the Marine Nationale to create a raiding force (designated the *Forces légères d'attaque*) at Bizerte, close to Italy. The 3rd Cruiser Division, joined by the *Emile Bertin*, arrived at Bizerte on 13 May 1939.

The Mediterranean Fleet came into being on 1 July. The 1st class cruisers formed the 3rd Squadron (*3e Escadre*) with the 1st Cruiser Division (*Algérie*, *Dupleix*, *Foch* and *Colbert*) and the 2nd Cruiser Division (*Duquesne* and *Tourville* – *Suffren* had just left for the Far East).

THE TRAINING CRUISERS

The school ship *Jeanne d'Arc* traditionally conducted the annual world cruise for officer cadets at the end of their studies at the *Ecole navale*. The *Pluton* was designed as a minelayer, but from her completion it was planned to use her as a school ship for the EATM, replacing the *Gueydon* for gunnery instruction at sea.

She was specially refitted for the role between October 1932 and April 1933. Attached to the training division, most of her activity involved brief sorties from Toulon to the gunnery training range at Salins d'Hyères. On 25 June 1939 *Pluton* arrived at Lorient for a second major refit. An increase in the number of officers under training meant that there was a requirement for a second school ship for officer cadets, and on 13 May *Pluton* was selected for the role. She was to have been attached to the *Ecole d'application* on 1 June 1940, changing her name in the process to *La Tour d'Auvergne*; she was due to accompany the *Jeanne d'Arc* on her 1940–1 world cruise. In the event *Pluton*, which blew up at Casablanca on 13 September 1939, would not be renamed, but in order to disguise her loss and confuse the enemy Intelligence services, the official communiqué used the name *La Tour d'Auvergne* in place of the name *Pluton*.[8]

From 29 August 1936 the *Duguay-Trouin* was attached to the Training Division (*Division d'instruction*) of the 1st Squadron, where she was used prima-

[8] The greatest confusion which resulted was in subsequent post-war secondary reference sources, some of which give the name of the ship when lost as *La Tour d'Auvergne*.

Below: *Duquesne* arrives in the anchorage at Algiers in early May 1930 for the naval review which marked the centenary of French rule in Algeria. *(Archives d'Outre-mer Aix-en-Provence, courtesy of Marc Saibène)*

FRENCH FLEET: ORGANISATION 1 FEBRUARY 1937

Escadre de l'Atlantique

2e DL: *Provence, Lorraine, Bretagne*
Béarn
2e escadre légère:
    Groupe des contre-torpilleurs:
        Emile Bertin
        6e DL: *Milan, Epervier*
        8e DCT: *L'Indomptable, Le Malin, Le Triomphant*
        10e DCT: *Le Fantasque, Le Terrible, L'Audacieux*
        Indisponible: *Vauban*
2e flottille de torpilleurs:
    Jaguar
    2e DT: *Fougueux, Basque, Frondeur*
    4e DT: *Bourrasque, Ouragan, Orage*
    5e DT: *Brestois, Foudroyant, Boulonnais*
    6e DT: *Cyclone, Siroco, Mistral*
    7e DT: *L'Alcyon, Typhon, Tornade*
    8e DT: *Bordelais, Trombe, Tramontane*
    Indisponible: *L'Adroit*
2e flottille de sous-marins:
    Bison
    Surcouf
    4e escadrille: *Persée, Poncelet, Archimède, Pasteur, Ajax,*
            Le Conquérant, Achille, Sfax, Casabianca, Agosta
    2e escadrille: *Minerve, Méduse, Amphitrite, Orphée,*
            Antiope, Amazone, La Sibylle
    Jules Verne

Escadre de la Méditerranée

1re DL: *Algérie, Dupleix, Colbert, Foch*
3e DL: *Duquesne, Tourville, Suffren, La Galissonnière*
Commandant Teste
3e escadre légère:
    5e DL: *Tartu, Vauquelin, Le Chevalier Paul*
    7e DL: *Gerfaut, Vautour, Albatros*
    9e DL: *Maillé Brézé, Kersaint, Cassard*
    3e DL: *Guépard, Valmy, Verdun*
1re flottille de torpilleurs:
    1re DT: *La Palme, Le Mars, Forbin*
    3e DT: *Le Fortuné, La Railleuse, Tempête*
1re flottille de sous-marins:
    Lion
    3e escadrille: *Actéon, Phénix, Espoir, Pégase, Monge, Protée*
    5e escadrille: *Vénus, Iris, La Vestale, La Sultane, Aréthuse,*
            Atalante, Doris
Division d'instruction:
    Courbet, Paris, Océan (ex *Jean Bart*), *Duguay-Trouin*
Train d'escadre:
    Le Gladiateur, Aube, Durance, Fraîche

Hors escadres:

En travaux: *Primauguet* (Lorient)
FNEO: *Lamotte-Picquet*
Maroc: *Simoun*
DNL: *Aigle*
Ecole navale: 12e DL: *Chacal, Léopard*
EATM: *Pluton*
EALM: 8e DL: *Tigre, Lynx, Panthère*

---

rily by the gunnery school. The division was designated 'Training Squadron' (*Escadre d'instruction*) from 1 October 1938; the latter was dissolved on 10 June 1939, and *Duguay-Trouin* was attached to the 5th Squadron at Lorient with a view to replacing *Pluton* in the rangefinder training role. These plans were derailed by the outbreak of war.

Duquesne, Tourville and *Suffren*, forming the 2nd Cruiser Division from November 1937, were attached to the gunnery school at Toulon in February 1938.

DEPLOYMENTS OVERSEAS

The premature loss of the *Edgar Quinet* meant that the smooth transition to the new school ship fitting out at Saint Nazaire could not take place as planned, and the 1930–1 training cruise for the *Ecole d'application* had to be undertaken by the three recently-completed 1st class cruisers. They formed a 1st Light Division which departed Brest on 6 October 1930 and returned to Toulon on 10 January 1931, having taken in Dakar, Rio de Janeiro, the French West Indies and Casablanca *en route*. The second phase of the annual cruise took place in the Eastern Mediterranean between 22 April and 10 July. The baton was then passed to the *Jeanne d'Arc*, which would embark on a further eight training cruises before the Second World War. She would leave Brest at the beginning of October and return at the beginning of July every year with the solitary exception of 1939, when due to the deteriorating international situation she returned early on 16 April

There was at least one cruiser deployed to the Far East. This ship ensured a semi-permanent presence in China, particularly at Shanghai during the Sino-Japanese War. The old armoured cruiser *Waldeck Rousseau*, which had been on station since 1929, was

replaced by the 8000-tonne *Primauguet*, which arrived in Indochina on 18 May 1932. She departed for metropolitan France on 10 January 1936, replaced by her sister *Lamotte-Piquet* which had arrived 29 December 1935. The latter ship remained moored at Shanghai from 11 August to 26 December 1937 during the hostilities between the Chinese and the Japanese, occasionally being near-missed by bombs. The *Lamotte-Piquet* would never leave the Far East station, where she was lost in 1945.

Whereas the *Duguay-Trouin* (end 1931) and the 4th

Below: *Algérie* is seen here during a visit to Naples 8–14 May 1935.

Right: *Gloire* arriving in New York on 10 July 1939 for the World's Fair 1939. *(Stephen Dent collection)*

Below: The 1st Light Division at sea in April 1934. In the foreground: a GL 810 floatplane on the starboard catapult of the *Foch*. In the background: *Colbert*, followed by *Tourville*.

Below: The 10,000-ton cruisers *Duquesne* (left) and *Suffren* (right) during a visit to Norfolk, USA, between 20 and 22 October 1931. The occasion was the inauguration of the monument to the British defeat at Yorktown. The ships, which embarked Marshal Pétain (representing the French government) and five descendants of La Fayette, de Grasse and Rochambeau, also visited Chesapeake Bay, New York and Newport before returning to Toulon via Oran. *(US Navy)*

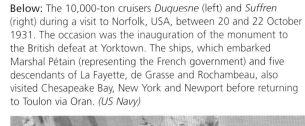

THE CRUISER DIVISIONS

FRENCH CRUISERS WERE NORMALLY ORGANISED in divisions of three ships. These divisions, termed 'Light Divisions' (*Divisions légères* or DL) from the late 1920s to the mid-1930s, also included the *contre-torpilleurs*. On 12 April 1937 these Light Divisions were variously rechristened Cruiser Divisions (*Divisions de croiseurs* or DC) or *Contre-torpilleur* Divisions (*Division de contre-torpilleurs* or DCT). In theory the three 8000-tonne cruisers (*Duguay-Trouin*, *Lamotte-Piquet* and *Primauguet*) were incorporated into a new 3rd DL between 19 November 1926 and mid-1932, but in reality, taking into account overseas deployments and spells in the dockyard, this 3rd DL comprised two units at best. The 2nd DL was formed with the *Duguay-Trouin* between 1 May 1934 and 1 July 1936, briefly joined by the *Lamotte-Piquet* from 15 March to 2 November 1935.

The 10,000-ton cruisers were incorporated into the 1st DL as and when they entered service. On 10 October 1934 the oldest ships (*Duquesne* and *Tourville*, joined by *Suffren* in early 1936) were regrouped into the 3rd DL, while the latest ships

(*Colbert*, *Dupleix* and *Algérie*, joined by *Foch* in 1936) formed the 1st DL. The *Foch* was part of the 3rd DL from October 1934 to 1 May 1936 during the refit of *Suffren*. The 1st Light Division (which in April 1937 became the 1st Cruiser Division) retained the four latest 10,000-ton cruisers virtually until the scuttling at Toulon, which resulted in the destruction of all four ships.

Between 25 May and 8 November 1937 the first three 10,000-ton cruisers passed from the 3rd Light Division to the 2nd Cruiser Division. The latter, which was interned at Alexandria from the end of June 1940 until June 1943, appears to have been rechristened the 1st Cruiser Division in mid-1943. The 1st DC was finally dissolved on 24 June 1944.

The 7600-ton cruisers were shared between the 3rd and (newly-formed) 4th Cruiser Divisions. The 3rd Division lost its 10,000-ton cruisers towards the end of 1937 to be replaced, on their entry into service, by *La Galissonnière* (October 1936), *Jean de Vienne* (April 1937) and *Marseillaise* (October 1937). The 3rd Cruiser Division disap-

peared when the fleet was scuttled at Toulon. The 4th DC, which was formed at Brest on 20 November 1937, comprised the *Georges Leygues*, *Montcalm* and *Gloire*; it survived until September 1943.

The 5th Cruiser Division was briefly formed in Indochina between 2 March 1939 and 12 August 1940. It comprised the *Lamotte-Piquet* and, for a short period, the *Primauguet*, replaced by the *Suffren*. The 6th Cruiser Division was formed from 28 August to 18 November 1939 with *Primauguet* and *Duguay-Trouin*. The 7th Cruiser Division was formed on 28 August 1939 with the *Jeanne d'Arc* and *Pluton*, but effectively ceased to exist following the loss of the latter ship on 13 September of the same year.

The 6th and 7th Cruiser Divisions were part of a newly-constituted 5th Squadron based at Lorient, which from 1 October 1938 regrouped in a Training Squadron (*Escadre d'instruction*) all the ships assigned to the naval schools. The Training Squadron became the 5th Squadron on 10 June 1940 and was dissolved on 18 November 1940.

Left: *Colbert* (left) and *Algérie* during a visit to Algiers. (*Patrick Maurand collection*)

Below: *Tourville* (two white bands on second funnel) at sea with the 1st Light Division on 28 June 1934. (*SHD Toulon, courtesy of Marc Saibène*)

Cruiser Division (early 1938) made only fleeting visits, a second cruiser was detached to the Far East from 1937 to ensure a permanent presence on the coast of China, forming with *Lamotte-Piquet* a 5th Cruiser Division. The *Primauguet* was deployed to the Far East from 22 November 1937 to 28 July 1939, and was then replaced by the *Suffren*, which arrived on 23 July 1939.

Apart from the customary activity in the Atlantic or the Mediterranean, generally associated with squadron manoeuvres, there were occasional overseas deployments by cruisers. *Primauguet* left Brest on 20 April 1927 for a world cruise. She visited Indochina from 17 June to 1 August, stayed for a month in Shanghai, went up the Yangtze River as far as Hankou, and visited other ports in China and Japan,

Above: *Montcalm* in the Saigon River on 12 January 1938. The 4th Cruiser Division was in Indochina from 12 January to 2 February 1938.

returning to Brest via the Panama Canal on 22 December 1927. *Duquesne* went on a tour of Africa from 31 January to 3 August 1929, taking in Dakar and the Cape and returning via Madagascar, Djibouti and the Mediterranean. Her sister *Tourville* went on a world cruise from 5 April to 24 December 1929, visiting the French West Indies, Polynesia, Indochina and Djibouti.

In the same year *Primauguet* deployed to Canada between 25 August and 27 October on a 'showing the flag' mission. The same ship and her sister *Lamotte-Piquet* sailed from Toulon on 17 January 1930. They

called in at Dakar, with *Primauguet* going on to the West Indies while *Lamotte-Piquet* visited the Gulf of Guinea as far as Pointe Noire. They returned to metropolitan France at the end of May. *Primauguet* subsequently deployed again to French West Africa as far as Conakry (Guinea) from 13 January to 10 April 1931 with the *contre-torpilleurs Tigre* and *Chacal*. Her sister *Duguay-Trouin* made a high-speed deployment to Indochina between 5 September and 22 December 1931.

Finally, the three cruisers of the 4th Division (*Georges Leygues*, *Montcalm* and *Gloire*) deployed to Indochina on an endurance cruise between 1 December 1937 and 14 April 1938. They then represented France at the New York World's Fair 1939, visiting New York between 10 and 18 July.

THE SPANISH CIVIL WAR

The Spanish Civil War began on 18 July 1936. The Marine Nationale initially ensured the safe evacuation of foreign nationals and refugees, then participated in the monitoring of maritime traffic destined for Spain. An international agreement intended primarily to combat 'piracy' by unknown (in fact Italian) submarines was signed at Nyons on 14 September 1937. The Mediterranean was divided up among the major European powers, each of which was charged with monitoring the zone it was allocated.

The cruisers *Duquesne*, *Suffren*, *Emile Bertin* and, at the end of August, *Colbert* were among the first ships involved. The *Duquesne* took charge of the first evacuations from Barcelona on 24 July, remaining in that

FRENCH FLEET: ORGANISATION 3 SEPTEMBER 1939

Forces navales indépendantes:

Force de raid (Brest):
    1ʳᵉ DL: *Dunkerque, Strasbourg*
    4ᵉ DC: *Georges Leygues, Montcalm, Gloire*
    2ᵉ escadre légère:
        6ᵉ DCT: *Mogador, Volta*
        8ᵉ DCT: *L'Indomptable, Le Triomphant, Le Malin*
        10ᵉ DCT: *Le Fantasque, Le Terrible, L'Audacieux*

Forces de haute mer (Toulon):
    2ᵉ escadre:
    Provence
    2ᵉ DL: *Lorraine, Bretagne*
    1ʳᵉ flottille de torpilleurs:
        1ʳᵉ DT: *La Palme, Le Mars, Tempête*
        3ᵉ DT: *Le Fortuné, Simoun, La Railleuse*
        7ᵉ DT: *Tramontane, Tornade, Typhon*
    3ᵉ escadre:
        1ʳᵉ DC: *Algérie, Dupleix, Foch, Colbert*
        2ᵉ DC: *Duquesne, Tourville*
    3ᵉ escadre légère:
        5ᵉ DCT: *Tartu, Vauquelin, Le Chevalier Paul*
        7ᵉ DCT: *Vautour, Albatros, Geerfaut*
        9ᵉ DCT: *Maillé Brézé, Kersaint, Cassard*

5e escadre:
    6ᵉ DC: *Duguay-Trouin, Primauguet*
    7ᵉ DC: *Jeanne d'Arc, Pluton* (28–31 Aug 1939)

Forces navales de région:

Forces maritimes du Nord:
    11ᵉ DT: *La Cordelière, L'Incomprise, Branlebas*
    1ʳᵉ escadrille d'avisos: *Amiral Mouchez, Arras, Yser*
    La Diligente, Belfort

Forces maritimes de l'Ouest:
    Forces navales de la 2ᵉ Région maritime (Brest):
    1ʳᵉ escadre:
    Paris, Courbet
        2ᵉ DCT: *Jaguar, Léopard, Panthère*
        2ᵉ flottille de torpilleurs:
            2ᵉ DT: *Fougueux, Frondeur, L'Adroit*
            4ᵉ DT: *Bourrasque, Ouragan, Orage*
            5ᵉ DT: *Brestois, Foudroyant, Boulonnais*
            6ᵉ DT: *Cyclone, Siroco, Mistral*
        4ᵉ escadrille:
            2ᵉ DSM: *Casabianca, Sfax, Achille, Pasteur*
            4ᵉ DSM: *Le Centaure, Argo, Pascal, Henri Poincaré*
            6ᵉ DSM: *Persée, Poncelet, Ajax, Archimède*
            8ᵉ DSM: *Agosta, Bévéziers, Ouessant, Sidi Ferruch*
        2ᵉ escadrille d'avisos:
        Belfort, Diligente
    Forces navales de la 5ᵉ Région maritime (Lorient):
        14ᵉ DT: *Bouclier, La Melpomène, La Flore*
        5ᵉ escadrille d'avisos

port for three weeks. *Emile Bertin* went to Bilbao in the north, and *Suffren* to Tangiers (Morocco). *Emile Bertin* was involved in the evacuation by the Republicans of Bilbao, Santander and Gijón between 4 and 12 May 1937, and *Suffren* took part in the evacuation of Barcelona between 24 and 28 January 1939.

NAVAL REVIEWS

On 3 July 1928 four of the newest cruisers, *Duguay-Trouin*, *Lamotte-Picquet*, *Tourville* and *Duquesne* took part in a naval review of seventy-seven ships off Le Havre. Another major naval review for which sixty-nine ships were assembled took place in Algiers on 10 May 1930 to celebrate the centenary of the arrival of the French in Algeria. The cruisers present were *Lamotte-Picquet*, *Primauguet*, *Duquesne*, *Suffren* and *Colbert*. The inauguration of the transatlantic passenger liner terminal at Cherbourg on 30 July 1933 provided the occasion for a naval review in which twenty-one ships of the 2nd Squadron participated. The only cruiser present was the *Lamotte-Picquet*, at that time the flagship of the squadron. On 27 June 1935, in the Bay of Douarnenez, there was an inspection of the fleet. The fifty-eight ships assembled for the occasion included the cruisers *Algérie*, *Dupleix*, *Foch*, *Duquesne*, *Tourville*, *Duguay-Trouin* and *Lamotte-Picquet*. The last great naval review of the inter-war period took place off Brest on 27 May 1937 following combined exercises involving the Atlantic and Mediterranean Squadrons in the presence of Navy Minister Pierre Gasnier-Duparc; forty-one ships took part, including the cruisers *Emile Bertin*, *Algérie*, *Foch*, *Colbert*, *Duquesne* and *Tourville*.

Above: The *Rade-Abri* at Brest in 1938 or early 1939. In the foreground are the *contre-torpilleurs* *Le Terrible*, *L'Audacieux* and *Le Fantasque* (10th DCT). Centre picture are the three cruisers of the 4th Division, probably in the order *Gloire*, *Montcalm* and *Georges Leygues*. Beyond them are the three old battleships of the 2nd Battleship Division, *Bretagne*, *Lorraine* and *Provence*. Beyond them, to the left of the picture, are the accommodation ships *Trémintin* (ex-armoured cruiser *Montcalm*), *Armorique* and *Gueydon* (ex-armoured cruiser), and on the right, two *contre-torpilleurs* of the *Jaguar* class are moored in front of the location of the future German submarine base.

3e Région maritime:
    4e DCT: *Tigre, Lynx, Panthère*
    13e DT: *Baliste, La Bayonnaise, La Poursuivante*
    3e escadrille d'avisos: *Lassigny, Amiens, Les Eparges, Dédaigneuse*
    Chasseur 1, Chasseur 2, Chasseur 3
    3e escadrille de sous-marins:
        1re DSM: *Le Héros, Le Glorieux, Le Tonnant, Le Conquérant*
        3e DSM: *Protée, Actéon, Fresnel, Achéron*
        5e DSM: *Espoir, Pégase, Monge*
        7e DSM: *Redoutable, Vengeur*
        13e DSM: *Doris, Thétis, Calypso, Circé*
        15e DSM: *Iris, Vénus, Pallas, Cérès*
        19e DSM: *Galatée, Naïade, Sirène, Argonaute*
        21e DSM: *Le Diamant, Perle*
    Gladiateur
    Aube, Durance, Fraiche, Forfait, Coetlogon, Rance, Boréal, Champlain

4e Région maritime:
    4e escadre (Forces légères d'attaque):
        3e DC: *Marseillaise, Jean de Vienne, La Galissonnière*
        Emile Bertin
        1re DCT: *Vauban, Lion, Epervier*
        3e DCT: *Guépard, Verdun, Valmy*
        11e DCT: *Bison, Milan*
    Secteur de Bizerte:
        12e DT: *La Pomone, Bombarde, L'Iphigénie*
        4e flottille de sous-marins:
            5e ESM:
                9e DSM: *Caïman, Morse, Souffleur*
                10e DSM: *Phoque, Espadon, Dauphin*
                11e DSM: *Marsouin, Requin, Narval*
            6e ESM:
                17e DSM: *Vestale, Sultane, Atalante, Aréthuse*
                20e DSM: *Turquoise, Rubis, Saphir, Nautilus*

Marine Maroc:
    9e DT: *Basque, Forbin*
    9e DSM: *Le Centaure, Pascal, Henri Poincaré, Argo*
    2e escadrille: *Psyché, Oréade, Méduse, Amphitrite, Danaé, Junon*

Dispositif d'Oran:
    Jules Verne
    8e DT: *Bordelais, L'Alcyon, Trombe*
    2e escadrille de sous-marins:
        12e DSM: *Minerve, Junon, Orion, Ondine*
        14e DSM: *Diane, Ariane, Eurydice, Danaé*
        18e DSM: *Psyché, Oréade, Méduse, Amphitrite*
    Commandant Teste (escadrilles HS1 et HB1)

Division Navale du Levant:
    D'Iberville
    11e DSM: *Marsouin, Narval, Requin*

Forces maritimes de l'Atlantique Ouest (Antilles):
    Jeanne d'Arc
    Surcouf
    Ville d'Ys

Forces navales d'Extrême-Orient:
    5e DC: *Lamotte-Picquet, Suffren*
    Rigault de Genouilly, Amiral Charner, Savorgnan de Brazza, Tahure

Marine Indochine:
    Marne

Station navale de l'océan Indien:
    Bougainville

Station navale du Pacifique:
    Dumont d'Urville

CHAPTER 10:

THE PERIOD 1939–1943

THE WAR WITH GERMANY, 3 SEPTEMBER 1939 TO 25 JUNE 1940

Putting the fleet on a war footing

The planned organisation for time of war was put in place on 27 August 1939. The Atlantic Fleet, which now comprised the 1st and 5th Squadrons, formed the *Force de raid* from its most powerful surface units: the battleships *Dunkerque* and *Strasbourg*, the cruisers *Georges Leygues*, *Montcalm* and *Gloire* (4th Cruiser Division), and the 2nd Light Squadron comprising the eight latest *contre-torpilleurs*. The *Force de raid* was a fast squadron composed exclusively of modern ships, and the British were quick to request its help in hunting down the German surface raiders. The other surface ships based at Brest, notably the torpedo boats, would generally be employed on escort duty. The 5th Squadron based at Lorient had a paper strength of two cruiser divisions: a 6th DC with *Duguay-Trouin* and *Primauguet* and, from 28 to 31 August, an ephemeral 7th DC comprising the *Pluton* and *Jeanne d'Arc*.

In the Mediterranean, the initial organisation consisted of the *Forces de haute mer* at Toulon with the 2nd and 3rd Squadrons. The 2nd Squadron comprised the three older battleships and the torpedo boats, the 3rd Squadron the six 1st class cruisers of the 1st and 2nd Cruiser Divisions, and the 3rd Light Squadron with nine *contre-torpilleurs*. At Bizerte, the *Forces légères d'attaque* (4th Squadron), comprised four cruisers (the 3rd Cruiser Division plus *Emile Bertin*) and, in theory, eight *contre-torpilleurs* – although the latter would never be at full strength. Italy's declaration of neutrality permitted the transfer of some ships based in the Mediterranean to the Atlantic.

The detached cruisers

The announcement of the sailing of German surface forces on 30 August 1939 prompted the despatch of the *Pluton* to lay a barrage of mines off Casablanca and a sortie by the *Force de raid* on 3 September to cover her. In the Mediterranean, on 31 August the 3rd Squadron covered the passage of a troop convoy to Corsica (the French feared an attack by the Italians), then regrouped at Oran before returning to Toulon on 19 September. Having ascertained that the Germans had not broken out into the Atlantic the *Force de raid* returned to Brest on the 6th. On the evening of 5 September *Georges Leygues* spotted a submarine on the surface and opened fire on the French submarine *Casabianca*, which promptly dived and made her escape.

Below, right: The wreck of the *Pluton* in the port of Casablanca. In the background: the submarine depot ship *Jules Verne*.

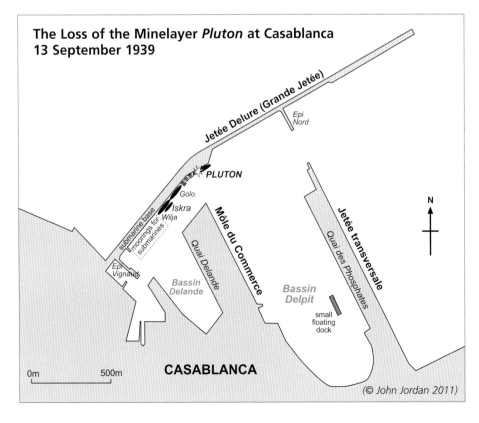

The Loss of the Minelayer *Pluton* at Casablanca
13 September 1939

CASABLANCA

(© John Jordan 2011)

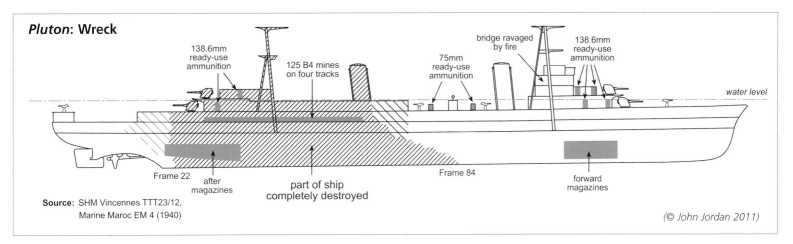

Pluton: Wreck

138.6mm ready-use ammunition

125 B4 mines on four tracks

bridge ravaged by fire

75mm ready-use ammunition

138.6mm ready-use ammunition

water level

Frame 22   after magazines

part of ship completely destroyed

Frame 84

forward magazines

Source: SHM Vincennes TTT23/12, Marine Maroc EM 4 (1940)

(© John Jordan 2011)

The *Pluton* arrived at Casablanca on 5 September. The mining operation was cancelled and disembarkation of the mines was begun on 13 September. Shortly afterwards, the accidental explosion of a mine caused the loss of the cruiser, which sank at her moorings. Of her crew 186 were killed or missing, and 73 were wounded. The wreck would not be broken up until 1952–3.

The *Emile Bertin*, attached independently to the *Forces légères d'attaque*, transported bank notes from Ajaccio to Beirut in the Levant. She was in Beirut from 19 to 23 September, and returned to Toulon on the 27th with 57 tonnes of gold evacuated from Poland. The cruiser was then under refit until December, after which she joined Force X at Dakar.

The *Lamotte-Piquet* remained in Indochina where she patrolled the local and Indonesian waters in a vain search for German raiders. She conducted two major patrols, from 12 to 31 December 1939 and from 15 January to 7 February 1940. The *Suffren* had arrived in Saigon on 23 July 1939. She also conducted patrols (8–20 November 1939, then 5–13 April 1940), and participated in the escort of troop convoys to Colombo (30 January 1940) and Singapore (February 1940). She left Saigon on 1 April 1940 and joined Force X at Alexandria.

The *Jeanne d'Arc* sailed from Brest on 3 September for the French West Indies. Based at Fort de France (Martinique), the cruiser escorted high-value merchantmen and conducted patrols in search of German shipping attempting to return to Germany. She returned to Brest on 26 April 1940.

The *Duguay-Trouin*, which had left Brest on 30 August, arrived at Dakar on 5 September. She escorted French ships and patrolled for German shipping out of Dakar. She returned to Lorient on 18 January 1940 for a major refit.

The *Primauguet*, returning from Indochina via Madagascar, operated out of Dakar during September and October. She arrived at Lorient for repairs on 28 October.

The hunt for the German surface raiders

The presence of German surface raiders revealed by the loss of the cargo ship *Clement*, which was known on 1 October 1939, led the Allies to despatch hunting groups into the Atlantic.

Force X, comprising the *Strasbourg* (from Brest), the cruisers *Algérie* and *Dupleix* (from Toulon), the British aircraft carrier *Hermes* and three *contre-torpilleurs*,

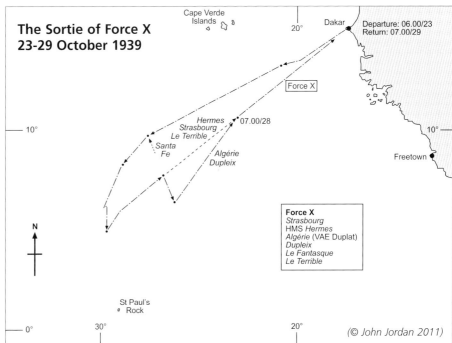

(© John Jordan 2011)

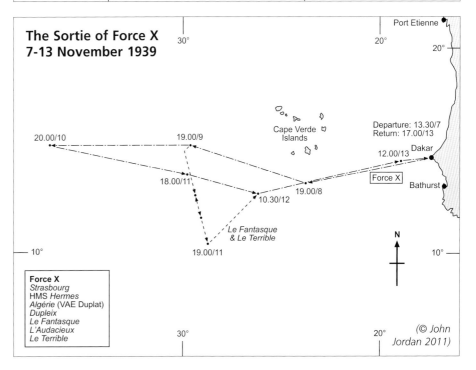

(© John Jordan 2011)

DEPLOYMENTS 1939–1940

	From:	Until:	Commanded by:	Composition:	Mission:
Force X	10 Oct 1936	18 Nov 1939	VAE Duplat	*Algérie* *Strasbourg* *Hermes* *Dupleix* *Le Fantasque* *L'Audacieux* + *Cassard* 12 Nov + *Milan* 12 Nov + *Foch* 13 Nov − Force Y (CA Moreau) 21 Nov	Search for surface raiders.
Force X	18 Nov 1939	15 Feb 1940	VAE Duplat	*Dupleix* *Foch* 13 Nov *Hermes* *Cassard* *Milan* − *Hermes* 24 Dec + *Bison* 30 Dec + *Epervier* 19 Jan + *Emile Bertin* 20 Jan − *Cassard* 21 Jan	Search for surface raiders (*Graf Spee*), then escort to Bermuda (*Dupleix* and *Foch* departed Dakar 23 Jan).
Force X	10 Mar 1940	10 Apr 1940	VAE Duplat	*Algérie* *Bretagne* *Victor Schoelcher* *Colbert* 12 Mar to 8 Apr	Transport of gold to Canada, escorted aircraft transports on return.
Force X	4 May 1940	10 Sep 1943	VA Godfroy	*Duquesne* *Provence* *Bretagne* *Lorraine* *Tourville* *Tigre* *Lynx* *Forbin* + *Suffren* 18 May − *Provence, Bretagne* 20 May − *Tigre, Lynx* 20 May + *Duguay-Trouin* 24 May + *Fortuné* 25 May + *Basque* 26 May + *Protée* 27 Jun	Operations in Eastern Mediterranean (Alexandria).
Force Y	18 Nov 1939	24 Nov 1939	CA Moreau	*Algérie* *Strasbourg* *Le Fantasque* *Le Terrible* *L'Audacieux*	Return to metropolitan France.

VAE	*Vice amiral d'escadre*	Squadron Vice-Admiral
VA	*Vice amiral*	Vice-Admiral
CA	*Contre amiral*	Rear-Admiral

Below: *Foch*, seen from the quarterdeck of *Algérie* in October 1939. Both ships would shortly be despatched to Dakar to hunt down German commerce raiders. *(Alain Marchand)*

was sent to Dakar, arriving there on 14 October. There were successive sorties to hunt down the German raider. The *Algérie* went south to Freetown on 19–20 October. Force X sortied at full strength from 23 to 29 October and again from 7 to 13 November. The cruiser *Foch* arrived from Toulon on 13 November, and the *Strasbourg* and *Algérie*, forming Force Y, left Dakar on 21 November to return to metropolitan France. Force X sailed from Dakar on 7 December with *Dupleix*, *Foch*, *Hermes*, the *contre-torpilleurs Milan* and *Cassard* and the British cruiser *Neptune*. The sortie took them to 850nm of Pernambuco when news of the interception of the *Graf Spee* off the River Plate on 13 December arrived. The French ships returned to Dakar to refuel so that they would be better able to position themselves in good time for an interception should the German raider succeed in evading the British cruisers blockading Montevideo, where she had taken refuge on

	From:	Until:	Commanded by:	Composition:	Mission:
Force Y	30 Jan 1940	15 Apr 1940	CA Bouxin	*Provence*	Replaced Force X at Dakar.
				Duquesne	
				Colbert	
				Emile Bertin	
				Bison	
				Milan	
				Epervier	
				+ *Le Héros* 8 Feb to 11 Apr	
				+ *Le Glorieux* 8 Feb to 11 Apr	
				+ *Le Tonnant* 8 Feb to 11 Apr	
				+ *Le Conquérant* 8 Feb to 11 Apr	
				− *Emile Bertin* 8 Feb	
				− *Bison* 13 Feb	
				− *Milan* 13 Feb	
				− *Epervier* 13 Feb	
				− *Colbert* 7 Mar to 8 Apr	
Force Y	4 Sep 1940	28 Oct 1940	CA Bourragué CA Lacroix	*Georges Leygues* *Montcalm* *Gloire* *Le Fantasque* *Le Malin* *L'Audacieux*	Planned operation in West Africa, based at Dakar.
Force Z	13 Nov 1939	27 Dec 1939	CA Marquis	*Marseillaise* *Lorraine* *Jean de Vienne*	Transport of gold to Canada, escorted aircraft transports on return.
Force Z	14 Feb 1940	12 Mar 1940	CA Derrien	*Emile Bertin* *Tartu* *Le Chevalier Paul* *Vauquelin* *Vautour* *Gerfaut* *Albatros* *Bison* *Milan* *Epervier* *Brestois* *Boulonnais* *Foudroyant* Five AMC	Planned operation in Norway (abandoned).
Force Z	5 Apr 1940	27 May 1940	CA Derrien	*Emile Bertin* up to 24 Apr *Montcalm* left 23 Apr *Tartu* *Maillé-Brézé* *Le Chevalier Paul* *Bison* *Milan* *Epervier* *Brestois* *Boulonnais* *Foudroyant* 1re DCX Eight auxilaries	Operations in Norway.

the 13th. In the event the *Graf Spee* was scuttled in the approaches to the port on 17 December. Force X, minus the *Neptune*, returned to Dakar on 16 December and could have left again on the 19th. Operations with the British had highlighted the general fragility of the equipment of the French ships and, in particular, their limited endurance. The latter could not be refuelled by underway replenishment, which was in its infancy in the Marine Nationale. Force X sortied again from 30 December 1939 to 5 January 1940. On 23 January *Dupleix* and *Foch* left Dakar and escorted a convoy from Bermuda to Morocco, then returned to Toulon.

Force X was replaced at Dakar by Force Y comprising the battleship *Provence* and the cruisers *Duquesne* and *Colbert*, which arrived on 30 January. The force sortied between 18–28 February and 6–16 March. The *Colbert* was detached from 7 March to 8 April to reinforce a new Force X which also comprised the cruiser *Algérie* and the battleship *Bretagne* and which was tasked with the transport of gold to Canada and, on the return journey, the escort of two cargo ships loaded with American planes. Force Y finally left Dakar on 11 April 1940.

In the North Atlantic the *Dunkerque*, *Georges Leygues*, *Montcalm* and three *contre-torpilleurs* sortied

---

Above: *Colbert* in North Africa. Detached to the 2nd Cruiser Division from 1 October 1939 to 1 May 1940, she had two black bands on her first funnel.
(*Pradignac & Léo*)

Below: *Gloire* and, in the background, *Georges Leygues* in North Africa during the Spring of 1940. In the foreground: a *contre-torpilleur* of the *Le Fantasque* class.
(*Pradignac & Léo*)

from 22 to 25 October 1939 to cover the passage of a convoy threatened by the *Deutschland*, whose presence in the North Atlantic was discovered only on 21 October. The sinking of the armed merchant cruiser *Rawalpindi* on 23 November by *Scharnhorst* and *Gneisenau* signalled the presence of other German battleships in the North Atlantic. The *Dunkerque*, *Georges Leygues*, and *Montcalm* sailed from Brest on 25 November and joined the British battlecruiser *Hood* in a patrol between Scotland and Iceland, in heavy weather. They returned on 3 December.

The *Gloire*, following a major refit at Cherbourg, sailed from Brest on 11 December with *Dunkerque*, which was transporting gold to Canada. During the return journey the two ships escorted seven liners carrying Canadian troops. They arrived at Brest on 30 December.

Apart from these missions, the activities of the cruisers at Brest and Toulon were divided between regular maintenance and exercises interrupted, as in peacetime, by short stays in Quiberon Bay and the anchorage at Hyères.

The Norwegian campaign
Allied intervention in the North had initially been envisaged during the 'Winter War' between Finland and the Soviet Union. A Force Z was have been led by *Emile Bertin*, which had been detached to Dakar from January to early February 1940. The cruiser arrived back in Brest on 17 February, but the operation was cancelled following the accord of 12 March between the Finns and the Russians. *Emile Bertin* subsequently sailed for Oran.

Hostilities in the North recommenced on 9 April 1940 with the German landings in Norway, which effectively short-circuited an Allied intervention agreed on 28 March and which began on that same day of 9 April with the laying of mines off the Norwegian coast. Force Z was recreated on 5 April, and *Emile Bertin* arrived at Scapa Flow on the 7th. On 9 April she was in company with British ships when the formation was bombed, the French cruiser being bracketed by three near-misses. On 19 April, *Emile Bertin* was escorting a convoy which was entering Namsos when a Ju 88 of II/KG 30 targeted her and released two 500kg bombs. One fell 10m to starboard, but the other struck the after deckhouse; it went straight through the lightly-built ship without exploding.

The cruiser returned to Scapa Flow on the evening of 20 April. She was replaced in Force Z by the cruiser *Montcalm*, detached from the *Force de raid*. The damage to *Emile Bertin* was repaired at Brest between 26 April and 18 May. The *Montcalm* took part in the sortie of 29 April to 5 May to cover the evacuation of Namsos. The formation, which comprised *Montcalm*, three British cruisers, three French armed merchant cruisers (AMCs), the *contre-torpilleur Bison* and eight British destroyers, was attacked by two German bombers around midday on 1 May. The AMCs, loaded

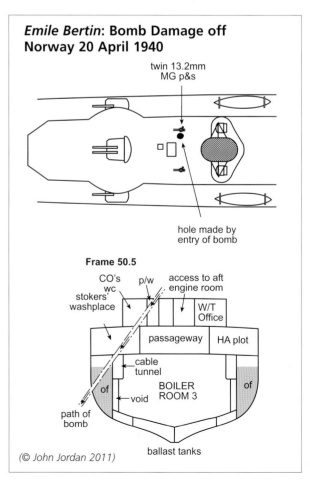

Emile Bertin: **Bomb Damage off Norway 20 April 1940**

(© *John Jordan 2011*)

with troops, left Namsos in the early hours of 3 May. The expected air attacks began around 08.30. Shortly after 10.00 a Stuka of I/St.G.1 began an attack on *Montcalm* but switched to the *Bison*, hitting her with a single bomb. The ship was cut in two by the explosion; her bow sank immediately, and the after part of the ship was despatched by the British destroyer *Afridi* once the survivors had been rescued. The *Afridi* would be sunk in her turn shortly before 14.00. The *Montcalm*, which returned to Brest on 15 May, had fired 800 rounds of 90mm, but without using her RPC system, which was considered unreliable.

The gold transports

The *Emile Bertin* conducted the first gold transport mission when she collected Polish gold from Beirut in September 1939. The purchase of war *matériel* (particularly aircraft) from the United States necessitated the shipping of gold as payment to Canada, from where it was transported to the USA. The first delivery was made by the Toulon-based cruisers *Marseillaise* and *Jean de Vienne* in November 1939, then by *Algérie* in March 1940. *Tourville* carried gold to Beirut to finance a Turkish loan.

The last transport missions involved the evacuation of the French gold reserves to prevent their capture by the Germans. On 21 May the *Jeanne d'Arc* and *Emile Bertin* left Brest with 212 tonnes of gold aboard. They joined up with the aircraft carrier *Béarn* from Toulon with a further 194 tonnes, and the three ships arrived at Halifax, Nova Scotia, on 1st June.

The *Emile Bertin* sailed again from Canada on 3 June, returned to Brest, embarking 290 tonnes of gold between 9 and 12 June, and returned to Halifax on

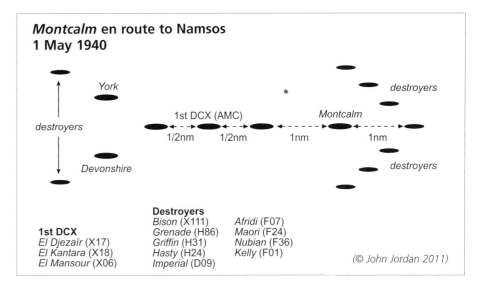

Montcalm en route to Namsos 1 May 1940

York

destroyers

Devonshire

1st DCX (AMC)

1/2nm   1/2nm   1nm   1nm

Montcalm

destroyers

destroyers

destroyers

1st DCX
El Djezaïr (X17)
El Kantara (X18)
El Mansour (X06)

Destroyers
Bison (X111)   *Afridi* (F07)
Grenade (H86)   *Maori* (F24)
Griffin (H31)   *Nubian* (F36)
Hasty (H24)   *Kelly* (F01)
Imperial (D09)

(© John Jordan 2011)

the 18th. On this occasion the gold remained on board, and faced with a refusal to allow the ship to sail, the cruiser made a forced exit on the evening of 21 June and sailed to Fort de France, Martinique, where she arrived 24 June. The *Jeanne d'Arc* and the *Béarn* left Halifax for Brest on 16 June with 106 US-built aircraft aboard, but with the situation in northern France deteriorating by the hour were ordered to make for Martinique; they arrived at Fort de France on 27 June.

The *Primauguet*, following repairs at Lorient, transported troops in the Mediterranean, then sailed for Casablanca, arriving on 13 March. She conducted patrols to monitor neutral traffic, then left Morocco on

Left: *Emile Bertin* escorting a convoy to Norway in April 1940. She was flagship of the French naval forces deployed to Norway, under the command of Rear-Admiral Derrien, until damaged by a bomb; she was replaced by the *Montcalm* of the 4th Cruiser Division. *(ECPAD)*

1 April to relieve *Jeanne d'Arc* in Martinique, arriving on 10 April. The cruiser disembarked her landing party at Aruba on 10 May. She sailed from Fort de France on 3 June, called in at Dakar and Casablanca and then headed for Brest but was diverted to the Gironde. There she stood ready to embark the President of the Republic, should the latter wish to leave metropolitan France. She was attacked by German aircraft while in the Royan anchorage, where she embarked 15 tonnes of gold on 23 June. She then sailed for Casablanca, arriving on 25 June.

The cruisers in the Mediterranean

The 1st class cruisers were all based at Toulon at the outbreak of war with the exception of *Suffren*, which was in Indochina. The three 2nd class cruisers of the 3rd Cruiser Division and the *Emile Bertin* were at Bizerte with the *Forces légères d'attaque*.

Tourville and *Colbert*, forming a 2nd Cruiser Division, sailed from Bizerte on 8 December to monitor shipping in the Eastern Mediterranean as far as Beirut. They returned to Bizerte on 26 and 28 December respectively. *Tourville* then transported gold to Beirut between 20 January and 7 February 1940.

The 3rd Cruiser Division transported two battalions of legionnaires and three regiments of African light infantry (*tirailleurs*) between North Africa and Marseille in March 1940. Each cruiser embarked 500–600 men for each trip. The first contingent left Oran on 3 March on board the *Marseillaise* and *Jean de Vienne*, which made four trips between 3 and 10 March. *La Galissonnière* made two trips between 8 and 12 March, and *Primauguet* a single trip between 8 and 9 March.

Right: *Duquesne* at Beirut some time between 21 May and 11 June 1940.
(Private collection, courtesy of Marc Saibène)

The *Force de raid* in the Mediterranean

With the position of Italy still uncertain, the *Force de raid* sailed for Mers el-Kebir with *Dunkerque*, *Strasbourg*, *Montcalm*, *Gloire* and five *contre-torpilleurs*, arriving on 5 April 1940. It left again on the 9th on the news of the German landings in Norway, arriving at Brest on 12 April. The *Force de raid* was back at Mers el-Kebir again, without the *Montcalm* (now involved in the Norwegian campaign) but with the *Georges Leygues*, on 27 April. The two cruisers were based at Oran.

On 30 April the 3rd Cruiser Division, now reassembled at Bizerte, covered the passage through the Sicilian Straits of the battleships *Provence*, *Bretagne* and *Lorraine*, which were on their way to Alexandria. They were joined *en route* by the British battleships *Royal Sovereign* and *Malaya*. The three cruisers of the 3rd DC subsequently made for Oran, where they joined the *Force de raid* on 2 May.

A major exercise on 9–10 May involved *Dunkerque*, *Strasbourg*, *Georges Leygues*, *Gloire*, *Jean de Vienne* and *La Galissonnière*. From 11 May the 4th DC was at Algiers, joined on 19 May by the *Montcalm*.

THE WAR WITH ITALY, 10 JUNE 1940 TO 25 JUNE 1940

The 'Battle of the Mirror Wardrobe'

On 12 June a force which was certainly the most powerful the French had yet sent to sea sailed from Mers el-Kebir, Oran and Algiers. It comprised four battleships, six cruisers (the 3rd and 4th DC at full strength), nine *contre-torpilleurs* and five fleet torpedo boats. Intelligence suggested that German naval forces might be about to enter the Mediterranean. The report was in error, as at this time *Scharnhorst* and *Gneisenau* were operating off Trondheim. The *Force de raid* established a barrier between the coast of Oran and Spain. The forces from Algiers (4th DC) joined the main body at dawn on 13 June. A Breguet Bizerte flying boat from Squadron E3 signalled a battleship and three destroyers 60nm from the *Force de raid*, which immediately headed towards the threat. In fact the position given by the seaplane was out by 60nm, which meant that the *Force de raid* was pursuing itself. This action against a phantom fleet would come to be referred to as the 'Battle of the Mirror Wardrobe' (*la bataille de l'armoire à glace*).[1]

On 17 June the Italian submarine *Dandolo* launched two torpedoes which passed between the *Jean de Vienne* and *La Galissonnière*. The submarine was located by a Loire 130 from *La Galissonnière*, but the aircraft was unarmed and the submarine was attacked by a second Loire 130 from the same ship, which dropped two bombs. Depth-charging by the cruiser and three torpedo boats followed; however, *Dandolo* survived not only this attack but the war.

The *Force de raid* returned to Mers el-Kebir on 13 June minus the 3rd Cruiser Division, which sailed for Algiers with two *contre-torpilleurs*. The 4th DC sortied from 19 to 22 June to cover the passage of a convoy. At 08.00 on 23 June the 4th Cruiser Division, in company with the 10th DCT, left Algiers to cover

---

[1] In a similar incident, on 27 July 1943 in the Aleutians, two American battleships and three cruisers fired 518 rounds of 14in and 487 of 8in shell against false radar echoes in the 'Battle of the Pips'.

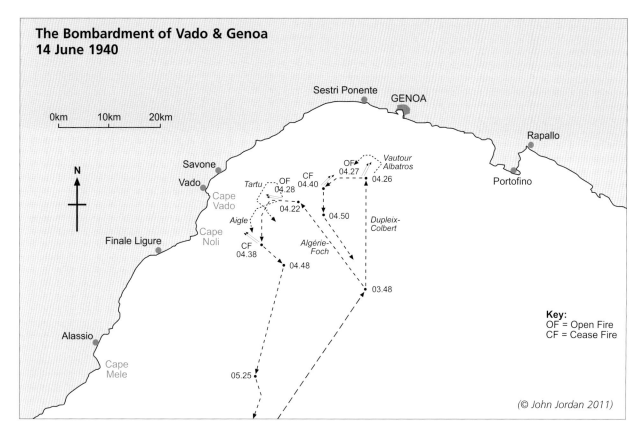

convoys and ships sailing independently between metropolitan France and North Africa. The hope of engaging Italian cruisers of the 7th Division[2] led the 3rd Cruiser Division to sortie from Algiers in company with the 8th DCT at 18.00 on the same day. The two formations joined up shortly after midnight on 24 June. The Italian ships were not found and the French ships were back at their moorings in Algiers around midday on 24 June.

The bombardment of Genoa (Operation 'Vado')

When Italy declared war on 10 June, the 3rd Squadron at Toulon comprised the four 10,000-ton cruisers *Algérie*, *Dupleix*, *Foch* and *Colbert* and eleven *contre-torpilleurs*, of which half had arrived from Brest since mid-May.

A bombardment of the Italian coast had been planned to take place as soon as Italy entered the war. Delayed for political reasons, it was sanctioned after the Italian bombing of Bizerte on 12 June. The operation, christened 'Vado', was finally undertaken during the night of 13/14 June by the 3rd Squadron, commanded by Vice-Admiral Duplat. Once the squadron neared its objectives it was divided into two groups:

Group Vado: the cruisers *Algérie* (VA Duplat) and *Foch*, with the *contre-torpilleurs Vauban*, *Lion*, *Aigle* (1th DCT), *Tartu*, *Chevalier Paul*, *Cassard* (5th DCT).

Group Genoa: the cruisers *Dupleix* (CA Derrien) and *Colbert* forming a 5th DC for the duration of the operation, with the *contre-torpilleurs Vautour*, *Albatros* (7th DCT), *Guépard*, *Valmy*, *Verdun* (3rd DCT).

---

[2] *Di Savoia* (Rear-Ad. Sansonetti), *D'Aosta*, *Attendolo* and *Montecuccoli*.

The cruisers fired on oil tanks and steel works between 04.26 and 04.40. The *contre-torpilleurs* were divided into bombardment divisions (5th and 7th DCT) and scouting/escort divisions (1st and 3rd DCT).

The Italian torpedo boat *Calatafimi*, which was escorting the auxiliary minelayer *Elbano Gasperi*, happened upon the French squadron. The minelayer escaped by following the line of the coast, and the torpedo boat opened fire and launched four torpedoes, but without result. A malfunction prevented the launch of the last two torpedoes, and the *Calatafimi* retired undamaged. The *contre-torpilleurs* fired on the shore battery at Cape Vado, which was silenced after a few minutes, then on the wireless station, the main road and a motor launch.

Four Italian motor torpedo boats were also at sea. *MAS 535* and *MAS 539*, 4nm to the east of Savona, attacked Group Vado. *MAS 534* and *MAS 538*, which were returning to Savona, turned back into open waters and also attacked Group Vado. Group Genoa also fired on MTBs whose identity remains uncertain. All the Italian MAS boats regained Savona after launching their torpedoes (*MAS 535* excepted), none of which found their target. *MAS 535* and *MAS 539* were hit by shell splinters which wounded three men but caused little other damage. *MAS 534* and *MAS 538* were virtually undamaged, with only one minor casualty. The French squadron retired as planned, the return to Toulon being marked by a breakdown in *Foch*'s steering which forced her to turn a complete circle to port; she subsequently had to be steered manually. The French squadron arrived back in Toulon shortly before midday on 14 June.

The final results were unimpressive. The French cruisers fired more than 500 203mm rounds and some 300 rounds of secondary ammunition (90mm and 100mm); the *contre-torpilleurs* fired 800 138mm rounds. Italian losses were nine civilians killed and thirty-four wounded. One-third of the French shells fell into the sea. At Vado, a gasometer and a fuel tank were set on fire. Some minor damage was inflicted on housing and factories in Vado, Savona, Abissola, Zinola and Quiliano. At Genoa the cruisers fired at the wrong targets – they fired on the valley of Lerone instead of that of Polcevera – but inflicted some damage on industrial buildings; the *contre-torpilleurs* hit the Ansaldo-Fossati factory at Sestri. All the damage was repaired in a few days.

The 3rd Squadron sortied from Toulon again 17–18 June to cover the passage of a convoy of seventeen ships from Marseille to Oran.

Force X in the Eastern Mediterranean
A Franco-British naval force was assembled in the Eastern Mediterranean to ensure control of this theatre in the event of war with Italy. The French ships formed a new Force X. Initially it comprised the battleships *Provence*, *Bretagne*, and *Lorraine*, the *contre-torpilleurs Tigre* and *Lynx* and the fleet torpedo boat *Forbin*, which arrived at Alexandria on 3 May. The cruisers *Duquesne* and *Tourville* arrived the following day, joined by the *Suffren* on 18 May (the 2nd Cruiser Division was now at full strength), but *Provence* and *Bretagne* sailed on 20 May for Bizerte, then Mers el-Kebir. The *Duguay-Trouin* arrived at Alexandria from Lorient on 24 May.

Tourville, *Suffren* and the *Forbin* sailed for Beirut, entering that port on 21 May, followed on the 27th by the *Duquesne* and the *Duguay-Trouin*. They were joined by the fleet torpedo boats *Le Fortuné* and *Basque* on 25 and 26 May. All the ships at Beirut sailed on 11 June for a raid in the Aegean, off the island of Crete, and returned Alexandria on 13 June without having encountered any enemy ships.

While the *Lorraine* was bombarding Bardia on 21 June, *Duguay-Trouin* and *Suffren* were despatched to the port of Tobruk, where three enemy cruisers were reported to be moored. These reports proved to be false, and the two French cruisers returned to Alexandria the same evening.

An operation against the coast of Sicily was planned for 23–26 June. Force X was preparing to get underway on the evening of 22 June when the operation was cancelled, and the French ships remained at Alexandria. The Armistice, which immobilised all French warships, came into force at 00.45 on 25 June.

AFTER THE ARMISTICE
From the Armistice to Mers el-Kebir
On 25 June 1940, the French cruisers were dispersed between the French West Indies and Indochina:

Toulon (metropolitan France): *Algérie, Dupleix, Foch, Colbert*.
Algiers (Algeria): *Marseillaise, Jean de Vienne, La Galissonnière, Georges Leygues, Montcalm, Gloire*.
Alexandria (Egypt): *Duquesne, Tourville, Suffren, Duguay-Trouin*.
Fort de France (Martinique): *Emile Bertin, Jeanne d'Arc* (arrived 27 June).
Casablanca (Morocco): *Primauguet*.
Saigon (Indochina): *Lamotte-Picquet*

The clauses of the Armistice stipulated the demobilisa-

tion and deactivation of the major part of the fleet – a small part of the fleet was to remain operational in order to protect French interests overseas – in designated ports which initially were to have been the ships' base ports in time of peace.

The wording of the Armistice gave rise to the subsequent tragic events at Mers el-Kebir. In summary, the French were devastated by their defeat, and believed that they had signed an honourable Armistice with the Germans (and Italians), whereas the British Prime Minister, Winston Churchill, considered the Germans under Hitler to be fundamentally untrustworthy, and that there was a risk that the French ships would somehow end up in the hands of the Germans, reducing the superiority of the Royal Navy over the navies of the Axis powers to zero. Discussions began between the Germans and the French to determine the ports in which the French ships were to be deactivated, and the thrust of these talks was that the Axis powers would agree to their deactivation where they were, in North Africa and Toulon. But by this time the British response had already been agreed.

On 3 July before dawn the British seized all the French ships which had taken refuge in British ports (there were no cruisers among them). At Mers el-Kebir, where four battleships and six *contre-torpilleurs* were currently assembled, an attempt to rally the French ships to the Allied cause failed and the British opened fire at 16.56. The battleship *Bretagne* was sunk with heavy loss of life and *Provence* and *Dunkerque* were seriously damaged and had to be beached, but *Strasbourg* got underway under a hail of shells.

The six 7600-ton cruisers and four *contre-torpilleurs* at Algiers sailed for Oran from 15.00. They were due to join the *Strasbourg*, which had sortied from Mers el-Kebir at 17.09, but they failed to locate her. Three cruisers (*Algérie, Foch* and *Colbert*) got underway at Toulon at 19.00, accompanied by twelve *contre-torpilleurs*. The cruisers from Algiers and from Toulon joined up at 04.45 on 4 July and arrived back in Toulon at 13.00, followed by the *Strasbourg* which, having skirted the coasts of Sardinia and Corsica, arrived in Toulon with her three *contre-torpilleurs* only at 20.00 that evening. There were now ten cruisers at Toulon. These ships remained operational and rotated between Toulon and the anchorage at Salins d'Hyères.

The cruisers at Dakar
Mers el-Kebir was a major upset; however, conflict with Britain was avoided. The deactivation of the fleet was suspended, and plans for its reorganisation discussed. The decision by the countries of French Equatorial Africa (Chad on 26 August, followed by Cameroon on the 27th and the Republic of the Congo on the 28th) to throw in their lot with the Free French of de Gaulle compelled the Vichy Government to react.

On 31 August it was decided to despatch the cruiser *Primauguet* and five sloops to Casablanca, and the Germans agreed to the despatch to Dakar of Force Y. Gabon, which had remained loyal to the Vichy Government, could serve as an operational base. The *Primauguet* left Casablanca with the oiler *Tarn* and the sloops *La Surprise* and *Gazelle* on 4 September; they arrived at Dakar on the 9th.

The cruisers *Georges Leygues, Montcalm* and *Gloire* (which still made up the 4th Cruiser Division) and the *contre-torpilleurs Le Fantasque, Le Malin* and *L'Auda-*

cieux (10th DCT) were grouped together in a new Force Y. They left Toulon on 9 September having disembarked their reservists and replaced them with volunteers. They passed through the Straits of Gibraltar on the morning of the 11th. The British, informed of their passage at the last minute, allowed them to proceed without hindrance. The lack of endurance, particularly of the *contre-torpilleurs*, compelled the French to call in at Casablanca for refuelling, a stay which was cut short by news that the battlecruiser *Renown* had left Gibraltar steaming west. The latter ship set off in pursuit of Force Y, which left the Moroccan port in a hurry at around 02.00 on the 12th, heading at speed for Dakar. The cruisers entered the latter port on 14 September. However, the *contre-torpilleurs*, which at these high speeds consumed vast quantities of fuel, were sent back to Morocco; they would reach Dakar only on 19 September.

The *Primauguet* and the *Tarn*, which were placed under the orders of Force Y, left Dakar on 14 September for Libreville in Gabon, where the tanker was to refuel Force Y. On 18 September the *Georges Leygues*, *Montcalm* and *Gloire* left Dakar and headed for the Gulf of Guinea.

As with Mers el-Kebir, a full history of the Dakar Expedition would be out of place here. The British and the Free French both wished to take Dakar, albeit for different reasons: the British wanted to make of use the port (and prevent the Axis powers gaining access to it), while the French wanted it for political reasons, to serve as a base on French soil for Free France, and as a rallying point for France's African colonies. It was envisaged that a combined British and Free French force would arrive off Dakar on 23 September and convince the local political and military authorities to rally to the Free French cause.

Unaware of the plans being drawn up on the other side of Channel, the three cruisers of Force Y headed for the Gulf of Guinea. They were intercepted at 09.00 on 19 September by the cruisers *Cumberland* and *Australia*, which proceeded to shadow the French ships as they made their way south. The *Primauguet* and the *Tarn* were intercepted in their turn shortly after 11.00 on the same day by the cruisers *Delhi* and *Cornwall*, which ordered the French to turn back to Casablanca. The commander of Force Y, Rear-Admiral Bourragué, accepting that combat with the British cruisers would be a pointless sacrifice, ordered the *Primauguet* to head for Morocco. The cruiser and the oiler subsequently entered Casablanca on 1 October, having been shadowed until 26 September.

Deprived of his oiler, the commander of Force Y decided to return to Dakar, but waited until 18.30 to turn back. Realising that the French were returning to Senegal, the British transmitted a flurry of messages requesting them to head for Morocco under the pretext that the Germans were at Dakar. A pursuit ensued in which the French, keeping to their course, began to slowly pull ahead. It was at this point that engine failure slowed the *Gloire*, which attempted to head for Conakry. Finally, under the guns of HMAS *Australia*, *Gloire* changed course for Casablanca, arriving during the evening of 24 September. The *Georges Leygues* and *Montcalm* succeeded in outrunning the *Cumberland*, the exchange of messages continuing until the British cruiser turned away in the night. The *Georges Leygues* and *Montcalm* entered Dakar at 07.30 on 20 September.

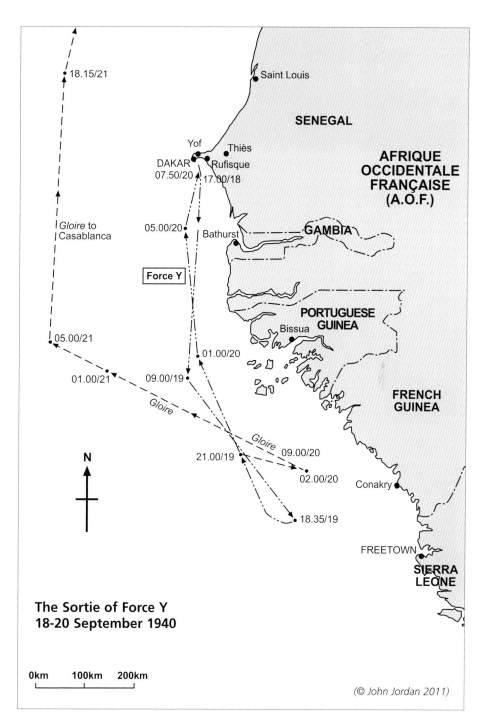

The Sortie of Force Y
18–20 September 1940

0km   100km   200km

(© John Jordan 2011)

The assault on Dakar

At dawn on 23 September, there were present at Dakar the battleship *Richelieu*, the cruisers *Georges Leygues* and *Montcalm*, three *contre-torpilleurs*, the modern fleet torpedo-boat *Le Hardi*, six sloops, three submarines, three patrol boats and five deactivated armed merchant cruisers. The British appeared off the port with the battleships *Barham* and *Resolution*, the aircraft carrier *Ark Royal*, the cruisers *Devonshire*, *Cumberland*, *Australia* and *Delhi*, and ten destroyers. The Free French naval forces comprised three sloops and two armed trawlers. Troops and their equipment were loaded onto a dozen transports. The British and Free French ships remained offshore, shrouded in mist; negotiations failed, a coastal battery opened fire at 10.05 and at 11.05 the British began their bombardment of the port, concentrating in particular

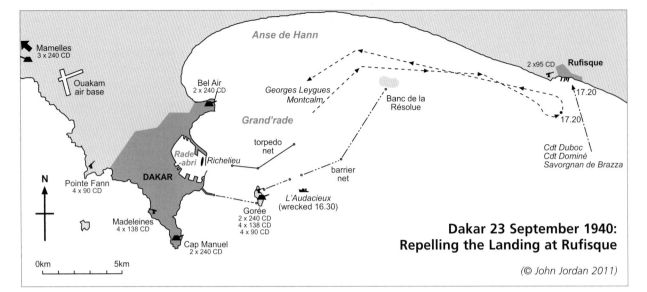

**Dakar 23 September 1940:
Repelling the Landing at Rufisque**

(© John Jordan 2011)

Below: *Georges Leygues* seen from the quarterdeck of a *contre-torpilleur* during the action at Dakar between 23 and 25 September 1940. Note the 138.6mm shell in the circular slide ready for loading into the breech of the after gun. *(ECPAD)*

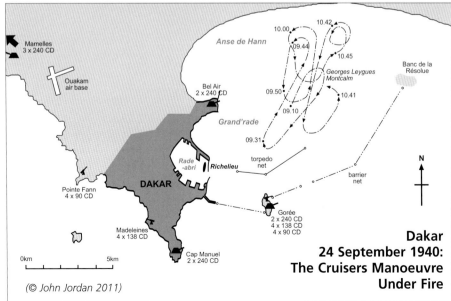

**Dakar
24 September 1940:
The Cruisers Manoeuvre
Under Fire**

(© John Jordan 2011)

on the *Richelieu*. The French ships at Dakar had been surprised, and needed to raise steam before moving to oppose the hostile forces arrayed against them. The cruisers eventually made for the Bay of Hann, where they manoeuvred between the coastal town of Rufisque and Gorée Island (see map) under the bombardment of the British ships, partially covered by smoke from the *contre-torpilleurs*, including the *L'Audacieux*, which was put out of action by the cruiser *Australia* at about 16.30. *Georges Leygues* and *Montcalm* conducted a reconnaissance as far as Rufisque at about 17.20, but the mist concealed the three FNFL sloops, whose attempt to land troops was being repelled at this time.

On 24 September, when the Free French had retired, the British fleet returned to bombard Dakar. The *Georges Leygues* and *Montcalm* resumed their manoeuvres in the 'rat run' between Rufisque and Gorée.

On 25 September, a repeat of the events of the previous two days was soon interrupted by the torpedoing of the *Resolution* by the submarine *Bévéziers*. The British then withdrew, under the fire of the French cruisers, with the *Resolution* in tow. The *Georges Leygues* had fired 623 rounds of 152mm and *Montcalm* 466.

The 4th Cruiser Division at Dakar
The British having been repelled, Force Y remained at Dakar, becoming the 4th Squadron on 28 October 1940. The Toulon-based *contre-torpilleur Le Terrible* replaced *L'Audacieux* on 26 February 1941, and *Gloire* rejoined from Casablanca on 29 March. Maintenance of the ships had now to be shared between Dakar, which had a dry dock, and Casablanca, which had limited repair facilities. In these conditions, the cruisers at Dakar took turns to be refitted at Casablanca: *Montcalm* from 26 April to 29 July 1941, followed by *Georges Leygues* from 26 August to 24 November, and *Gloire* again from 3 April to 12 July 1942. The trips to Casablanca in August 1941 and April 1942 were utilised to bring back Belgian gold (100 and 75 tonnes) to Dakar.

A chronic shortage of fuel limited the activities of the cruisers to a short training sortie off Gorée initially once a week, subsequently reduced to once a month. Other sorties were made to cover the merchant ships which still regularly plied between Morocco, Senegal and the Ivory Coast and occasionally the French West Indies.

The seizure by the British of the banana boat *Fort de France*, in transit from the French West Indies to Morocco, led to a sortie by the *Georges Leygues* and *Montcalm* on 8 April 1941, but the ship was recaptured and brought back by the *Primauguet*. A second sortie, this time by the *Georges Leygues* and *Gloire* on 14-15 May, failed to locate the cargo ship *Bourbonnais*, which had been captured by the British on 13 May.

The *Gloire* sortied again to assist the cargo liner *Eridan* which, released by the British, was escorted by the cruiser back to Dakar on 9 June 1941. On 13 September 1942, it was again the *Gloire* which sailed; together with the sloop *Annamite* she picked up 1041 survivors from the British liner *Laconia*, sunk by the German *U 156* on 12 September. The cruiser refuelled at Dakar on the 21st, then sailed again for Casablanca to disembark the survivors. She remained at Casablanca from 25 September to 17 October 1942.

When the Allied landings in North Africa (Operation 'Torch') took place in November 1942, the three cruisers of the 4th Division were still at Dakar.

The cruisers in the West Indies

Following the Armistice, the French West Indies were under continuous close surveillance by the Americans, who doubted the neutrality declared by the Vichy government. The *Jeanne d'Arc*, which had arrived at Fort de France (Martinique) on 27 June 1940, sailed for Pointe à Pitre (Guadeloupe) on 29 June to help maintain order amid the disturbances which followed the Armistice. The cruiser would remain in Guadeloupe except for a sortie to Martinique in October 1940, four short deployments in 1941 to Les Saintes and Fort de France, and a short sortie in April 1942.

The *Emile Bertin* remained at Fort de France. She sortied briefly in October 1940. She joined *Jeanne d'Arc* on short deployments to Martinique, Les Saintes and Guadeloupe in late January and early May 1941. She made one more sortie between 30 March and 7 April 1942, then remained moored quay-side at Fort de France.

Negotiations between the local authorities and the Americans resulted in an agreement on 15 May 1942 under which the two cruisers in the West Indies were to be immobilised after the dismantling of certain items of machinery (butterfly valves and regulators aboard *Jeanne d'Arc*, gearing pinions aboard *Emile Bertin*), which were sent to Casablanca.

The *Lamotte-Piquet* in Indochina

In Indochina, *les oubliés du bout du monde* ('the forgotten ones at the end of the world') were finally cut off from metropolitan France when the British captured a convoy on 3 November 1941 off The Cape.

Following the defeat of June 1940 the French government, lacking the means to defend its territory, was compelled on 22 September 1940 to accept a military agreement permitting Japanese use of the airfields in Indochina and the port of Hai Phong, and the passage of Japanese troops across the Tonkin River.[3]

Border incidents with neighbouring Siam degenerated into open warfare in January 1941. On 19

---

[3] The British and the Americans were consulted but declined assistance.

November 1940 the navy had constituted a temporary standing force comprising the cruiser *Lamotte-Piquet* and the sloops *Amiral Charner*, *Dumont d'Urville*, *Marne* and *Tahure*. A naval action, to be combined with a land operation, was decided on 17 January. The force based around *Lamotte-Piquet* was to attack part of the Siamese fleet based at Koh Chang.

The battle of Koh Chang

The French ships, organised as three sections with the cruiser making up a single section, failed in their attempt to surprise the Siamese, who had been alerted by a Loire 130 reconnaissance plane. Both sides opened fire at about 06.15, with *Lamotte-Piquet* herself opening fire at 06.19. At 06.20 she launched three torpedoes, one of which certainly struck the coast-defence ship *Sri Ayuthia*, From 06.54 she concentrated her fire on the coast-defence ship *Dhonburi*. At 07.48 she launched another three torpedoes, one of which may have struck the *Dhonburi*. The order to cease fire was given at 08.00.

The Siamese lost the coast-defence ships *Dhonburi*

Above: *Georges Leygues* at Dakar. The photo was taken some time between September 1940 and August 1941. The ships retained their pre-war funnel bands. *(Pradignac & Léo)*

Below: *Jeanne d'Arc* in the French West Indies in late 1939/early 1940. The cruiser had embarked two Loire 130 seaplanes. The commanding officer, Captain Rouyer, had a false bow wave painted to make it appear that the ship was underway and at speed. *(Philippe Caresse collection)*

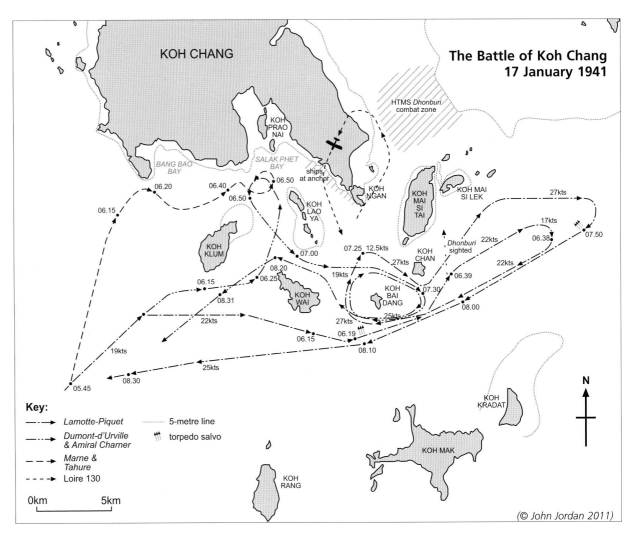

The Battle of Koh Chang
17 January 1941

KOH CHANG

HTMS *Dhonburi*
combat zone

KOH PRAO NAI

BANG BAO BAY

SALAK PHET BAY

ships at anchor

06.20

06.40

06.50

06.50

06.15

KOH NGAN

KOH MAI SI LEK

KOH MAI SI TAI

27kts

17kts

06.38

07.50

KOH LAO YA

KOH KLUM

07.00

07.25 12.5kts

27kts

19kts

Dhonburi sighted

22kts

KOH CHAN

22kts

06.39

08.20

06.25

08.31

06.15

KOH WAI

KOH BAI DANG

07.30

08.00

22kts

27kts

25kts

06.15

06.19

08.10

19kts

08.30

25kts

05.45

N

KOH KRADAT

Key:

- *Lamotte-Piquet*
- *Dumont-d'Urville* & *Amiral Charner*
- *Marne* & *Tahure*
- *Loire 130*
- 5-metre line
- torpedo salvo

KOH MAK

KOH RANG

0km   5km

(© John Jordan 2011)

and *Sri Ayuthia* (the latter would be raised), and the torpedo boats *Trad* (salvaged), *Chonburi* and *Songhkli*; the French ships withdrew without sustaining damage despite Siamese air attacks, and the *Lamotte-Piquet* returned to Saigon on 18 January.

The conflict with Siam ended on 28 January after mediation by the Japanese, followed by a peace treaty on 9 May 1941. On 9 December of the same year

Japan would impose a defence agreement on the French permitting the occupation of Indochina by the Japanese Army.

The *Lamotte-Piquet* conducted a number of coastal patrols up to June 1941. The deteriorating condition of the ship, and in particular of the boilers, meant that she was badly in need of a refit, and the ship was docked at Osaka, Japan, from 15 to 27 September

Right: *Lamotte Picquet* from the Australian-manned armed merchant cruiser HMS *Kanimbla*, Mekong River, Saigon, 28 June 1940. *(Con Cannon)*

1941. Repairs to the boilers were made in stages between March and September 1942. However, the ship no longer went to sea, principally because of a shortage of fuel. During early 1943 she was moored in the Donnai Province, facing the pyrotechnics at Thanh-Tya-Ha and, placed in 'special reserve', housed the naval school for the Annamite region.

Between 10 and 20 January 1945 the US Navy's Task Force 38 conducted a raid in the southern China Sea. Its planes attacked all Japanese shipping together with other ships present. On 12 January the *Lamotte-Piquet* was attacked by aircraft from Task Group 38.2, comprising the aircraft carriers *Lexington*, *Hancock* and *Hornet*. She capsized to port.

The *Primauguet* in Morocco

Following the Armistice, with the Atlantic ports of metropolitan France in the Occupied Zone, Casablanca became the primary French outlet to that ocean. A small naval force had been based there since the Armistice, and the incomplete battleship *Jean Bart* was moored quay-side. The cruiser *Primauguet* left Casablanca in company with the oiler *Tarn* on 14 September 1940 but, intercepted by the British, returned to Morocco on 1st October

The cruiser remained at Casablanca, conducting a number of training sorties and participating in the retrieval of the banana boat *Fort de France* in April 1941 (see above). She was at Dakar for docking from 2 to 17 November 1941, then began a major refit at Casablanca which lasted until 15 March 1942. She became flagship of the 2nd Light Squadron, which was formed at Casablanca on 19 April 1942 with three *contre-torpilleurs* and seven fleet torpedo boats. From that time there was a monthly training sortie, and *Primauguet* began a minor refit on 4 October 1942.

The battle of Casablanca

On 8 November 1942 the Allies landed in Morocco and Algeria (Operation 'Torch'). French forces resisted until 10 November.

While the two *contre-torpilleurs* and five fleet torpedo boats available (2nd Light Squadron) got underway to confront the American ships between Casablanca and Fedala, where the landings were taking place. *Primauguet* hastily reassembled as far as possible the equipment and machinery which had been dismantled during her refit and got underway. She left harbour shortly before 10.00 and headed for Fedala with the other ships of her squadron, which had reassembled off Casablanca. *Primauguet* opened fire on the US battleship *Massachusetts* at 10.35. The French formation manoeuvred between the port of Casablanca and Fedala, farther up the coast, under the fire of the US cruisers *Augusta* and *Brooklyn*, then the cruisers *Tuscaloosa* and *Wichita* and their destroyers. The French cruiser was hit at 11.20 by three shells which failed to explode, and at 11.45 a near-miss close to the stern resulted in some minor flooding. A shell from the *Primauguet* struck the *Massachusetts* at 11.57. Then at 12.30 *Primauguet* sustained a hit in a boiler room, followed at 12.40 by a bomb hit. Admiral Gervais de Lafond, who left the *contre-torpilleur Milan* when that ship was put out of action, then raised his flag on the cruiser at 12.58.

The *Primauguet* returned to Casablanca, and at 13.28 was moored 1000m off the entrance to the port.

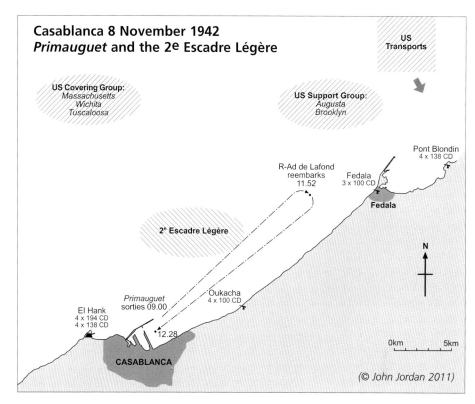

Casablanca 8 November 1942
Primauguet and the 2e Escadre Légère

US Transports

US Covering Group:
Massachusetts
Wichita
Tuscaloosa

US Support Group:
Augusta
Brooklyn

Pont Blondin
4 x 138 CD

R-Ad de Lafond
reembarks
11.52

Fedala
3 x 100 CD

Fedala

2e Escadre Légère

N

Primauguet
sorties 09.00

'Oukacha
4 x 100 CD

El Hank
4 x 194 CD
4 x 138 CD

12.28

CASABLANCA

0km   5km

(© John Jordan 2011)

She was attacked again at 14.40 by nine Dauntless dive-bombers and was hit by at least three bombs, one of which killed her commanding officer on the bridge. The cruiser was moored closer to land at 15.53, being struck again by a shell during the manoeuvre. At 16.50 she was subjected to another aerial assault, and the bridge was again hit. At about 17.00 the cruiser went aground facing the Roches Noires. Fires took hold and the crew was taken off shortly before 18.00. She would burn throughout the night.

The *Primauguet* suffered eighty-five dead and numerous wounded. She had fired 512 155mm rounds. The wreck, which remained in position, would be sold in 1951 and broken up.

The *Forces de Haute Mer* at Toulon

Despite Italian demands for the deactivation of the French fleet in accordance with the provisions of the Armistice, events in the Gulf of Guinea and at Dakar were to mean that a large part remained operational.

On 20 September the despatch of reinforcements for Force Y at Dakar was forbidden. The French had planned to send the cruisers *Algérie*, *Foch*, *Dupleix* and *Marseillaise* with five *contre-torpilleurs* and three fleet torpedo boats to the West African port, with departure scheduled for 22 September.

On 25 September the *Forces de haute mer* (FHM) were created at Toulon under the command of Vice-Admiral Jean Laborde, who flew his flag in the *Strasbourg*. The initial composition was:

– *Strasbourg* (flag)
– *Algérie*, *Foch*, *Dupleix* (1st DC)
– *Marseillaise*, *La Galissonniére* (3rd DC)
– Nine *contre-torpilleurs* in three divisions

The cruisers *Colbert* and *Jean de Vienne* were deactivated and placed in care and maintenance (*en gardiennage*).

Above: *Foch* during underway replenishment trials in 1941, while serving with the *Forces de haute mer* (FHM) at Toulon. UNREP trials were conducted by the Marine Nationale from 1936, but the alongside replenishment technique was only fully operational in France after 1945. *(Henri Landais collection)*

The *Forces de haute mer* would keep broadly the same composition throughout the period 1940–2: *Strasbourg*, three 1st class and two 2nd class cruisers, together with the 3rd Light Squadron with around ten *contre-torpilleurs* and, from November 1940, three newly-completed fleet torpedo boats of the *Le Hardi* class. This fleet, often referred to by French historians as the 'Toulon Fleet', was effectively the deterrent force of the Vichy government. Both the British and the Germans feared that it might fall into the hands of the other.

Virtually cut off from the industries of northern France, which were in the Occupied Zone, the fleet was difficult to maintain, and was limited to minor and major refits requiring docking, together with small improvements to close-range air defences, generally by cannibalising all available *matériel*. A shortage of fuel limited sea time. With the exception of rare training sorties by individual ships or divisions, the ships of the FHM were initially limited to a single major sortie per month, economising on fuel by mooring at Les Salins d'Hyères. By 1942 sorties were limited to one every two months.

The composition of the cruiser divisions changed throughout the period:

– *Colbert* replaced *Dupleix* on 1 January 1941;
– *Jean de Vienne* replaced *La Galissonnière* on 15 March 1941;
– *Dupleix* replaced *Foch* on 4 October 1941.

The ships which were decommissioned were placed in care and maintenance (*en gardiennage*). They retained a skeleton crew.

The FHM made its first sortie from 16 to 18 October 1940. The second sortie, on 6–8 November, was to cover the return of *Provence* from Mers el-Kebir.

On 29 June 1941 *Foch*, accompanied by the *contre-torpilleurs Cassard* and *Tartu*, left Toulon for Algiers, where she embarked a battalion of Algerian Light Infantry. The latter was disembarked at Marseille ready for a deployment to the Levant via Salonika.

The *Jean de Vienne* sailed on 9 January 1942 to search for the cargo ship *Jumièges*, and to bring back the survivors of the liner *Lamoricière*, which had sunk

in a storm. The sloop *L'Impétueuse*, which had taken part in the rescue, transferred the survivors to the cruiser. They were disembarked at Marseille on the 12th.

The final sortie of the cruisers at Toulon was by the *Marseillaise* and *Jean de Vienne*, which sailed for the anchorage at Hyères with the *Strasbourg* on 4 November 1942. The return to Toulon, which for the cruisers was to have been on the 11th, was brought forward to the 7th when the passage of a British convoy from Gibraltar sailing eastwards was reported.

The Cruisers at Alexandria

The British refused to permit any sortie by the French ships of Force X after 23 June 1940. On the morning of 3 July, the day of Mers el-Kebir, Admiral Cunningham submitted to Admiral Godfroy an ultimatum requesting either that the ships be placed under British command, or that they be deactivated at their moorings and the crews repatriated, or that they be scuttled. Despite unhelpful instructions from their superiors – Churchill insisted on the sinking of the ships, Darlan on their escape under fire – the two admirals, who knew and respected one another, took time to discuss the possible options. These discussions ended in a signed agreement on 7 July to the effect that the ships would be immobilised with reduced crews (314 per cruiser). The obturators of the guns were to be removed and deposited with the French consulate in Alexandria.

Despite some problems (the desertion of personnel

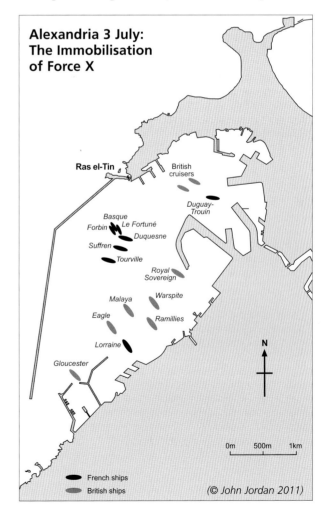

Alexandria 3 July: The Immobilisation of Force X

(© John Jordan 2011)

to the Free French, the replacement of Cunningham by Admiral Harwood in May 1942, the evacuation from Alexandria of the Mediterrean Fleet in July 1942), Force X would remain at Alexandria until 1943. The ships were maintained throughout the period, and certain members of the crews were even relieved during 1942.

THE FLEET IS SCUTTLED AT TOULON
27 NOVEMBER 1942

Following the Allied landings in North Africa, the Germans invaded the Unoccupied Zone on 11 November 1942. The FHM, ready to sail for North Africa to oppose the Allied forces, remained at Toulon, which became a fortified camp. Admiral de Laborde, the C-in-C, maintained good relations with the Germans and subsequently refused to sail for Africa when requested to do so by Admiral Darlan.

On 27 November the Germans invaded the fortified camp. The operational cruisers of the FHM were moored at the Milhaud finger piers, with the exception of the *Jean de Vienne* and *Dupleix* which were in the Missiessy Basin. The cruisers in care and maintenance were in the dockyard: the *La Galissonnière* at Missiessy and the *Foch* at Castigneau (see plan). The German forces were delayed when they lost their way as they penetrated into the dockyard, giving the French time to sound the alarm and to order the pre-arranged scuttling of the fleet.

The *La Galissonnière* was in Dock no.3 at Missiessy. The sluice gates were opened and the cruiser was floated out so that her bow blocked the dock gates. The *Jean de Vienne*, in Dock no.1, was scuttled in the same way. These were the first ships to be encountered by the Germans; their scuttling, apart from their sinking, involved only the destruction of key items of equipment by sledge-hammer and holes cut in bulkheads.

Farther along the quay the *Dupleix* was in commission. The scuttling measures were interrupted when the Germans came on board. The planned destruction measures, notably the detonation of the explosives, were completed, but the flooding of the ship was interrupted. Fires took hold on the ship, punctuated by numerous explosions, and the ship burned until 6 December.

The *Foch*, in care and maintenance, sank after the condensers and the sea cocks were opened. Only the

guns were destroyed using explosives.

At Milhaud, the cruisers *Colbert*, *Algérie* and *Marseillaise* were in line with the *Strasbourg*, bows south. The *Colbert*, at pier no.5, had not yet been to sea since her modernisation (see Chapter 5). Her guns

Above: The French ships interned at Alexandria, which included four cruisers, were forced to remain there for some three years. Seen here are *Duguay-Trouin* (foreground) with the 1500-tonne submarine *Protée* alongside, and *Suffren* with the destroyer *Basque* alongside.

Left: A close-up of *La Galissonnière* following the scuttling. She appears relatively undamaged above decks, but is seated firmly on the bottom of dock no.3.

Colbert: DEM Installation

The first radar of French design and manufacture was designated *Détecteur Electro-Magnétique* or D.E.M. In the installation aboard *Colbert*, the four small dipole antennae, each on its own rotating frame, were fitted on yards projecting from just below the foretop at 45-degree angles; two were for transmission, the other two for reception; the ME 140 transmitter and MR 126 receiver were developed and manufactured by the Sadir Company; trials were cut short by events, but early tests indicated a detection range against aircraft of 50km with a bearing accuracy of ±1° and a range accuracy of ±50m under favourable conditions. Of the ships scuttled at Toulon, only the cruisers *Colbert* and *Algérie*, both of which had recently received AA upgrades, and the flagship *Strasbourg* had been fitted with D.E.M. radar.

(© John Jordan 2010)

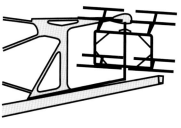

Sadir ME140/MR126 Antenna: Dimensions

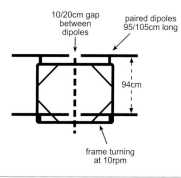

10/20cm gap between dipoles

paired dipoles 95/105cm long

94cm

frame turning at 10rpm

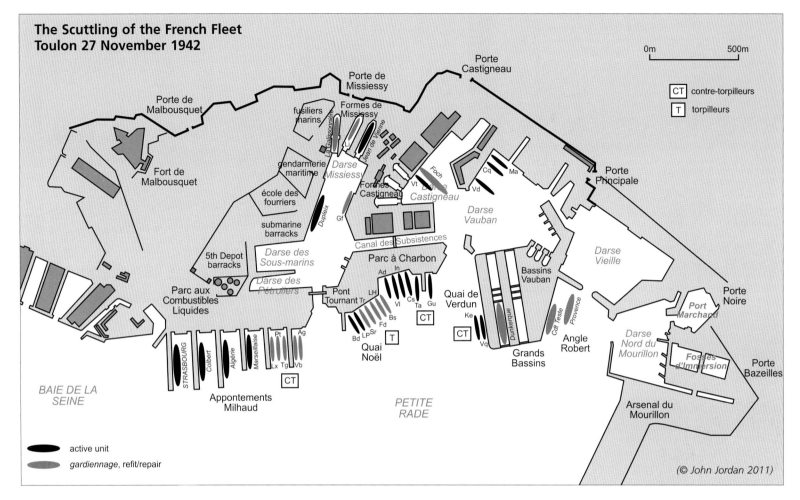

The Scuttling of the French Fleet
Toulon 27 November 1942

CT contre-torpilleurs
T torpilleurs

● active unit
● *gardiennage*, refit/repair

(© John Jordan 2011)

Right: *Colbert* during the scuttling at Milhaud finger pier no.5. The fire first took hold close to the tripod foremast. Clearly visible in this view is the newly-constructed *pergola* in place of the mainmast, with the after light AA guns mounted atop it.

had been spiked with explosives (35kg per 203mm gun) which were now detonated, and fire spread throughout the ship as she settled on the bottom. At pier no.4 the *Algérie* also detonated the explosive charges in her guns. The sea cocks were opened, and a fire spread from the fuel tanks, which were full, throughout the ship. *Algérie* burned until 16 December. Aboard the *Marseillaise*, at pier no.3, the critical parts of the machinery and guns were destroyed using explosive charges and the ship was flooded. A fire broke out and the cruiser, listing 45 degrees to port, sank to the bottom. The fire was extinguished on 3 December.

None of the seven cruisers scuttled at Toulon ever went to sea again. The *Algérie, Dupleix, Foch, Colbert*

Far right: *Jean de Vienne* was partially floated out of Missiessy dock no.1, which she had entered on 8 November following the last sortie of the FHM, before being scuttled, making not only the ship but the dock unusable.

Right: *La Galissonnière* was scuttled in the same way as her sister *Jean de Vienne*, blocking Missiessy dock no.3. The cruiser was not set on fire; the smoke is from the *Dupleix*, which was moored farther down the quay (see plan).

Far left: *Dupleix* burns fiercely following the detonation of the scuttling charges. The arrival of the Germans prevented the flooding of the magazines, thereby facilitating the spread of the fires.

Left, top: The ruined bridge structure of *Colbert* with the DEM (radar) antennae prominent at the ends of the yards. Note the two 37mm CAD on the platform installed above the bridge.

Far left, middle: Turret II of *Dupleix* following the scuttling. The numerous explosions aboard (notably the magazines and the torpedoes) resulted in casualties and a significant amount of damage to the dockyard area around the ship.

Left, middle: The after part of *Dupleix* after the fires had been extinguished. In the foreground: one of the four twin 90mm HA mountings.

Far left, bottom: *Colbert* partly on fire after her scuttling at pier no.5.

Below: *Foch*, which was *en gardiennage* in the Castigneau basin at the time of the scuttling, had her sea cocks opened and settled upright on the bottom. She appears relatively undamaged compared to the cruisers moored at the Milhaud finger piers, but all delicate fire control apparatus and machinery dials had been destroyed with sledge-hammers.

Right: *Marseillaise* during the scuttling, on fire and listing. All the key items for the boilers, the turbines and the guns were destroyed.

Far right: The after part of *Marseillaise* in the aftermath of the fires. In the foreground: the second funnel. The ship could not be salvaged.

Right: *Marseillaise* at Milhaud pier no.3, after the fires had died down..

Far right: *Algérie* lies scuttled at Milhaud finger pier no.4, once the fires had been extinguished. Note the DEM radar antennae on the yards of the forward tower.

Far right: Two German sailors on the forecastle of the scuttled *Colbert*. Each of the 203mm guns was destroyed using a 35kg charge of *mélinite* (picric acid).

Below: *Algérie* lies scuttled at Milhaud pier no.4; she remained on the bottom and burned until 16 December 1942. In the background the funnels of *Colbert* and *Strasbourg* can be made out.

and *Marseillaise* were deemed to be irrecoverable. The *Foch* was broken up before the Liberation and the others after the war, the last, *Algérie*, being sold for scrap on 21 December 1956.

The only partial scuttling of *La Galissonnière* and *Jean de Vienne* allowed them to be quickly refloated. The Italians attempted to refurbish them, and incorporated them into their fleet (at least on paper) as the *FR 12* and *FR 11* respectively. They were still at Toulon on 9 September 1943 when the armistice with Italy was signed, and were seized by the Germans. Work on the ships was halted, the Germans having other priorities than to reactivate vessels for which they would have no fuel.

The *Jean de Vienne* was to have left for La Spezia on 15 September 1943. She was struck by two bombs during an Allied air raid on 24 November and capsized.

The wreck would be righted in late 1945, refloated in 1948 and broken up.

The *La Galissonnière* was struck by a single bomb during the same air raid. She was handed over to the French who moored her in Lazaret Bay close to Toulon. She was sunk, heeling over to starboard, during an American air raid on 18 August 1944. The wreck, which was raised in 1954, was demolished in 1955 and 1956.

THE FORCES OF NORTH AFRICA REJOIN THE ALLIED CAUSE

Following the actions in North Africa and the scuttling at Toulon, the French Navy was left with only ten cruisers including the *Lamotte-Piquet*, stranded in the Far East. The Free French had no cruisers.

The French forces of North Africa joined the Allied cause following the ceasefire declared on 10 November 1942. The three cruisers at Dakar (*Georges Leygues*, *Montcalm* and *Gloire*) belonged to the forces of West Africa, which recognised the authorities in Algiers on 23 November. Force X at Alexandria joined the Allied cause on 17 May 1943 with its four cruisers: *Duquesne*, *Tourville*, *Suffren*, and *Duguay-Trouin*.

In the French West Indies, it was only on 30 June 1943 that Admiral Robert, faced with increasing hostility from the population and many servicemen, decided to abandon his post as High Commissioner.

Moreover, incidents had taken place aboard the two cruisers, which had been blockaded since 30 June 1940, with many members of the crews keen to rejoin the war. The French West Indies rallied to the Allied cause on 14 July, when a representative of the authorities in Algiers arrived in Fort de France aboard the *contre-torpilleur Le Terrible*.

Above: *Emile Bertin* in the French West Indies. She would remain there for three years following the Armistice, before being modernised in the United States. (*Pradignac & Léo*)

FRENCH POLITICS AND THE WAR IN 1943

THE FRENCH DEFEAT OF JUNE 1940 RESULTED IN A new national government led by Marshal Pétain, which took office on 16 June. Admiral François Darlan, Chief of the Naval General Staff since 1 January 1937, took on the additional role of Navy Minister in the government. The Armistice with Germany and Italy came into force on 25 June. The seat of government was to be Vichy, a provincial spa town in the centre of France which remained in the Unoccupied Zone, known as the *zone libre*. Initially Pétain, who legally became head of state on 11 July, was popular, notably for having been one of the rare commanders of the First World War who made every effort to spare the blood of the men under his command.

The Vichy government, convinced that Germany would ultimately win the war, attempted to position itself in such a way as to limit the adverse consequences for France of a future peace treaty. At the same time, in England General de Gaulle, with the support of Churchill, was creating Free France (*France Libre*) as an entity embracing all Frenchmen who rejected the Armistice; his appeal to his countrymen was broadcast on 18 June 1940,. Following the seizure of the French ships which had fled to Britain and the bombardment of Mers el-Kebir by the British fleet, the Free French and the Vichy French would come into conflict at Dakar (23 to 25 September 1940), in Gabon (17 October to 11 November 1940) and in the Levant (Syria and the Lebanon, 8 June to 14 July 1941).

Admiral Darlan, who for more than a year was head of the French government (from 9 February 1941 to 17 April 1942), became C-in-C of all the armed forces on 16 April 1942. Believing that the German attack on the USSR was a strategic error

which made an ultimate Axis victory unlikely, he foresaw an Allied intervention in North Africa in the Spring of 1943. He anticipated that the French would again enter the war against the Axis and sent out feelers to the Americans.

The Vichy forces, although taken by surprise, strenuously opposed the Anglo-American landings in Algeria and Morocco which took place on 8 November 1942 (Operation 'Torch'). The cease-fire in North Africa on 10 November, and the invasion by the Germans of the southern zone of France, which had hitherto been free of occupation, effectively divided the French into three camps:

– The French of metropolitan France, now occupied by the Germans. The small army maintained following the armistice was disbanded and the fleet at Toulon was scuttled on 27 November. Dissatisfaction with the Vichy government was growing, and the Resistance, increasingly supported and sustained by the Allies and the Free French, was gaining in strength, boosted in numbers by former army and navy personnel.
– The French of North Africa, quickly joined by French West Africa (*Afrique Occidentale Française*, or AOF), were commanded first by Admiral Darlan (assassinated on 24 December 1942), then by General Giraud, who was supported by the Americans. French forces based in Tunisia rejoined the fight against the Axis from 18 November 1942. The naval forces which had survived the battles of November were joined by the ships at Dakar (24 November 1942), then by those at Alexandria (17 May 1943) and the West Indies (14 July 1943). Together they made up the *Forces maritimes d'Afrique* (FMA, otherwise known as the *Marine barbaresque*).

– The Free French, still supported by the British but practically ignored by the Americans. Following its recognition by the resistance movements in metropolitan France, *France Libre* officially became *France Combattante*, but the historical name continued to be widely used.

From November 1942 Algiers became the centre of intrigues and battles for influence between Pétainists, Giraudists, Gaullists, monarchists and those nostalgic for the Third Republic. General de Gaulle arrived in North Africa on 30 May 1943. On 3 June, the French Committee for National Liberation (*Comité français de libération nationale*, or CFLN) was set up under the dual presidency of de Gaulle and Giraud. The latter was effectively dismissed from the CFLN on 31 July, and legally deposed on 9 October, but assumed the post of C-in-C of French forces from 31 July 1943 until 8 April 1944 when he was finally removed.

The Armed Forces of Africa and the Free French Forces were merged on 4 August 1943. The 'Marine Nationale' grouped now embraced the *Forces maritimes d'Afrique* (FMA: 36,000 men) and the former *Forces navales françaises libres* (FNFL: 6000 men), which now became the *Forces navales en Grande Bretagne* (FNGB). A genuine merging of the two forces would take some time due to the accumulation of bad feeling between them since 1940.

On 3 June 1944 the CFLN became the GPRF (*Gouvernement provisoire de la République Française*). The Vichy government fell on 20 August, and Pétain was relocated to Germany to head a government in exile. The GPRF, headed by De Gaulle, was legally recognised by the United States, the British and the Soviets only on 21 October 1944.

CHAPTER 11

THE PERIOD 1943–1945

THE MODERNISATIONS IN THE USA

Following the re-entry into the war against the Axis of the French Forces of Africa, negotiations between the authorities in Algiers (Darlan, then Giraud) and the Americans ended with a decision to modernise these forces. The naval forces (FMA), which in practice were now under Allied command, were divided into two groups:

– The battleship *Richelieu*, four cruisers and four *contre-torpilleurs* were to be modernised in the United States. These were the most modern units, of which the oldest had entered service only in 1936. An agreement was signed on 21 January 1943.
– The other ships would be refitted locally in North Africa using the available facilities, with improve-

ments limited to the fitting of 40mm and 20mm AA guns, together with the installation of a navigation radar.

The general staff at Algiers inundated the Americans with requests for assistance in the rebuilding of an ocean-going fleet comprising aircraft carriers, cruisers and destroyers, but the latter were prepared to transfer only a half-dozen destroyer escorts (DEs) and coastal units (sub-chasers and minesweepers).

The first ships to leave for the USA were the *Richelieu* and the cruiser *Montcalm*, which left Dakar on 30 January 1943. *Montcalm* was modernised at Philadelphia Navy Yard from 15 February to 5 August. The ship underwent a complete overhaul and had a new anti-aircraft outfit installed. The 90mm, 37mm

Opposite, bottom: View from the bridge of *Gloire* during her modernisation at the Brooklyn Navy Yard in 1943. The numbers in white indicate the new items of equipment fitted. Note the rails to limit the training arcs of the newly-fitted 20mm Oerlikon guns [2], the ready-use ammunition lockers [1] and the US Navy-style life rafts [5]. *(US Navy)*

Montcalm August 1943

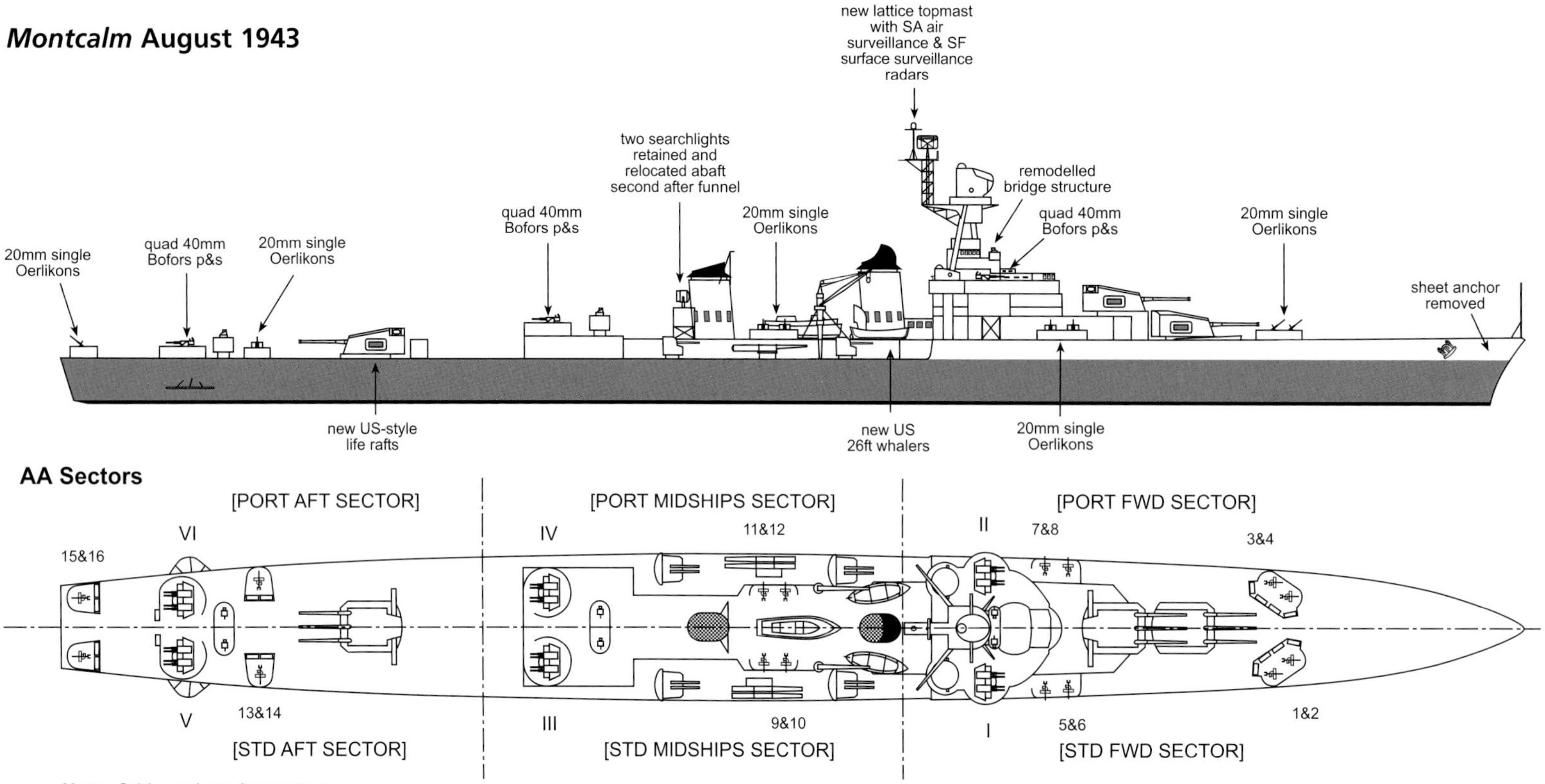

(© John Jordan 2010)

Note: Odd-numbered mounts to starboard, even-numbered to port.

There were numerous detail differences between *Montcalm*, *Georges Leygues* and *Gloire* as modernised. *Montcalm*, the first to be taken in hand at the Philadelphia Navy Yard, had her forward quad 40mm mountings in an extension of the bridge wings, whereas in the other two ships they were in tubs mounted slightly lower, presumably to clear the HA director on after bearings. *Montcalm* would be similarly modified after the war. *Gloire*, which was modernised at the Brooklyn Navy Yard, was the only cruiser of the four modernised in the USA not to have a lattice topmast for the SA and SF radars; instead the SA was mounted atop a light pole topmast, while the SF thimble radome was mounted on a platform extending from the forward leg of the tripod foremast. This was the position adopted for the SF radome for her two sisters post-war, when the new quadruped foremast was stepped around the fore-funnel (see drawing p.215). Other differences concerned the positioning of the life rafts and the configuration of the gun tubs.

Emile Bertin November 1943

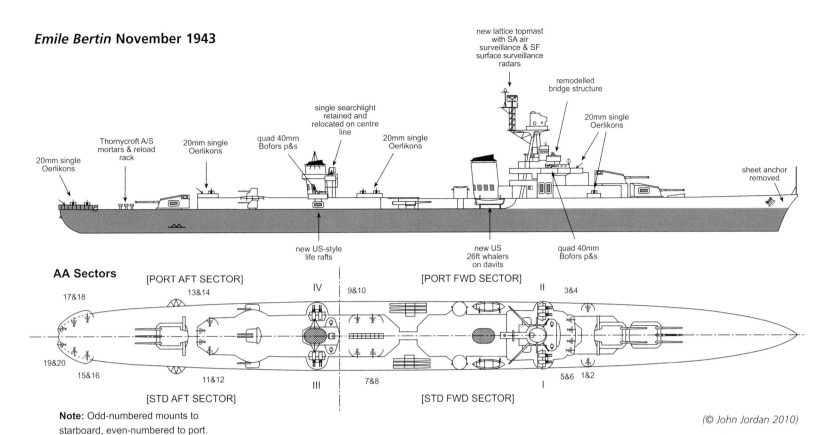

new lattice topmast
with SA air
surveillance & SF
surface surveillance
radars

remodelled
bridge structure

single searchlight
retained and
relocated on centre
line

20mm single
Oerlikons

Thornycroft A/S
mortars & reload
rack

20mm single
Oerlikons

quad 40mm
Bofors p&s

20mm single
Oerlikons

20mm single
Oerlikons

20mm single
Oerlikons

sheet anchor
removed

new US-style
life rafts

new US
26ft whalers
on davits

quad 40mm
Bofors p&s

AA Sectors

[PORT AFT SECTOR]

17&18

13&14

IV

9&10

[PORT FWD SECTOR]

II

3&4

19&20

15&16

11&12

III

7&8

[STD AFT SECTOR]

5&6 1&2

I

[STD FWD SECTOR]

Note: Odd-numbered mounts to
starboard, even-numbered to port.

(© John Jordan 2010)

and 13.2mm guns, together with the catapult and
other aviation facilities, had been disembarked at
Dakar. The 90mm twin mountings would eventually be
reinstalled, but would be complemented by six
quadruple 40mm Bofors and sixteen single 20mm
Oerlikons. *Montcalm* received an SF surface radar
which could be used for fire control of the main guns,
and a short-range SA air surveillance radar. However,
the Americans refused to release the latest fire control
radars, even those which currently equipped their
destroyers.

The *Georges Leygues* replaced the *Montcalm* at
Philadelphia from 2 July to 8 October 1943, while the
Gloire was modernised at the Brooklyn Navy Yard from
22 July to 7 November. The *Emile Bertin*, arriving from
Martinique following the reassembly of her machinery

US Naval Radars

as fitted to *Emile Bertin* and
the three 7600-tonne cruisers

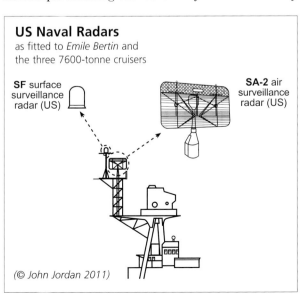

SF surface
surveillance
radar (US)

SA-2 air
surveillance
radar (US)

(© John Jordan 2011)

BS56328

Above: Views from the forecastle (left) and from the second funnel looking forward. The distinctive zebra-pattern camouflage was unique to *Gloire*; the other three cruisers all wore the US Navy's Measure 22. Note in the left-hand photo the distinctive black blast bags, with their mobile gun port shields [5], and the antenna for the SA air surveillance radar [20]. Number [21] denotes the quad Bofors mountings fitted in the bridge wings. *(US Navy)*

using the parts stored at Casablanca (see Chapter 10), arrived at Philadelphia on 30 August. She underwent a modernisation similar to that of the other cruisers with four quadruple 40mm Bofors and twenty single 20mm Oerlikons, and SA and SF radars. She left the Navy Yard on 18 November for trials, then sailed for Fort de France to re-embark her torpedoes and arrived at Dakar 2 January 1944.

The other cruisers, in effect the *Jeanne d'Arc* and the ships from Alexandria, were relatively elderly and worn out, and the Allies refused to invest in extensive modifications which would have delayed the completion of more modern, high-performance units in the predominantly US and British shipyards. The modernisations embarked upon from early 1943, beginning with the *Montcalm*, presented a number of

difficulties. The French used the metric system and also had little idea of the standardisation typical aboard US warships. The Americans were astonished to find that there were no fewer than six separate galleys aboard the French ships (for the admiral, senior officers, junior officers, chief petty officers, petty officers and medical staff, and seamen).

The first of the older cruisers to upgrade her AA capabilities was the *Jeanne d'Arc* which, after sailing from the West Indies via Puerto Rico and Bermuda, was in Algiers from 17 to 18 September, embarking six 40mm Bofors, seventeen 20mm Oerlikons and an SF radar before sailing for Corsica.

The *Duguay-Trouin* was in refit at Casablanca from 14 September to 12 October 1943. Her aviation installations, some of the 13.2mm Hotchkiss MG and two of her torpedo tube mountings were disembarked and fifteen 20mm Oerlikons fitted.

The three 10,000-ton cruisers from Alexandria underwent their first modifications at Dakar or at Casablanca between January and March 1944. A full modernisation was projected for a later date, but in the end had to be curtailed when the Americans refused to

RADARS INSTALLED USA 1943

Model	Function	Frequency	Range	Accuracy	Resolution
SA-2	Air surveillance	1.36m (P-band)	68,000m	30m/1°	150m/25°
SF	Surface surveillance	10cm (S-band)	22,000m	70m/2°	50m/6°

Source: Norman Friedman, *Naval Radar* (London: Conway Maritime Press, 1981).

Above: *Montcalm* on 26 July 1943. She is shown returning from her first sea trials following her modernisation at the Philadelphia Navy Yard. *(US Navy)*

Below: *Montcalm* on 30 July 1943, about to depart the Philadelphia Navy Yard following her modernisation. The silhouette of the ship is much changed, notably with the suppression of the aircraft hangar and mainmast. *(US Navy)*

Right: An aerial view of *Georges Leygues* on 29 September 1943 following her modernisation at the Philadelphia Navy Yard. Particularly prominent are the quadruple 40mm Bofors mountings located in tubs above the stern, amidships (in place of the aircraft hangar) and in the bridge wings, backed up by single 20mm Oerlikon guns. Each of the Bofors mountings has its own associated Mk 51 director.

Below: The bridge and tripod foremast of *Montcalm* following her modernisation in the United States. Note the SA and SF radar antennae atop the new lattice topmast, and the 40mm quad Bofors mounting in a prominent tub extending from the bridge wings. *(US Navy)*

Left: *Emile Bertin* on 17 December 1943, working up off Norfolk, USA. The centre gun of turret II was disembarked for proving trials with the new 152mm ammunition manufactured in the United States, to enable firing tables for the American shells and charges to be drawn up. Of the four cruisers modernised in the USA, *Emile Bertin*, *Montcalm* and *Georges Leygues* all received the US Navy's Measure 22 paint-scheme: Navy Blue hull and Haze Gray upperworks with Deck Blue for horizontal surfaces. *(US Navy)*

Left: *Tourville* in the port of Casablanca, probably in late 1943 following her arrival from Alexandria via Dakar. At Dakar she had embarked a single Loire 130 (atop the catapult), and two Latécoère 298 torpedo floatplanes from Squadron 1S. The latter could not be catapulted and were due to be ferried to Arzew, Algeria, where they would reinforce Squadron 4S. *(US Navy)*

Left: *Duguay-Trouin* and *Jeanne d'Arc* moored to the Delure Jetty at Casablanca on 14/15 September 1943. *Jeanne d'Arc* had arrived from the French West Indies on 9 September, and *Duguay-Trouin* from Alexandria on 14 September. *Jeanne d'Arc* would leave for the Mediterranean on 15 September. *(US Navy)*

supply the necessary equipment, notably the quadruple 40mm Bofors for which tubs had already been constructed (see drawing of *Tourville* 1945).

The modifications of early 1944 undertaken at Casablanca and Dakar involved the replacement of the 37mm cannon and 13.2mm MG by 40mm Bofors and 20mm Oerlikon single mountings, the disembarkation of the aviation installations and the torpedo tubes and, for the *Suffren*, the shortening of the mainmast.

THE HUNT FOR THE BLOCKADE RUNNERS
The French cruisers at Dakar were tasked with reinforcing the anti-raider barrier formed by Allied cruisers on the line Freetown–Pernambuco (Brazil). The line in the west was held by the American light cruisers based at Recife (*Omaha, Cincinnati, Marblehead* and *Memphis*). Out of range of Axis aircraft, the French cruisers did not need a modern AA outfit and were therefore immediately available for this task.

After a few exercises in December 1942 and January 1943, the first patrol was conducted by *Georges Leygues*, from 28 January to 7 February. The latter ship and her sister *Goire* would undertake eight and seven patrols respectively before they sailed for their modernisation in the USA. The *Montcalm*, the first of the three to be modernised, entered the roster in November 1943 on her return from the USA and following a short stay in the Mediterranean.

PATROLS FROM DAKAR 1943–1944

Cruiser	Left Dakar	Returned	Remarks
Georges Leygues	28 Jan 1943	7 Feb 1943	1st patrol 28 Jan–3 Feb, Freetown 3–6 Feb, 2nd patrol 6–7 Feb
Gloire	9 Feb 1943	20 Feb 1943	1st patrol 9–14 Feb, Freetown 14 Feb, 2nd patrol 15–20 Feb
Georges Leygues	15 Feb 1943	21 Feb 1943	Bathurst 15–16 Feb
Georges Leygues	28 Feb 1943	10 Mar 1943	Freetown 1–4 Mar, 4th patrol 4–10 Mar
Gloire	11 Mar 1943	16 Mar 1943	3rd patrol
Gloire	20 Mar 1943	26 Mar 1943	4th patrol
Georges Leygues	25 Mar 1943	31 Mar 1943	5th patrol
Georges Leygues	31 Mar 1943	8 Apr 1943	6th patrol
Gloire	5 Apr 1943	10 Apr 1943	5th patrol
Georges Leygues	9 Apr 1943	15 Apr 1943	7th patrol; intercepted Portland
Gloire	23 Apr 1943	30 Apr 1943	6th patrol
Georges Leygues	28 Apr 1943	5 May 1943	8th patrol
Gloire	5 May 1943	9 May 1943	7th patrol
Suffren	18 Sep 1943	23 Sep 1943	1st patrol
Duquesne	26 Sep 1943	30 Sep 1943	1st patrol
Tourville	2 Oct 1943	6 Oct 1943	1st patrol
Duquesne	13 Oct 1943	17 Oct 1943	2nd patrol
Tourville	16 Oct 1943	20 Oct 1943	2nd patrol
Suffren	18 Oct 1943	21 Oct 1943	2nd patrol
Suffren	2 Nov 1943	8 Nov 1943	3rd patrol
Montcalm	8 Nov 1943	14 Nov 1943	1st patrol
Suffren	11 Nov 1943	22 Nov 1943	4th patrol 11–18 Nov, Freetown 18–21 Nov, 5th patrol 21–22 Nov
Tourville	17 Nov 1943	21 Nov 1943	3rd patrol
Duquesne	20 Nov 1943	14 Nov 1943	3rd patrol
Montcalm	23 Nov 1943	29 Nov 1943	2nd patrol
Tourville	28 Nov 1943	2 Dec 1943	4th patrol
Duquesne	1 Dec 1943	12 Dec 1943	4th patrol 1–5 Dec, Freetown 5–8 Dec, 5th patrol 8–12 Dec
Montcalm	5 Dec 1943	9 Dec 1943	3rd patrol
Tourville	9 Dec 1943	13 Dec 1943	5th patrol
Georges Leygues	11 Dec 1943	17 Dec 1943	9th patrol
Gloire	14 Dec 1943	20 Dec 1943	8th patrol
Montcalm	14 Dec 1943	20 Dec 1943	4th patrol
Duquesne	18 Dec 1943	22 Dec 1943	6th patrol
Tourville	19 Dec 1943	23 Dec 1943	6th patrol
Georges Leygues	21 Dec 1943	28 Dec 1943	10th patrol
Duquesne	27 Dec 1943	31 Dec 1943	7th patrol; with Suffren
Suffren	27 Dec 1943	4 Jan 1944	6th patrol
Gloire	1 Jan 1944	9 Jan 1944	9th patrol
Georges Leygues	5 Jan 1944	14 Jan 1944	11th patrol
Duquesne	6 Jan 1944	13 Jan 1944	8th patrol
Emile Bertin	7 Jan 1944	13 Jan 1944	1st patrol
Montcalm	10 Jan 1944	2 Feb 1944	5th patrol 10–20 Jan, Freetown 20–24 Jan, 6th patrol 24 Jan–2 Feb
Suffren	10 Jan 1944	22 Jan 1944	7th patrol 10-16 Jan, Freetown 16–20, 8th patrol 20–22 Jan
Tourville	17 Jan 1944	18 Jan 1944	Patrol cancelled 18 Dec
Tourville	28 Jan 1944	10 Feb 1944	7th patrol 28 Jan–2 Feb, Freetown 2–6 Feb, 8th patrol 6–10 Feb
Emile Bertin	30 Jan 1944	5 Feb 1944	2nd patrol
Suffren	2 Feb 1944	9 Feb 1944	9th patrol
Georges Leygues	3 Feb 1944	13 Feb 1944	12th patrol
Montcalm	10 Feb 1944	20 Feb 1944	7th patrol
Duquesne	12 Feb 1944	19 Feb 1944	9th patrol
Suffren	17 Feb 1944	9 Mar 1944	10th patrol 17–25 Feb, Recife 25 Feb–4 Mar, 11th patrol 4–9 Mar
Georges Leygues	21 Feb 1944	25 Feb 1944	13th patrol

The cruisers from Alexandria sailed for Dakar via the Cape: *Duquesne* and *Tourville* on 18 August 1943, *Suffren* and *Duguay-Trouin* on 3 September. The three 10,000-ton cruisers took part in patrols against the blockade runners, and also called in at Casablanca. *Suffren* sailed for her first patrol on 18 September. The *Emile Bertin* conducted two patrols in January/early February 1944, and the last patrol was by *Georges Leygues* in late February of the same year. Some patrols were broken by a brief stay in Freetown. The force was boosted by the arrival of the Italian cruisers *Luigi di Savoia Degli Abruzzi* and *Emanuele Filiberto Duca d'Aosta* at Freetown on 6 November 1943. As relations between the French Navy and the Italians were somewhat strained, they remained based at Freetown. The Italian cruisers would return to the Mediterranean in April 1944.

The only success of the French cruisers while engaged in these patrols was the interception of the German blockade runner *Portland*. Knowing that four ships had left Bordeaux for Japan in March 1943, the Allies lay in wait for them. One ship turned back, two

broke through the line, and the *Portland* was intercepted by *Georges Leygues* on the evening of 12 April 1943 and scuttled herself at night after forty-one rounds of 90mm had been fired. The Germans were confident that their radar detectors would enable them to avoid the patrolling cruisers but *Georges Leygues*, which had yet to be modernised, was as yet not equipped with radar.

RETURN TO THE MEDITERRANEAN
The liberation of Corsica
The operation to retake Corsica launched by General Giraud after the Armistice with Italy was undertaken by the French practically unaided, the other Allies providing only limited logistic support. It was primarily a matter of reinforcing and sustaining the Resistance fighters and troops from Algeria, the first of which disembarked at Ajaccio on the night of 12/13 September aboard the submarine *Casabianca*.

The *Jeanne d'Arc*, having made her way to the Mediterranean from the West Indies, sailed from Algiers (following the reinforcement of her light AA) on the evening of 19 September with 1200 passengers, accompanied by the *Le Fantasque* and the fleet torpedo boats *Tempête* and *L'Alcyon*. She made three trips between Algiers and Ajaccio (Corsica) between 19 September and 2 October. With the liberation of Corsica secured, the island was supplied from Algeria by normal mercantile convoys. The cruiser would make two further round trips to Ajaccio between 31 October and 15 November. She then left for Dakar for docking in December.

The *Montcalm*, following her modernisation in the USA, had arrived at Dakar on 16 August. She sortied from 31 August to 5 September to intercept the Spanish cargo ship *Monte Albertia*. She left Dakar again on 17 September, embarked 1250 men at Algiers, and sailed with *Le Fantasque* for Ajaccio, arriving at midnight on 22 September. The *Le Fantasque* went aground while entering the port, and the cruiser disembarked her troops then tried, in vain, to refloat the *Le Fantasque* – she was not successfully refloated until the 25th. The *Montcalm* returned to Algiers, sailing again for Ajaccio on 26 September with the British destroyer *Pathfinder*, carrying 750 troops and their equipment. Returning to Algiers on the evening of the 24th, the cruiser remained there until 10 October, then was at Mers el-Kebir until 26 October, returning to Dakar on the 30th.

The Italian Front
The *Gloire* left Dakar 17 January 1944 and, via Mers el-Kebir and Algiers, entered Naples on 30 January. The cruiser then carried out bombardments in support of the Allied ground forces off Formia on 3 and 4 February, firing a total of 826 rounds of 152mm. The Americans brought in 300 shells manufactured in Chicago by plane.

The *Gloire* was subsequently used as a fast troop transport between North Africa and Italy. She carried between 1000 and 1500 men on each crossing, making four round trips between 5 and 24 February.

Concentration at Mers el-Kebir
The French cruisers, with the exception of the elderly 10,000-ton ships virtually placed in reserve at Casablanca, were assembled in the Mediterranean in

Left: A bow view of *Tourville* at Casablanca. She was in the port from 27 October to 10 November 1943, and then again from 25 May to 3 June 1944. She is moored with her stern to the Delure Jetty which forms the outer wall of the harbour. *(US Navy)*

Jeanne d'Arc June 1944

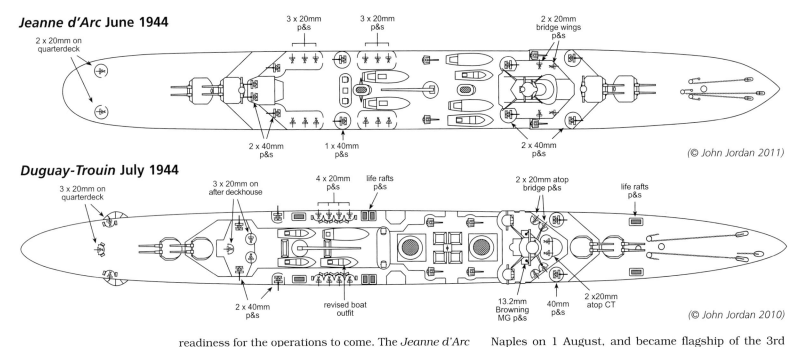

2 x 20mm on quarterdeck

3 x 20mm p&s

3 x 20mm p&s

2 x 20mm bridge wings p&s

2 x 40mm p&s   1 x 40mm p&s

2 x 40mm p&s

(© John Jordan 2011)

Duguay-Trouin July 1944

3 x 20mm on quarterdeck

3 x 20mm on after deckhouse

4 x 20mm p&s

life rafts p&s

2 x 20mm atop bridge p&s

life rafts p&s

2 x 40mm p&s   revised boat outfit

13.2mm Browning MG p&s   40mm p&s   2 x20mm atop CT

(© John Jordan 2010)

readiness for the operations to come. The *Jeanne d'Arc* arrived in the Mediterranean on 3 January. She transported troops for the British to Syracuse, and was then in refit at Casablanca from 20 January to 8 May, She was docked at Oran at the end of May, and was again utilised as a troop transport between Oran, Gibraltar, Ajaccio and Cagliari in June and July.

The *Duguay-Trouin*, following a stay at Dakar from 3 to 11 September 1943, was in refit at Casablanca from 14 September to 12 October, then remained at Oran until 15 January 1944 where she was modernised, receiving six 40mm single Bofors and twenty 20mm Oerlikons (see drawing). She was employed as a troop transport from late January to the end of February, worked up at Mers el-Kebir in March, was refitted at Sidi Abdallah (Bizerte) in April, then again transported troops between the North African ports, Ajaccio and Naples. She was at Oran in July, and was incorporated into a new 3rd Cruiser Division on 1 August.

The *Emile Bertin* arrived at Algiers from Dakar on 16 February 1944. She then worked up at Mers el-Kebir, and transported troops between Algiers and Naples, then Ajaccio in April. She conducted bombardments off Anzio between 27 and 29 May, and again in early June. She was in refit at Bizerte from late June to the end of July. She transported troops from Bizerte to

Naples on 1 August, and became flagship of the 3rd Cruiser Squadron the following day. She underwent a short refit at Bizerte from 15 June to the end of July, then transported 800 men to Naples on 2 August.

The *Gloire* was at Algiers and Mers el-Kebir in March, undertook three troop transport missions to from Mers to Ajaccio in April. A turbine failure kept her immobilised at Algiers from 27 April to 23 June.

The *Georges Leygues* arrived at Mers el-Kebir from Dakar on 6 March 1944, followed by the *Montcalm* on the 9th.

THE NORMANDY LANDINGS

The French Navy deployed three cruisers to support the landings in Normandy (Operation 'Overlord'). The *Georges Leygues* and *Montcalm* took part in fire support missions against the German shore fortifications (Operation 'Neptune'). *Duquesne*, which sailed from Dakar via Casablanca, arrived at Greenock on 1 May; she brought with her ammunition for the two 7600-ton cruisers. Because they lacked a modern AA battery the 10,000-ton cruisers could not be deployed in range of enemy land-based aircraft, but *Duquesne* nevertheless remained available.

The *Georges Leygues* and *Montcalm* sailed from Mers el-Kebir on 14 April. They parted company on 17 April, the former going to North Shields and the second to Greenock. They joined up again at Greenock on 7 May, embarked a number of items of equipment (navigation radars, radio sets, jammers for German glide bombs) and worked up in that area with a primary focus on fire support. A rehearsal for the forthcoming operation took place off Belfast at the end of May. The two French cruisers left Belfast on 3 June; they were to be part of a Force C, covering the 1st US Infantry Division on a Normandy beach christened 'Omaha'. The two cruisers, moored off Port en Bessin, fired in support of the troops from 6 to 11 June. The *Georges Leygues* fired a total of 1008 152mm shells in twenty-seven separate bombardments, and *Montcalm* 843 152mm shells in thirty-eight.

Out of range of the current objectives and with their magazines emptied, the two cruisers left the Normandy coast on the evening of the 15th, and headed for

Below: *Emile Bertin* working up off Mers el-Kebir on 8 March 1944. In the background: an American destroyer of the *Benson* class.

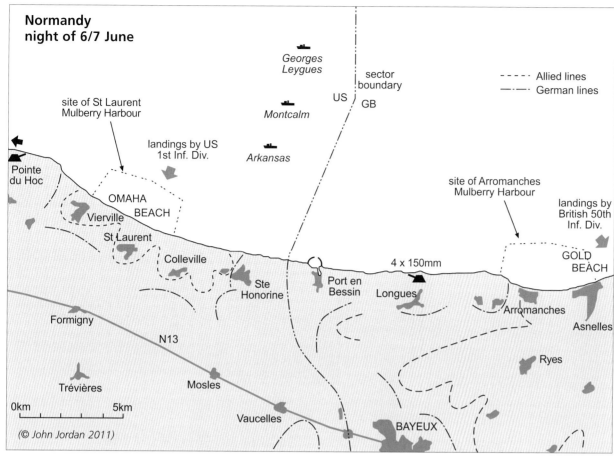

Normandy
night of 6/7 June

site of St Laurent
Mulberry Harbour

landings by US
1st Inf. Div.

Georges
Leygues

sector
boundary

US   GB

Allied lines
German lines

Montcalm

Arkansas

Pointe
du Hoc

OMAHA
BEACH

Vierville

St Laurent

Colleville

Ste
Honorine

Port en
Bessin

4 x 150mm

Longues

site of Arromanches
Mulberry Harbour

landings by
British 50th
Inf. Div.

GOLD
BEACH

Arromanches

Asnelles

Formigny

N13

Trévières

Mosles

Ryes

0km   5km

(© John Jordan 2011)

Vaucelles

BAYEUX

Below: The stern of *Duguay-Trouin* in August 1945. Turret IV is masked by the shield of a 20mm Oerlikon. Above turret III two 40mm Bofors guns are pointing skywards. *(ECPAD)*

Milford Haven (south coast of Wales). They returned to Algiers on 15 July.

The *Duquesne*, which left part of her crew in the UK, sailed from Greenock on 25 August and arrived at Casablanca on the 29th. She subsequently served as a transport, calling in at Casablanca, Gibraltar, Oran, Greenock and Cherbourg, and returning to Casablanca from 1 to 14 November. She then sailed for Toulon, Oran, Brest and Plymouth (8 December), where she joined the FNTF (see below).

THE LANDINGS IN PROVENCE

The landings in Provence (Operations 'Anvil'/'Dragoon') on 15 August 1944 were supported by a large part of the French fleet. Only the 10,000-ton cruisers were not engaged, again due to their lack of modern AA batteries; their activation would also have made heavy demands on personnel at a time when the Allies already had plenty of ships available for fire support.

The 4th Cruiser Division was reconstituted on 15 July with the three 7600-ton cruisers. The *Gloire* made a round trip to Naples on 24 June, then was immobilised at Mers el-Kebir until 20 July. She made another round trip to Naples on 22 July and was at Malta from 26 July to 13 August. The *Georges Leygues* and *Montcalm* left Algiers on 22 July, called in at Mers el-Kebir, and were at Taranto from 28 July to 11 August. They were attached to Task Force 85 which was tasked with supporting the landings at La Nartelle, to the east of Sainte Maxime (Zone Delta).

Georges Leygues fired 271 rounds on 15–16 August, and *Montcalm* 241 rounds. The two cruisers remained off the coast except for brief spells in Corsica for replenishment. From 20 August they

FOUR MORE LIGHT CRUISERS

THE THIRTY-TWO FRENCH *CONTRE-TORPILLEURS* WERE SIGNIFICANTLY LARGER SHIPS
than the majority of destroyers and torpedo boats built by the other major powers between
the wars. They displaced between 2126 tons and 2884 tons standard, whereas other contemporary destroyers were generally around 1500 tons (with a higher figure of 1850 tons for
'leaders'). In 1943 the French Navy still retained four *contre-torpilleurs* of the *Le Fantasque*
class, completed in 1936. Conceived primarily for raiding in the Mediterranean, they displaced
2569 tons standard and were armed (as completed) with five 138mm guns and nine 550mm
torpedoes in triple tubes; all had exceeded 42 knots on trials. Three ships had been
modernised (40mm/20mm AA and radar) in the United States in 1943. The first unit to be
modernised, *Le Fantasque*, returned to the Mediterranean in late July 1943, followed by
Le Terrible in mid-August and by *Le Malin* in January 1944. The fourth, *Le Triomphant*, which
had been seized by the British in June 1940, was modernised only between February and May
1945. The first three ships formed a new 10th Division of *contre-torpilleurs* (DCT), which
carried out raids in the Aegean then the Adriatic, being placed under the British 12th Cruiser
Squadron at Alexandria in mid-November. Their initial classification of 'destroyer' in the Allied
fleet proved to be a handicap, particularly when it came to priority for replenishment. In size
and performance they were closer to the Allied cruisers than to the destroyers. Thus on
28 September 1943 the General Staff approved their reclassification as 'light cruisers', and the
10th DCT became the 10th DCL (*Division de croiseurs légers*).

played a significant part in the battle for Toulon,
engaging in a duel with the batteries of the Saint-
Mandrier peninsula, and notably with the battery at
Cape Cepet – of the four 340mm in twin turrets of the
original battery only a single gun remained in service,
the others having been sabotaged or damaged by
bombs. On the first day *Georges Leygues* was struck
by a 138mm shell from the Sainte Elme battery which
destroyed one of the after starboard 40mm mountings
(casualties: one dead, fifteen men wounded). The
Germans at Saint-Mandrier surrendered on
28 August.

The *Gloire* was incorporated into Task Force 84
which covered the landing in Cavalaire and

Below: *Emile Bertin* at the Sidi Abdallah naval dockyard, Bizerte, in September 1944. There is a destroyer escort (DE) alongside.

Pampelonne Bays (Zone Alpha). She fired a total of
1527 rounds of 152mm between 15 and 26 August, of
which 236 rounds were fired on 15–16 August alone.

The *Emile Bertin* and *Duguay-Trouin* were part of TF
87 covering the landings at Cape Dramont and Agay,
to the east of Saint-Raphaël (Zone Camel). *Emile Bertin*
sailed from Palermo on 13 August. At dawn on 15
August she took up her position in the Gulf of Fréjus
and bombarded the air base at Saint-Raphaël, firing
530 rounds on 15–16 August. She remained off the
coast of Provence, with passages to Corsica to
replenish and a round trip to Algiers on 31 August.

The *Duguay-Trouin* left Palermo on 13 August and
operated from 15th to 17th off La Napoule, then
Cannes. She replenished twice at Propriano, then
participated in the bombardments of the Saint-
Mandrier Peninsula. She was at Mers el-Kebir, then at
Algiers from 31 August to 4 September.

The *Jeanne d'Arc* did not participate in the landings
in Provence and remained at Malta from 9 to 16
August, called in at Naples and Ajaccio and arrived in
Algiers on 22 August. She sailed on 28 August with
members of the Algiers government and their accompanying civil servants, disembarking them in
Cherbourg on 1 September. A second round trip
between Algiers and Cherbourg was accomplished
between 14 and 18 September to bring the personnel
of the Navy Ministry to metropolitan France. The
cruiser was then in maintenance at Algiers from 1 to
20 October.

THE LAST MONTHS OF THE WAR
Task Force 86

The front on the Franco-Italian border stabilised at the
beginning of 1944. The Germans and the Italians of
the Italian Social Republic (ISR) of Mussolini remained

in control of the Gulf of Genoa and had at their disposition reduced naval forces which included Linsen radio-controlled motor-boats filled with explosives, MTBs, midget submarines and human torpedoes.

On 1 September 1944, Task Force 86 (initially under the command of the American Admiral Davidson then, from 16 September, of the French Admiral Auboyneau) was created to support the troops fighting the Axis forces on the coast and to blockade enemy naval forces in the Gulf of Genoa. The 4th Cruiser Division was incorporated into TF86. The *Montcalm* conducted a shore bombardment against the forces on Mount Agel, on the border between France and Monaco, on 4 September.

On 13 September what remained of the French fleet entered Toulon. The anchorage was littered with so many wrecks that it could accommodate only the *Georges Leygues* and *Emile Bertin*. The cruisers, which from this point on could again be based at Toulon, would divide their duties between fire support on the coast and troop transport missions. A cruiser was maintained on alert in the Gulf of Saint Tropez, ready to respond to any call for fire support, while a second remained in reserve at Toulon, ready to sail at short notice.

The *Montcalm* made a round trip to Algiers from 25 September to 9 October, then conducted a fire support mission off Ventimiglia, in the Gulf of Genoa, on 3 November. The *Georges Leygues* made a round trip to Algiers from 19 September to 3 October, and bombarded the Italian coast on 24 October. She was at Casablanca from 28 October to 5 November. The *Gloire* was at Algiers, then Casablanca from 17 to 29 October, refitting at Oran in November. The *Emile Bertin* was at Bizerte for repairs to a propeller shaft

from 18 to 28 September, and was then 'duty cruiser' off Provence from 30 September to 4 October. The *Duguay-Trouin* returned to the coast of Provence in early September and conducted a fire support mission on the 8th. She moored in the anchorage at Toulon on 15 September. Having been duty ship at Saint-Tropez between 22 and 25 September, she was at Oran at the beginning of October.

Above: The foredeck of *Montcalm* towards the end of 1944. There are 20mm Oerlikons on the forecastle and abeam the bridge structure, and 40mm quad mountings in the bridge wings to port and starboard. Note the prominent black blast bags fitted in the United States, with their internal shields covering the gun ports. *(ECPAD)*

Left: *Gloire*, still sporting her distinctive zebra camouflage, returns to the fleet at Toulon on 13 September 1944.

THE ATLANTIC POCKETS

AT THE END OF AUGUST 1944 THE GERMANS EVACUATED MOST OF MAINLAND FRANCE, but left troops in fortified positions (*Festung*) on the coast to prevent the Allies from utilising the French ports. The Allies, in view of the losses sustained when Brest was retaken on 19 September, decided against retaking these last pockets of resistance, which were instead blockaded by the French with American support. The French would have liked to retake these positions, mainly for political reasons, but lacked the means to do so, and would begin such operations only in April 1945.

The fortified positions, from north to south, were formed around the ports of:

– Dunkirk, occupied until the German surrender in May 1945;
– Le Havre, taken by the British on 12 September 1944;
– Cherbourg, taken by the Americans on 27 June 1944;
– Saint Malo, taken by the Americans on 17 August 1944;
– Brest, taken by the Americans on 19 September 1944;
– Lorient & Ile de Groix, occupied until the German surrender;
– Quiberon & Belle Ile, occupied until the German surrender;
– Saint-Nazaire, occupied until the German surrender;
– La Pallice-La Rochelle and the Ile de Ré and Ile d'Oléron, occupied until the German surrender (except for Ile d'Oléron, taken by the French on 1 May 1945);
– Royan & La Coubre (*Festung Gironde Nord*), liberated by the French on 18 April 1945;
– Le Verdon & Pointe de Grave (*Festung Gironde Sud*), liberated by the French on 20 April 1945.

On the Mediterranean coast, the fortresses of Toulon and Marseille were taken by the French on 27 and 28 August 1944 respectively.

The 'Flank Force'

On 4 November 1944 Task Force 86 was replaced by the 'Flank Force', under the command of Rear-Admiral Jaujard, the American and British contribution to the force declining. The *Georges Leygues* and *Montcalm* remained part of the Flank Force until the end of April 1945.

Georges Leygues bombarded Ventimiglia on 8, 9 and 17 November. She was docked at Oran at the end of November, and was at Naples from 28 December to 5 January. She bombarded Pietro-Ligure on 10–11

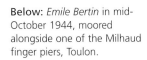

Below: *Emile Bertin* in mid-October 1944, moored alongside one of the Milhaud finger piers, Toulon.

January, Porto Maurizio on 15 January, called in at Algiers in mid-February, then bombarded San Remo on 22 February and 2–3 March. Her 152mm guns fired 1424 rounds between October 1944 and March 1945, by which time the barrels were completely worn out. The cruiser would undergo a major refit at Casablanca from 23 April.

The *Montcalm* bombarded San Remo on 20 November, then was docked at Oran from 10 to 17 December. She bombarded San Remo and Bordighera on 15 January, called in at Algiers in early February, again bombarded Bordighera on 2 and 8 March, returned to Algiers between 6 and 10 April, and conducted a final bombardment against San Remo on 23 April. The barrels of her guns were by this time completely worn out (she had fired 3659 rounds – 400 per gun!). She made a return trip to Beirut, staying there between 6 and 9 May.

The *Gloire*, arriving from Cherbourg, joined the Flank Force at Toulon on 7 March 1945. She conducted three bombardments (against San Remo and Ventimiglia) between 20 March and 10 April.

The *Emile Bertin* executed a bombardment on 7 October, called in at Naples on the 17th, conducted further bombardments between 28 and 31 October, then went on a voyage which took in Algiers, Piraeus, Alexandria and Oran, embarking troops in the latter port and returning to Toulon on 15 December. She made a round trip to Beirut in late December, and conducted a final bombardment against a viaduct between Ventimiglia and Bordighera on 7 January. She was in refit from 22 January to 16 September 1945.

The *Duguay-Trouin* was back at Saint-Tropez from 16 to 20 October, called in at Oran and Gibraltar, and transported 500 men from Casablanca to Brest, where she arrived on 14 November. She returned to Casablanca on the 25th and then embarked on a mission along the coast of Africa which took her, via Dakar, as far south as Pointe Noire. She returned to

Toulon on 14 January 1945. She then sailed for Bizerte via Algiers, arriving on 24 January and began a major refit, which included the replacement of the barrels of her 155mm guns. She left again on 22 March, calling in at Algiers and Oran on her way to Toulon, where she arrived on 5 April. She rejoined the Flank Force and fired against enemy communications in the vicinity of Ventimiglia on 9 April. On 23 April she bombarded the ports of Oneglia and Porto Maurizio on 23 April. She left the Flank Force on 5 May, the Germans in Italy having capitulated.

The *Jeanne d'Arc* was incorporated into the Flank Force at Toulon on 22 October. She conducted four bombardment missions against the Italian coast between 26 October and 30 November, transported troops from Algiers to Toulon between 7 and 8 December, and conducted two further bombardments on 9 and 19 December. Damaged by severe weather on the night of 31 December/1 January, between Algiers and Toulon, the cruiser was under repair until 20 January. She conducted four more bombardments between 6 February and 2 March before undergoing a refit at Bizerte. She conducted two transport missions between Toulon and North Africa, then returned to Bizerte, remaining there from 21 April to 2 May. She transported troops from Toulon to Beirut, then served as a transport in the western Mediterranean until 15 October 1945. The 3rd Cruiser Division was dissolved on 20 September 1945.

THE FNTF

A small naval force, the French Naval Task Force (FNTF), was constituted on 8 December 1944 to support the retaking of the German-held Atlantic pockets and to prevent communication between those pockets and Spain.

The *Duquesne* and *Gloire* arrived in Brest from Oran on 4 December 1944. *Gloire* made a round trip to New York between 7 and 31 December to collect a consign-

ment of banknotes. She remained available at Brest, Plymouth and Cherbourg until 1 March 1945, then rejoined the Flank Force at Toulon.

The *Duquesne* was due to bombard Belle Ile on 13 January, but the mission had to be cancelled due to poor visibility. After a passage to Plymouth, she sailed for Cherbourg where she remained from 20 January to 3 April; her condensers were overhauled and two boilers retubed. She then participated in the operations against the Royan and Pointe de Grave pockets, firing off 938 203mm rounds on 15 and 16 April. The cruiser replenished her ammunition at

Above: *Duquesne* mooring close to the Ile d'Oleron during the operations to retake the island between 28 April and 1 May 1945. *(ECPAD)*

Left: *Gloire* at sea between November 1944 and June 1946. Her original zebra-pattern disruptive camouflage has been replaced by the two-tone US Navy Measure 22 carried by her two sisters and the *Emile Bertin*. *(US Navy)*

Casablanca between 21 and 23 April, then fired a further 522 203mm rounds against the Ile d'Oléron on 30 April in support of the French landings.

The FNTF was disbanded on 28 May 1945.

TO INDOCHINA

From 1943 the surviving French merchant marine was incorporated into the Allied 'pool' of merchant shipping. The French retained control only over a few small ships for local traffic. It was essentially the cruisers which ensured the transfer of personnel between metropolitan France and the overseas territories.

Indochina posed problems. The French had been expelled on 9 March 1945 in a Japanese *coup de force* which resulted in massacres and the internment of all French nationals in Indochina. The French government now installed in Paris wished to take back control of Indochina, and to participate in the last months of the war against Japan to re-establish France's status as a major power. The Americans had no wish to see the French return to Indochina and needed no help to defeat Japan. French military options were in reality extremely limited, while metropolitan France was in ruins. The naval forces for such long-range operations would have to be constituted

Suffren Spring 1944

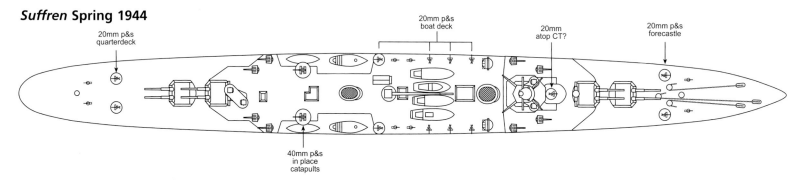

Suffren April 1945

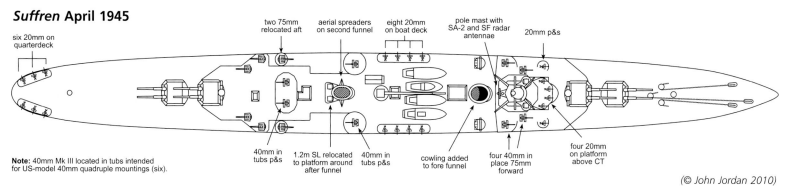

Note: 40mm Mk III located in tubs intended for US-model 40mm quadruple mountings (six).

(© John Jordan 2010)

Duquesne 1945

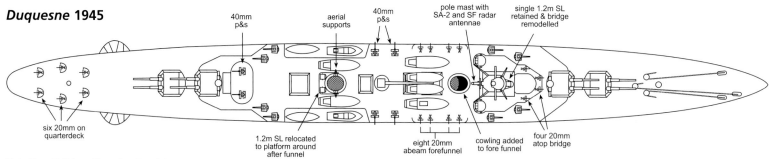

Note: 40mm Mk III located in positions intended for US-model 40mm quadruple mountings (four).

Tourville 1945

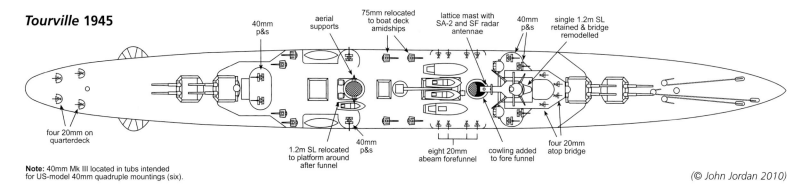

Note: 40mm Mk III located in tubs intended for US-model 40mm quadruple mountings (six).

(© John Jordan 2010)

essentially from the nine ships modernised in the United States in 1943, and it would have been difficult to provide the necessary logistic support.

When the Japanese surrender was announced on 15 August 1945, the battleship *Richelieu* and the light cruiser *Le Triomphant* were in the Indian Ocean under British command. The other cruisers were either in refit or would need refitting before they could be deployed to the Far East. The four modernised ships would need to be supported in part by the older 10,000-ton units, which would be used as fast transports.

The *Suffren*, which was part of the 1st Cruiser Division (dissolved on 24 June 1944), arrived at Casablanca on 17 April 1944. She was practically deactivated, and maintenance and modernisation work was undertaken within the limited resources available. She was ready for sea only on 21 April 1945. She sailed for Oran, then called in at Toulon, Algiers and Oran and was again in refit from June to August. She left Toulon on 29 June, delivered equipment intended for *Richelieu* at Diego-Suarez and disembarked a light Intervention Corps at Colombo. She returned to Toulon on 26 August but left again on 12 September with troops for Indochina. The 1st Cruiser Division was reactivated on 15 September 1945.

The *Gloire* was utilised for transport missions between Algiers, Marseille, Oran, Casablanca and Cherbourg. She arrived at Saint-Nazaire, where the docks remained intact, on 13 August 1945. A major refit at Bizerte was postponed, and the cruiser left again on 10 September for Indochina. The *Emile Bertin* was to serve as leader for the division of light cruisers for raids against Japanese communications. She underwent a major refit at Toulon from the end of January to September 1945. The *Tourville* arrived at Casablanca on 25 May 1944, and sailed for Bizerte in early June, arriving on the 6th to be placed in reserve. She arrived at Toulon on 28 November 1944, and served as a support ship for escort forces while undergoing a refit which began on 1 December 1944 and ended on 17 November 1945. The *Duquesne* underwent a major refit at Brest from 14 June to 15 November 1945.

The *Duguay-Trouin* was at Algiers on 9 May 1945. The situation in Algeria was deteriorating, and the cruiser disembarked her landing company and conducted a bombardment aimed at intimidating the rebels on 9 May near Bougie. She transported 150 men from Algiers to Bougie on 15 May, then sailed again for Toulon. She conducted several troop transport missions up to October 1945, with passages to Toulon, Marseille, Algiers, Oran, Bizerte, Naples, Casablanca, Dakar and Tangiers. She was then refitted at Toulon

The Campaign in Indochina 1945-1954

0   300km

(© John Jordan 2011)

from 23 October to 10 March 1947.

The *Montcalm* was refitted at La Seyne from 23 May 1945 to 16 January 1946. Her sister *Georges Leygues* was refitted at Casablanca from 23 April 1945 to 29 January 1946. All the French cruisers except the two last-named would be deployed to Indochina between June 1945 and May 1947.

CHAPTER 12

THE PERIOD
1945–1956

AFTER THE WAR, THE FRENCH NAVY HAD ONLY nine surviving cruisers. The oldest cruisers (the three 10,000-ton ships and the *Duguay-Trouin*) ended their service careers in Indochina, the *Jeanne d'Arc* resumed her role of school ship, and the remaining four, modernised in the USA in 1943, would be the main elements of a fleet in transition pending the completion of new ships from the post-war programmes.

THE CRUISERS IN INDOCHINA

Most of the ships which were to have participated in the war against Japan would be engaged in what would become the war in Indochina. Only the British supported the French, who returned to Saigon (subsequently renamed Hô-Chi-Minh-Ville in French, Ho Chi Minh City in English) in late September 1945. The French nationals who had been imprisoned by the Japanese were liberated and were joined by new arrivals. Incidents, contacts and discussions with the Vietnamese independence movement resulted in a number of serious incidents which began in Hai Phong on 20 November 1947 and an outbreak of hostilities on 19 December of the same year. The war in Indochina would end following the Geneva agreements of 20 July 1954 with a cease-fire, the application of which was spread, depending on the region, over the period 20 July to 7 August, and the departure of the last French forces in April 1956.

Gloire and *Suffren* were the first cruisers to be deployed to Indochina. *Gloire* sailed from Brest on 12 September 1945 and arrived at Saigon on 15 October with 330 troops and some equipment. *Suffren* arrived

on 19 October with a reduced crew of 130 and 440 troops as passengers. The two cruisers disembarked their landing companies and left for France on 27 and 30 October respectively, embarking personnel who had been in Indochina since before the war. The three 10,000-ton cruisers and the cruisers on passage to Indochina were grouped together in a reconstituted 1st Cruiser Division from 15 September 1945 to 18 February 1947.

Emile Bertin arrived in Saigon on 21 November 1945. Her landing company was also disembarked. The cruiser then visited Hong Kong (19 to 21 December) and Shanghai (24 December to 3 January 1946). She patrolled the coasts of Annam at the end of January, making a diversion towards Nha Trang on 3 March prior to the landings at Tonkin of 6 March. She was in Ha Long Bay from 5 to 26 March, notably during the operations at Hai Phong on 6 March (Operation 'Bentré'). Troops were put ashore at Hai Phong from 8 March following an incident with the Chinese, who had occupied the north of Indochina following the Japanese surrender. The *Emile Bertin* fired on the battery at Appowan,[1] which had fallen into the hands of the insurgents, on 7 April and participated in a naval review on the 24th following talks between Ho Chi Minh, the leader of the Vietnamese independence movement, and Admiral Thierry d'Argenlieu, French High-Commissioner in Indochina. The cruiser visited Singapore and Manila and was at Yokosuka, Japan,

---

[1] The battery, located on Appowan Island and guarding the approaches to the major port of Hai Phong, comprised three older-model 138mm guns.

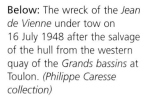

Below: The wreck of the *Jean de Vienne* under tow on 16 July 1948 after the salvage of the hull from the western quay of the *Grands bassins* at Toulon. *(Philippe Caresse collection)*

DEPLOYMENTS TO INDOCHINA 1922–1956

	Left France	Arrived Indochine	Left Indochine	Returned France
Montcalm	15 Jan 1921	22 Mar 1921	27 Jun 1922	16 Aug 1922
Colmar	19 Jun 1922	7 Sep 1922	?? Nov 1924	11 Feb 1925
Jules Michelet	12 Oct 1922	19 Apr 1923	10 May 1923	11 Jul 1923
Victor Hugo	[as *Jules Michelet*]		[as *Jules Michelet*]	
Jules Ferry	27 Sep 1923	21 Nov 1923	21 Sep 1925	10 Nov 1925
Jules Michelet	15 Jun 1925	?? Jul 1925	?? May 1929	10 Jul 1929
Primauguet	20 Apr 1927	9 Aug 1927 (Flag FNEO)	7 Oct 1927	22 Dec 1927
Waldeck Rousseau	10 May 1929	22 Jun 1929	?? May 1932	3 Jul 1932
Duguay-Trouin	5 Sep 1931	16 Oct 1931	14 Nov 1931	22 Dec 1931
Primauguet	15 Apr 1932	18 May 1932	10 Jan 1936	26 Feb 1936
Lamotte-Picquet	2 Nov 1935	29 Dec 1935	Sunk 12 Jan 1945	
Primauguet	4 Oct 1937	22 Nov 1937	28 Jul 1939	15 Sep 1939
4e DC	1 Dec 1937	2 Jan 1938	2 Mar 1938	14 Apr 1938
Suffren	26 Jun 1939	23 Jul 1939	1 Apr 1940	Force X
Suffren	26 Jun 1945	Colombo 2–4 Aug 1945		26 Aug 1945
Gloire	21 Sep 1945	13 Oct 1945	30 Oct 1945	22 Nov 1945
Suffren	21 Sep 1945	19 Oct 1945	27 Oct 1945	21 Nov 1945
Emile Bertin	11 Oct 1945	21 Nov 1945	2 Jul 1946	29 Jul 1946
Tourville	5 Dec 1945	16 Jan 1946	2 Jul 1946	27 Jul 1946
Duquesne	22 Dec 1945	25 Jan 1946	4 Oct 1946	6 Nov 1946
Gloire	4 Feb 1946	23 Feb 1946	6 Apr 1946	10 May 1946
Suffren	9 Feb 1946	25 Feb 1946	18 Feb 1947	24 Mar 1947
Tourville	4 Oct 1946	30 Nov 1946	15 Nov 1947	11 Dec 1947
Duquesne	22 Dec 1946	17 Jan 1947	16 Apr 1947	16 May 1947
Duguay-Trouin	9 May 1947	13 Nov 1947	22 Sep 1951	22 Oct 1951
Gloire	28 May 1954	20 Jun 1954	27 Aug 1954	12 Oct 1954
Montcalm	28 May 1954	20 Jun 1954	18 May 1955	6 Jul 1955

from 15 to 30 May. *Emile Bertin* left Saigon on 2 July and arrived back in Toulon on 29 July.

Tourville arrived on 16 January 1946 with 610 passengers and 50 tonnes of equipment. Only 203mm turrets II and III were manned. The cruiser carried out a first bombardment (thirty-four rounds of 203mm and 321 of 75mm) at Cam Ranh and Cap Padaran between 23 January and 9 February. She participated in Operation 'Bentré' and in the naval review on 24 March in Ha Long Bay. She then sailed for Saigon, called in at Nha Trang, returned to Ha Long Bay, and was in Shanghai at the beginning of June. She left Saigon on 2 July, arriving back at Toulon on the 27th.

Duquesne arrived in Saigon on 26 January 1946. She sailed on 28 February for the retaking of Tonkin. She was in Ha Long Bay on 6 March and took part in the naval review there on the 24th. She made a round trip to Hong Kong and Shanghai late March/early April, and two round trips between Saigon and Tonkin. She again visited Hong Kong and Shanghai in May, made two round trips between Saigon and Tonkin in early August and mid-September respectively, and left for Toulon on 4 October.

Gloire returned to Saigon on 23 February 1946 with personnel and munitions. She went to Tourane (now Da Nang) and Ha Long Bay, reembarked her landing company at Cam Ranh and left Saigon for Toulon on 16 April.

Suffren sailed from Toulon again on 9 February 1946 and arrived at Saigon on the 26th. She sailed for Ha Long Bay on 20 March and participated in the review on the 24th. She was at Saigon in early April, then returned to Ha Long Bay at the end of April and in June repatriated troops who had remained in China, visiting Hong Kong, Chinwangtao and Shanghai. She was at Saigon late July/early August,

then returned to Ha Long Bay. She carried out transport missions between Saigon and Tonkin in October. Following incidents in Hai Phong, she transported 500 troops to Tonkin between 25 and 27 November. On 28 November she fired sixty-nine rounds of 203mm against the Appowan battery. She transported troops to Tourane in early December then participated in operations in the Tourane, Hue and Qang Tri sectors until early February (transport missions, and bombardments during which she fired ninety-two rounds of 203mm). She left Saigon on 18 February 1947 and arrived in Toulon on 24 March.

Tourville made a return trip to North Africa at the end of September 1946, then left again for the Far East via Madagascar and La Réunion. She arrived at Saigon on 30 November, disembarking 1379 passengers and 277 tonnes of equipment. She carried out bombardments at Tourane in late December 1946 and January 1947, and a fire-support mission off the coast of Annam in late March. She was subsequently employed for transport missions between Saigon and Ha Long Bay until September, broken by a lengthy stay in Saigon in July and August. Relieved by the *Duguay-Trouin*, she left Saigon on 15 November for Toulon, arriving on 11 December 1947.

Duquesne sailed from Toulon 22 December 1946 and arrived in Saigon on 17 January 1947. Following a transport mission to Tonkin, she provided fire support for operations around Tourane, notably in March when she fired 475 rounds of 75mm. She left Indochina on 16 April and arrived back in Toulon on 16 May 1947.

Duguay-Trouin was in Algeria on 9 May 1945 and intervened in the Bougie area when the Setif rebellion took place; she disembarked her landing company and carried out a bombardment to intimidate the rebels. She returned to Toulon on 16 May, and then under-

Below, left: The stern of *Montcalm* during her major refit at La Seyne from May 1945 to January 1946. New barrels were fitted in the 152mm and 90mm guns at this time. The American 40mm quads fitted in place of the former hangar are particularly prominent in this view. *(ECPAD)*

Below, right: *Gloire* in 1948 with, from top to bottom, the antennae for the British Type 281 (topmast) and Type 284 (front of director) radars, and the American SF (below foretop). *(ECPAD)*

took transport missions between Toulon, Marseille, Algiers, Oran, Bizerte, Naples, Casablanca and Dakar. She was at Tangiers on 11 October to deliver the Mendoub (representing the Sultan of Morocco) to that port following the departure of the Spanish, who had occupied it since 1940. The *Duguay-Trouin* had travelled 22,270nm and moored on 101 occasions between 22 March and 23 October 1945. The cruiser was effectively worn out, and was refitted at Toulon from 1 November 1945 to March 1947. She departed Toulon on 9 May 1947 and sailed directly to Madagascar, where an insurrection had broken out on the night of 29/30 March, arriving at Diego Suarez on 28 May. She operated along the Madagascan coasts, disembarking a commando unit when required and firing her guns in the approaches to Diego Suarez. She left Diego Suarez on 27 October and arrived at Saigon on 13 November 1947. On 4 December she was off Tonkin. She oper-

ated along the coast between Cochinchine Province in the south and Tonkin in the north, with stays of varying length in Saigon for leave and maintenance. Her missions were essentially fire support, the transporting of personnel and equipment, and 'showing the flag' visits. She embarked on a tour of the French Indian Ocean territories in late October/early November 1948, and was docked at Singapore. She finally left Indochina on 22 September 1951, arriving back at Toulon on 22 October. She had travelled 70,000nm in four years. Her place in Indochina was taken by the carrier *Arromanches* (ex-HMS *Colossus*). There would be no further deployments of cruisers to the Far East before June 1954.

THE NAVAL FORCES IN METROPOLITAN FRANCE

After the war ended, the available cruisers were utilised primarily for the transport of personnel. The three 7600-ton cruisers and *Emile Bertin*, which were worn out from their active war service, were refitted, initially with a view to their deployment in the Far East against the Japanese.

The three 7600-ton cruisers were modernised beginning in June 1945. The work focused on renewing the barrels of their guns and the installation of a quadruped mast between the bridge structure and the fore-funnel. This work was completed for *Georges Leygues* on 19 January 1946, for *Montcalm* on

NAVAL FORMATIONS AFTER THE WAR

AFTER THE DISSOLUTION OF THE FNTF AND THE FLANK Force in May 1945, French naval forces were reorganised. In the Far East, following a few adjustments, the naval forces were divided into two theoretically independent commands: the *Forces maritimes d'Extrême-Orient* (FMEO), and the *Commandement de la Marine en Indochine* (or *Marine Indochine*). The 1st Cruiser Division was formed on 15 September 1945 with the cruisers *Duquesne*, *Tourville* and *Suffren*. In theory this was a command independent of the FMEO which was to become the *Division navale d'Extrême-Orient* (DNEO) when the 1st DC was dissolved on 18 February 1947.

The naval forces based in metropolitan France were reorganised on 11 January 1947 as three tactical groupings: battleship, aircraft carriers and cruisers:

– Battleship group: *Richelieu* (the *Lorraine* had been decommissioned and *Jean Bart* was still fitting out).
– Carrier group: *Arromanches*, *Dixmude* and two escorts.
– Cruiser group: *Georges Leygues*, *Montcalm*, *Gloire* and the light cruisers *Le Fantasque*, *Le Malin*, *Le Terrible* and *Le Triomphant*.

The Navy was to be capable of providing an 'intervention force' at the request of the United Nations, and a first *Force d'intervention* (FI) was formed from 20 May to 13 June 1947 on the occasion of the fleet cruise to the coasts of Africa; it comprised *Richelieu* plus the cruiser, carrier and submarine groups. The FI was revived from 9 April and 28 June 1948.

The *Escadre* was created at Toulon as a permanent force on 19 April 1949; it combined the carrier and cruiser groups with the *Groupe d'action anti-sous-marine* (GASM) comprising the escorts and submarines in commission.

The 4th Cruiser Division, extant since 20 November 1937 with a brief interruption between 22 September 1943 and 15 July 1944, comprised the *Georges Leygues*, *Montcalm*, and *Gloire*. It became the 2nd Cruiser Division on 19 April 1949 and was dissolved on 20 October 1954.

The light cruisers, incorporated into the *groupe des croiseurs*, at first continued to form the 10th DCL, although there were rarely more than two of the four ships in commission at any given time. It became the 1st DCL on 1 January 1948 and effectively disappeared in October 1949, after which only a single ship generally remained in service.

1 February 1946 and for *Gloire*, delayed by two deployments to Indochina, on 30 April 1947. These cruisers would remain in service for some ten years, and would be tasked with training a new generation of sailors who would man the new ships built under naval programmes of the 1950s. Transport missions would become the exception, being superseded by fleet exercises. The ships would undergo one last major refit, marked by the installation of a new pole mainmast: *Gloire* at Toulon December 1949 to December 1950; *Montcalm* at Bizerte February 1951 to May 1952; and *Georges Leygues* at Bizerte January 1953 to April 1954.

These three ships, which still made up the 4th Cruiser Squadron, were based at Toulon. In practice, two of the three cruisers were in commission, of which one was flagship of the *Escadre* (see box feature) in the absence of a battleship following the decommissioning of *Richelieu* on 1st April 1949. The second of the two cruisers was generally flagship of the 4th, then of the 2nd Cruiser Division.

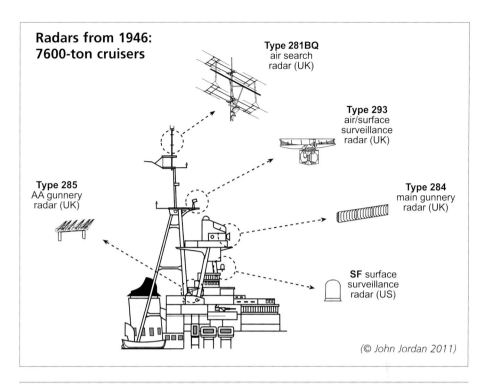

Radars from 1946: 7600-ton cruisers

Type 281BQ air search radar (UK)

Type 293 air/surface surveillance radar (UK)

Type 285 AA gunnery radar (UK)

Type 284 main gunnery radar (UK)

SF surface surveillance radar (US)

(© John Jordan 2011)

RADARS INSTALLED 1946–1947

Model	Function	Frequency	Range	Accuracy	Resolution
Type 281BQ	Air search	3.5m	120–150nm	n/a	n/a
Type 293	Air/surface surveillance	10cm (S-band)	15–17nm	50m/0.5°	n/a
Type 284P	Main gunnery	50cm (L-Band)	22,000m	25m/0.2°	150m/1°
Type 285P	Secondary gunnery	50cm (L-Band)	15,000m	45m/0.25°	150m/1.5°

Source: Norman Friedman, *Naval Radar* (London: Conway Maritime Press, 1981).

Beyond the customary running for trials and work-up, activities comprised fleet exercises, often between the coast of Provence and Corsica, sometimes as far as the coasts of North Africa and, in practice, one sortie into the Atlantic per year. The ships also took part in the first inter-Allied exercises under the North Atlantic Treaty Organisation (NATO), which was formed on 4 April 1949.

Jeanne d'Arc embarked on a new training cruise for the *Ecole d'application* on 10 September 1946. The cruise took her initially to the eastern Mediterranean, then to the Gulf of Guinea and the French West Indies,

Above: *Montcalm* in 1946 with the new quadruped mast fitted during her refit at La Seyne.

and ended with her return to Brest on 19 April 1947. She would from this point on be based at Brest, embarking on an annual training cruise which generally took place between November and early June. From the 'campaign' of 1952–3 she would be accompanied by a sloop – initially the *aviso colonial La Grandière*, followed by the newly-completed *aviso-escorteur Commandant Rivière* in 1959-61 and her sister-ship *Victor Schoelcher* from late 1961. She embarked on two world cruises in 1955–6 and 1959–60. The latter was marked by a collision with the *Commandant Rivière* during the night of 17/18 April off Dakar. There were two dead and six injured aboard the cruiser, which was repaired at Dakar and resumed her cruise in mid-May. During the cruise of 1962–3 the starboard propeller shaft fractured on 8 December following a passage through the Panama Canal. The cruiser crossed the Pacific from Balboa to Tokyo on a single shaft and was repaired at Hong Kong in early March. The last campaign of *Jeanne d'Arc* ended at Brest on 8 June 1964.

Emile Bertin paid off following her return from

Below: *Georges Leygues* moored off the Côte d'Azur in 1952. By this time the cruisers had an all-over light grey livery in place of the post-war two-tone scheme. *(Jean Labayle Couhat collection)*

Indochina and was in refit until 1 July 1947. She was then attached to the *Groupe des écoles* at Toulon for service with the Gunnery School. In a normal month she would make between five and seven sorties. She made a round trip to North Africa in late November 1947 to repatriate the remains of General Leclerc,[2] who had been killed in an air crash on the 28th. She participated in a cruise to North Africa with the 4th Cruiser Division in March 1949, then carried out practice firings of her guns off Arzew in June. She was docked for maintenance at Bizerte July/August 1949, and carried out landing trials with a Bell 47 helicopter

[2] Philippe Leclerc de Hautecloque (1902–47) participated in the rallying of French Equatorial Africa to the Free French cause, fought against the Italians in the south of Libya, commanded the 2nd Armoured Division which liberated Paris in August 1944, and signed the Japanese surrender document for France in 1945. After his death in a plane crash near Colomb-Béchard on 28 November 1947 he was made a Marshal of France in 1952.

Montcalm 1954

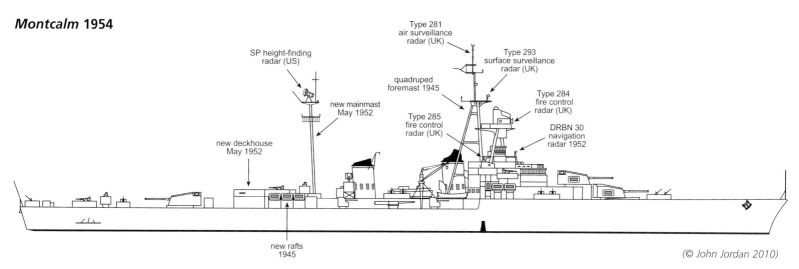

SP height-finding
radar (US)

Type 281
air surveillance
radar (UK)

Type 293
surface surveillance
radar (UK)

quadruped
foremast 1945

new mainmast
May 1952

Type 284
fire control
radar (UK)

Type 285
fire control
radar (UK)

DRBN 30
navigation
radar 1952

new deckhouse
May 1952

new rafts
1945

(© John Jordan 2010)

There continued to be numerous detail differences between *Montcalm*, *Georges Leygues* and *Gloire* following the post-war modernisations of 1945–7, when a quadruped foremast carrying surveillance radars of British origin was stepped around the forefunnel, and the early 1950s, when the after deckhouse was extended and a new mainmast fitted. Initially all three ships had the SF thimble radome (US) on a platform beneath the foretop; it would later be replaced by a DRBN 30 navigation radar of French design and manufacture. *Gloire* was the first to have a pole mainmast fitted (1950), but the American SP height-finding radar (for fighter and AA fire control) was not available until 1953, when it was fitted in *Montcalm* and *Georges Leygues* only. *Georges Leygues*, the last of the three to remain in service, would have her British Type 284 gunnery fire control radar replaced by the French-developed DRBC 11A in January 1955, and the British Type 281 air search radar replaced by the French DRBV 20 from January 1956. There were also small variations in the positioning of life rafts and the configuration of the outriggers for radio antennae on the second funnel.

in the autumn of 1950. She deployed to North Africa in February 1951 and again in late July, visiting Malta and Naples in early August. She returned to Toulon on 13 August 1951 and was decommissioned; she would never sail again.

Georges Leygues was flagship of the 4th Cruiser Division from 25 March to 1 October 1946. She carried out transport missions to North Africa in early 1946 (5370 passengers in March alone), and participated in the evacuation of the French administration in Syria and Lebanon in July. She visited Boston and Philadelphia in September, made a round trip to North Africa with the French Minister for Defence in October, and transported a UN delegation to Greece in late January 1947. She was again flagship of the 4th

Cruiser Division from 1 March to 1 October 1947, becoming part of the *Force d'intervention* in June 1947, which led her as far as Casablanca. The cruiser returned to the USA in November 1947, embarking a consignment of gold for the outward journey, and returning to Casablanca with the ex-German destroyer *Z 39* under tow. She was in refit at Bizerte until mid-October 1948, and again served as flagship of the 4th Cruiser Division from 1st November of that year until 19 April 1949. She carried out further transport missions between metropolitan Franca and North Africa in November. Incorporated into the *Escadre*, she was flagship of the 2nd Cruiser Division from 19 April 1949 to 1 October 1952. She embarked the President of the Republic for a visit to North Africa late

Below: *Montcalm* in May 1953. She has just been fitted with a new mainmast to carry the American SP height-finding radar at a major refit at Bizerte February 1951 to May 1952.

May/early June 1949, accompanied the Mediterranean Squadron to Brest in June, then participated in Exercise 'Verity' in early 1950 and Exercise 'Symphonie' in the western Mediterranean in March 1950. She embarked on a cruise to the Channel in May/June 1950, and took part in Exercise 'Activity' in late June/early July. She transported a consignment of gold to Pointe Noire in late February/early March 1951, took part in Exercise 'Symphonie II' in October, transported motorised guards to Tunisia in late January 1952, participated in NATO exercise 'Grand Slam' late February/early March and then took part in the fleet cruise which took in Lisbon, Brest, Cherbourg and Le Havre late May/early June 1952. She entered Bizerte on 15 January 1953. *Georges Leygues* underwent a major refit at Bizerte from January 1953 to January 1954. Placed in reserve at Bizerte, she was recommissioned on 10 November 1954 to become flagship of the Mediterranean Squadron pending the availability of the *De Grasse*. She joined the *Escadre* at Toulon on 30 December 1954 and served as flagship from 11 January 1955 until September 1956. She participated in Exercise 'Medflex 2' at the end of

January 1955, and in exercises in North Africa in March and May/June. In late August she landed a commando unit at Collo in Algeria, then took part in exercises with the *Escadre* in the western Mediterranean in late September/early October. Following further exercises in late February/early

Below: *Gloire* in May 1953. The SP radar aerial planned for installation atop the mainmast would never be installed.

March 1956, she was in North Africa at the end of March, and carried out a shore bombardment on 4 April. She participated in an inter-Allied exercise in mid-April, then in Squadron cruises to the eastern Mediterranean in early May and the Atlantic, as far as Dakar and Monrovia, in late May/early June. She was docked in July, and then detached from the *Escadre* in readiness for the planned operation in Egypt.

Montcalm was flagship of the 4th Cruiser Division from 1 August 1945 to 26 March 1946, from 1 October 1946 to 1 March 1947, and from 1 October 1947 to 1 November 1948. In February 1946 she sailed for the French West Indies where she reembarked the 300 tonnes of gold at Martinique landed by the *Emile Bertin* in 1940 and repatriated it to Cherbourg. Her new 152mm guns were fitted only in April 1946. She transported recently-demobilised troops to Madagascar and

La Réunion in May, took part in the evacuation of Lebanon in late August, and returned to the USA and the French West Indies in April/May 1947. She was part of the *Force d'intervention* in May/June 1948. She was moored in the anchorage at Brest, along with the *Gloire*, for the naval review of 30 May 1948. She became flagship of the *Escadre* on its formation 19 April 1949, and continued in this role until 15 January 1951. She took part in a sortie into the Atlantic which

THE *ESCADRE* (TOULON) 1 OCTOBER 1949

Groupe des porte-avions
Carriers: *Arromanches, Dixmude*
Torpedo Boats: *Hova, Marocain, Sénégalais*
Air Squadrons: 1F, 12F, 4F

Groupe des croiseurs
Cruisers: *Georges Leygues, Montcalm, Gloire*
Light Cruisers : *Le Fantasque, Le Terrible, Le Malin, Le Triomphant*

GASM (*Groupe d'action anti-sous-marine*)
Torpedo Boats: *Lorrain, Alsacien*
Torpedo Boats : *Algérien, Tunisien*
Frigates: *L'Escarmouche, Croix de Lorraine, Tonkinois, La Surprise*
Escorts: *Dague, Coutelas*
Submarines: *Le Glorieux, Junon, Millé, Laubie, La Créole, L'Africaine, 2518,* midget submarine group
Depot Ship: *Gustave Zédé*
Accommodation Ship: former carrier *Béarn.*

ended with Exercise 'Verity' in early July 1949. She then participated in Exercises 'Symphonie' (March 1950) and 'Activity' (late June 1950). She underwent a major refit at Bizerte from late February 1951 until June 1952.

Montcalm was again flagship of the *Escadre* from 1 October 1952 to 1 June 1954. Along with *Gloire* she participated in Exercises 'Long Step' (November 1952), 'Lander One' (February 1953), 'Rendez-Vous' and 'New Moon' (March 1953), the Atlantic Spring cruise of the squadron of May/June 1953, and Exercises 'Atout III' (February 1954) and 'Medflex Able' (late March 1954). She sailed from Toulon on 25 April 1954 for the Spring cruise but was recalled, along with *Gloire*, on 8 May 1954.

Following her deployment to Indochina (see below),

Montcalm returned to Toulon on 6 July 1955. She transported troops between Marseille, Casablanca and Oran in August/September 1955 and stayed for two months from 20 September to 15 November 1855 in Philippeville, Algeria, where massacres had taken place on 20 August. The cruiser returned to Toulon, then sailed again for North Africa in early December. She underwent a major refit at Bizerte from 1 February 1956 to 15 February 1957. In early 1957 she embarked on trials during which she again reached 33 knots, operated off the Algerian coast in February, and carried out a final shore bombardment against rebel positions on 2 March. She returned to Bizerte on the evening of 2 March 1957.

Gloire was flagship of the 4th Cruiser Division from 1 April 1945 to 1 August 1945. On her return from Indochina on 22 November 1945 the cruiser carried out six transport missions between metropolitan France and North Africa in January 1946. She again deployed to Indochina from February to April 1946, then underwent a major refit at Bizerte from June 1946 to April 1947 during which she received a quadruped foremast. She was again employed on troop transport missions in May and June (Marseille, Casablanca, Saint-Nazaire, Oran and Toulon). She was in refit at Toulon from September to November, and towed the *Duquesne* from Toulon to Oran in late January 1948. She then took part in exercises with *Montcalm*, returning to Toulon only on 20 February. In mid-April she took the Navy Minister to Algeria, then became part of the *Force d'intervention*, which operated off the coasts of North Africa before taking part in a naval review in the anchorage at Brest on 30 May 1948.

Gloire again transported troops and personnel to North Africa in late 1948, and was incorporated into

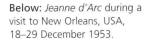
Below: *Jeanne d'Arc* during a visit to New Orleans, USA, 18–29 December 1953.

the *Escadre*. Unusually, all three cruisers were available in late 1949, and all took part in Exercise 'Verity' in early July. *Gloire* was in refit at Toulon for almost the whole of 1950. The barrels of her 152mm guns were replaced, and she received a new mainmast. She was flagship of the *Escadre* from 15 January 1951 to 1st October 1952. She participated alongside *Georges Leygues* in Exercises 'Progress' (early June 1951), 'Symphonie II' (October 1951), 'Sans Atout' (May 1952), and in the Atlantic sortie by the *Escadre* in May/June 1952.

From 1 October 1952 to 20 October 1954 *Gloire* would be flagship of the 2nd Cruiser Division. Together with the *Montcalm* she would take part in Exercises 'Rendez-Vous' and 'New Moon' (March 1953), in the Spring cruise of 1953, and in Exercise 'Sans Atout III' in February 1954. And with *Montcalm* she was recalled from the Spring sortie on 8 April 1954 and returned to Toulon.

RETURN TO INDOCHINA

The deteriorating military situation in Indochina following the siege of Dien Bien Phu, which was taken by the Viet Minh on 7 May 1954, prompted a deployment of the two cruisers of the 2nd Cruiser Division. The *Montcalm* and *Gloire* sailed from Toulon on 28 May 1954 and arrived at Saigon on 20 June.

Gloire left Saigon on 28 June and operated off the coast of Annam province, then covered the retreat of French ground forces from the Tonkin delta. Following the cease-fire, *Gloire* was at Saigon, made two round trips to Ha Long Bay and left Saigon for France on 15 September. She had fired a total of ninety-four rounds of 152mm and 217 of 90mm since 1 April.

Montcalm operated off the coast of Annam and in Ha Long Bay between 5 and 20 July, which marked the cease-fire in this zone. *Montcalm* was in Ha Long Bay at the beginning of August and took part in the final evacuation of Tonkin by the French, which was completed on 15 May 1955. *Montcalm* left Saigon for Toulon on 31 May 1955.

SUEZ

The nationalisation of the Suez Canal by Colonel Nasser on 26 July 1956 provoked a reaction from the French and the British. An operation against Egypt to re-establish Franco-British control over the canal was agreed following discussions which included the Israelis, and was finally launched after numerous delays.

Georges Leygues was detached from the *Escadre* to be employed as the command ship for the *Force navale d'intervention* (FNI), which would be formed from French units and would operate alongside a British formation. Vice-Admiral Lancelot raised his flag on the cruiser on 8 August. *Georges Leygues* worked up during August with a view to an intervention in Egypt. The FNI eventually sailed for the eastern Mediterranean in late October. *Georges Leygues* was detached for a fire support mission against Rafah (Gaza Strip) on the night of 31 October / 1 November. She fired 352 rounds of 152mm in support of the Israeli forces. She replenished at Cyprus, then covered the Franco-British landings at Port Said and Port Fouad on 6 November without needing to fire her guns. Operations ended with the cease-fire on 6 November. The cruiser did not leave Port Said until 22 December, the last French ship to sail following the embarkation

of Franco-British troops. She returned to Toulon on 27 December 1956, then sailed for Bizerte via Algiers in late January 1957.

THE DEACTIVATIONS

Duquesne was placed in reserve at Toulon on 1 September 1947. She was attached to the Amphibious Operations Training Centre (*Centre d'instruction des opérations amphibies*, or CIOA) at Arzew. She was modified for her new role as command post, school and barracks at Oran between February and August 1948, then moored at Arzew from 30 August. She was stricken on 2 July 1955 (she became *Q 52*), towed to Mers el-Kebir in August 1955 and put up for sale on 27 July 1956.

Tourville arrived at Brest on 23 December 1947. She was placed in special reserve on 1 January 1948. She served as a floating barracks for the flotilla of the 2nd Maritime Region, alongside the battleship *Paris*, then the *Richelieu*. She housed the School of Officers of the Reserve (*Ecole des officiers de réserve*, or EOR), then the navigation school (*Ecole de manoeuvre*). She was placed in reserve B on 28 April 1961, stricken on 8 March 1962 (she became the *Q 312*), and towed from Brest to Toulon from 15 January to 4 February 1963. She was broken up at La Seyne.

Suffren arrived at Toulon on 24 March 1947, and was decommissioned and placed in reserve on

Above: *Georges Leygues* at Port Said in November 1956. In the background the British destroyer depot ship *Tyne*, which was serving as a command ship. She is now fitted with the French DRBV 20A and DRBC 11A air surveillance fire control radars (see drawing caption p.217). *(ECPAD)*

Below: *Duquesne* at Arzew during the early 1950s following her modification at Oran as a support ship for the Amphibious Operations Training Centre (CIOA). *(Marc Saibène collection)*

Right: The Angle Robert at Toulon between 1959 and 1962 with the cruisers *Montcalm* and *Suffren* serving as (stationary) school ships and a newly-completed *aviso-escorteur* of the *Commandant Rivière* class. The battleship *Jean Bart*, normally moored alongside, is absent, docked for maintenance.

1 October. Moored at the Angle Robert, the cruiser served as a hulk for the gunnery school then, from 1961, for the sonar school. She was renamed *Océan* on 1 January 1963, the name *Suffren* having been allocated to a new guided missile frigate under construction at Lorient. Becoming surplus to requirements with the regrouping of the training schools at Saint-Mandrier, where the *Centre d'instruction naval* (CIN) was opened in 1971, the cruiser was moved into the dockyard. *Océan* was stricken on 24 March 1972, becoming *Q 494*. She was moored at Brégaillon and put up for sale on 5 November 1975. She left Toulon on 22 February 1976 to be broken up at Valencia.

Emile Bertin began her deactivation on 15 August 1951 and completed it on 25 October. She was moored at the Angle Robert at Toulon, and utilised as an accommodation ship for the training establishments

until September 1959. She was stricken on 27 October 1959, becoming the *Q 173*. She was sold on 17 March 1961 and broken up at La Seyne.

Duguay-Trouin was placed in reserve at Toulon on 15 December 1951, stricken on 29 March 1952, sold on 27 March 1953 and broken up.

Gloire, which had returned from Indochina on 12 October 1954, arrived at Bizerte on 17 November and was subsequently placed in special reserve A in March 1955. She was finally decommissioned on 1st November 1955, placed in reserve B on 5 October 1956 and stricken on 2 January 1958, becoming *Q 101*. She was sold for scrap on 7 November of that year.

Montcalm was at Bizerte when she was placed in reserve on 4 March 1957. She was towed to Toulon in July 1959 and replaced *Emile Bertin* at the Angle Robert. She was utilised by the ASW school and finally

Right: *Tourville* in 1953/1954 when she was serving as an accommodation ship for the School of Reserve Officers (EOR) at Brest. Alongside is the sub-chaser *P 694* (ex-*CH 121*, ex-US *SC 515*) and behind *Tourville* the transport *Ile d'Oleron* (the ex-German *München*) and the sailing ship *Duchesse Anne* (also ex-German, now preserved at Dunkirk).

Left: *Jeanne d'Arc* towards the end of her career, in 1959. *(Courtesy of Stephen Dent)*

Below: Old and new: the Angle Robert at Toulon on 15 August 1964, with the *escorteur d'escadre D'Estrées*, the battleship *Jean Bart*, the *Océan* (ex-*Suffren*), the *Montcalm*, and the anti-aircraft cruiser *Colbert*. In one of the two large graving docks can be see the fleet oiler *La Seine*. At the top of the picture on the left: the coastal patrol boat *La Combattante*, on which the President of the Republic, Charles de Gaulle, had embarked for a review of the ships in the dockyard to commemorate the twentieth anniversary of the landings in Provence.

Above, left: *Jeanne d'Arc* following her paying off; the 155mm guns have been disembarked.

Above, right: *De Grasse* in dock no.4 at Brest in 1964 just before her conversion to a command ship for the French nuclear test centre (CEP) in the Pacific. *(Jean Moulin)*

Below, left: *De Grasse* dressed overall during the late 1950s. *(Courtesy of Robert Dumas)*

Below, right: *De Grasse* as a command ship; the photo was taken at Papeete during the 1968 deployment. *(Jean Moulin)*

deactivated on 30 September 1969. Stricken on 31 December 1969, she became *Q 457*. She was sold for scrap on 21 May 1970, and broken up at La Seyne alongside the battleship *Jean Bart*.

Georges Leygues was placed in reserve A at Bizerte on 1 April 1957, then in special reserve B on 27 April 1959. She was brought back to Toulon on 18 June 1959, used as a target for AS 20 air-launched missiles, then sold for scrap at Toulon on 17 March 1961.

Jeanne d'Arc was decommissioned and became *Q 381* on 6 July 1964. The name *Jeanne d'Arc* was taken over on the same day by the helicopter-carrying cruiser *La Résolue*, which also took on her mission as a school ship for officer cadets, and was to remain in service until 2010. *Q 381* was stricken on 25 March 1965 and was broken up at La Seyne in 1966. She had travelled 740,000nm, a record for the ships of her generation.

THE LAST CRUISERS

The continuation of the naval programme following the completion of the 7600-ton cruisers was to comprise three improved units displacing 8000 tons with a main armament of nine 152mm guns (see Chapter 7). The first, *De Grasse*, authorised under the 1937 Estimates, was the only ship to be laid down; she would be completed post-war to a radically modified design. The other two ships, *Châteaurenault* and *Guichen*, autho-

rised in 1938, were ordered but would not be laid down due to the events of 1940 and would be cancelled.

The large wartime programme of 1 April 1940 included three cruisers of 14,770 tons armed with nine 203mm guns (see Chapter 8). None was ordered due to the events of the following months, and the Minister did not even have sufficient time to select three names from the six proposed (*Saint Louis*, *Henri IV*, *Charlemagne*, *Brennus*, *Charles Martel* and *Vercingetorix*). The class is, nevertheless, generally referred to as the *Saint Louis* class.

The decree of 1 April 1940 also included a light cruiser, apparently as a numerical replacement for the minelaying cruiser *Pluton* lost in September 1939; no details have been found. The ship was cancelled on 27 May 1940 and replaced by six destroyers which would almost certainly have been ordered from the USA, fifteen ships of the *Woolsey* (*Livermore*) class having been included in the programme of April 1940.

Two new light cruisers were integrated into the cruiser force in 1948. In accordance with the peace treaty between Italy and France, the Italians were to hand over two light cruisers of the 'Capitani Romani' class: the *Attilio Regolo* was renamed *Châteaurenault* and the *Scipione Africano* became the *Guichen*. The ships were reclassified as *destroyer-escorteur de 1re classe* in 1951, rebuilt and modernised 1951–4, and reclassified *escorteur d'escadre* ('fleet escort' – the

Châteaurenault: Profile and Plan Views

Profile and plan views of *Châteaurenault* as first completed, based
on the official plans produced at La Seyne 4 February 1955.

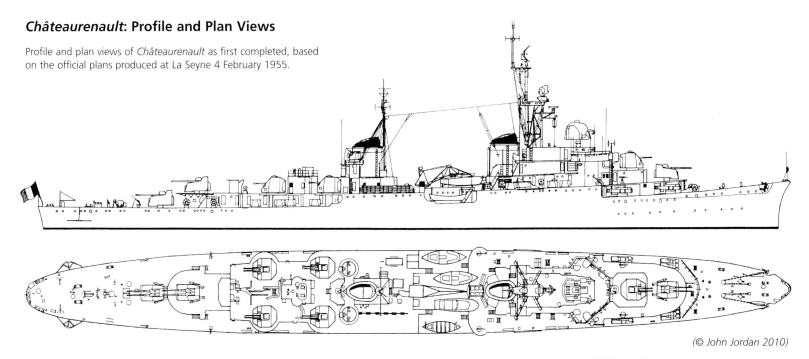

(© John Jordan 2010)

GENERAL CHARACTERISTICS: *CHÂTEAURENAULT* & *GUICHEN* FOLLOWING CONVERSION AT LA SEYNE 1951-4

Displacement:	3680 tons standard
	5500 tonnes full load
Length:	138.7m pp, 141.8m oa
Beam:	14.4m
Draught:	4.1m
Machinery:	Four boilers, 26kg/cm² (320°C); two-shaft Belluzzo geared steam turbines; 110,000CV; speed 39kts
Oil fuel:	1400 tonnes; radius 3600nm at 18kts
Armament:	Six 105mm/65 SK C/33in twin mountings L C/37;
	ten 57mm/60 Mle 1951 HA in twin mountings Mle 1948;
	twelve 550mm torpedo tubes in four triple mountings Mle KT 50
Electronics:	*Surveillance radars:* DRBV 20A, DRBV 11
	Navigation radars: DRBN 31
	FC radars: 1 DRBC 11, 2 DRBC 30
	Sonars: DUBVA 1A/B
Complement:	353

Below: *Guichen* at Malta in
1956 *(Leo van Ginderen
collection)*

Above, left: *Colbert* is towed to the fitting-out quay at Brest after being floated out of the Salou building dock on 24 March 1956. *(ECPA)*

Above, right: *Colbert* as completed as a conventional anti-aircraft cruiser. She is seen here moored at one of the *appontements Milhaud* on 7 August 1969. *(Jean Moulin)*

same designation as the new French-built units of the T47 type) in 1955. *Guichen* was stricken in 1961 and *Châteaurenault* in 1962.

The studies and projects for fleet renewal following the Second World War envisaged new cruisers. A study for a ship with four triple 152mm turrets requested in March 1945 was abandoned in January 1948. The naval plans drawn up in 1946 and 1947 envisaged the formation of three, then two blue-water combat groups (or Task Forces) of which one would be placed at the disposal of the United Nations. The Navy wanted to have six conventional cruisers and six anti-aircraft cruisers in service by 1960. In the event the Marine Nationale secured funding only to complete the *De Grasse* and to build a new purpose-designed AA cruiser, *Colbert*, authorised in 1953.

De Grasse was laid down at Lorient on 28 August

1939. Her construction, interrupted by the arrival of the Germans in June 1940, proceeded slowly during the occupation with a view to freeing up the slipway; there was also a proposal to complete her as an auxiliary aircraft carrier. The hull was completed and launched on 11 September 1946 and towed to Brest in 1951; she would be completed as an anti-aircraft cruiser armed with sixteen 127mm and twenty 57mm guns. She began trials on 17 August 1954 and entered service on 3 September 1956. She became flagship of the *Escadre* in place of the *Georges Leygues*, and took no part in the Suez operation of October/December 1956. She embarked on a world cruise in 1962. In 1964–5 she was converted to a command ship for the *Centre d'expérimentation du Pacifique* (CEP), and operated as such during the nuclear tests at Mururoa and Fangataufa from 1966 to 1972. She was decommis-

Colbert: Profile & Plan views

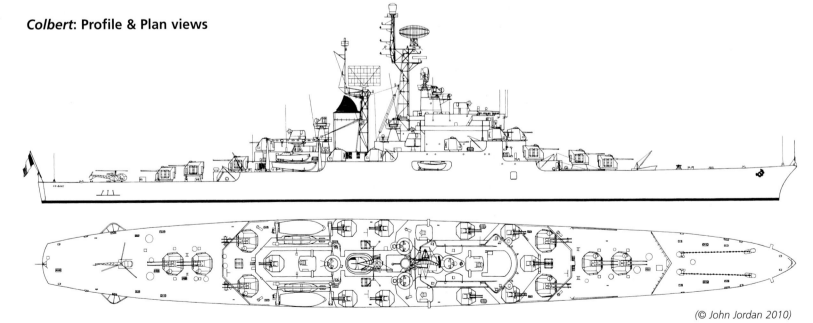

(© John Jordan 2010)

Profile and plan views of *Colbert* as first completed, based on the official plans produced by Brest Naval Dockyard and dated 6 July 1959. A design history of this ship would be out of place in this book. However, the authors felt it would be useful for the reader to have these plans, previously unpublished, and the accompanying table of characteristics to illustrate the degree of 'cross-pollination' between this and the final configuration of the *De Grasse*. *Colbert* had a more modern outfit of radars, but otherwise the major differences between the two ships as completed lay in the adoption of a transom stern for *Colbert*, and the below-decks arrangements, which included combined machinery spaces on the American pattern in place of the traditional alternating boiler and engine rooms of the pre-war French cruiser designs.

BUILDING DATA AND GENERAL CHARACTERISTICS: ANTI-AIRCRAFT CRUISER *COLBERT*

Name	Builder	Laid down	Launched	In service
1953 Programme				
Colbert	Arsenal de Brest	9 Jun 1954	24 Mar 1956	5 May 1959

Displacement:	9084 tons standard
	9280 tonnes light
	11,587 tonnes full load
Length:	175m pp, 180.5m oa
Beam:	19.7m wl
Draught:	6.0m, 6.5m max.
Machinery:	Four Indret boilers, 45kg/cm^2 (450°C); two-shaft Parsons geared steam turbines; 86,000CV; speed 32kts
Oil fuel:	1708 tonnes*; radius 7100nm at 18kts, 1900nm at 33kts
Armament:	Sixteen 127mm/54 Mle 1948 in twin mountings (4800 rounds);
	twenty 57mm/60 Mle 1951 HA in twin mountings (30,000 rounds)
Electronics:	*Surveillance radars*: DRBV 22A, DRBV 20A, DRBI 10B
	Navigation radars: DRBN 31
	FC radars: 4 DRBC 31B, 4 DRBC 31A,
	ESM: ARBA 10B, ARBR 10B, ARBR 20, RRBM1&2, AN/SPR 1
	Sonar: DSBV 1
Protection:	*Belt*: 50–80mm
	Deck: 50mm
Complement:	977 (as flagship)

* Includes 137t used for protection of the machinery spaces (sections I & L).

sioned on 28 February 1973, became *Q 521* and was broken up in Italy in 1975.

The anti-aircraft cruiser *Colbert* was built at Brest to a design based on that of *De Grasse*. Initially referred to by the project designation 'C53', she was launched at Brest on 24 March 1956 and entered service on 5 May 1959. Based at Toulon, she served as flagship of the *Escadre* (renamed *Escadre de la Méditerranée* on 15 September 1965), then was modernised between 1970 and 1972, her 127mm guns being replaced by the French Masurca area defence missile system and two single 100mm automatic DP guns. Redesignated *croiseur lance-missiles*, she was based at Brest from 1973 to 1976, then Toulon, and was finally decommissioned on 24 May 1991. *Colbert* became a floating museum at Bordeaux in 1993, but she was closed to the public at the end of 2006 and stricken. She has been awaiting breaking up at Brest since 2007. *Colbert* was the last of the French cruisers, their successors being the new 'frigates' (*frégates*).

Below: *Colbert* finds her last resting place in the naval 'cemetery' at Landevennec in Britanny. Prior to this she had been a museum ship at Bordeaux from 1993 to 2007. On either side of her are the former *escorteurs d'escadre* *La Galissonnière* and *Duperré*. (*Jean Moulin*)

SOURCES

TECHNICAL

Campbell, John, *Naval Weapons of World War Two* (London: Conway Maritime Press, 1985 reprinted 2002).

Dumas, Robert, 'Genèse des croiseurs de 10 000 t', *Marine no.41* (Bourg-en-Bresse: Marines Editions, 1996).

Friedman, Norman, *Naval Radar* (London: Conway Maritime Press, 1981).

Guiglini, Jean, *Les Marques Particulières des Navires de Guerre Français (1900-1950)* (Vincennes: Service Historique de la Marine, 2002).

Guiglini, Jean & Moreau, Albert, *Les croiseurs de 8 000 T* (Bourg-en-Bresse: Marines Editions, 1996).

Guiglini, Jean & Moreau, Albert, *Les croiseurs Jeanne d'Arc & Pluton* (Bourg-en-Bresse: Marines Editions, 1999).

Garier, Gérard & du Cheyron, Patrick, *Les croiseurs lourds français Duquesne & Tourville* (Outreau: Lela Presse, 2003).

Garier, Gérard, *Les croiseurs français de 10 000 tW Tome 1: Suffren & Colbert* (Outreau: Lela Presse, 2010).

Giorgerini, Giorgio & Nani, Augusto, *Gli Incrociatotori Italiani* (Rome: Ufficio Storico della Marina Militare, 1964).

Jordan, John, *Warships After Washington* (Barnsley: Seaforth Publishing, 2011).

Jordan, John & Dumas, Robert, *French Battleships 1922-1956* (Barnsley: Seaforth Publishing, 2009).

Lassaque, Jean, *Le croiseur Emile Bertin* (Bourg-en-Bresse: Marines Editions, 1996).

Moulin, Jean, *Les croiseurs de 7 600 tonnes* (Bourg-en-Bresse: Marines Editions, 1993)

Moulin, Jean, *Les Projets de Croiseurs C5 1939-1940* (self-published as booklet 1989).

Moulin, Jean, *Dates de Construction, Bâtiments des programmes de 1922 à 1940* (self-published as booklet 1999).

Moulin, Jean & Maurand, Patrick, *Le croiseur Algérie* (Nantes: Marines Editions 1999).

Raven, Alan & Roberts, John, *British Cruisers of World War Two* (London: Arms & Armour Press, 1980).

Plans and other documentation from the Centre d'Archives de l'Armement (CAA), Châtellerault, and from the Service Historique de la Défense, département marine (http,//www.servicehistorique.sga. defense.gouv.fr/02fonds-collections/banquedocuments/planbato/planbato/central.php)

HISTORICAL

Antier, Jean-Jacques, *La Flotte se Saborde, Toulon 1942* (Paris: Presses de la Cité, 1992).

Auphan, Admiral Gabriel, & Mordal, Jacques, *La Marine française pendant la seconde guerre mondiale* (Editions France-Empire, 1959).

Caroff, C F, *La campagne de Norvège 1940* (Paris: Service Historique de la Marine, 1955).

Caroff, C V, *Les Débarquements Alliés en Afrique du Nord* (Paris: Service Historique de la Marine, 1960).

Caroff, C V, *Le théâtre Atlantique*, 2 volumes (Paris: Service Historique de la Marine, 1958 et 1959).

Caroff, C V, *Le théâtre Méditerranéen*, 2 volumes (Paris: Service Historique de la Marine, 1960).

Lemonnier, Admiral André, *Croiseurs en action* (Editions France Empire, 1959).

Masson, Muracciole, Villardi de Montlaur, *La participation de la Marine française aux débarquements de Normandie et de Provence* (Paris: Service Historique de la Marine, 1969).

Mordal, Jacques, *La bataille de Dakar* (Editions Ozanne, 1956).

The archives of the Service Historique de la Défense: Département Marine at Vincennes, Paris (Activities/Operations); Centre d'archives de l'armement et du Personnel civil (CAA) at Châtellerault (Design/Plans).

INDEX

NOTE ABOUT THE INDEX

The main body of the index consists predominantly of names of ships, people and places. For ships the nationality and type of vessel are in parentheses; for places the location/country is given; the personalities, with the exception of national leaders, are French unless otherwise stated. There are also 'thematic'

entries for the following: **aicraft**, **formations**, **guns**, **radars** and **torpedoes**. Sections of the book which focus on a particular system, or on a particular aspect of a ship or class of ship are in **bold** type; *bold italics* are used for a major illustration of a ship or weapons system, and also for key maps.

A

Abruzzi class (It. cruisers) 143, 149
aircraft
  CAMS 37A 13-14, **51**
  FBA 17 13, **37**
  Gourdou Leseurre (GL) 810/811/812 13-14, **61**
  Gourdou Leseurre (GL) 832 **38**
  Loire 130 14, **140**
  Loire 210 14, **140**
  Latécoère 298 201
Adventure (Br. minelayer) 83
Afridi (Br. destroyer) 181
Aigle (Fr. *contre-torpilleur*) 183
Albatros (Fr. *contre-torpilleur*) 179,183
Alexandria, Egypt 177, 182, 184, 190-1, *190* [map], 195
Algérie (Fr. cruiser) 8, 10-16, 18-19, 21, 23, 48, 53, 69-70, 82, 94, **107-20**, 121, 123, 125, 127-8, 144, 150-1, 154, 159-60, 162-3, 166, *169*, 171, 169-70, *173*, 173-5, *175*, 177-9, *178*, 181, 183-4, 189, 191-2, *193-4*
Algiers, Algeria 109, 170, 173, 175, 182-4, 190, 195, 196, 198, 203-9, 211, 214, 221
Alsace class (projected French battleships) 162
Amiral Charner (Fr. sloop) 187-188
Amiral Sénès (Fr. destroyer, ex-Ger. *S113*) 17
Annamite (Fr. sloop) 187
Applevage (Fr. manufacturer) 52
Arethusa class (Br. cruisers) 24
Arromanches (Fr. aircraft carrier) 214-5, 220
ASDIC 128 (French 'Alpha') 13, 20
Atago class (Jap. cruisers) 114
Ateliers et Chantiers de la Loire (St. Nazaire) 9, 124
Ateliers et Chantiers de St. Nazaire-Penhoët 8-9, 90-3, 97, 99, 123-4
Attilio Regolo (It. cruiser) 224
Auboynau, Rear-Admiral Philippe 207
Augusta (US cruiser) 189
Australia (Aus. cruiser) 185-6

B

Basque (Fr. destroyer) 178, 184, 190, *191*
Béarn (Fr. aircraft carrier) 165, 171, 181, 220
Bévéziers (Fr. submarine) 186
Bison (Fr. *contre-torpilleur*) 178-81
Bourbonnais (Fr. cargo ship) 187
Bourragué, Rear-Admiral Pierre 185
Breguet (Fr. manufacturer) 85, 87-8, 96, 99, 104-5, 112, 182
Brest Naval Dockyard **8-9**, 25-6, 30, 42, 44, 55, 59-60, 64, 70-2, 77, 79, 108, 110, 122, 124, 227
Bretagne (Fr. battleship) 8, 25, 165, 168, 171, 174, *175*

Brooklyn (US cruiser) 189
Brooklyn Navy Yard, USA 196-7

C

C4 French cruiser project 82, 107, 110, 159-60
C5 French cruiser project 159-63
Calatafimi (It. torpedo boat) 183
Casabianca (Fr. submarine) 203
Casablanca, Morocco 170-1, *176* [map], 176-7, 181-2, 184-7, 189, 198, 201-5, 207-8, 210-1, 214, 217, 220
Cassard (Fr. *contre-torpilleur*) 171, 174, 178, 183, 190
Castor (Fr. minelayer) 83
Chacal (Fr. *contre-torpilleur*) 165, 171, 174
Chamois class (Fr. M/S sloops) 153
Châteaurenault (Fr. cruiser) 146-7, 149, 157
Châteaurenault (Fr. Fleet Escort) **224-6**
Chevalier Paul (Fr. *contre-torpilleur*) 169, 171, 174, 179, 183
Chonburi (Siamese torpedo boat) 188
Cincinnati (US cruiser) 202
Colbert (Fr. cruiser L1928) 8, *10*, 13, 15, 18-23, 58-60, **63-9**, 70-2, 74-7, 79, 82, 102, 109, 118, 120, *129-31*, 165-6, *169*, 169-71, *172-3*, 173-5, *180*, 182-4, 189-92, *192-4*
Colbert (Fr. cruiser L1956) *223*, **226-7**
Colmar (Fr. cruiser) 167
Commandant Rivière (Fr. sloop) 216, *222*
concentration dials 22, 34, 37, 50, 74, 79, 89, 116-7, 140
Condé (Fr. cruiser) 167
Condottieri (It. cruisers) 96, 121, 126-7
Cornwall (Br. cruiser) 185
Cot, Pierre (Fr. Air Minister 1933-37) 21
Courbet class (Fr. battleships) 25
Cumberland (Br. cruiser) 185
Cunningham, Vice-Admiral Sir Andrew (GB) 190-1

D

D'Argenlieu, Vice-Admiral Thierry 212
Dakar, Senegal 166, 168, 170, 172, 174, 177-82, 184-7, *186* [maps], 189, 195, 196-8, 201-4, 208, 211, 214, 216, 219
Dandolo (It. submarine) 182
Darlan, Admiral François 22, 145, 190-1, 195
Davidson, Rear-Admiral Lyal (US) 207
De Gaulle, General Charles 184, 195, 223
De Grasse (Fr. cruiser) 8-10, 12, 14-8, 21, 124, **143-58**, 218, 224, *224*, 226-7
De Laborde, Vice-Admiral Jean 189, 191
Delhi (Br. cruiser) 185
Derrien, Rear-Admiral Edmond 179, 181, 183
Dhonhuri (Siamese coast defence ship) 187-8

dispositif 'K' (shell colorant) 48, 102. 168
Dixmude (Fr. aircraft carrier) 215, 220
Duguay-Trouin (Fr. cruiser) 8, 12-14, 16-23, **24-40**, 41, 43-53, 64, 89-90, 92, 94-5, 101, 105, 164-6, 168, 170-1, 173-5, 176-8, 184, 190, *191*, 195, 198, *201*, 203-6, **204** [1944 config.], *207*, 208, 211, 212-4, 222
Dumont d'Urville (Fr. sloop) 187-8
Dunkerque (Fr. battleship) 150, 154, 161, 165, 168, 174, 176, 179-80, 182, 184, 192
Dupleix (Fr. cruiser) 15-16, 18, 20, 23, 55, 57, 63, 65, 71-2, 74, **77-82**, 166, *169*, 169-71, 173-5, 177-9, 183-4, 189-92, *193*
Duquesne (Fr. cruiser) 8, 10, 12-17, 19-20, 23, 25, 29, 37, **41-53**, 54-5, 57-62, 65-6, 69, 79, 107, 110, 165-6, 169-71, *170*, *172*, 173-5, 178-9, *182*, 184, 190, 195, 202, 204-5, 209, 211, **210** [1944-5 config.], 213, 215, 220, *221*, 221
Duplat, Vice-Admiral Emile 177-8, 183

E

Ecole d'application du tir à la mer (EATM) 88, 167, 170-1
Ecole navale 169-71
Edgar Quinet (Fr. cruiser) 165, 167, 171
Elbano Gasperi (It. aux. minelayer) 183
Elan class (Fr. M/S sloops) 153
Emanuele Filiberto Duca d'Aosta (It. cruiser) 203
Emile Bertin (Fr. cruiser) 6, 8, 12-14, 17-18, 65, 81, **96-106**, *136*, 166, 168, 170-1, 174-5, 176-82, **180** [damage], *181*, 184, 187, 195, **197** [1943 config.], 197, *201*, 202, 203-4, 208, *206*, *208-9*, 211, 212-4, 216, 219, 222
Epervier (Fr. *contre-torpilleur*) 178-9
Eridan (Fr. liner) 187
Ernest Renan (Fr. cruiser) 165, 167

F

Fessenden u/w telephone 20
Foch (Fr. cruiser) 8, *12*, 15-16, 18, 20-1, 23, 57, 63, **69-77**, *131*, 165-6, *169*, 169-71, *172*, 173-5, 178-9, *178*, 183-4, 189-90, *190*, 191-2, *193*, 194
Forges et Chantiers de la Gironde (Bordeaux) 8-9, 85, 124
Forges et Chantiers de la Méditerranée (La Seyne) 8-9, 124-5
Forbin (Fr. destroyer) 178, 184, 190
formations (squadron and above)
  2e Escadre (2nd Squadron) 165, 167, 174
  3e Escadre (3rd Squadron) 165, 171, 174
  2e Escadre légère (2nd EL) 165, 168, 171, 174, 189
  3e Escadre légère (3rd EL) 174
  Escadre de l'Atlantique 167
  Escadre de la Méditerranée 169
  Escadre (Toulon post-war) 215, 217, 221, 226-7
  'Flank Force' 208-9
  Flotte de l'Atlantique 167
  Flotte de la Méditerranée 169
  Force X 177 [Dakar], 184 [Med]
  Force Y [Dakar] 178-9, 184-7
  Force Z [Norway] 179-81
  Force navale d'intervention (FNI) 215. 217, 219, 221
  Force de raid 174, 176, 180, 182,
  Forces de haute mer (FHM) 176, 189-90
  Forces légères d'attaque 170, 175-7, 182
  Forces maritimes d'Extrême Orient (FMEO) 215

French Naval Task Force (FNTF) 205, 209-10, 215
  Groupe d'action anti-sous-marine (GASM) 215, 220
Fort de France (Fr. cargo ship) 189
Furutaka class (Jap. cruisers) 41

G

Georges Leygues (Fr. cruiser) 8, 9, 124-6, 128-31, *135*, 142, 166, 168, 173, 175, 176, 179-80, *180*, 182, 184-7, *186*, 195, 196-7, *200*, 201-8, 211, 214-8, 221, 224, 226
Gervais de Lafond, Rear-Admiral Raymond 189
Giraud, General Henri 195, 196, 203
Gloire (Fr. cruiser) 23, 124-6, 128, 132, 166, 168, *172*, 173-5, 176, 179-80, 182, 184-7, 195, *196*, 196-8, 202-6, *207*, 207-9, 211, 212-22, *214*, *218*
Gneisenau (Ger. battleship) 180, 182
Godfroy, Rear-Admiral René-Emile 178, 190
gold transports 181-2
Graf Spee (Ger. *Panzerschiff*) 178-9
Guépard (Fr. *contre-torpilleur*) 165, 171, 183
Gueydon (Fr. cruiser) 165-6, *170*, 175
Guichen (Fr. cruiser) 9, 146-7, 149, 224
Guichen (Fr.Fleet Escort) **224-6**
guns
  203/45 Mle 1924 **48-9**, **114-5**
  155/50 Mle 1920 **31-2**
  152/55 Mle 1930 **100-2**
  138.6/40 Mle 1923 **86-7**
  100/45 Mle 1930 **115-6**
  100/45 Mle 1933 **153-4**
  100/55 Mle 1945 155
  90/50 Mle 1926 **65**
  75/50 Mle 1922 **32-3**
  40mm Bofors 197-8, 200, 202, 205
  37mm CAS Mle 1925 **49**
  37mm CAD Mle 1933 **102-3**
  37mm ACAD Mle 1935 **161**
  20mm Oerlikon 198, 202, 205
  13.2mm Hotchkiss MG **116**
  13.2mm Browning MG 69, 77, 82, 120
Guyot-du Temple boilers 45, 59, 72

H

Hancock (US aircraft carrier) 189
Harwood, Vice-Admiral Sir Henry (GB) 191
Hawkins class (Br. cruisers) 41
Hermes (Br. aircraft carrier) 177-8
Hipper class (Ger. cruisers) 162
Hood (Br. battlecruiser) 180
Hornet (US aircraft carrier) 189

I

Indochina 37, 171, 173-4, 177, 182, 184, 187-8, **211** [map], 212-6, 220-2
Indret (Fr. naval propulsion establishment) 12, 28-9, 46, 110-1, 124-5

J

Jaujard, Rear-Admiral Robert 208
Jean Bart (Fr. battleship) 8, 9, 155, 165, 189, 215, 222-3, 224
Jean de Vienne (Fr. cruiser) 8, 14, 123-5, 127, 131-2, 166, 169, 175, 179, 181-2, 184, 189-92, 194, *212*
Jeanne d'Arc (Fr. cruiser) 8, 13, 85, **89-95**, 105, *132*, 166-8, 170-1, 173-7, 179-80, 182, 187, 198-9, *199*, 201, 203, **204** [1944 config.], 206, 209, 212, 215-6, 220, 223-4

Joffre (Fr. aircraft carrier) 53
Jules Michelet (Fr. cruiser) 167, 213
Jumièges (Fr. cargo ship) 190

K

Karlsruhe class (Ger. cruisers) 24
Kent class (Br. cruisers) 15, 44-5, 60, 114
Koh-Chang, Thailand 187-9

L

L'Alcyon (Fr. destroyer) 165, 171, 175, 203
L'Audacieux (Fr. *contre-torpilleur*) 171, 174-5, 177-9, 188
L'Impétueuse (Fr. sloop) 190
La Galissonnière (Fr. cruiser) 8, 10-12, 14-16, 20-21, 40, 65, 101-2, **121-8,** *133,* **137-42**, 143-5, 149-54, 166, 169-71, 175, 182, 189-191, *191-2,* 194-5
La Grandière (Fr. sloop) 216
La Tour d'Auvergne (Fr. cruiser) 85, 170
Laconia (Br. liner) 187
Lamoricière (Fr. liner) 190
Lamotte-Piquet (Fr. cruiser) 8, 17, 21, 23, 24-5, 27, *28,* 29-30, *35,* 36, *37,* 37, *39,* 39-40, 165-6, 168, 171, 173-5, 177, 184, 187-9, *188,* 195, 213
Lancelot, Vice-Admiral Pierre 221
Le Fantasque (Fr. *contre-torpilleur*) 168, 171, 174, 177-9, *180,* 184, 203, 206, 215, 220
Le Fortuné (Fr. destroyer) 165, 171, 174, 178, 184, 190
Le Malin (Fr. *contre-torpilleur*) 171, 174, 179, 184, 206, 215, 220
Le Terrible (Fr. *contre-torpilleur*) 171, 174-5, 177-8, 195, 206, 215, 220
Le Triomphant (Fr. *contre-torpilleur*) 171, 174, 206, 211, 215, 220
Leander (Br. cruiser) 121, 124
Lexington (US aircraft carrier) 189
Leygues, Georges (Fr. Navy Minister 1917-1933) 25, 124
Lion (Fr. *contre-torpilleur*) 165, 171, 175, 182-3
London class (Br. cruisers) 54
Lorient Naval Dockyard **8-9,** 27-8, 30, 44, 39, 83-5, 124. 146-7
Lorraine (Fr. battleship) 165, 168, 171, 174, *175,* 178-9, 182, 184, 192, 215
Louisville class (US cruisers) 107
Luigi di Savoia Duca Degli Abruzzi (It. cruiser) 203
Lynx (Fr. *contre-torpilleur*) 165, 171, 175, 178, 184
Lyon class (projected Fr. battleships) 101

M

Malaya (Br. battleship) 181,190
Marblehead (US cruiser) 202
Marne (Fr. sloop) 165, 175, 187-8
Marseillaise (Fr. cruiser) 14, 18, 124-6, 128, *133-5, 141,* 142, 166-7, 169-70, 173, 175, 179, 181-2, 184, 189-92, 194, *194*
MAS boats (It.) 183
Massachusetts (US battleship) 189
Mélinite (explosive) 32, 49, 102
Memphis (US cruiser) 202
Mers el-Kebir, Algeria 182, 184-5, 190, 195, 203-6, 221
Metz (Fr. cruiser) 167
Milan (Fr. *contre-torpilleur*) 171, 175, 178-9, 189
Mogador (Fr. *contre-torpilleur*) 150-1, 168, 174

Montcalm (Fr. cruiser) 22, 124-5, *126,* 128-9, *138,* 146, 166, 168, 173-5, *174-5,* 176, 179-82, 184-7, 195, **196** [1943 config.], 197-8, *199-200,* 201-5, 207-8, *207,* 211, 213-5, *214,* **217** [1954 config.], 219-21, *222,* 222, *223*
Monte Albertia (Spa. cargo ship) 203
Mulhouse (Fr. cruiser) 165, 167
Myoko class (Jap. cruisers) 114

N

Neptune (Br. cruiser) 55, 178-9
Nelson class (Br. battleships) 74
New Orleans class (US cruisers) 107
Normandie class (Fr. battleships) 8, 101
Norwegian campaign 180-1

O

Omaha (US cruiser) 202
Operation 'Anvil' 205
Operation 'Bentré' 212-3
Operation 'Dragoon' 205
Operation 'Neptune' 204
Operation 'Overlord' 204
Operation 'Torch' 187, 189, 195
Operation 'Vado' 183-4
Oran, Algeria 172, 175, 176, 180, 182, 184, 204-5, 207-9, 211, 214, 220-1

P

Painlevé (Fr. aircraft carrier) 53
Parsons turbines 12, 28, 30, 91, 93, 99, 111, 124-6, 227
Pathfinder (Br. destroyer) 203
Pensacola class (US cruisers) 107
Philadelphia Navy Yard, USA 196, 199-200
Pluton (Fr. cruiser) 8, **83-9,** 91, 96, 105, *133,* 165-6, 170-1, 173-4, 176-7, **177**
Pola (It. cruiser) 121
Pollux (Fr. minelayer) 83
Portland (Ger. cargo ship) 202-3
Primauguet (Fr. cruiser) 20, 23, *25,* 25-6, 29-31, *30, 34,* 36-40, *38,* 44, 51, *55,* 64, 165-6, *167,* 171, 173-75, 176-7, 181-2, 184-5, 187, 189, 213,
Provence (Fr. battleship) 165, 168, 171, 174, *175,* 178-9, 182, 184, 190, 192,

R

Rateau-Bretagne turbines 12, 46, 59, 72, 91, 110-1, 124-6, 147, 151, 166
Rawalpindi (Br. AMC) 180
radars
    DEM air surveillance (Fr.) **193**
    DRBN 30 navigation (Fr.) 217
    SA-2 air surveillance (US) **197**
    SF surface surveillance (US) **197**
    SP height-finding (US) 217
    Type 281BQ LR air surveillance (GB) **215**
    Type 284 main gunnery control (GB) **215**
    Type 285 AA fire control (GB) **215**
    Type 293 surface surveillance (GB) **215**
Renown (Br. battlecruiser) 185
Resolution (Br. battleship) 185-6
Richelieu (Fr. battleship) 143-5, 150, 153-5, 160, 185-6, 196, 211, 215, 221
Robert, Rear-Admiral Georges 195
Royal Sovereign (Br. battleship) 182

S

Saint Louis (Fr. cruiser) **159-63**, 224
Sautter-Harlé (Fr. manufacturer) 50, 83, 85, 87,
    102-5, 138, 161
Scharnhorst (Ger. battleship) 180, 182
Scipio Africano (It. cruiser) 224
Sidi-Abdallah Naval Dockyard, Bizerte (Tunisia) 204,
    206
Songhkli (Siamese torpedo boat) 188
Sri Ayuthua (Siamese coast defence ship) 187-8
Strasbourg (Fr. cruiser) 165, 167
Strasbourg (Fr. battleship) 168, 174, 176-8, 182, 184,
    189-92, *194*
Suffren (Fr. cruiser) 8, 10-21, 23, 29, 48, **54-62**,
    63-7, 69-72, 75, 79-80, 85, 98, 107, 109-10, 112,
    123, *130*, 154, 165-6, 169-71, 173-5, 177-8, 182,
    184, 190, *191*, 195, 202-3, **210** [1944-5 config.],
    211, 212-3, 215, 221-2, *223*
superheating 12, 44, 82, 96-7, 99, 107, 111, 151
Surcouf class (Fr. fleet escorts) 157-8

T

Tahure (Fr. sloop) 165, 175. 187-8
Tarn (Fr. oiler) 184-5, 189
Tartu (Fr. *contre-torpilleur*) 165, 171, 174, 179, 183,
    190
Tempête (Fr. destroyer) 165, 171, 174, 203
Thionville (Fr. cruiser) 165, 167
Tigre (Fr. *contre-torpilleur*) 165, 171, 174-5, 178, 184
Torpedoes
    550mm Mle 1919D 19

550mm Mle 1923D 19, 30, **34**, 37, 43-4, 51, 54,
    72, 93-4, 99, 110, 117, 124
Toulon Naval Dockyard 191-5 [scuttling], **192** [map]
Tourville (Fr. cruiser) 8, 10, 20, 23, 37, 41-53, *52-3*,
    165-6, 169-71, *172-3*, 173-5, 178, 181-2, 184, 190,
    195, *199*, 202-5, 209, **210** [1944-5 config.], 211,
    213, 215, 221, *222*
Trad (Siamese torpedo boat) 188
Trento (It. cruiser) 45, 46
Trieste (It. cruiser) 54

U

U 156 (Ger.submarine) 187

V

Valmy (Fr. *contre-torpilleur*) 165, 171, 175, 183
Vauban (Fr. *contre-torpilleur*) 165, 171, 175, 183
Vauquelin (Fr. *contre-torpilleur*) 165, 174, 179
Vautour (Fr. *contre-torpilleur*) 165, 171, 174, 179, 183
Verdun (Fr. *contre-torpilleur*) 165, 171, 175, 183

W

Walser hydrophones 20, 26, 36
Waldeck Rousseau (Fr. cruiser) 165, 167, 171, 213
Washington Treaty (1922) 14, 25, 41, 44, 55, 69, 96,
    107
West Indies 177, 184, 187, 195
Woolsey class (US destroyers) 224

Z

Zara class (It. cruisers) 53, 107